Model experts

MANCHESTER
1824

Manchester University Press

Model experts

Wax anatomies and Enlightenment in Florence and Vienna, 1775–1815

ANNA MAERKER

Manchester University Press

Published by Manchester University Press
Altrincham Street, Manchester M1 7JA, UK
www.manchesteruniversitypress.co.uk

British Library Cataloguing-in-Publication Data
A catalogue record for this book is available from the British Library

Library of Congress Cataloging-in-Publication Data applied for

ISBN   978 0 7190 8205 4 hardback
ISBN   978 0 7190 9739 3 paperback

First published 2011
This paperback edition first published 2015

Typeset in 11/13 Bulmer MT
by Servis Filmsetting Ltd, Stockport, Cheshire
Printed in Great Britain
by TJ International Ltd, Padstow

for Simon

Contents

List of figures and plates   *page* viii
Acknowledgements   ix
List of abbreviations   xi

Introduction: model practices and expertise in state service   1

Part I: Politics of nature and politics of the body

1   The politics of nature and the foundation of the Royal Museum   19
2   Bodies and the state in eighteenth-century Tuscany   50

Part II: Articulating expertise in everyday practice

3   Accuracy and authority in model production   83
4   Model reception and the display of expertise   118

Part III: Changing model contexts and interpretations

5   The rejection of the Florentine anatomical models in Vienna   151
6   Regime changes in Tuscany and at La Specola, 1790–1814   185

Conclusion   209
Bibliography   220
Index   245

List of figures and plates

Figures

1 Map of Florence.   *page* 2
2 The Royal Museum of Physics and Natural History ('La Specola')
   in Florence.   3
3 Detail of a female wax model with real hair.   4
4 Giovanni Fabbroni (1752–1822).   32
5 Gaetano Zumbo, *Trionfo del tempo*.   35
6 Showroom XXIX with anatomical wax models at the Royal
   Museum of Physics and Natural History ('La Specola') in Florence.   51
7 Obstetric phantom in leather and wood, eighteenth-century Italy.   54
8 Modellers' tools and journals, La Specola.   87
9 Fontana's model in wood, La Specola.   134
10 The reconciliation of medicine and surgery.   170

Plates

I   Tanya Marcuse, Wax Bodies No. 49, 'La Specola', Florence.
IIa Wax bust of Emperor Leopold II of Austria (1747–92), formerly Grand
    Duke Pietro Leopoldo of Tuscany.
IIb Plaster bust of Felice Fontana (1730–1805).
IIc Painted plaster bust of Clemente Susini (1754–1814).
III 'Anatomical Venus', La Specola.
IV 'Lo scorticato' (The flayed man).

Plates appear between pages 148 and 149

Acknowledgements

This book and its author have benefited from the generous support of many individuals and institutions, and I am glad to be able to thank them here. Thus, in roughly chronological order, thanks to Christoph Meinel and the staff and students of the Chair of History of Science, Regensburg, and to the staff and students of the Department of History and Philosophy of Science, Cambridge, especially Simon Schaffer, Tatjana Buklijaš, Nick Hopwood, and Liba Taub. The Department of Science & Technology Studies at Cornell provided the perfect environment to develop the project, thanks in particular to my advisory 'dream team' Peter Dear, Michael Dennis, Isabel Hull, and Michael Lynch, to fellow dissertators Sonja Schmid and John Downer, and to the regulars of the Science Studies Research Gathering and the European History Seminar.

In Florence, thanks to Marta Poggesi, Saulo Bambi and colleagues at the Museo Zoologico 'La Specola', to Mara Miniati, Patrizia Ruffo, Angela Bandinelli and staff at the Istituto e Museo di Storia della Scienza, to Peter Becker and the staff and students of the European University Institute, and to the helpful archivists at the Archivio di Stato. In Vienna, I appreciated the hospitality and support of Sonia Horn and the Collections Department of the Medical University. Thanks also to Manfred Skopec for a tour of the Josephinum, and to the late Rita Furrer for a behind-the-scenes visit to her model restoration workshop. In Berlin, I am grateful to the Max Planck Institute for the History of Science for an inspiring working environment, especially to the members of Otto Sibum's research group 'Experimental History of Science', and to the organisers and participants of the 'Wandering Seminar'. At Oxford Brookes University, thanks to the staff and students of the History Department and the Centre for Health, Medicine and Society for their kind support and emergency coffee breaks. In London, I am grateful to the staff of the Wellcome Library and the Science Museum for their help.

I am happy to acknowledge financial support from a Dissertation Improvement Grant of the National Science Foundation, an International

Dissertation Research Fellowship of the Social Science Research Council, a Luigi Einaudi Fellowship of the Institute for European Studies at Cornell, and the Wellcome Trust Strategic Award 'Health Care in Public and Private' of the Centre for Health, Medicine and Society at Oxford Brookes University. I am grateful to the editors of *History of Science*, *Nuncius*, the *British journal for the history of science*, and *From Private to Public: Natural Collections and Museums*, for permission to reproduce material from previous publications.

For crucial feedback on the project I am obliged to the organisers and participants of two inspiring workshops, 'Figurationen des Experten' at the Humboldt University, especially Tom Broman, Eric Engstrom, Volker Hess, and Ulrike Thoms, and 'Instruments and material culture in early modern science' at Harvard, especially Jean-François Gauvin, Mario Biagioli, and Jim Bennett.

Tanya Marcuse very kindly shared photographs from her witty and thoughtful series 'Wax Bodies' (www.tanyamarcuse.com). Sam Alberti, Simone Contardi, Liz Hallam, Renato Mazzolini, Rebecca Messbarger and Renato Pasta generously provided critical insights on individual sections. Peter Dear had the dubious pleasure of commenting on various iterations of the entire manuscript well beyond the call of doctor-fatherly duty, and did so with unfailing analytical acumen.

Simon Werrett provided intellectual, emotional and physical nourishment when it was needed. This book is for him.

List of abbreviations

ABA	Archivio dell'Accademia delle Belle Arti, Florence
AFS	Accademia dei Fisiocritici, Siena
AGF	Archivio Storico delle Gallerie Fiorentine, Florence
ASCP	Archivio Storico Civico, Pavia
ASF	Archivio di Stato, Florence
BNCF	Biblioteca Nazionale Centrale, Florence
BSW	Bibliothek der Stadt Wien, Vienna
HHS	Österreichisches Staatsarchiv, Abteilung Haus- Hof- und Staatsarchiv, Vienna
IMSS–ARMU	Istituto e Museo di Storia della Scienza, Florence: Archive of the Royal Museum of Physics and Natural History
JJC	John Johnson Collection of Printed Ephemera, Bodleian Library, Oxford
LS	Museo Zoologico 'La Specola', Florence
WSA	Wiener Stadtarchiv, Vienna

Introduction: model practices and expertise in state service

On his visit to Florence in 1817, the French novelist Stendahl was overcome by the city's abundance of spectacular art and architecture: 'Absorbed in the contemplation of sublime beauty . . . I had palpitations of the heart, . . . Life was drained from me. I walked with the fear of falling.'[1] Tourists who wish to avoid a bout of *stendhalismo*[2] would do well to venture south of the river Arno beyond Palazzo Pitti, formerly the residence of Tuscany's Grand Dukes (figure 1).

There, the traveller will find the Zoological Museum 'La Specola' (figure 2).

After passing through several turns of the museum's terracotta corridors, filled with taxidermised animals and the smell of formaldehyde, the visitor encounters a vast collection of objects, which are not to be found in an ordinary natural history museum or, indeed, anywhere else in the world. Room upon room is brimming with models of human bodies and body parts in coloured wax. They are considered by some to be artistic achievements rivalling the masterpieces on display in the local art galleries and churches. These anatomical wax models include life-sized bodies of men and women at various degrees of dissection, upright and reclining; miniature figurines of flayed men in various poses, demonstrating the muscle layers; enlarged or isolated studies of anatomical details – a hand, a heart, a brain – all of them displayed in elegant wooden showcases behind glass, mounted on cushions or on gilded pedestals (plate I).

The visitor may take pleasure in the methodical arrangement of objects: full body models in the middle of the room, complemented by models and drawings of details along the walls, invite the visitor's glance to move back and forth between the whole and its parts. He or she might enjoy identifying the overarching theme of each room – the nervous system, perhaps, the muscles, or the reproductive system. Freshly primed by the appreciation of local art, the traveller might also discover resonances with celebrated paintings and sculptures: an enraptured saint, a bashful Venus, a reclining Adam. Medical professionals may admire the precision of the anatomical display; others might marvel at the

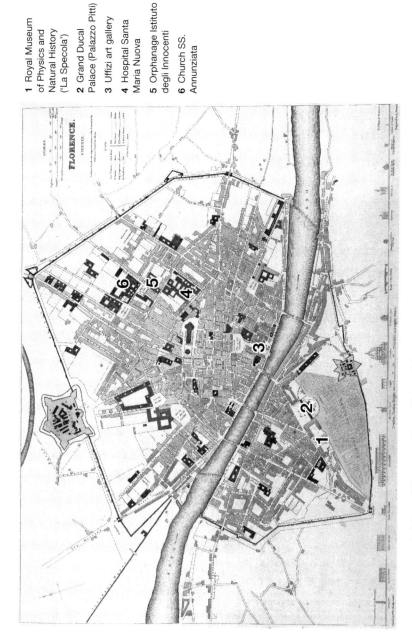

1 Royal Museum of Physics and Natural History ('La Specola')

2 Grand Ducal Palace (Palazzo Pitti)

3 Uffizi art gallery

4 Hospital Santa Maria Nuova

5 Orphanage Istituto degli Innocenti

6 Church SS. Annunziata

1 Map of Florence. From *Maps of the Society for the Diffusion of Useful Knowledge* (1844). (Bodleian Library, University of Oxford. Shelfmark: 2027 b.36, vol. 2, no. 178)

Veduta del Real Museo di Fisica, e d'Istoria Naturale dalla parte del Real Giardino di Boboli

2 The Royal Museum of Physics and Natural History ('La Specola') in Florence. (N.A. cart. 6, tav. 111, Biblioteca Nazionale Centrale, Florence. Su concessione del *Ministero per i Beni e le Attività Culturali della Repubblica Italiana.*)

expressive gestures of the figures or the minute details of the waxen bodies, adorned with real hair (figure 3).

The artificial bodies are lifelike even under the clinical neon lights. Only the occasional sun beam, stealing in from a gap in the heavy curtains, reveals the transparency of the waxen bones.

La Specola has been open to the public since 1775 when it was founded as the Royal Museum of Physics and Natural History by the Tuscan Grand Duke Pietro Leopoldo in an attempt to institutionalise natural knowledge and to further public education.[3] It survived many turbulent episodes in the political history of Tuscany, including rapid regime changes in the wake of the French Revolution, the unification of Italy, the rise of Fascism and the uncertainties of the post-war era. Since its foundation, the vast collection of anatomical wax models has fascinated audiences from all walks of life – old and young, rich and poor, local and foreign. Anatomists and modellers have emulated, historians and critics have interpreted, and artists have been inspired by them. Scholars from a wide range of disciplines have provided insights into their aesthetic features, uncovering artistic tropes and conventions of gesture, implicit assumptions about gender roles and the uncanny qualities of waxen flesh.[4]

However, these perspectives frequently obscure other important elements

3 Detail of a female wax model with real hair. (Alexander Ablogin, Sammlungen der Medizinischen Universität Wien/Collections of the Medical University Vienna)

of the models' history, which this book recounts, especially the political, social and cultural context of the anatomical waxes' production and use. The apparent serenity of the artificial anatomies obscures the fact that they were surrounded by human interactions and frequent controversy when they emerged in the context of an optimistic and radical attempt at political reform in the age of enlightened absolutism. The models owe their existence to the actions and aspirations of a wide range of individuals – sovereigns and servants, anatomists and artists, from the zealous reformer Grand Duke Pietro Leopoldo and his court scientist Felice Fontana to the museum's sweeper and dogsbody Giacinto Guidetti. At the time of their conception, the anatomical models were supposed to contribute to the Grand Duke's policy of public enlightenment: an attempt to use science to secure public happiness and to create the enlightened citizen. It is the purpose of this book to uncover the people and practices that contributed to the emergence of La Specola's unique model collection and to its survival. Taking the museum's enlightenment mission seriously, the book shows how practices of model production and model use shaped the emerging role of the expert in state service, and concomitant notions of the public.

Model Experts argues that the anatomical models of La Specola were political in a number of ways, in particular as an element of government reforms. New scholarship has highlighted the importance of reformist politics for the development of scientific culture and institutions in eighteenth-century Tuscany.[5] The Tuscan Grand Duke Pietro Leopoldo founded the Royal Museum of Physics and Natural History in an attempt to make his subjects happy by making them civilised. The new museum was one of a series of enlightened reform measures undertaken during his reign. Following the conviction of the Grand Duke and his advisers that only adherence to natural law could guarantee the sovereign's political legitimacy and the public's happiness, the museum was meant to be a place where expert naturalists could produce natural knowledge in state service, and enlighten the public to understand and accept these laws. The Grand Duke's reforms were inspired by eighteenth-century political theories based on the assumption that the laws of nature were unproblematically accessible and should be used as the basis for political action.[6] The display of natural specimens and artificial anatomies at the new museum should demonstrate this claim, and turn model audiences into model citizens.

Thanks to the well-developed bureaucracy of eighteenth-century Tuscany and the Royal Museum's status as a state institution, this book's analysis of modelling in state service can draw on comparatively rich administrative source material for the reconstruction of interactions in modelling practice and model reception at the new institution. In addition, the model collection's popularity with visitors generated a large number of written accounts of the exhibition. *Model Experts* explores this rich source material to develop a detailed micro-historical analysis of model production, and model use in the larger context of political reform and regime change. Focusing on the practical aspects of anatomical modelling, *Model Experts* supports the argument that representations of nature are not unproblematic mirrorings of an independent reality, but rather the outcomes of historically and locally specific processes of construction.[7] The analysis foregrounds the relationship between epistemological and practical problems in the production and use of anatomical models. It thus speaks to recent scholarship on scientific representation, which has illuminated aspects such as the role of mechanical means of image production for the historical emergence of a new category of objectivity, the processes leading to the reification of invisible entities, claims about proper scientific method implicit in types of models, and the choices involved in simplifying the features of teaching models.[8]

Three-dimensional models, in particular, have recently attracted attention as points of contention, which provide access to scientific practice and a broader perspective on problems of representation.[9] In order to illuminate the relationship between model practices and model politics, *Model Experts* engages particularly with the ambivalence of the notion of the model, and with the observation by Barnes, Bloor, and Henry that scientific modelling is 'purposive and goal-oriented'. Models are ambivalent objects – both a (descriptive) 'representation of structure' and a (prescriptive) 'object of imitation'.[10] Models of entities as diverse as molecules, human bodies, and national economies serve as representations of nature or other law-governed systems; these may be used to serve as bases for prescriptive measures. Thus, models can be political in different ways. They may form part of explicitly (party-) political projects, but also support or subvert power structures in a less obvious manner.[11] Barnes, Bloor and Henry argue that 'A successful model is a pragmatic accomplishment, something which those who evaluate it take to serve their purposes.'[12]

This insight draws attention to two related issues: the purposes of a model, and the criteria by which it is evaluated. It thus opens up questions of particular importance for scientific activity in state service: Who determines what these purposes and criteria are, how, and why? Model production at La Specola, an early case of scientific modelling in state service, illuminates the relationship between different actors who were involved in model production, negotiations of responsibility and authority between scientists and the state which employed them, and the institutional and disciplinary contexts in which models were evaluated.

These everyday practices were related to fundamental problems of science in state service. Three main issues shaped the fate of La Specola's models and its model experts: What are the ramifications of science as a model for political action? What are the practical contributions of science and technology to state building? What should be the role of the scientist as an expert in state service?

Analyses of liberal democratic states such as Yaron Ezrahi's *The Descent of Icarus* (1990) have investigated the role of science as a template for modern politics. According to this interpretation, the idea of political action as accessible acts that can be witnessed and assessed by the public is based on, and structurally similar to, a view of scientific observations of natural processes as unproblematically observable and intelligible events. This image of nature and science can only work as a basis for political legitimacy if one assumes a stance of 'naive realism': the assumption that there are absolute standards upon which political action can be assessed when it is witnessed by an 'attestive public'.[13] However, such stances are not restricted to the liberal democracies of Ezrahi's analysis. In the age of absolutism two important theoretical frameworks put forward similar views: the early modern natural law tradition and physiocracy. Both schools of thought claimed that good government should follow the laws of nature, because adherence to these laws would ensure the establishment and maintenance of social harmony and public happiness. Natural law theorists had to grapple with the problem of political authority that was inherent in this claim: How could descriptive statements about nature be turned into normative prescriptions, and who should be in charge of realising these prescriptions? How could it be ascertained that the central authority adhered to the laws of nature? The foundation of La Specola, as part of the Tuscan sovereign's political 'experiments', was an attempts to address these problems in political practice.

At the same time, the notion of science as a model for political action raises questions about the constitution of 'the public' that witnesses both scientific and political action. Importantly, the framework of natural law already requires the creation of an 'attestive public' that is capable of assessing, and to some degree even legitimising, both forms of action. Therefore, the present analysis of how the public was created and shaped at the museum does not draw exclusively on analyses of contemporary issues of science and legitimacy in science and technology studies. It also engages with recent historiography on the late eighteenth century concerned with conceptual issues of the emerging public sphere, and works in museum studies, which have investigated historical practices of public education and attempts to shape public engagement with natural knowledge.[14]

However, science may be influential in a polity not only as a conceptual resource for the legitimising recourse to laws of nature. In addition, the very techniques developed by scientific disciplines may play an important role for the practical demands of governance and state building. Scholars have pointed especially to the role of techniques such as standardisation, counting, census and measurement, mapping, examination, and observation for practices of governance.[15] Recent publications on natural knowledge in eighteenth-century Tuscany assert the importance of science and technology for enlightened state-building efforts.[16] However, historical understandings of the 'utility' of natural knowledge change, and in Florence, model experts would rearticulate the utility of the artificial anatomies to ensure their survival under changing political regimes. When transferred to a different local context in Vienna in the 1780s, to be used at a controversial new surgico-medical academy, the Florentine models' claim to utility was undermined. The models' transfer to Austria and their fate under changing regimes in Tuscany therefore afford a critical re-evaluation of established claims in science and technology studies concerning the role of representations as elements which contribute centrally to the mobility and universality of modern science.[17]

In particular, the book argues that model production and model use were opportunities to address a third central issue: the role of the scientist as an expert in state service. While the state can make use of scientists' knowledge and skills for specific aims, the existence of this knowledge poses problems of control: How can scientists' judgements be assessed, if those in power do not possess the same kind of expertise? How can it be ascertained that scientists' own agenda coincides with, or at least does not contradict, that of the government? Influential attempts to theorise this problem for contemporary liberal democracies have framed it in terms of the place of scientific experts as a separate order of society, as an 'estate' (Don K. Price) or a 'fifth branch' (Sheila Jasanoff).[18] While sociologists have recently proposed a taxonomy of expertise, historical investigations have highlighted the fact that the notion of the expert was not available in early modern Europe.[19] Eighteenth-century Tuscany was no exception: the 'expert' was not an actors' category, although naturalists occasionally used the adjective *esperto* (expert, skilful, experienced) to justify their claims to authority. None of the scientists, anatomists, artists or administrators at La Specola thus referred to themselves explicitly as experts. However, the problem of special knowledge and its control was as pertinent for late-eighteenth-century Tuscany as it is for modern polities. Thus, the present study supports recent investigations into the genealogy of the persona of the expert, which argue that its establishment was an important element of the formation of the modern state.[20] Recent works have analysed the uses of expertise in early modern Europe, from engineering projects to legal deliberations, and the spaces in which claims to expertise were articulated, such as courtrooms, customs offices, building sites, or academies.[21] As a public institution, the Florentine museum with its model workshop and exhibition was another important space where notions of expertise, its public, and its place in the polity were defined. Because this articulation took place in everyday practices of model production and display, the present analysis adopts sociologist Erving Goffman's dramaturgical approach to the establishment of social identities, using a performative idiom to analyse the constitution of experts' roles vis-à-vis the state and the public.[22] In this book, articulations of expertise are themselves the subject of investigation; the term 'expert' is, therefore, used broadly to refer to someone who claims authority to make evaluations and prescriptions on the basis of his or her (exclusive) access to natural knowledge.[23]

But what, exactly, was the basis for expert authority? The book argues that articulations of authority could change rapidly in the face of conceptual and practical problems. Investigating the long history of the persona of the scientist, Steven Shapin has recently suggested that 'familiarity, trust, and the recognition of personal virtues' continued to play a central role for the production of natural knowledge well into late modernity.[24] *Model Experts* investigates this claim by focusing on changing articulations of expertise in everyday practices of knowledge making during a transitional period between early and late modernity.

Analysing the relationship between modelling and expertise, *Model Experts* asks a core set of questions. In what ways were the models supposed to be useful for the state, and who defined this utility? How and why did definitions of utility change? How did practices of model production and use articulate notions of expertise and public? How did the models' institutional and political contexts shape negotiations of scientific authority in state service? The focus of the analysis is on the decades from La Specola's foundation in 1775 to the Restoration in 1814–15 in order to pursue a comparative analysis of the roles of models and experts under changing political regimes. The analysis is divided into three parts which address, respectively, the ideological context in which the models were conceived, the articulation of the utility of models and experts in everyday practice at the museum, and their fate under changing institutional contexts and political regimes.

Part I: Politics of nature and politics of the body, considers the era of the foundation of the Royal Museum, and investigates how the museum and its anatomical models were supposed to contribute to Grand Duke Pietro Leopoldo's enlightened reforms and the creation of public happiness. Chapter 1, 'The politics of nature and the foundation of the Royal Museum', explains why the Tuscan sovereign undertook the foundation of a public science museum. It identifies La Specola as part of the 'political experiments' of the Grand Duke, a zealous enlightener inspired by the physiocrats. One of the main tenets of physiocratic theory was that adherence to the laws of nature would also be the solution to problems of social order. One of its main problems, then, was the creation of a society that was able to perceive and follow these laws. The questions of how nature could be unproblematically observed and represented and how the public could be educated in such a way as to understand these representations became central to political practice. The chapter argues that La Specola was one attempt to institutionalise expertise in state service and public science education. Comparing the museum to other institutions such as the Agricultural Academy and the Chamber of Commerce, the chapter shows that this institutionalisation created problems concerning the control of experts and the limits of their authority – a problem that remained salient in everyday practice at the new museum.

Chapter 2, 'Bodies and the state in eighteenth-century Tuscany', investigates how the museum's anatomical models were supposed to contribute to Pietro Leopoldo's efforts to address problems of legitimacy and to achieve public happiness by following natural law. To understand the Grand Duke's willingness to finance an enterprise as expensive as the model workshop, the chapter explores why different groups and individuals in Tuscany (such as physicians, surgeons, obstetricians, and government officials) were interested in the body. A main focus is the work of Tuscan physician Antonio Cocchi who was central in developing suggestions for medical reform in Tuscany during the Regency, before Pietro Leopoldo's accession. The chapter argues that the sovereign's reform efforts concerning anatomy in state service, including reforms at the General Hospital and the establishment of the model collection at La Specola, built on these earlier discussions, and widened the scope of anatomical expertise.

Part II: Articulating expertise in everyday practice highlights how practices of model production and model use at the museum shaped practitioners' roles as experts in state service, and articulated notions of the public. Chapter 3, 'Accuracy and authority in model production', investigates how the ongoing struggle between the museum's naturalists and its artisans concerning questions of workplace authority and discipline (a struggle which involved a fair bit of name-calling and threats) prompted different articulations of naturalists' roles as experts in state service. This struggle connected practical and conceptual issues of modelling, which fundamentally concerned the collection's suitability as a tool for public enlightenment: What should be the relationship between models and the public? How could the models' accuracy be guaranteed? Who could claim expertise? The abrasive director Felice Fontana tried to maintain his directorial authority vis-à-vis both his subordinates at the workshop and his superiors at court by claiming for himself a special faculty of attention. By contrast, his more affable assistant Fabbroni articulated his position as an expert in state service in a very different and ultimately more effective way, stressing a history of reliable service rather than special faculties. The artisans, finally, used their special practical skills as a powerful leverage to secure their position.

Chapter 4, 'Model reception and the display of expertise', turns to the museum's 'frontstage': the exhibition. The public museum as a new form of institution for the production and exhibition of natural knowledge required the simultaneous creation of a new audience: the museum visitor. The museum naturalists' early expectations that suitable teaching tools such as the anatomical waxes would by themselves create an enlightened public were sorely disappointed when visitors instead reacted to the models in a variety of idiosyncratic ways. Where some visitors saw evidence of the wisdom and benevolence of the Creator, others responded somewhat more profanely to the bodies on display, and objects such as monstrous foetuses and wax models of female genitals had to be protected from roving hands. In response to this interpretive flexibility,

Fontana and Fabbroni once more developed strategies which articulated the role of the expert in different ways. Fontana maintained that a suitable presentation would be sufficient, and he turned to the production of detachable models in wood. In contrast, Fabbroni claimed that models could only be useful tools for public education if they were accompanied by the instructions of an expert. He thus accorded a very different place to the expert in the process of public education – one that denied the possibility of visitors discovering underlying natural laws for themselves.

Part III: Changing model contexts and interpretations investigates the Florentine models' fate under changing circumstances, to show that the survival of models and model experts depended on their local political and cultural context. The artificial bodies' interpretive flexibility was used by different social groups to support their claims to public utility. This flexibility, in part, accounts for the models' failure to become accepted as useful tools of public enlightenment in the different institutional and cultural context of the Viennese medico-surgical academy Josephinum, which is the topic of Chapter 5, 'The rejection of the Florentine anatomical models in Vienna'. The Austrian emperor Joseph II had requested wax models from the Florentine workshop for his newly founded surgico-medical academy, an institution established mainly for the training of military surgeons. Like its Tuscan counterpart, the expensive Viennese model collection raised considerable public interest after its arrival in the mid-1780s. However, in Vienna the anatomical waxes became controversial immediately: In a public skirmish with the Josephinum's surgeons over the public utility of their expertise, local physicians denounced the models as vulgar. They chimed in with a printed satire, *Monkeyland*, which eloquently ridiculed the anatomical waxes as 'pretty toys' and its users at the new surgeons' academy as uncivilised 'butcher's apprentices'. The chapter argues that surgeons eager to stress their usefulness for the state accordingly renounced the models' utility (despite their acknowledged accuracy) in order to distance themselves from the received image of the coarse surgeon, and to side with middle-class doctors and their claim to sophistication.

Chapter 6, 'Regime changes in Tuscany and at La Specola, 1790–1814', returns to La Specola to describe the fate of the model collection during the turbulent years between the French Revolution and the restoration of the Grand Duchy in 1814. It analyses how museum directors rearticulated the utility of the museum, its experts and its models for the state in order to ensure the continuing survival of the institution and its costly modelling activities under different regimes plagued by chronic budget shortages. Here, the same interpretive flexibility which troubled Pietro Leopoldo's plans to use the models for public enlightenment proved to be an advantage. Regime changes could be both an opportunity and a threat for naturalists' own agendas concerning the shaping of the museum, its cadre of expert naturalists and its model collection as tools for public education. This chapter argues that the naturalists' success hinged on their ability to align their own ideas for the collection's purpose with those of the new government. This strategy was most successful when their ideas were congruent with the French (post-) revolutionary regime, which highlights the continuities between enlightened absolutism and the French Revolution.

Finally, the conclusion examines the continuing relevance of the Florentine models for representations of the body and articulations of expertise in state service. It analyses the consequences of the models' materiality for practices of production, administration, use and display, and addresses the ramifications of their interpretive flexibility for their own trajectories as well as for subsequent modelling enterprises, up to the present. As a project that prompted various articulations of expertise in state service, the Florentine model collection and the human interactions that surrounded it highlight the fragility and context-dependency of expert authority, experts' precarious position between the state and the public, and the persistence of fundamental conceptual problems at the core of expertise.

Notes

1 'Absorbé dans la contemplation de la beauté sublime, . . ., j'ávais un battement de coeur, . . . la vie était épuisée chez moi, je marchais avec la crainte de tomber'. Stendhal, *Rome, Naples et Florence* (3rd edn, Paris: Delaunay, 1826), vol. 1, p. 102.
2 Graziella Magherini, *La sindrome di Stendhal* (Florence: Ponte alle Grazie, 1989).
3 The name 'La Specola' came into use when the museum added an astronomical observatory (*specola*) in the late eighteenth century. As this is the name it is known by today, the book uses 'La Specola' and 'Royal Museum' interchangeably.
4 For interpretations of the models' features, see e.g. Mario Bucci, *Anatomia come arte* (Florence: Edizioni d'Arte Il Fiorino, 1969); Ludmilla Jordanova, *Sexual visions: images of gender in science and medicine between the eighteenth and twentieth centuries* (Madison: University of Wisconsin Press, 1989); Georges Didi-Huberman, (1999a), 'Wax flesh, vicious circles', in *Encyclopaedia Anatomica. Vollständige Sammlung anatomischer Wachse. Museo di Storia Naturale dell' Università di Firenze, sezione di zoologia La Specola* (Cologne: Taschen, 1999), pp. 64–74; Georges Didi-Huberman (1999b), *Ouvrir Vénus – nudité, rêve, cruauté* (Paris: Gallimard, 1999). For a brief overview of eighteenth-century wax modelling, see also Joan B. Landes, 'Wax fibres, wax bodies, and moving figures: artifice and nature in eighteenth-century anatomy', in Roberta Panzanelli (ed.), *Ephemeral*

bodies: wax sculpture and the human figure (Los Angeles: Getty Research Institute, 2008), pp. 41–66.

5 For groundbreaking work on the institutional history of La Specola and its political context see the works of Simone Contardi and Renato Pasta, especially Simone Contardi, *La Casa di Salomone a Firenze. L'Imperiale e Reale Museo di Fisica e Storia Naturale (1775–1801)* (Florence: Olschki, 2002); Renato Pasta, *Scienza politica e rivoluzione. L'opera di Giovanni Fabbroni (1752–1822) intellettuale e funzionario al servizio dei Lorena* (Florence: Olschki, 1989).

6 These theories include physiocracy and early liberalism. See e.g. Steven Kaplan, 'Physiocracy, the state, and society: the limits of disengagement', in Peter Katzenstein, Theodore Lowi, and Sidney Tarrow (eds), *Comparative theory and political experience* (Ithaca and London: Cornell University Press, 1990), pp. 23–62; Yaron Ezrahi, *The descent of Icarus. Science and the transformation of contemporary society* (Cambridge, Mass.: Harvard University Press, 1990).

7 For an overview of constructivism in historical studies of science see Jan Golinski, *Making natural knowledge: constructivism and the history of science* (Cambridge: Cambridge University Press, 1998). For representation as practical achievement see e.g. Michael A. Dennis, 'Graphic understanding: instruments and interpretation in Robert Hooke's "Micrographia"', *Science in context 3* (1989), pp. 309–64. For an analysis of the problem of realism with special reference to museums see Ludmilla Jordanova, 'Museums: representing the real?', in George Levine (ed.), *Realism and representation. Essays on the problem of realism in relation to science, literature, and culture* (Madison: University of Wisconsin Press, 1993), pp. 255–78.

8 Lorraine Daston and Peter Galison, 'The image of objectivity', *Representations* 40 (1992), pp. 81–128; Alberto Cambrosio, D. Jacobi, and P. Keating, 'Ehrlich's "beautiful pictures" and the controversial beginnings of immunological imagery', *Isis* 84 (1993), pp. 662–99; Christoph Meinel, 'Molecules and croquet balls', in Soraya de Chadarevian and Nick Hopwood (eds), *Models: the third dimension of science* (Stanford: Stanford University Press, 2004), pp. 242–75; Nick Hopwood, 'Giving body to embryos: modeling, mechanism, and the microtome in late-nineteenth-century anatomy', *Isis* 90 (1999), pp. 462–96; Eric Francoeur, 'The forgotten tool: the design and use of molecular models', *Social studies of science* 27 (1997), pp. 7–40.

9 de Chadarevian and Hopwood (eds), *Models: the third dimension*; Hopwood, 'Giving body'.

10 *Oxford English dictionary*. For the ambivalence of models see also James R. Griesemer, 'Three-dimensional models in philosophical perspective', in de Chadarevian and Hopwood (eds), *Models: the third dimension*, pp. 433–42.

11 For different politics of modelling see e.g. Nick Hopwood, 'Artist versus anatomist, models against dissection: Paul Zeiller of Munich and the Revolution of 1848', *Medical history* 51 (2007), pp. 279–308; Ludmilla Jordanova, *Sexual visions*; Rebecca Messbarger, 'As who dare gaze the Sun: Anna Morandi Manzolini's wax

anatomies of the male reproductive system', in Paula Findlen, Wendy Wassyng Roworth, and Catherina M. Sama (eds), *Italy's eighteenth century: Gender and culture in the age of the Grand Tour* (Stanford: Stanford University Press, 2009), pp. 251–74; Simon Schaffer, 'Fish and ships: models in the age of reason', in de Chadarevian and Hopwood (eds), *Models: the third dimension*, pp. 71–105.

12 Barry Barnes, David Bloor, and John Henry, *Scientific knowledge. A sociological analysis* (Chicago: University of Chicago Press, 1996), pp. 108–9.

13 Ezrahi, *Descent of Icarus*, p. 76.

14 For a valuable historiographical perspective on the concept of the public sphere see Harold Mah, 'Phantasies of the public sphere: rethinking the Habermas of historians', *Journal of modern history* 72 (2000), pp. 153–82; a useful critical review of recent developments in museum studies is Randolph Starn, 'A historian's brief guide to new museum studies', *The American historical review* 110:1 (2005), pp. 68–98.

15 Michel Foucault, *Discipline and punish* (New York: Vintage Books, 1995 [1975]); Benedict Anderson, *Imagined communities* (London and New York: Verso, 1991 [1983]); James C. Scott, *Seeing like a state: how certain schemes to improve the human condition have failed* (New Haven: Yale University Press, 1998); Ken Alder, *Engineering the revolution: arms, enlightenment, and the making of modern France, 1763–1815* (Princeton: Princeton University Press, 1997).

16 See e.g. the contributions in Renato Pasta (ed.), *La politica della scienza: Toscana e stati italiani nel tardo Settecento* (Florence: Olschki, 1996).

17 See especially Steven Shapin, 'Pump and circumstance: Robert Boyle's literary technology', *Social studies of science* 14 (1984), pp. 481–520; Bruno Latour, 'Drawing things together', in Michael Lynch and Steve Woolgar (eds), *Representation in scientific practice* (Cambridge, Mass.: MIT Press, 1990), pp. 19-68.

18 Don K. Price, *The scientific estate* (Cambridge, Mass.: Harvard University Press, 1965); Sheila Jasanoff, *The fifth branch. Science advisers as policymakers* (Cambridge, Mass.: Harvard University Press, 1990).

19 Harry Collins and Robert Evans, *Rethinking expertise* (Chicago: University of Chicago Press, 2007).

20 See e.g. the contributions in Volker Hess, Eric Engstrom and Ulrike Thoms (eds), *Figurationen des Experten: Ambivalenzen der wissenschaftlichen Expertise im ausgehenden 18. und frühen 19. Jahrhundert* (Frankfurt: Peter Lang, 2005); Christelle Rabier (ed.), *Fields of expertise: a comparative history of expert procedures in Paris and London, 1600 to present* (Newcastle: Cambridge Scholars Publishing, 2007); and in *Osiris* 25 (2010), 'Expertise and the early modern state' (ed. Eric Ash).

21 For engineering projects, see e.g. Frédéric Graber, 'Inventing needs: expertise and water supply in late eighteenth- and early nineteenth-century Paris', *British journal for the history of science* 40 (2007), pp. 315–32; Chandra Mukerji, 'Cartography, entrepreneurialism, and power in the reign of Louis XIV: the case of the Canal du Midi', in Pamela H. Smith and Paula Findlen (eds), *Merchants and marvels: commerce, science, and art in early modern Europe* (New York and London: Routledge,

2002), pp. 248–76; for legal deliberations in courts, see e.g. Silvia De Renzi, 'Medical expertise, bodies and the law in early modern courts', *Isis* 98 (2007), pp. 315–22; Tal Golan, *Laws of men and laws of nature: the history of scientific expert testimony in England and America* (Cambridge, Mass.: Harvard University Press, 2004); for customs, see William J. Ashworth, *Customs and excise: trade, production, and consumption in England, 1640–1845* (Oxford: Oxford University Press, 2003).

22 Erving Goffman, *The presentation of self in everyday life* (New York 1959). See also Stephen Hilgartner, *Science on stage. Expert advice as public drama* (Stanford 2000), and Charles Thorpe, 'Disciplining experts: scientific authority and liberal democracy in the Oppenheimer case', *Social studies of science* 32 (2002), pp. 525–62.

23 For a valuable overview of analytical approaches to the historical emergence of expertise, see Eric Ash, 'Introduction: expertise and the early modern state', *Osiris* 25 (2010).

24 Steven Shapin, *The scientific life. A moral history of a late modern vocation* (Chicago and London: University of Chicago Press, 2008), p. 1.

Part I

Politics of nature and politics of the body

1

The politics of nature and the foundation of the Royal Museum

In 1765, the Austrian prince Peter Leopold (1747–92) (plate IIa) succeeded his father Francis Stephen of Habsburg-Lorraine as Grand Duke of Tuscany, at only eighteen years of age. Arriving at his new Florence residence from Vienna, the young sovereign was confronted with a country in disarray, a political patchwork of competing secular and religious authorities, struck by poverty, famine and illiteracy. The Habsburg-Lorraine dynasty was still new to Tuscany – the young Grand Duke's father had reigned *in absentia* since the demise of the Medici in 1737, and the glorious memory of the Medicean past was still fresh in many Tuscan minds, and visible throughout the capital. Over the following decades, the well-educated Habsburg prince, now known to his Tuscan subjects as Pietro Leopoldo, embarked on a wide range of reform measures to support the legitimacy of his rule and to further the common good.

Pietro Leopoldo considered natural knowledge and its dissemination central in securing a new ruling dynasty and creating a viable state with contented subjects. The young sovereign's perspective was shared, and in the early years of his reign decisively influenced, by trusted advisers such as Franz Xaver Rosenberg, head of the Tuscan government from 1766 to 1771.[1] At the time of Pietro Leopoldo's accession, Tuscany could already look back on a long tradition of scholarship, institutionalised in learned academies. Pietro Leopoldo's government appropriated established scholarly traditions and institutions in his efforts at state building. However, the Grand Duke met with a territory that was not only politically heterogeneous, with many conflicting authorities, but also a place which hosted many competing discourses and displays of natural knowledge. Mountebanks, itinerant lecturers and academicians alike claimed knowledge of nature; they presented nature and its wonders to the public in market squares, churches, private homes and in learned publications. To police these voices, the sovereign and his advisers initiated efforts to streamline not just Tuscan government, but also education and the production of natural knowledge. They aimed to create a public that would not only understand the laws of nature and accept policies based on them, but also to create a cadre of experts who would produce and disseminate natural knowledge in state service. These efforts included the reform and new foundation of institutions such as the Chamber of Commerce, the agricultural Accademia dei Georgofili, and the Royal Museum of Physics and Natural History. The Royal Museum, which aimed to 'enlighten the public and make it happy by making it educated', was one of the Grand Duke's most well-known measures internationally.[2]

Directed by court physicist Felice Fontana, a mentor of Pietro Leopoldo as a young regent, the museum represented a microcosm of creation, from collections of minerals and plants to stuffed animals, physical instruments and chemical apparatus. Moving beyond the Medici *Wunderkammer*, the new museum, which opened to the public in Florence in 1775, was from the outset explicitly public and soon received international acclaim. It became subsequently known as 'La Specola' for its astronomical observatory, although this colloquial title also captured what was expected of the visitor: 'to speculate, contemplate, view, or observe a thing attentively'.[3] A vast collection of anatomical wax models particularly fascinated local and foreign visitors: the Royal Museum soon became famous among educated Europeans for these three-dimensional representations of human bodies and body parts, life-sized, enlarged and *en miniature*, which depicted normal anatomy in an idealised and strangely attractive manner. The museum's educational mission was further supported by controlling and curtailing popular and religious spectacle in Tuscany, effectively giving the new museum almost a monopoly on the public display of nature and its laws.

The first part of this book, 'Politics of nature and politics of the body', analyses the Tuscan sovereign's reasons for developing a project as costly as the museum and its model collection. In the context of eighteenth-century political thought, La Specola and its models can be understood as an attempt to use natural knowledge to address the problem of political legitimacy, and to achieve that elusive goal of enlightened reform, *pubblica felicità* or public happiness, by educating the public about nature and the body.[4] However, the institutionalisation of natural knowledge in state service was difficult. This chapter compares three of Pietro Leopoldo's efforts to institutionalise expertise in state service, at the agricultural Accademia dei Georgofili, the Chamber of Commerce, and the museum, to highlight that the existence of these institutions and its members, who could claim special knowledge of nature and its laws, raised questions about the function and power of experts in the enlightened absolutist polity.

Grand Duke Pietro Leopoldo's politics of nature: Tuscany as a laboratory of enlightened reform

At his accession to the Tuscan throne, following Francis Stephen's death in 1765, Grand Duke Pietro Leopoldo was faced with a country plagued by famine, heavily in debt, and in need of political and administrative reform.[5] In 1737, an era had come to an end in Tuscany: Grand Duke Gian Gastone, last of the Medici rulers, had died without an heir. Following the territorial shuffles of the War of Polish Succession, Tuscany went to Duke Francis Stephen of Lorraine, consort-to-be of future Austrian empress Maria Teresa of Habsburg, but the country remained independent from their imperial domains. Owing to his Viennese duties as royal consort and Holy Roman Emperor, Francis Stephen was absent from his Tuscan domains for almost 30 years. During this regency period, Tuscany was little more to its incumbent sovereign than a cash cow for the vast Habsburg empire. The state's heterogeneous political constitution, the result of Tuscany's emergence from the Florentine city state and its gradual accumulation of adjacent territories since the Middle Ages, was left unchanged.

Unlike his father, Pietro Leopoldo set upon the business of ruling the state in earnest, and took residence in Florence. Arriving in Tuscany, he witnessed the effects of famine and deprivation, as well as the competing local allegiances and authorities in the capital and the country: the rivalries between formerly independent city states like Florence and Siena, and the influence of the numerous guilds, religious orders, and lay confraternities. Inspired by the latest developments in political thought and natural philosophy, and guided by his advisers Rosenberg, Angelo Tavanti, Pompeo Neri, and Francesco Maria Gianni, the young Grand Duke soon initiated numerous reforms, which made Tuscany the model state of enlightened absolutism in the eyes of contemporaries. The eighteen-year-old sovereign was well versed in natural history and experimental natural philosophy, and he conceived of political action as a form of problem solving that could be tackled by experimental methods. Thus, he used Tuscany explicitly as a political laboratory for legal, economic, administrative, and social reform – an approach which his mother's advisers had recently applied with success in Austria.[6] On his legal reforms, for example, the Grand Duke remarked that 'a good legislation is like sound natural philosophy, it must be founded on experiment; the laws too should be tried'.[7] Intellectuals and sovereigns throughout Europe followed Tuscan political experiments with much interest. The physiocrats courted Pietro Leopoldo's attention early on; the French physiocrat Mirabeau dedicated his 1769 work *Les économiques* to Pietro Leopoldo, applauding the ambition of this 'shepherd-prince' ('Prince-pasteur') to follow 'the sublime science of the laws of nature' and to 'provide to our brothers knowledge of the rights and duties of Man'.[8]

Knowledge, and especially knowledge of nature, was indeed at the core of Pietro Leopoldo's reform plans. The natural law tradition was the main framework for the Grand Duke's understanding of legitimacy, rights and obligations within the polity. It was based on the dual assumption that nature was a system governed by universal laws, and that the human subject was a rational being capable of perceiving these laws.[9] According to this tradition, the legal norms governing society should be derived from, and harmonious with, the perceived natural order of the world. This approach faced a problem with regard to the source of obligation: the laws derived from nature remained descriptive. The obligation for members of society to obey these rules, however, could not be derived from such a set of descriptive statements. In order to make these descriptive statements normative, then, legal theorists resorted to a transcendent authority, that is, God, or accepted the (in principle inarticulable) nature of authority as a given.[10] Later developments of natural law based the source of obligation on the assumption of a contract between all members of society, according to which, members of society transferred their power to a central source of authority by mutual assent. This authority was responsible for the enforcement and formulation of the legal principles derived from the order of nature. Although this contractual relationship did not necessitate any specific form of government, in the early modern period it was taken to legitimise absolutist rule.[11] Ultimately, this form of legitimacy was based on the consensus of all members of the polity.

This approach opened up a number of practical problems concerning the organisation of governance. The localisation of sovereignty, in particular, was not unequivocal. In the contractual approach the power of the members of the polity was completely transferred to the sovereign. However, this power of the ruler was, in principle, restricted to guaranteeing the adherence to laws that were already fully determined by principles of natural order. Thus, eighteenth-century political actors such as Prussian king Frederick II argued that sovereigns were no more than 'slaves of their means'.[12] In addition, the natural law approach left open the question of how the sovereign's adherence to these laws of good order should be ascertained. Who should control the sovereign, and how? What were the possibilities of action for subjects if their ruler did not adhere to the laws prescribed by nature?

A number of reform measures from the 1760s onwards made attempts at practical solutions to these problems of authority and control. In Pietro Leopoldo's framework, it was necessary to create natural knowledge in the government and in the population alike. The sovereign had to be able to perceive and understand the laws of nature on which his political actions had to be based in order to be legitimate. At the same time, his subjects had to receive similar education that would enable them not only to accept natural law as the basis for the sovereign's authority, but also to assess his actions.

A more recent conceptual development – the new doctrine of physiocracy – shared Pietro Leopoldo's conviction that natural knowledge was central to the creation of public happiness.[13] Physiocracy was a systematic attempt in the mid-eighteenth century to develop concrete rules for the reform of society according to the laws of nature. Like the natural law tradition, it was 'predicated upon absolute deference to the imperious laws of nature'.[14] The physiocrats' main tenets were the right of property and the assumption that agriculture was the (primary) source of a society's wealth. From these principles, physiocrats derived laws pertaining not only to economic policy, but also to other areas of 'good order', such as political participation, administration, and education.[15] The practical implementation of physiocratic doctrine therefore required fundamental changes in the polity. The liberalisation of the grain trade, for instance, a core element of physiocratic doctrine, redefined the role of the sovereign, as the protector of his subjects' livelihood, from protector of fixed grain prices to guarantor of free trade. In the case of Tuscany, these redefinitions would meet with strong resistance from parts of the population who perceived the reforms as an abandonment of the Grand Duke's protective role towards his subjects. Given the fundamental nature of these changes, and the possibility of strong resistance, the physiocrats therefore called for a strong sovereign, a 'legal despot'[16] who could implement changes against public resistance for the public good. Tuscan intellectuals and functionaries shared the physiocrats' perspective in this regard: they considered monarchy to be the only form of government sufficiently powerful to carry through far-reaching reforms, and to guarantee that all subjects would benefit equally from those changes.[17]

While Tuscan intellectuals and functionaries like Francesco Maria Gianni remained sceptical of physiocratic orthodoxy, they pursued a pragmatic and eclectic approach in adopting some of its elements for the Tuscan polity.[18] The main economic reform, starting with the liberation of the grain trade in 1767, abolished local custom duties, corporations, and privileges and monopolies. While a strong stress was placed on the support of agriculture, the Tuscan government deviated from strict physiocratic doctrine in its additional support of manufacture and trade. The homogenisation of administration was achieved mainly through a far-reaching reform of local government, which in 1769 replaced the patchwork of local authorities by a central *Camera delle Comunità*.[19]

Institutionalising expertise in state service: the Accademia dei Georgofili and the Chamber of Commerce

In addition to such economic and administrative reforms, Pietro Leopoldo undertook the reform and foundation of institutions for the production and dissemination of natural knowledge, such as the reformed agricultural academy Accademia dei Georgofili, the new Chamber of Commerce (*Camera di Commercio*), and the new Museum of Physics and Natural History. These institutions were to be home to cadres of experts who would create and disseminate natural knowledge in state service. Issues concerning the control and use of natural knowledge, which natural law theorists and physiocrats had raised on the conceptual level, were now raised in practice, in the relationship between the sovereign and his experts. The development of these three institutions illustrates how Pietro Leopoldo responded to these practical issues, careful to maintain his authority and to prevent the emergence of powerful expert groups with claims to natural knowledge by curtailing their responsibilities or abolishing them.

In his institutional measures, Pietro Leopoldo could draw on a large number of long-standing private academies and learned societies.[20] Some of them had already served informally as sources of information and advice, for example for ad hoc assessments of governmental mining enterprises during the Regency. However, the new sovereign took a strong interest in reconstituting the academies permanently, and creating additional institutions designed to make natural philosophy and natural history useful for the state. Similar to the economic and administrative reforms, the reform and creation of learned institutions aimed for increased, but not total homogenisation and centralisation. The Grand Duke's intervention led to the abolition of some of the older academies, which did not fit his idea of useful knowledge, such as the famous Accademia della Crusca, which was concerned with care for the Tuscan language. Others, like the relatively new agricultural Accademia dei Georgofili, were reorganised internally to promote the public good in the service of the state. Newly founded state institutions such as the Chamber of Commerce and the Royal Museum of Physics and Natural History were directly subordinate to the sovereign. At some of these institutions the issue of autonomy was contentious; in the case of the Camera, this issue would even lead to its abolition. Thus, the relationship between the Grand Duke and the institutions that produced natural knowledge reveal a persistent tension between the authority of Nature, and the authority of the sovereign.

The Accademia dei Georgofili (Greek: 'friends of farming'), founded in 1753, was initially a private association of scholars and landowners interested in the development of agriculture as a means for social improvement. Publishing prolifically in, for instance, the *Magazzino toscano* and the *Giornale fiorentino d'agricoltura*, the Georgofili were among the most important proponents for agricultural reform in Italy.[21] They actively attempted to shape the state, putting forward in their publications strategies for economic reform and agricultural innovation.[22] During the famine years of 1764–67 the academicians put forward plans for government intervention aimed at the liberalisation and support of trade and commerce, which did at least in part coincide with the actual measures subsequently taken by the government. This 'convergence between cultural forces and the government' was reflected in the Academy's institutional reform in 1767, which included the election of officials who provided standing links to the government.[23] However, the coincidence between the measures proposed by the Georgofili and those taken by the government does not imply that Pietro Leopoldo was generally inclined to grant agency to the academicians on the basis of their scientific expertise, or to institutionalise this expertise on a larger scale. The sovereign persistently refused to create a national academy of science similar to those established in France or Prussia, a proposal that had been put forward repeatedly during the 1770s and 1780s by the Georgofili and other scholars, including court scientist Felice Fontana.[24]

Pietro Leopoldo's refusal reveals, on the level of political practice, the tension inherent in theories of state based on the laws of nature. The Grand Duke publicly demonstrated his adherence to Nature as a way to support his legitimacy, and he was genuinely convinced of Nature's importance for creating the public good and furthering public happiness. At the same time, however, instead of one central national academy of science, Pietro Leopoldo maintained a variety of separate institutions devoted to the production and dissemination of natural knowledge. He thus avoided the emergence of a single organisation which might one day turn Pietro Leopoldo's legitimising strategy against him by claiming significant political authority for itself on the basis of claims to natural knowledge.

Despite Pietro Leopoldo's refusal of the Georgofili's more far-reaching institutional plans, the agricultural academy remained among the government's most important supporters. In the following decades the sovereign encouraged public discussion of those of his measures that had met with resistance.[25] In these discussions he could rely on the support of the Georgofili and their well-developed publication channels. In addition, Pietro Leopoldo continued to call upon the Georgofili as sources of information.[26] At the same time, however, the Grand Duke restricted the academies' competencies. Especially during the 1780s, most academies were reformed further towards stronger governmental control and internal specialisation. Larger academies such as the Georgofili and the Fisiocritici – a broadly natural philosophical society in Siena – were equipped with two government officials nominated by the sovereign, a superintendent and a representative of the ruler. Pietro Leopoldo further circumscribed the responsibilities of the academies' experts. With regard to the Accademia dei Fisiocritici, for instance, he punningly insisted that 'the Academy has to cover discoveries' (and nothing else).[27] Similarly, the Georgofili's prize competitions no longer included general political and moral questions, but focused specifically on technical and agricultural practices.[28]

The conflict between the experts' struggle for political agency and government control was more pronounced during the short history of the Camera di Commercio, Arti e Manifatture, which was abolished when its members claimed significant political authority on the basis of their expertise. The Chamber of Commerce was part of the array of measures for the liberalisation of commerce in the late 1760s and early 1770s. This included reducing the influence of the powerful local guilds. To this end, the Grand Duke 'unified' the artisanal corporations of Florence, and installed his Camera di Commercio as their head office.[29] The Camera's appointed task was to 'improve manufacturing and commerce' in the Grand Duchy, and thus to carry out the transition from a corporate-based economy of artisanal production to a free market economy. While expected to protect, control and support artisans and traders 'with all facilities necessary for inciting their industry', the Camera was to attend to the 'constant and uniform rules' of the new liberalised economy 'directed at the universal good of the state', and to publish accounts of innovations in commerce and production.[30]

The Camera's members affirmed economic reforms as the most important instrument of political action, and adherence to the laws of nature as indispensable to the reforms' success. They regarded technological progress as an indispensable element of successful economic reform. Like most Florentine intellectuals and functionaries, they supported – in principle, at least – the sovereign's absolute power as necessary for the introduction of reform measures.[31] Nevertheless, the members of the Camera attempted to create a space of agency for themselves. Similar to the Georgofili, here too a push towards technological specialisation in state service came from within the institution itself: the Camera's members envisioned themselves as the kernel of an emerging technological elite, and proposed the foundation of an institution for the support of technological development after the image of the Society of Arts in London.[32]

Like similar plans for the foundation of an academy of science put forward by the Georgofili, these were rejected by the sovereign. Pietro Leopoldo increasingly distrusted the growing enthusiasm of the Camera to shape economic policy. The main point of contention was the distribution of agency in the implementation of reform measures. The Camera seemed to envision a division of tasks by which they would determine the contents of new reforms, and the sovereign would provide the authority and power for their actual implementation. The sovereign, however, insisted that he alone was in a position to make decisions concerning reform. As he assured his brother, Austrian emperor Joseph II, 'it is only the sovereign who can oversee all the different branches [of administration] at the same time, without predilection for anything but the general good of the whole state'.[33] Accordingly, on 29 May 1781 the sovereign ordered the Camera to be dissolved within a year. Thus, the fate of the Camera was strikingly similar to the development of the academies when brought under government control. Here too the sovereign initially relied on the shared interests and ideological preconceptions of the Camera's experts, but prevented their more far-reaching claims for political agency.

Sensationalism and public enlightenment

A more lasting foundation by the Grand Duke was the Royal Museum of Physics and Natural History, which served the dual function of institutionalising expertise and public enlightenment in state service. The Tuscan politics of nature required that the public understand and accept natural law as the basis of political action. At the new museum, Pietro Leopoldo could realise some of his most dearly held beliefs, especially the tenets of sensationalism. The foundational text of this theory of learning was John Locke's 1689 *Essay Concerning Human Understanding*, in which Locke refuted the concept of innate ideas and argued instead that knowledge was the product of a combination of sensation and reflection.[34] Subsequent elaborations of this argument increasingly stressed the central role of sensation in particular. The main proponent of a radically reductionist interpretation of sensationalism, the French philosopher Etienne Bonnot de Condillac, claimed that sensation had primacy in learning, since 'sensation calls out all the faculties of the soul'.[35] Enlightenment theorists and practitioners considered education central to the creation of a civilised, happy society, and they shared a strong optimism regarding the power of education – the assertion by French philosopher Claude Adrien Helvétius that 'education can do anything'[36] represented the view of many of his contemporaries. The widespread interest in education was shared by monarchs, functionaries, and intellectuals; and Tuscany under Pietro Leopoldo was no exception. The Tuscan journal *Novelle Letterarie*, for instance, voiced the opinion that

> governments and sovereigns have to promote and procure public education. The man who grows up ignorant, if he remains in this state, is always a bad citizen . . .

he does not love and respect the law . . . he does not serve the purpose to which the natural order has destined him.[37]

Accordingly, public education should rest on 'everything which explains history, which deciphers the secrets of nature, which shows to man the use of his faculties, and his destiny on earth'. Of primary importance 'for all individuals' was the overarching 'science of order', which would teach the populace that 'everything in the world is connected, and everything is determined by unchangeable laws', and that, therefore, the promotion of the public good was in every individual's interest.[38] The journal's editor until 1777, Giuseppe Pelli (1729–1808), practised this conviction in the power of education: he adopted a young orphan, and submitted her to a rigorous educational regimen. Pelli's experiment in enlightenment at home eventually bore fruit: his adopted daughter Teresa (who married museum director Fontana's second-in-command Giovanni Fabbroni in 1782) became Florence's foremost *salonnière*.[39] Many Tuscan functionaries applied similar convictions to the Tuscan public as a whole; Pietro Leopoldo's adviser Gianni, for example, asserted that education 'will in a few years change the customs of an entire nation'.[40] A few decades later, in 1797 museum deputy director Fabbroni (who owed his own upward mobility to the improving power of education) urged Pietro Leopoldo's son and successor Ferdinando III to continue his father's legacy, reminding him of the strong link between knowledge and legitimacy: public education, he stressed, was 'the primary foundation not only of national industry, and character, but also of good social order, and the firm basis of the sovereign's magnificence'.[41]

Pietro Leopoldo shared both this belief in the power of education to create good order, and sympathies for post-Lockean epistemology. His own sons read Locke as part of their curriculum.[42] Developing a reform of the educational system, the Grand Duke corresponded with the Swiss educator Pestalozzi in the late 1780s, and exchanged information with other Habsburg rulers on educational institutions.[43] It was felt that, in theory, all Tuscans should be educated according to the same universal principles, and the education of subjects and sovereigns should be complementary to solve the problem of legitimacy. Education would develop a 'good common sense' in both ruler and ruled; this would make the sovereign wise and benevolent, and teach his subjects to submit to his rule willingly.[44] In a more radical vein, the Grand Duke hoped that a reform of the educational system and of cultural institutions more broadly would contribute to his attempts to homogenise the Tuscan populace of Florentines, Pisans, Sienese and others as citizens united under one sovereign, and to make the boundaries between different social groups, especially between the nobility and the emerging middle class, more permeable.[45] The Grand

Duke thereby pre-empted some of the major tenets that would characterise educational reform in France during the Revolution. This stance contributed further to Tuscan liberals' conviction that enlightened despotism was the form of government most conducive to the realisation of their aims.[46]

The Grand Duke's children received an education with a strong natural philosophical and natural historical component in order to develop their 'common sense'.[47] Empiricism and visual aids were central to this development: In his 'Notes on education' ('Notes sur l'éducation', 1775), the Grand Duke stressed that 'natural history and physics have to be taught to children with drawings and facts'.[48] Accordingly, museum director and court physicist Felice Fontana, who had guided Pietro Leopoldo's own chemical experiments, gave lessons at least to his eldest sons Francesco (who was to succeed Joseph II as Austrian emperor) and Ferdinando (who was to succeed his father in Tuscany).[49] The new museum and its garden became sites of royal education, a 'scientific "gymnasium" for the archdukes', in line with the Grand Duke's conviction that learning should be immediate, object-oriented, and not primarily from books.[50] French visitor Dupaty, who was inclined to present Tuscany as a model state for enlightened politics, reported approvingly:

> I met this morning, when I was walking in the botanic garden, a little child, to whom a professor was distinguishing the plants; it was one of the duke's children. One is pleased to see a monarch's offspring amidst the scenes of nature.[51]

The establishment of the Royal Museum of Physics and Natural History 'La Specola'

The new Museum of Physics and Natural History (figure 2) was the perfect place to apply sensationalist theories of learning and perception in the service of public enlightenment and political legitimation, offering encounters with a wide range of natural objects to the Grand Duke's children and his subjects. The sovereign tried to ensure the museum's success in a number of ways, providing a building near the grand-ducal palace, instruments and *naturalia* from the Medici collection and financial support for further acquisitions, and employing a renowned natural philosopher as its director. Like other institutions such as the Chamber of Commerce and the Accademia dei Georgofili, however, the museum had to deal with a number of problems arising from expertise in state service. At La Specola, issues of autonomy and control were continually present in more or less explicit and far-reaching ways. Like other scholars, museum director Fontana unsuccessfully raised plans for a national academy of science. On the level of everyday museum practice, contentious

issues between court administration and museum experts included the owner-
ship of specimens, the control of the museum's finances, and even the accuracy
of models, investigated further in Chapter 3.

With the Tuscan throne, the Habsburg-Lorraine dynasty had inherited
the Medici's substantial collections of art, scientific instruments, globes, and
naturalia.[52] Some of these objects went to Vienna at Francis Stephen's
instigation. His son and successor Pietro Leopoldo would have encountered
them there. The prince showed a lifelong interest in scientific developments,
famously engaging in chemical experimentation himself. Soon after his arrival
in Tuscany, mentored by his court physicist Felice Fontana, Pietro Leopoldo
developed the idea of transforming and consolidating the grand-ducal collections into a public science museum. Collections were used for a variety of
learned and political purposes in early modern Europe. Noblemen and well-to-
do commoners kept collections of marvels both artificial and natural in private
cabinets of curiosities, central elements of early modern self-fashioning. These
Wunderkammern served to display the marvels of God's creation, but they also
demonstrated, more or less ostensibly, the sophistication and affluence of their
owners.[53] Individual visitors were given access to these private collections only
by permission of the owner.[54] Other important points of reference for Pietro
Leopoldo and his advisers may have been the collections of Italian learned
institutions such as the Bologna Academy of Sciences and the University of
Padua. While these collections were not accessible to the general public, they
shared with the envisioned Florentine museum the aim of being comprehensive
inventories of natural and natural philosophical objects.[55]

In an attempt to create a new form of scientific collection and display, suitable for public enlightenment, the grand-ducal collections were enlarged,
modified, and relocated to a separate building. Two similar contemporary
projects were undertaken elsewhere to further public knowledge of nature; they
later came to serve as comparisons for La Specola's naturalist-administrators in
their attempts to improve the Florentine museum as a place of instruction for
the common good. The British Museum in London was founded by an act of
Parliament in 1753 on the basis of the private collection of Sir Hans Sloane,
and opened to the public in 1759. However, this museum was not dedicated
exclusively to natural and natural philosophical objects.[56] More similar to
the Tuscan museum in terms of content was the slightly later transformation,
during the French Revolution, of the Paris Jardin du Roi into the Muséum
d'histoire naturelle, a place to turn French subjects into citizens of the new
republic through public enlightenment.[57]

In 1771 Pietro Leopoldo acquired a building to house the new institution –
Palazzo Torrigiani, suitably close to the Grand Duke's palace, and adjacent to

the Boboli Gardens.[58] The sovereign entrusted the museum to Felice Fontana (plate IIb) whose international reputation as a natural philosopher and wide network of correspondents could help secure the new institution's success. Fontana (1730–1805), a notary's son from Pomarolo near Rovereto in northern Italy, had studied mathematics, natural philosophy and anatomy at various Italian universities.[59] Working as a tutor to a young patrician in Bologna, he established contacts with the renowned Istituto di Bologna. His first publication, in 1760, was a defence of Haller's theory of irritability; throughout his career the phenomenon of life was one of Fontana's main interests.[60] In 1765 he started teaching at the Tuscan University of Pisa, and in 1766 he became an ordinarius in physics, grand-ducal physicist, and supervisor of the Grand Duke's cabinet. His interests ranged from chemistry and electricity to botany and medicine.

In his research on human and animal bodies, Fontana combined anatomical description with physiological experimentation, for instance in his investigation of the movements of the iris (*Dei moti dell'iride*, 1765) and his analysis of snake venom (*Richerche fisiche sopra il veleno della vipera*, 1767). Fontana soon became one of the most famous Italian natural philosophers of his day; his fame secured the reputation of the Grand Duke's new museum among naturalists and the reading public. However, Fontana's abrasive character and his paranoid tendencies quickly alienated him from the intellectual community of Florence, which regarded the foreign (i.e. non-Tuscan) interloper with hostility. Fontana's opposite number in the grand-ducal art collection, the director of the Uffizi Gallery Giuseppe Pelli, was not alone in considering Fontana to be 'a man of talent and reputation, but of a harsh and false character, and too prone to empty promises'.[61] The northerner's personal and professional relationships in Florence were fraught with tension. A dispute over the replication of Lavoisier's analysis of water between Fontana and rival experimenter Ferdinando Giorgi, fought with polemical posters and pamphlets in the mid-1780s, escalated in the city until the chief of police Giuseppe Giusti stepped in to end the 'distasteful affair'.[62] Fontana soon saw conspiracy everywhere, venting his suspicions to his royal patron Pietro Leopoldo in letters of increasing desperation. At La Specola, the director's conflicts with modellers, fellow naturalists and administrators would repeatedly endanger the Grand Duke's vision for the museum in ways investigated further in Part II.

Despite these local difficulties, Fontana maintained a large international network of correspondents, among them anatomists such as Paolo Mascagni and Antonio Scarpa, renowned instrument makers like Nairne and Blunt in London, naturalists such as the president of the Royal Society Joseph Banks, the secretary of the Swedish Patriotic Society Adolf Modeer, botanist

4 Giovanni Fabbroni (1752–1822). (Wellcome Collection, London)

Humphry Marshall in Pennsylvania, and experimentalists Joseph Priestley and Jan Henrik Van Swinden.[63] For the new museum, the natural philosopher made use of his correspondence network to obtain new specimens. This traffic in objects could cause problems in determining the status of possessions: did unsolicited gifts belong to Fontana, or to the museum? Fontana insisted that everything he received went to the museum.[64] At the same time, however, the director frequently transferred specimens and instruments from the public museum to his house without accounting for them, treating, in effect, the museum like a repository of objects provided by his royal patron for the natural philosopher's personal use. This mismatch between Fontana's self-image as the Grand Duke's client, following early modern conventions of patronage, and his position as state employee of an enlightened absolutist regime would lead to conflict with the court administration, especially in the context of the production of anatomical models investigated further in Chapter 3.

In the late 1770s, Fontana travelled to England and France to commission new instruments. The Grand Duke demonstrated his support for the museum by giving Fontana carte blanche to shop for public enlightenment in the capitals of scientific instrument-making, Paris and London. Fontana was accompanied on this journey by his assistant Giovanni Fabbroni (figure 4), who would become a central figure for the museum and Tuscan politics, developing a vision of expertise in state service that conflicted with Fontana's.

Fabbroni (1752–1822) had personally experienced the improving power of education, and took the museum's political mission to heart.[65] In his youth, he did not have the means to attend university. However, he frequented the Florentine Accademia del Disegno and the hospital Santa Maria Nuova for free classes in chemistry and mechanics, anatomy and botany. In 1769, the ambitious teenager presented his discovery and microscopic investigation of a new plant to Fontana, who took him on as his student and assistant. In 1773, Fabbroni was officially employed at the emergent museum as Fontana's assistant.[66] Like Fontana, Fabbroni established an international network of correspondents; he became a member of the Georgofili, where he presented work ranging from experimental chemistry to economic analyses.[67] 'Well-built, well-mannered, and friendly', he soon won the favour of influential Florentines.[68] Uffizi director Giuseppe Pelli agreed to Fabbroni's marriage to his only child, his adopted daughter Teresa. He was not a 'great catch' financially, conceded his father-in-law, but he was talented and 'capable of good progress'.[69] This socially unequal match met with approval from the Grand Duke.[70] An English visitor observed that, 'The levelling system of the Tuscan Government, that embraces every opportunity to humble the Nobility, views with pleasure, and encourages with zeal, alliances that prejudice might condemn, and prudence disapprove.'[71] The Grand Duke himself was godfather to their first child, Leopoldo.

During his long and distinguished career Fabbroni never mentioned his family background. The reason for his silence may well have been an association with an institution that had long carried the stigma of ignobility: the theatre. Contemporaries remarked that Fabbroni was an excellent dancer and musician – a rare set of skills in someone of humble birth, which has led Fabbroni's biographer Renato Pasta to suggest that he may have been brought up by professional performers. In the late 1780s, when the relationship between the collaborators had deteriorated considerably, Fontana certainly seemed to relish an opportunity to hint at his assistant's former association with a dishonourable profession when he told the Grand Duke that an artisan at the museum had called Fabbroni an 'infamous theatre dancer'.[72] Whatever his background, Fabbroni was clearly well aware of the performative aspects of his work at the museum, evident in his attempts to act in accordance with his role as a public servant and to stage manage the public display of anatomical models. His keen efforts to realise Pietro Leopoldo's vision for the museum, frequently different from Fontana's approach, are investigated further in Chapters 3 and 4.[73]

In addition to shopping trips and acquisitions through correspondence, the new museum benefited from attempts to systematise the various collections that Pietro Leopoldo had inherited. Works of art, in particular, were simultaneously united at the Uffizi to form a publicly accessible exhibition of sculptures and paintings.[74] Deliberations on the appropriate place for objects gave museum employees an opportunity to define the remits of their expertise and the purpose of their institutions. The Uffizi collection was relieved of items that were no longer deemed appropriate for a grand-ducal gallery, especially those that did not fit the art critic Johann Joachim Winckelmann's recent call for 'noble simplicity and sedate grandeur'.[75] Objects considered too gaudy for display among the marbles and paintings, such as coloured wax busts and marvels, were purged from the collection, and the *naturalia* were transferred to La Specola.[76] The separation of objects of art from objects of nature was not always obvious: a set of Chinese sex toys ('Venus spheres'), for instance, which had initially been given to the Uffizi, was passed on to the Royal Museum since the Uffizi's director Giuseppe Pelli considered it more relevant for natural philosophical speculations (but apparently at La Specola it was never put on display).[77] Another borderline case were the wax figures produced by the seventeenth-century modeller Gaetano Zumbo for the Medici. Zumbo's dramatic miniature studies of bodily decay, pest and syphilis victims, poignant scenes in the *memento mori* tradition drawing on southern Italian nativities (figure 5), required more deliberation between museum, gallery and court to establish how these objects could contribute to public enlightenment.

Following Winckelmann, the Uffizi had rejected these morbid displays as being inappropriate for exhibition among the art gallery's marble sculptures. La Specola's naturalists did not consider the miniatures' value as anatomical representations too highly. Nevertheless, after some deliberation, Zumbo's waxes were included in the Royal Museum's exhibition, albeit in a separate room. Museum naturalists argued that the models could contribute to the museum's task of celebrating Tuscan artisanal traditions as a showpiece for high achievements in wax modelling – skills which La Specola's own anatomical modelling workshop built on.[78]

The Grand Duke's generous financial support provided for a number of museum employees in addition to Fontana's assistant Fabbroni. Employees came from a wide range of backgrounds, including naturalists and physicians, as well as court servants and local artisans, and these different perspectives would frequently create conflict at the museum. Custodian Luigi Gagli, who was in charge of the museum's general care, had previously been a footman at the grand-ducal court, and had no scientific or medical background.[79] Local naturalists and physicians worked at the museum on a temporary basis for

5 Gaetano Zumbo, *Trionfo del tempo*. (Saulo Bambi, Museo di Storia
Naturale, Florence)

specific projects. The anatomist Paolo Mascagni (1755–1815) contributed
to the production of anatomical models of the lymphatic system and became
an important supporter of Fontana's plans for the museum. Local physician
Tommaso Bonicoli (1746–1802) regularly prepared body parts for model
production hired on a day basis, and was called upon by Fabbroni to provide
evidence to counteract Mascagni's testimonies.

Other than Fontana and Fabbroni, the only naturalist to be employed on a
permanent basis was physician Attilio Zuccagni (1754–1807), who had first
been employed at the museum in 1773 as a medical student. In the course
of administrative reforms at the museum in 1789 he was named prefect of
the museum's botanical garden; and his expertise was usually called upon to
evaluate and classify botanical and zoological specimens.[80] In addition, the
museum's employees included artisans producing models and instruments,
and servants who worked as porters, cleaners, and guards.[81] The artisans'
status as permanent employees, rather than temporary day workers, would
subsequently cause disciplinary problems in anatomical model production,
investigated further in Chapter 3.

In its early decades, the museum was shaped according to the shared ideas of museum director Felice Fontana and the sovereign. Fontana, who as director was immediately subordinate to the sovereign himself, stressed empiricism, and distanced his own work strongly from the erudite tradition represented by Tuscan naturalists such as Giovanni Targioni Tozzetti, which he judged to be lacking in utility. He conceived of natural philosophy as a body of knowledge that was, in principle, accessible to everybody if presented in a simple, unadorned manner. In a memorandum of 1780 the director accordingly argued that for the museum to fulfil its task as an instrument of public education, no instructor was needed. A systematic presentation of natural objects, complete with simple written explanations, would enable any visitor to understand the underlying natural philosophical principles in an autodidactic fashion: 'knowing how to read [was] sufficient for anyone at the museum to learn about natural history'.[82] This understanding should lead not only to the knowledge of facts, but especially to an active grasp of natural laws, which would in effect enable visitors to develop their own natural philosophy for the benefit of innovation and social progress.

In the museum, visitors walked through the exhibition representing a microcosm of creation, from the mineral kingdom through the vegetable and animal kingdom, including humanity, to instruments and machines. Thus, Fontana insisted, the museum's collection represented an organic whole no part of which could be understood separately. A purely descriptive knowledge of natural history without a simultaneous understanding of the underlying 'physics' in the sense of law-like behaviour, he stressed, would not result in applicable, useful knowledge. Therefore, scientific disciplines could not be studied in isolation if they were to contribute to the public good.[83] Fontana's view was supported by local publications such as the *Novelle Letterarie* , which argued that true advancement of natural knowledge had to unite natural history as a description and physics as an explanation of nature:

> the first element of science to form a philosopher would be natural history, which embraces all objects that the universe presents to us; the second would be physics, which is the only [discipline] that has the ability to read in this great book.[84]

Fontana shared and shaped some of the basic assumptions of Pietro Leopoldo's initiatives, in particular the view of the fundamental importance of natural knowledge for public education. According to the director, (self-) instruction in natural philosophy was more useful for developing one's moral judgement and reasoning than formal logic.[85] In addition, Fontana agreed with the sovereign's assumption of technological progress as an important basis for economic development. The museum not only acquired instruments and specimens, but also produced instruments and anatomical models at its own workshops. At the instruments workshop, Fontana aimed to create instrument-makers who combined artisanal skills and knowledge of mechanics, emulating the renowned specialists whom he had met on his travels to London and Paris in an attempt to strengthen local industry.[86] In addition, the museum presented historical instruments previously owned by Galileo or the Accademia del Cimento, and Zumbo's wax miniatures, with the aim of showcasing Tuscany's scientific and artisanal tradition, as well as providing evidence of scientific and technological progress, in this way promoting a sense of Tuscan national unity.

The museum further reinforced this message by reserving one part of the exhibition for Tuscany's natural resources, thus addressing one of the central problems of physiocracy with regards to the boundaries of territories. A problem which arises from any political theory based on the assumption of universal natural laws is where to draw boundaries to the territory ruled. As Pietro Leopoldo's adviser Gianni had criticised, physiocratic doctrine in its 'chimera of universal communion' did not provide a superior arbiter that protected the safety of individual nations from takeovers which were potentially justifiable by drawing on universal laws of nature.[87] At the museum, Tuscany was defined as a clearly circumscribed, autonomous political entity; it constituted the fourth reign presented at the museum. In addition to the three kingdoms of nature (mineral, vegetable, animal), La Specola displayed the riches of the Tuscan nation both in natural possessions and in scientific and artisanal traditions, exemplified for instance in one of Galileo's original lenses, which was put on display as a 'learned relic to be venerated by Tuscans'.[88]

Like the Chamber of Commerce and the learned academies, the museum did not achieve permanent autonomy. Pietro Leopoldo denied Fontana's plans for the creation of an academy of science just as he had denied similar plans of the Georgofili and the Camera. However, he did not curb the museum's responsibilities. Unlike the Camera, the newly created museum had not been endowed with much explicit agency from the outset since the museum's naturalists had not been asked to develop policy strategies. The fact that the institution was directed by a foreigner (that is, a non-Tuscan) who depended on the sovereign's support for lack of local allies, ensured that, at least during the museum's early years, no demands for greater influence on policies regarding natural resources, or on public science education, arose from the museum staff. Individual cases of museum activities such as the establishment of the museum's anatomical model collection, investigated in Chapter 2, show that, on occasion, museum naturalists used their position as creators and administrators of natural knowledge to articulate state interests.[89] However, this agency was highly contingent upon actors' ability to mobilise rhetorical and other resources in their negotiations with the grand-ducal court – as well as on the sovereign's willingness to listen.

Policing spectacle

In addition to material support for the new institution, Pietro Leopoldo tried to ensure the success of the museum by attempting to control the museum's cultural context. He ruthlessly policed alternative venues for learning, such as itinerant shows and religious spectacles, thus making his new Museum of Physics and Natural History quite literally the only show in town.

Florence offered a variety of opportunities to encounter *naturalia*, real and artificial human bodies. This variety posed a potential threat to the Grand Duke's mission of public enlightenment. Like many of his contemporaries, Pietro Leopoldo was well aware of the fine line between education and entertainment.[90] In the sovereign's mind, entertainment had to be firmly controlled in order to contribute to public enlightenment rather than remaining an idle diversion. Pietro Leopoldo's austerity was famous (or, according to some contemporary commentators, infamous): 'state and magnificence make no part of the expense of the Grand Duke of Tuscany, and the salaries of his household approach nearer to parsimony than extravagance'.[91] The Grand Duke's interventions were not restricted to schools and universities. In agreement with Enlightenment intellectuals, the Grand Duke conceived of the stage as a moral institution for the formation of the rational citizen.[92] Accordingly, the sovereign aimed to utilise public spectacle and entertainment to further his social reform, an approach which was applauded by local intellectuals.[93]

Tuscan spectacle included processions sponsored by guilds, fraternities and religious orders, the carnival, athletic games, and plays by local and itinerant troupes. The court celebrated events such as the visits of foreign monarchs, royal births, and coronations, which were open to all members of the public 'if decently dressed'. These celebrations were highly organised and included dance, theatrical machines and illuminations, as well as enrolling the local clergy for processions and donations to the poor.[94] Other venues catered more specifically to audiences' interest in nature.[95] Most educated Tuscans were familiar with natural historical specimens through the private cabinets of local collectors.[96] Less privileged Florentines had to be content with travelling shows in order to encounter marvels such as exotic animals and monsters.[97] However, in his quest for the creation of an enlightened, civilised, and productive society, between 1767 and 1789, Grand Duke Pietro Leopoldo issued increasingly strict prohibitions of 'occasions for useless dissipations and deceptions', including limitations on various forms of popular culture such as the Carnival, card games, and processions.[98] On 1 February 1780 he declared that

> it is not permitted in any city, region, castle, or other place of the Grandduchy to exhibit spectacles, and to exercise any of their arts and skills, to charlatans, mountebanks, storytellers, puppeteers, tricksters, jugglers, and all those, who display jokes of nature, machines, animals, or who sell secrets, and to any other foreign persons who roam to procure their livelihood in a similar manner.[99]

Transgression of this order was punished severely with six months in prison, and exile from Tuscany for repeat offenders. In a similar vein, on the same day the Grand Duke also published new restrictions for local theatres. To combat the 'excessive dissipation created by the theatres, which could increase in disadvantage to manufacture and good habits', Pietro Leopoldo prohibited cheap spectacles such as acrobatics and foreign troupes, and required government permission for all theatre events.[100]

This prohibition seems to have been enforced quite rigorously during the 1780s, at least in Florence.[101] In 1781, Pelli remarked that that year's carnival had been of a rather 'new species' without the usual entertainments and spectacles.[102] Among the few exceptions to the new anti-spectacular legislation were permissions for charitable reasons, granted, for instance, to one Giovanni Cecchini to show monkeys in the streets of Florence for money, and supposedly educational events such as balloon flights, including experiments conducted by Fontana in Pisa for the instruction and entertainment of Pietro Leopoldo's sons.[103] From 1784, balloonists were only granted a licence in order 'to make new and useful experiments'.[104] Thus the Grand Duke's legislation abolished frivolous entertainment in favour of equally spectacular, but educational alternatives – most prominently the new museum. Pietro Leopoldo tried to control his experts and his public: at La Specola, he could do both in the same space.

Conclusion

As a place for public enlightenment, for the training of artisans, and a home for expertise in state service, the Royal Museum of Physics and Natural History was an institution designed to realise Pietro Leopoldo's politics of nature. Public education should create citizens who could attest to the sovereign's adherence to natural laws, and who were willing to participate actively in the reconstruction of the state according to the dictates of Reason. Demonstrations of technological development such as models of improved windmills and kitchens provided a link between the sovereign and the state, which legitimised the ruler as the executor of natural laws.[105] Simultaneously, such displays justified the localisation of sovereignty with the Grand Duke as the guarantor of the necessary technological development, who supported institutions such as the workshops at the museum, and public education, which would improve artisanal practice and further innovation. Thus, the exhibitions worked towards providing the link between Tuscan nature and the new ruling dynasty by displaying national ingenuity, national resources as an integrated whole and the dynasty as the force to guarantee the productivity of these national resources and the population.

The three cases of the museum, the agricultural academy the Georgofili, and the Chamber of Commerce highlight the difficulties of institutionalising natural knowledge in state service. At these institutions emerged experts who could lay claim to natural knowledge which, according to the Grand Duke's own convictions, should be the basis for political action. This potential raised questions about the function of experts and the limits of their power. The sovereign's response was to promote those institutions of knowledge production that suited his ideas about useful knowledge, while simultaneously setting limits on experts' responsibilities in order to curb their potential claims to political power. The institutions which survived the Grand Duke's cull did so at the expense of increased specialisation.

Renato Pasta has argued that the case of the academies, the Chamber, and the museum highlight the 'antinomy of late absolutism', the difficult balance between the sovereign's power and the authority of public opinion.[106] Pasta takes institutions of knowledge production to stand in for the general public; thus, in his analysis increasing centralisation and a focus on public education act as 'shortcuts' towards public opinion. The question of how much the public (that is, in Pasta's account, the experts) should take an active role in political decision making is solved by leaving decisions to the sovereign. Public education ensures that the populace does indeed arrive at the same 'public opinion' as the sovereign, thus legitimising his actions after the fact. This interpretation highlights how central publishing and education were to the sovereign's legitimising strategy; it also equates the expert naturalists at the new or reformed institutions with the public. The case of La Specola's everyday activities, investigated in the following chapters, supplements this interpretation with an analytical perspective recently developed in science and technology studies, which engages with the problematic notion of the public sphere and its relationship to scientific expertise. This perspective draws attention to the fact that the conflation of experts and the public is at the heart of experts' legitimising strategy.

Historian Harold Mah has highlighted the impossibility of any one individual or institution speaking for 'the public', as any such claim can be refuted with reference to the speaker's particular subject position. Claims to speak for the public are therefore inherently unstable. Recent work in the history of science and in science studies has shown that this instability is frequently visible in the actions of scientists in state service.[107] These experts characteristically articulate their position in ambivalent ways, at times claiming to represent the public, at other times claiming privileged access to special knowledge. The problem of sovereignty, then, is not restricted to the question of how to create, know, and realise public opinion in the framework of absolutist rule. In addition, political actors in late enlightened absolutism such as the Tuscan Grand Duke had to consider a third element in political decision making: the expert. This approach thus explicitly acknowledges the existence of, and tension between, two different conceptions of knowledge: public opinion as knowledge in principle accessible to everyone, versus expert knowledge as exclusive. Part II investigates how, at the new museum, the tension between these two conceptions of knowledge shaped everyday practice both 'frontstage', in the exhibition, and 'backstage', in the model workshop.

Notes

1 See e.g. Adam Wandruszka, *Leopold II.* (2 vols, Vienna and Munich: Herold, 1963), vol. 1, pp. 171–82 ('Die Ära Rosenberg').

2 '[P]er illuminare il suo popolo e per renderlo felice col farlo più culto', Anon., *Saggio del Real Gabinetto di Fisica, e di Storia Naturale di Firenze* (Rome: Giovanni Zempel, 1775), p. 4.

3 'Specolare/speculare', in Joseph [Giuseppe] Baretti, *A dictionary of the English and Italian languages*, vol. 1 (London, 1760).

4 For Italian theorists' ideas on the use of natural philosophy for the creation of public happiness in the second half of the eighteenth century see Luigino Bruni and Pier Luigi Porta, 'Economia civile e pubblica felicità in the Italian Enlightenment', *History of political economy 35*, annual supplement (2003), pp. 361–85.

5 Eric Cochrane, *Florence in the forgotten centuries 1527–1800. A history of Florence and the Florentines in the age of the Grand Dukes* (Chicago and London: University of Chicago Press, 1973), especially p. 343 ff.

6 Wandruszka, *Leopold II.*, p. 179.

7 Quoted in Charles Dupaty, *Sentimental Letters on Italy* (London: Crowder and Bew, 1789), pp. 99–100.

8 '[D]e s'élever jusqu'à la science sublime des loix de la nature'; 'procurer à nos Frères la connoissance des droits & des devoirs de l'homme', Victor de Riquetti, marquis de Mirabeau, *Les économiques* (Amsterdam, 1769), 'Epitre', pp. iii–viii. The first publication of Jean Charles Léonard Simonde de Sismondi, the 'father of political economy' was an account of his observations of Tuscan reform politics (*Tableau de l'agriculture toscane*, 1801). Maxine Berg, *The machinery*

question and the making of political economy, 1815–1848 (Cambridge: Cambridge University Press, 1980); Wandruszka, *Leopold II.*, vol. 1, p. 261.

 9 Karl-Heinz Ilting, 'Naturrecht', in Otto Brunner, Werner Conze, and Reinhart Koselleck (eds), *Geschichtliche Grundbegriffe. Historisches Lexikon zur politisch-sozialen Sprache in Deutschland* (Stuttgart: Klett-Cotta, 1978).

10 Peter Dear, 'Mysteries of state, mysteries of nature: Authority, knowledge and expertise in the 17th century', in Sheila Jasanoff (ed.), *States of knowledge. The co-production of science and social order* (London and New York: Routledge, 2004), ch. 11, pp. 206–24.

11 For an influential reading of early modern natural law theories, which foregrounds their authoritarian nature, see Richard Tuck, *Natural rights theories. Their origin and development* (Cambridge: Cambridge University Press, 1979). But see more recently Heinz Duchhardt, 'Die Absolutismusdebatte – eine Antipolemik', *Historische Zeitschrift* 275 (2002), pp. 323–31.

12 Möller, Horst. *Vernunft und Kritik. Deutsche Aufklärung im 17. und 18. Jahrhundert* (Frankfurt am Main: Suhrkamp, 1986).

13 The term 'physiocracy' (from the Greek: 'rule of nature') was coined in 1767 by Du Pont de Nemours to describe the doctrine developed by Quesnay and Mirabeau.

14 Steven Kaplan, 'Physiocracy, the state, and society: The limits of disengagement', in Peter Katzenstein, Theodore Lowi, and Sidney Tarrow (eds), *Comparative theory and political experience* (Ithaca and London: Cornell University Press, 1990), p. 23.

15 Elizabeth Fox-Genovese, *The origins of physiocracy. Economic revolution and social order in eighteenth-century France* (Ithaca and London: Cornell University Press, 1976), p. 9 ff; Kaplan, 'Physiocracy'. For a more recent re-evaluation of physiocracy as a theory of social and political order and its impact on religion, the military and the law see the contributions in *Studi settecenteschi* 24 (2004), 'Fisiocrazia e proprietà terriera', ed. Manuela Albertone. For physiocracy's subversive potential see the contribution by Vieri Becagli, 'Georg-Ludwig Schmid d'Auenstein e i suoi *Principes de la législation universelle*: oltre la fisiocrazia?', pp. 215–52, and M. Albertone, 'Introduzione', pp. 11–22, especially p. 19.

16 Kaplan, 'Physiocracy', p. 24.

17 By the late eighteenth century, political theorists and practitioners had departed from orthodox physiocratic doctrine to assume more liberal positions. See e.g. Zeffiro Ciuffoletti, 'I moderati toscani e la tradizione leopoldina', in Clementina Rotondi (ed.), *I Lorena in Toscana* (Florence: Olschki, 1989), pp. 121–38.

18 Cochrane, *Florence*, pp. 447–53.

19 Wandruszka, *Leopold II.*, p. 271.

20 See e.g. Eric Cochrane, *Tradition and enlightenment in the Tuscan academies, 1691–1800* (Chicago: University of Chicago Press, 1961).

21 Renato Pasta, 'L'Accademia dei Georgofili e la riforma dell'agricoltura', *Rivista storica italiana* 105 (1993), pp. 484–501, p. 490.

22 Pasta, 'Georgofili', p. 494.

23 After Pasta, 'Georgofili', p. 488, see also Franco Venturi, *Settecento riformatore* (Turin: Einaudi, 1969–84), 5 vols, vol. 1, pp. 336ff.

24 For a draft of Fontana's plan see Instituto e Museo di Storia della Scienze: Archive of the Royal Museum (IMSS–ARMU), Filza di negozi dell'anno 1789A, fols 433–43.

25 Wandruszka, *Leopold II*, p. 187.

26 See ibid., p. 186; Pasta, 'Georgofili', p. 491.

27 '[L]o scopo dell'Accademia sono le scoperte'. Quoted from Vieri Becagli, 'Economia e politica del sapere nelle riforme leopoldine. Le Accademie', in Giulio Barsanti, Vieri Becagli, and Renato Pasta (eds) *La politica della scienza. Toscana e stati italiani nel tardo settecento* (Florence: Olschki, 1996), pp. 35-66, on p. 41.

28 Pasta, 'Georgofili', p. 498.

29 Daniele Baggiani, 'Progresso tecnico e azione politica nella Toscana leopoldina: La Camera di Commercio di Firenze (1768–1782)', in Barsanti et al. (eds), *Politica della scienza*, pp. 67–99.

30 '[A]umentare le manifatture ed il traffico del nostro Gran-Ducato'; 'tutte le facilità che sono necessarie ad eccitare la loro industria'; 'massime costanti ed uniformi'; 'indirizzante al bene universale dello stato'. Preamble of Pietro Leopoldo's *motu-proprio* of 1 February 1770; quoted from Baggiani, 'Progresso tecnico', p. 69.

31 Baggiani, 'Progresso tecnico', pp. 90–1.

32 Ibid, pp. 87–8.

33 '[I]l n'y a que le Souverain qui peut avoir en vue toutes les différentes branches à la fois, sans avoir de prédilection pour aucune que pour le bien général de tout l'État'. Letter from Pietro Leopoldo to Joseph II, n.d. (late August 1782); quoted from Alfred von Arneth (ed.), *Joseph II. und Leopold von Toscana. Ihr Briefwechsel von 1781 bis 1790* (Vienna: Wilhelm Braumüller, 1872), p. 134.

34 Harvey Chiswick, *The limits of reform in the Enlightenment: Attitudes toward the education of the lower classes in eighteenth-century France* (Princeton: Princeton University Press, 1981), pp. 38–45.

35 '[L]a Sensation enveloppe toutes les facultés de l'âme'; Condillac, *Traité des sensations* (London [Paris?] 1754), p. 128.

36 '[L]'education peut tout', *De l'homme* (1773). Cited from Chiswick, *Limits of reform*, p. 40, n. 30.

37 '[I] Governi, ed i Sovrani debbono promuovere e procurare la pubblica istruzione. L'Uomo che nasce ignorante, se si conserva in questo stato, è sempre un cattivo Cittadino. . . . egli non ama e non rispetta le leggi, . . . egli non serve a quello a che lo à destinato l'ordine naturale'. *Novelle letterarie*, no. 1 (1777).

38 '[T]utto quello che spiega la storia dei tempi, che decifra i segreti della natura, che indica all'uomo l'uso delle sue facoltà, e il suo destino sopra la terra, è quello sopra di cui deve posare la pubblica istruzione . . . In quest'ultima branca di dottrine tiene in primo luogo la scienza dell'Ordine, la quale presa nella sua vera estensione non è propria solo per le Classi dei Direttori della Società, ma per tutti

gl'Individui. Per fare il bene bisogna che ne sentano la convenevolezza, e bisogna che conoscano come questo bene venga a ridondare sopra di loro. Tutto è legato nel mondo, e tutto è disposto con leggi fisse e invariabili'. *Novelle letterarie*, no. 1 (1777).

39 Maria Augusta Morelli Timpanaro, *Autori, stampatori, librai. Per una storia dell'editoria in Firenze nel secolo XVIII* (Florence: Olschki, 1999), p. 204.

40 '[La scuola] muterà in pochi anni i costumi di un'intera nazione', quoted from Luciana Bellatalla, *Pietro Leopoldo di Toscana granduca-educatore. Teoria e pratica di un despota illuminato* (Lucca: Maria Pacini Fazzi, 1984), p. 56.

41 'La pubblica Educazione, primo fondamento, non solo della nazionale industria, e carattere, ma del buon ordine Sociale, e base inconcussa del Sovrano Splendore'. IMSS–ARMU, Filza di negozi dell'anno 1797, fol. 10–11 (doc. 4).

42 Charles Dupaty, *Sentimental letters on Italy, written in French by President Dupaty, in 1785* (London: Crowder and Bew, 1789), p. 92. For Pietro Leopoldo's interest in public education and his pro-Lockean position see Bellatalla, *Pietro Leopoldo*, especially pp. 16–17 and 20–1, and Contini, 'La naissance n'est qu'effet du hazard', in Sergio Bertelli and Renato Pasta (eds) *Vivere a Pitti. Una reggia dai Medici ai Savoia* (Florence: Olschki 2003).

43 For the theory and practice of national education in eighteenth-century Tuscany, see for example Gian Bruno Ravenni, 'Il Settecento tra lumi e rivoluzione. L'educazione del popolo, dalle feste agli opuscoli, al teatro', in *La Toscana e l'educazione. Dal Settecento a oggi: tra identità regionale e laboratorio nazionale*, ed. Franco Cambi (Florence: Le Lettere, 1998), pp. 91–102.

44 Bellatalla, *Pietro Leopoldo*, pp. 29 and 37.

45 Dupaty, *Sentimental letters*, p. 140: 'There is but one class of subjects in Tuscany, and but one master.'

46 For education in the French Revolution with emphasis on science education, see Charles C. Gillispie, *Science and polity in France: The revolutionary and Napoleonic years* (Princeton: Princeton University Press, 2004), especially pp. 110–29, 'The Condorcet plan for national education'; more general also Robert R. Palmer, *The improvement of humanity. Education and the French Revolution* (Princeton: Princeton University Press, 1985).

47 Österreichisches Staatsarchiv, Abteilung Haus- Hof- und Staatsarchiv, Vienna (HHS), F.A. Sammelbände 15, fols 24–99: 'Punti Diversi di S.M. l'Imperatore relativam.e all'Educazione dell'Arciduca Francesco'; Stanislao Canovai and Gaetano del Ricco, *Elementi di fisica matematica dedicati all'Altezze Reali di Ferdinando-Giuseppe, Carlo-Luigi, Alessandro-Leopoldo Arciduchi d'Austria, Principi di Toscana ec.ec.ec.* (Florence: Pietro Allegrini, 1788).

48 'L'histoire naturelle la phisyque [sic] doivent être enseignées aux enfants avec les dessins et par des faits'. Pietro Leopoldo, *Notes sur l'éducation* (1775), HHS, folder 55; quoted from Bellatalla, *Pietro Leopoldo*, p. 43.

49 Vienna HHS, F.A. Sammelbände 15, 'Memorie relative alli studj fatti da S.A.R. l'Arciduca Francesco, nelle Mattematiche, Metafisica, e Fisica sperimentale'

(1784), especially fol. 77, 'Prospetto delle Lezioni della fisica particolarm.e sperimentale dell'Ab.te Fontana'. For a statement by Fontana, see e.g. ASF, Imperiale
e Reale Corte Lorenese, 360, no. 284 I, 'Memoria dl Cav. Fontana in sua giustificazione' (n.d.), p. 52.

50 '"[P]alestra" scientifica . . . per gli arciduchi', Alessandra Contini, '"La naissance
n'est qu'effet du hazard". L'educazione delle principesse e dei pricipi alla corte
leopoldina', in Bertelli and Pasta (eds), *Vivere a Pitti*. pp. 389–438, p. 409.

51 Dupaty, *Sentimental letters*, p. 103. For Pietro Leopoldo's insistence on the
immediacy of learning, see also Bellatalla, *Pietro Leopoldo*, p. 25.

52 Silvio Bedini, 'The fate of the Medici-Lorraine scientific instruments', in *Patrons,
artisans and instruments of science, 1600–1750* (Aldershot and Brookfield:
Ashgate/Variorum, 1999), n.p.

53 Jay Tribby, 'Body/building: Living the museum life in early modern Europe',
Rhetorica 10:2 (1992), pp. 139–63.

54 Oliver Impey and Arthur MacGregor (eds), *The origins of museums: The cabinet
of curiosities in sixteenth and seventeenth-century Europe* (Oxford: Clarendon
Press, 1985); Paula Findlen, *Possessing nature: museums, collecting and scientific
culture in early modern Italy* (Berkeley: University of California Press, 1994).

55 Accademia delle scienze, *I materiali dell'Istituto delle Scienze* (Bologna: CLUEB,
1979).

56 Edward Miller, *That noble cabinet. A history of the British Museum* (London:
Andre Deutsch, 1973).

57 Emma C. Spary, *Utopia's garden. French natural history from Old Regime to
Revolution* (Chicago and London: University of Chicago Press, 2000).

58 For a description of Palazzo Torrigiani's architectural features see Alberto Forti
(ed.), *L'Imperiale e Regio Museo di Fisica e Storia Naturale di Firenze: indicazioni
per un metodo di lettura e per una soluzione museografica* (Florence: Angelo
Pontecorboli, 1995).

59 Peter K. Knoefel, *Felice Fontana. Life and works* (Trento: Società di Studi
Trentini di Scienze Storiche, 1984); Renato G. Mazzolini, 'Fontana, Gasparo
Ferdinando Felice', in *Dizionario biografico degli Italiani* (Rome: Istituto della
Enciclopedia Italiana, 1997), vol. 42, pp. 663–9.

60 Mazzolini, 'Fontana'. See e.g. also Fontana's *Richerche filosofiche sopra la fisica
animale* (1775). Studies of Fontana's chemical research include Ferdinando
Abbri, *Science de l'air: Studi su Felice Fontana* (Cosenza: Brenner, 1991), and
Simon Schaffer, 'Measuring virtue: eudiometry, enlightenment and pneumatic
medicine', in Andrew Cunningham and Roger French (eds) *The medical enlightenment of the eighteenth century* (Cambridge: Cambridge University Press, 1990),
pp. 281–318.

61 'Felice Fontana Fisico di S.A.R. [è] Uomo di talento e che hà un nome, ma è di
un carattere duro, finto, e portato troppo al ciarlatanismo'. IMSS–ARMU, Pelli,
'Efemeridi', Serie II, vol. VIII (1780), fol. 1434v, 27 September 1780.

62 Cochrane, *Florence*, pp. 429–30; Biblioteca Nazionale Centrale, Florence

(BNCF), manuscript collection NA 1050, Pelli, 'Efemeridi', Serie II, vol. XIV, 2717v (1786).

63 For Fontana's correspondence see e.g. Knoefel, *Felice Fontana*, pp. 109–59; Mazzolini, 'Fontana'; a typical list of addressees is contained in the index to IMSS–ARMU, Filza di negozi dell'anno 1789B.

64 IMSS–ARMU, Filza di negozi dell'anno 1790, fol. 88–91 (doc. 10), Fontana's report: 'Quelli [strumenti] poi che si mandano a me da miei amici li ho sempre messi nel R. Museo, perchè li ho sempre riputato cose di S.A.R. venendomi naturalmente regolata, perchè sono al Suo reale servizio.'

65 For the life of Giovanni Fabbroni see Renato Pasta, *Scienza politica e rivoluzione. L'opera di Giovanni Fabbroni (1752–1822) intellettuale e funzionario al servizio dei Lorena* (Florence: Olschki, 1989).

66 IMSS–ARMU, Filza di negozi dell'anno 1794, fols 269–87 (doc. 57), 'Copia della Portata fatta dai Soggetti impiegati a Ruolo Stabile nel Real Museo di Fisica rimessa alla Reale Segreteria della Corona, e di Corte il dì 31. Luglio 1794. Portate fatte dai medesimi Soggetti Separatam', fol. 276.

67 See Pasta, *Scienza politica rivoluzione*, pp. 186–95.

68 '[D]i bella figura, di dolci maniere, e di tratto gentile', Pelli, 'Efemeridi', Serie II, vol. IX, 1516v (1781).

69 'Non è un gran partito'; 'in stato di fare dei buoni progressi'. Pelli, 'Efemeridi', Serie II, vol. IX, 1592v, 1593 (1781).

70 Pelli, 'Efemeridi', Serie II, vol. IX, 1600v (1781).

71 Peter Beckford, *Familiar letters from Italy, to a friend in England*, vol. 1 (London: J. Easton, 1805), p. 237.

72 Pasta, *Fabbroni*, p. 2. 'infamoso ballerino di teatro': ASF, Imperiale e Reale Corte Lorenese, fol. 119, 'Memoria del Cav. Fontana in sua giustificazione', p. 7v.

73 For Fabbroni's performance of his role as expert naturalist in state service see also Anna Maerker, 'The tale of the hermaphrodite monkey: classification, state interests and natural historical expertise between museum and court, 1791–94', *British journal for the history of science* 39:1 (2006), pp. 29–47.

74 For the early history of the Uffizi see Miriam Fileti Mazza and Bruna Tomasello, *Galleria degli Uffizi 1758–1775: la politica museale di Raimondo Cocchi* (Modena: Panini, 1999), Miriam Fileti Mazza and Bruna Tomasello, *Galleria degli Uffizi 1775–1792: un laboratorio culturale per Giuseppe Pelli Bencivenni* (Modena: Panini, 2003); L. Pellegrini Boni, 'Strutture e regolamenti della Galleria nel periodo di Pietro Leopoldo', in *Gli Uffizi: quattro secoli di una galleria. Convegno internazionale di studi. Fonti e documenti* (Florence: Olschki, 1982), pp. 267–311.

75 '[E]dle Einfalt', 'stille Größe'; Johann Joachim Winckelmann (1755), *Gedanken über die Nachahmung der griechischen Werke in der Malerei und Bildhauerkunst*. Quoted from the English translation *Reflections on the painting and sculpture of the Greeks* (London: Millar and Cadell, 1765), p. 30.

76 AGF, filza II (1769–1770), doc. 47.

77 BNCF, manuscript collection NA 1050, Pelli, 'Efemeridi', Serie II, vol. 3 (1775), fol. 481r.

78 IMSS–ARMU, Filza di negozi dell'anno 1793, fols 189–205.

79 IMSS–ARMU, Filza di negozi dell'anno 1794, fol. 269–87 (doc. 57): 'Copia della Portata fatta dai Soggetti impiegati a Ruolo Stabile nel Real Museo di Fisica rimessa alla Reale Segreteria della Corona, e di Corte il dì 31. Luglio 1794. Portate fatte dai medesimi Soggetti Separatam', fol. 279.

80 IMSS–ARMU, Filza di negozi dell'anno 1794, fol. 269–87 (doc. 57): 'Copia della Portata fatta dai Soggetti impiegati a Ruolo Stabile nel Real Museo di Fisica rimessa alla Reale Segreteria della Corona, e di Corte il dì 31. Luglio 1794. Portate fatte dai medesimi Soggetti Separatam', fol. 277.

81 For a complete list of museum employees at the time of its opening see ASF, Imperiale e Reale Corte Lorenese, 343, no. 56, decree of 21 February 1775.

82 '[B]asta saper leggere per imparare di presenta la storia naturale da chicchessia dentro il Real Museo'. Biblioteca Rosminiana, Rovereto, Manoscritti di Felice Fontana, faldone 28.B.110, fol. 8r–8v, quoted from Simone Contardi, 'Felice Fontana e l'Imperiale e Regio Museo di Firenze. Strategie museali e accademismo scientifico nella Firenze di Pietro Leopoldo', in Ferdinando Abbri and Marco Segala (eds) *Il ruolo sociale della scienza (1789–1830)* (Florence: Olschki, 2000), p. 45, see also p. 54.

83 Contardi, 'Felice Fontana', pp. 47–8.

84 '[I]l primo elemento della Scienza per formare un Filosofo, sia la Storia Naturale, la quale abraccia tutti gli oggetti che ci presenta l'Universo; il secondo la Fisica, la quale sola à la facoltà di leggere in sì gran libro', *Novelle letterarie*, no. 1 (1782).

85 Simone Contardi, 'Unità del sapere e pubblica utilità: Felice Fontana e le collezioni di fisica dell'Imperiale e Regio Museo', in Barsanti, Becagli, and Pasta (eds) *La politica della scienza*, pp. 279–94, p. 281.

86 Simone Contardi, 'L'artigianato fiorentino al servizio della scienza', in Riccardo Spinelli (ed.) *La grande storia dell'Artigianato* (Florence: Giunti, 2002), vol. 5 (Il Seicento e il Settecento), pp. 85–99.

87 '[A] questa chimera di communione universale non intervengono come contraenti tutte le nazioni, e non esiste un tribunale dove reclamare l'inosservanza di un tale contratto immaginario'. Gianni in a letter to the Grand Duke, 9 July 1782. Quoted from Daniele Baggiani, 'Progresso tecnico e azione politica nella Toscana leopoldina: La Camera di Commercio di Firenze (1768–1782)', in Barsanti et al. (eds) *Politica della scienza*, pp. 67–99, p. 97, n.78.

88 Pelli, BNCF, NA 1050, 'Efemeridi', Serie II, vol. 3 (1775), 469v.

89 See also Maerker, 'Hermaphrodite monkey'.

90 See e.g. *Gazzetta Toscana,* no. 42 (1803).

91 Beckford, *Familiar letters*, vol. 1 (1805), p. 236.

92 Wandruszka, *Leopold II.*, vol. 2, 'Nationalerziehung und Kulturpolitik', pp. 151–63.

93 *Novelle letterarie*, no. 45 (1789): review of Idelfonso Valdastri, *Due discorsi*

filosofici e politici, l'uno sull'influenza degli spettacoli nelle Nazioni, l'altro su quella de'Viaggi nell'educazione (Modena, 1789).

94 Luigi Zangheri, *Feste e apparati nella Toscana dei Lorena, 1737–1859* (Florence: Olschki, 1996) ('vi fu ammesso ogni ceto di persone "purché decentemente vestite"'), p. 43.

95 Bernadette Bensaude-Vincent and Christine Blondel (eds), *Science and spectacle in the European Enlightenment* (Aldershot: Ashgate, 2008).

96 See e.g. BNCF, manuscript collection NA 1050, Pelli, 'Efemeridi', Serie I, vol. XXVIII, fol. 54, 12 September 1771, for Pelli's visit to the private cabinet of Antonio Fabbrini.

97 Pelli, 'Efemeridi', Serie II, vol. 3 (1775), mentions the public display of an elephant in Florence.

98 Ravenni, *Settecento*, p. 101.

99 '[V]olendo la R.A.S. per quanto sia possibile togliere al popolo le occasioni di dissiparsi inutilmente, e di essere ingannato, ha determinato che in avvenire non si permetta il fermarsi in qualunque Città, Terra, Castello, o altro luogo del Granducato e dare spettacoli, ed esercitare qualsiasi delle loro arti, ed industrie, ai Chiarlatani, Cantimbanchi, Cantastorie, Burattinai, Circolatori, Giocolatori, ed a tutti quelli, che portano in mostra scherzi di natura, Macchine, Animali, o che vendano segreti, ed a qualunque altra Persona forestiera, che vada vagabonda a procacciarsi il Vitto con alcun simile mestiere. . . . I Trasgressori saranno sottoposti alla pena di sei mesi di Carcere, ed all'esilio perpetuo dal Granducato, pena altrettanto tempo di Carcere, e l'Esilio in caso d'inosservanza'. *Bandi, e ordini da osservarsi del Granducato di Toscana pubblicati in Firenze dal dì primo Gennaio MDCCLXXX. a tutto Dicembre MDCCLXXXI. raccolti posteriormente per ordine successivo dei tempi con il sommario dei medesimi disposto con ordine alfabetico di materie e di tribunali*, vol. 10 (Florence: Cambiagi, 1782).

100 '[L]a R.A.S. volendo riparare all'eccessiva dissipazione che producono i Teatri, la quale potrebbe sempre più aumentare in pregiudizio delle manifatture, e del buon costume, ha prescritto che . . . sia osservato il seguente Regolamento . . . I. Siano esclusi dal rappresentare nei Teatri di Toscana i Comici Italiani Forestieri, o siano Istrioni, i Giocolatori di corda, e di Equilibrj, ed ogni forestiere che esibisca nei Teatri qualunque altro genere di spettacolo; saranno eccettuati i soli Professori forestieri di Musica, e di Ballo, ed i Comici Francesi, ogni altra Compagnia Comica nei Teatri di Toscana dovrà essere nazionale. . . . IV. Ed il Ministro . . . abbia l'avvertenza che non siano troppo moltiplicate le Rappresentanze peggiori piccole, e di vil prezzo . . . IX. . . . dovranno sempre domandarsi le solite permissioni per l'apertura dei Teatri, per le maschere, e per le Feste di ballo'. *Bandi, e ordini*, vol. 10.

101 Pelli, a diligent chronicler of public events in Florence, did not mention any spectacles other than a balloon flight and occasional theatre visits in the three volumes of the 'Efemeridi' consulted as samples for the 1780s (1780, 1781, 1788).

102 'Ecco che finisce il tempo del Carnevale, che in quest'anno è stato di una nuova

specie perché senza divertimenti, e senza spettacoli'. Pelli, 'Efemeridi', Serie II, vol. IX, 1548 (1781).

103 Accademia dei Fisiocritici, Siena (ASF), Presidenza del Buongoverno 1784–1808, Affari comuni, 'Affari di polizia', Filza 84, no. 24, 'Supplica di Giovanni Cecchini' (1789) (monkey show); Zangheri, *Feste e apparati*, p. 146 (balloon).

104 '[P]er fare nuovi, ed utili esperimenti', broadsheet of 13 April 1784, in ASF, Segreteria di Finanze, Affari prima del 1788, pezzo 479, folder 1784. For the description of a (failed) balloon ascent in Florence, November 1788, see BNCF, manuscript collection NA 1050, Pelli, 'Efemeridi', Serie II, vol. XVI (1788), fol. 3239. See also Zangheri, *Feste e apparati*, p.145, for a successful ascent on 23 January 1784.

105 For these and other examples of improved technologies displayed at La Specola see e.g. IMSS–ARMU, Filza di negozi dell'anno 1794, fol. 134 (doc. 66).

106 Pasta, 'Scienza e istituzioni', p. 27.

107 Jürgen Habermas, *Strukturwandel der Öffentlichkeit* (Frankfurt: Suhrkamp, 1990 [1962]); Harold Mah, 'Phantasies of the Public Sphere: Rethinking the Habermas of Historians', *Journal of Modern History* 72 (2000), pp. 153–82; Thomas Broman, 'The Habermasian public sphere and "science in the Enlightenment"', *History of science* 26 (1998), pp. 123–49; Volker Hess, Eric Engstrom, and Ulrike Thoms (eds), *Figurationen des Experten: Ambivalenzen der wissenschaftlichen Expertise im ausgehenden 18. und frühen 19. Jahrhundert* (Frankfurt: Peter Lang, 2005).

2

Bodies and the state in eighteenth-century Tuscany

The most spectacular aspect of the new Museum of Physics and Natural History was its collection of anatomical wax models. Modellers at the museum's own workshop produced thousands of anatomical waxes, which continue to fascinate visitors to the present day: life-sized, miniaturised, and enlarged three-dimensional representations of whole bodies and body parts. Artisans and anatomists collaborated to make models in coloured, varnished waxes, which gave the artificial bodies a lifelike colouring and sheen. With its malleability, softness, and shiny surface, wax held deeply entrenched connotations of flesh and generation for eighteenth-century audiences.[1] In addition, the life-sized whole body models, in particular, presented lively poses, gestures, and expressions, which heightened the sensation of an encounter with living bodies. The 'anatomical Venus' – the model of a pregnant woman whose abdomen opens to reveal the foetus inside – looks at the spectator with a languid gaze (plate III). Models were frequently reminiscent of the famous works of art that were on display elsewhere in the city, or at other stages of the Grand Tour. 'Lo Scorticato', for instance, a reclining figure of a skinned man, recalls Michelangelo's Adam.[2] Other models included series of embryonic development, models of individual organs, and studies of spatial relationships between body parts from different angles and perspectives. Numerous rooms at the museum were filled with wax models, displayed in decorative showcases on cushions or pedestals (figure 6 and plate I).

The production of these vast series was time-consuming and costly – the workshop employed numerous artisans, artists and anatomists, and used expensive materials such as precious metals, pigments, and Venetian wax of the highest quality. Overall, the production of models accounted for half of the museum's considerable budget – a remarkable expense in the light of Pietro Leopoldo's distrust of public entertainment and his infamous frugality. While the Grand Duke was evidently filled with reformist zeal, he was equally determined to save money. His efforts to economise did not spare local sensi-

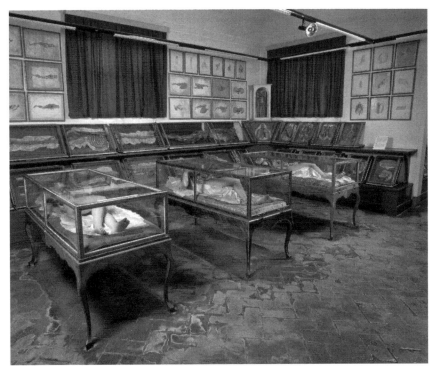

6 Showroom XXIX with anatomical wax models at the Royal Museum of Physics and Natural History ('La Specola') in Florence. (Saulo Bambi, Museo di Storia Naturale, Florence)

bilities, as a Florentine delegation learnt when they approached the sovereign with the proposal of erecting a statue in the Grand Duke's honour. They had collected donations to express their gratitude for recent legal reforms, but Pietro Leopoldo, flying into one of his characteristic fits of rage, rejected their proposal as a waste of money. Attempts to placate their irate sovereign with the alternative of an eminently useful public fountain were in vain, and the delegation left, ordered to return the donations.[3]

This chapter analyses how Tuscan debates on the utility of medicine, anatomy, and artificial bodies, which preceded Pietro Leopoldo's accession, shaped the Royal Museum. These debates articulated how different kinds of medical expertise, objects and institutions could be useful to the state. Their development shows that the new Grand Duke's policies built on ideas that had already been raised in the first half of the eighteenth century, most prominently by the Tuscan physician and intellectual Antonio Cocchi, whose proposals for medical improvement were partly adopted in reforms during the Regency and through Pietro Leopoldo's reign. Tuscan debates about the uses of medical expertise and knowledge of the body encouraged a number of individuals to develop projects for the public use of artificial anatomies. The concluding section of this chapter highlights the case of Florentine obstetrician Giuseppe Galletti, who put forward an idea for the production of obstetric wax models to museum director Fontana – a suggestion which led to the establishment of the modelling workshop at La Specola, albeit under a different framework more concerned with normal human anatomy, and rearticulated to address Pietro Leopoldo's concerns for legitimacy and public happiness. Where Chapter 1 explored the general functions accorded to natural knowledge for the state, this chapter highlights more specifically the uses of anatomical expertise.

Medicine and the state in enlightened debate: Antonio Cocchi

In the eighteenth century, European intellectuals and politicians increasingly foregrounded the importance of medicine for the state. The main aim of medicine in state service, they argued, was the creation and maintenance of healthy citizens – productive workers and fertile women who would increase the country's revenue and its military power. These arguments made anatomical knowledge central, and frequently discussed the utility of artificial bodies. Exemplary for this development was the discipline of obstetrics, which was central to enlightened debate for its role in preserving both mothers and their offspring for the polity. A growing population, theorists argued, would increase state revenue as well as strengthen military power by increasing the size of the army.[4] Anatomy, philosophy, and politics were thus often inseparable in eighteenth-century discussions of reproduction, which articulated the roles of mothers and foetuses in different, sometimes conflicting ways. Physicians from Turin anatomist Giovanni Battista Bianchi to Austrian public health innovator Johann Peter Frank, but also theologians and philosophers, redefined the foetus as a human being and a citizen. As a consequence, some articulations of foetal identity and autonomy, expressed in new anatomical representations, supported an interpretation of the mother as a vessel, while her perceived influence on the foetus was simultaneously diminished.

In contrast, other scholars who entered the debate celebrated the active role of mothers for the well-being of their offspring.[5] Despite these conflicting perspectives, new anatomical and physiological conceptualisations of reproduction had practical consequences in legal and medical reforms. The pregnant woman's body was now increasingly protected by law, for example against the husband's right to physical punishment, in order to protect the unborn child and future citizen.[6] Political concerns for population growth also motivated changes in the training and licensing of midwives around Europe.[7] Many states attempted to wrestle away the licensing of midwives from the Church, and governments introduced anatomical instruction. In Italy, some prominent physicians such as Bologna professor of obstetrics Luigi Galli campaigned to improve the anatomical training of midwives and to elevate their professional standing.[8] Efforts to increase midwives' anatomical knowledge, and to distribute it more widely, could be supported by the production and circulation of artificial anatomies, as in the case of the celebrated French midwife Mme du Coudray.[9] Ordered by Louis XV to tour the French provinces on an educational mission, she took with her an obstetric 'phantom' – a live-sized model of a female torso made from leather and wood, mounted on a real pelvis, together with a leather doll of a foetus, on which midwives and obstetricians could practice manual intervention in the womb.[10] Since around 1700, obstetricians around Europe experimented with different materials and designs in attempts to perfect these models for obstetric training (figure 7). Artificial bodies thus became part of various initiatives to improve society through anatomical knowledge.

In their attempts to promote population growth through the knowledge of the body, reformers targeted those institutions and professions most central to public health care and medical expertise.[11] In Tuscany, the government could draw on a wide range of long-established medical institutions to implement its measures. Florence, in particular, was home to a large number of medical and welfare institutions. Religious organisations, guilds and other donors had set up a wide range of charities in Florence since the Middle Ages.[12] Already in the fifteenth century, Leon Battista Alberti boasted that

> In Tuscany, in keeping with the long-standing local tradition for religious piety, wonderful hospitals are to be found, built at vast expense, where any citizen or stranger would feel there to be nothing amiss to ensure his well-being.[13]

The hospital Santa Maria Nuova was the largest and most important of the city's medical institutions. It became a focal point of Habsburg reforms, first tentatively during the Regency, and more forcefully since Pietro Leopoldo's accession in the mid-1760s, culminating in a new set of rules and regulations in the 1780s. A secular charitable institution founded in 1288 by patrician Folco Portinari (the father of Dante's Beatrice, as Grand Tourists liked to point out), the hospital provided free care for the sick and the infirm as well as medical training for physicians and surgeons. The hospital was a vast institution – in the 1780s it provided more than 1000 beds to accommodate both male and female patients, a pharmacy and laboratory, rooms for teaching and dissection, and a garden of medicinal plants (*giardino dei semplici*), which provided herbs for the pharmacy (*spezieria*).[14] Financially, Santa Maria Nuova was supported by

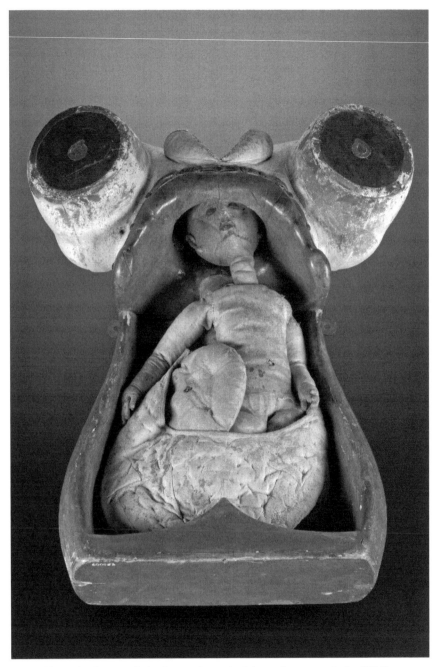

7 Obstetric phantom in leather and wood, eighteenth-century Italy. (Wellcome Collection, London)

its significant endowment, including 18 farms, 339 manors, 28 mills, residential properties both in the city and in the countryside, and numerous workshops.

Santa Maria Nuova had long been a place for medical instruction. Physicians with doctorates from the nearby universities in Pisa and Siena came to Florence to receive further education from some of the hospital's renowned practitioners, and surgeons trained there. In the mid-eighteenth century physician Antonio Cocchi reported that

> some of the hospital's most distinguished ordinated physicians perform as its public instructors in medicine, however without any particular remuneration. Out of courtesy, they have established the custom to admit to their school on their daily rounds all students or lovers of this profession who want to make practical experiences.[15]

At the time, Santa Maria Nuova already hosted 90–100 students, as well as admitting lay audiences to public lectures.[16] However, this training was not formalised.

Antonio Cocchi (1695–1758) was a central figure for debates about the political uses of medicine in Tuscany. His insistence on the utility of anatomical knowledge, in particular, would later influence Pietro Leopoldo's reform measures concerning medicine, governance, and public education.[17] Cocchi, who was 'well-built, strong, and studious', had graduated in medicine from the University of Pisa, and pursued further studies at the Florentine hospital, Santa Maria Nuova.[18] His academic interests were wide-ranging, and in the 1720s he travelled around Europe to meet some of the luminaries of the day, visiting Fontenelle in France, Newton in England, and Boerhaave in Holland.[19] In his observations on England, the anglophile Cocchi articulated a utilitarian and empirical philosophy concerned with 'pubblica felicità'.[20] This concern motivated his reflections on the utility of anatomical expertise, which was close to the position later adopted by Pietro Leopoldo.

Like many physicians in early eighteenth-century Florence, Cocchi advocated a 'Galileian', iatromechanist approach to medicine, and he became a vocal advocate for anatomy in state service. His home government recognised his potential utility, and in 1726 he was recalled from London by the last Medici Grand Duke Gian Gastone, who made him Chair of theoretical medicine at the University of Pisa, and later Chair of anatomy at the Florence Studio Fiorentino. The physician contributed not only to professional medical education, but also to public health, especially since he was elected to the Florentine Collegio Medico, the municipal body responsible for public health supervision in the city. The new Regency government of the Habsburg-Lorraine dynasty shared the Medici's trust in the erudite physician, and

Cocchi became the first antiquarian of the Uffizi Gallery, and anatomy lecturer and surgeon at the hospital Santa Maria Nuova. In addition, he was called upon as government adviser to report on the spas of Pisa at the request of Emperor Francis Stephen.

Cocchi was a central figure among Florentine intellectuals, friendly with many local and foreign scholars. He published on a wide range of subjects, including treatises on hospitals and health, spa waters and the failure of the Regency government's attempt to establish a settlement in the swampy Maremma region.[21] The physician had the support of his peers, but he did not enjoy favours from the city's traditional high society. The British government representative in Tuscany Sir Horace Mann reported in 1741 that Cocchi was offered the position of inspector and regulator of Santa Maria Nuova, but had to decline it because he could not afford to take on an unpaid post.[22] Mann concluded that "tis terrible a man of his worth and who might be so useful to society should be so neglected'.[23] This neglect was characteristic of the attitude of the Tuscan nobility, who had little affection for those who had to work for a living. With government officials and scholars, however, Cocchi enjoyed an excellent reputation as 'a learned anatomist, an able physician, a man of deep erudition, [and] an elegant writer'. On his death in 1758, Cocchi was buried in Santa Croce in a mausoleum for celebrated Tuscans, and his bust was placed among statues of Galileo, Michelangelo and Machiavelli.[24]

In his prominent position at the nexus of erudite debate and government policy making, Cocchi was influential in shaping the role of medicine in enlightened Tuscany. In publications such as his preface to Lorenzo Bellini's *Discorsi di anatomia* (1741–44), Cocchi pursued the mission 'that anatomy shall never lose the favour of the public'.[25] He argued that the value of medicine was not just its immediate application to individuals, but also as a tool for policy, public health, evaluation and the control of territory and population – his own study on mortality in the failed Maremma colony being just one example of this use of medicine for political purposes. To optimise medicine's utility for the state, Cocchi advocated a close collaboration between doctors, natural philosophers and government administrators.[26] In this effort, Tuscany could draw on its celebrated scientific tradition. A century earlier, the physician claimed, Galileo had set free natural philosophy from 'barbarism' and 'blindness'.[27] But Tuscany was also the birthplace of a new 'scientific medicine' (*medicina scientifica*), characterised by observation and deduction. Cocchi argued that former Pisan professor of mathematics Giovanni Alfonso Borelli had 'reduced the theorems of physiology to exact demonstration'.[28] The Bologna physician Marcello Malpighi had introduced a natural historical approach to anatomy, 'excluding final causes and reducing material effects to physical necessity'.[29]

For Cocchi, drawing on the work of predecessors such as Borelli and Malpighi, the analytical method was 'the only [method] which could promote human knowledge, especially in anatomy'. This approach meant to 'describe with sincere and full exactness the parts and the fabric of things, and thus deduce by simple and secure discourse their tendency to produce certain effects, and their necessity to produce them under certain circumstances'.[30] Thus, the physician argued,

> Anatomy becomes nothing other than natural history, which is the principal part of physics, and in which the intellect is only patient, its task consisting in receiving the images of that which is understood by the senses without any additions of its own invention.[31]

Cocchi claimed that the anatomical method, characterised by information gathering through the senses, the analytical-deductive identification of physical causes, and the rejection of speculation, was useful for the achievement of public happiness in a number of ways. It would improve the practice of medicine and surgery and thus increase the population, and it could usefully be applied to improve our knowledge of natural resources as well as our understanding of the arts.

> The uses which knowledge of the fabric of the human body, and those of other animals, has for a variety of arts which are most useful to civil society, are innumerable, be it by measuring their forces with the conjunction of the similarities or analogies of parts, be it by discovering the location and the quality of liquids which are healthy or poisonous to man, and the artifice of their arms and instruments.[32]

Thus, the application of this anatomical approach to other practices and disciplines would dispel ignorance.[33] Anatomy, Cocchi concluded, is 'easy and certain, useful for the contemplation of nature, for medicine, surgery, and public life'.[34] For him, the political utility of anatomy was both in the content of anatomical knowledge, which could be applied to practical problems, and in its epistemological approach, which could be adapted in other fields to make knowledge production more reliable. Unlike Pietro Leopoldo a few decades later, Cocchi did not consider the uses of natural knowledge for legitimatory purposes.

Medicine in the Tuscan press

While many of Cocchi's suggestions were not realised immediately, after his death in 1758, his concerns with medicine for the common good were kept alive in Tuscan public discourse, especially through the local press. The discussion received an additional boost after the arrival of the scientifically minded Grand Duke Pietro Leopoldo in 1765. The sovereign's use of natural knowledge met with approval from local intellectuals who praised reform measures such as the foundation of the Royal Museum. Tuscany developed a lively publishing scene, which commented on developments in medicine and science, praising the benefits of medical progress for public enlightenment and the common good.[35] In solemn editorials, in book reviews and in laboured verse, erudite journals like the *Novelle Letterarie*, under the editorship of Uffizi director Giuseppe Pelli from 1770 to 1777, celebrated natural knowledge as a means to develop faculties of rational observation, and as the basis for public happiness and productivity.[36] The news-oriented *Gazzetta Toscana* reported on Tuscan public lectures on subjects from anatomy to physics, experiments and scientific publications, new instruments and machines, as well as reporting monstrous foetuses born locally.[37] Journal authors across the spectrum celebrated the present as 'the century of science', now that its practitioners had 'given method to good studies, and preference to useful knowledge over that which is fruitless and inconclusive'. They praised natural philosophers and the sovereign for their efforts 'to discover those truths which are of interest for the public good and that of individuals'. Such a maxim, they assured their readers, was 'capable of bringing about the most enormous changes' in society.[38] Like Cocchi, they claimed that Tuscany in particular was ready to benefit from such progress because of its scientific legacy.[39] And, like Cocchi, the journalists proposed that natural knowledge be applied simultaneously to bodies physical and metaphorical: medical and scientific progress would enhance 'the physical and moral state of man, the prosperity and well-being of the body politic, and of government'.[40] Commentators particularly highlighted the use of scientific medicine for improving the health of the population, and advocated knowledge about the body for everyone.

The proliferation of medical periodicals highlights the centrality of medical concerns for local intellectuals since Pietro Leopoldo's accession. Since the 1760s and 1770s, Tuscany saw the emergence of a wide range of (albeit frequently short-lived) medical journals for professionals and lay audiences. They openly declared their aims with indicative titles such as the *Giornale di Firenze, opera periodica che ha per primo oggetto la conservazione del corpo umano* ('Journal of Florence, a periodical whose primary objective is the preservation of the human body').[41] The image of useful knowledge promoted by these journals stressed the importance of empirical studies: positively reviewed works were praised for their focus on observation and experiment, especially when presented in a systematic and accessible manner.[42] Authors celebrated La Specola as the most complete, and the most useful collection of its kind in Europe.[43] Fontana's work on snake venom was hailed as a perfect example of the fruitful unity of natural philosophy and natural history, uniting the disciplines in 'a series of the most numerous experiments and observations' to produce 'a very evident proof' of his claim that the venom was organic, not inorganic.[44] Both the *Novelle* and the *Gazzetta* put forward an image of 'physics' as an empirical, experimental enterprise which could be useful for society in a number of ways: physics as an endeavour to understand the law-like behaviour of natural systems was the basis for a rational medicine, for the improvement of industry and for the introduction of good legislation. This attitude motivated discussions on public health issues such as the improvement of burial practices.[45]

As part of their quest to improve bodies physical and bodies politic, journal authors promoted medical knowledge for the general public, but also increasingly extolled the trustworthiness and value of doctors' professional expertise. In Tuscany, as elsewhere in early modern Europe, university-educated physicians were in competition with a wide range of less erudite healers such as herbalists, wise women, and bone-setters.[46] The local press applauded the efforts of physicians like Buchan and Tissot to produce accessible medical works for lay people as a way to reduce the pernicious influence of medical charlatans. Concerning William Buchan's *Domestic Medicine* (1769), for example, the authors of the *Novelle Letterarie* asserted that this work would 'enable anyone to take care of his own health'.[47] At other points, however, the *Novelle Letterarie* delimited the potential of these works. In their subsequent review of the same Italian translation of Buchan, they qualified that only 'persons . . . endowed with sufficient talent and good sense' could benefit from the book enough to take care of their own health.[48]

The local press, in concert with local doctors, contributed to the increasing stress placed on the need for medical expertise, as embodied in the university-trained doctor. The Florentine physician Lorenzo Pignotti in his 1784 *Istruzioni Mediche per le genti di campagna* (*Medical Instructions for the peasantry*), for instance, asserted that the efforts of Buchan, Tissot and others were useless in practice since they overtaxed lay people, and that physicians should instead highlight to the populace the limits of lay knowledge, educating them not to trust 'charlatans' and 'wise women', and instructing them on when to call a doctor.[49] To support the doctors' quest for medical authority Tuscan journals often described local physicians' accomplishments, encouraging the population to entrust their health to these licensed medical practitioners. It was, they proclaimed, 'just, and [our] duty, that the public be informed of the ability of those [medical] professionals who have given a real trial of their knowledge in difficult treatments'.[50]

Medical reforms in Tuscany before Pietro Leopoldo's accession

In the eighteenth century, Tuscan intellectuals and policy makers widely agreed on the importance of healthy, productive bodies, and of anatomical knowledge for the state. Already in the first half of the century, under the last Medici and the Regency, the government and individual functionaries had introduced some reform measures. However, medical improvements were not always accepted unquestionably. The British government representative Horace Mann reported on popular resistance to the introduction of smallpox inoculation during the Regency, noting

> a strong objection to it among the poor people, who most devoutly hope that the smallpox will ease them of the burden of their children, whom they cannot main-tain. I literally don't exaggerate, and they make no mystery of owning it. Both spring and autumn the inoculation is performed in an hospital at the Emperor's expense, but very few carry their children; and [prime minister] Marshal Botta, who is shocked at the motive of their repugnance, does not think it permitted in conscience to remove it at the expense of a crown each, which would be sufficient bribe. Now who is most to blame![51]

Such instances of resistance to medical reforms further highlighted the importance of public enlightenment. Ideally, an educated public should under-stand and accept the measures imposed by the government. Healthcare reforms in Tuscany even before Pietro Leopoldo's arrival, therefore, usually targeted institutions providing professional medical care, and professional and public education. Measures frequently centred on the disciplines that were most pre-valent in enlightened debates about medicine in state service: anatomy, surgery, and obstetrics. At the Conservatorio di Orbatello, a fourteenth-century founda-tion for the elderly poor and unwed mothers, a *motuproprio* of 1763 founded a school for obstetrics for surgeons and midwives, used by the medical students at Santa Maria Nuova.[52] Santa Maria Nuova, by far the largest of the Florentine hospitals, was the centre of early reforms. Michele Mariani, administrator from 1669 to 1707, introduced measures such as the introduction of individual beds for patients at his institution.[53]

A few decades later, in 1741, the new Habsburg government charged Antonio Cocchi with an appraisal of Santa Maria Nuova, and guidelines for its reform. In his *Relazione dello Spedale di Santa Maria Nuova di Firenze* of 1742, Cocchi commented on many aspects of hospital life, which would become important for later reforms, such as food, hygiene, ventilation, and water supply; he also advocated the exclusion of mental patients. Cocchi fur-ther suggested a formalisation of functionaries' roles under the direction of the sovereign, and an extension of the formerly marginal role of the medical personnel. The head of medical care, selected by the sovereign, should be a secular professional of honest character with surgical knowledge. In Cocchi's vision, 'the eye of the physician' (*l'occhio del medico*), rather than religious orders, should rule over the hospital. Not many suggestions of the *Relazione* were realised, but some measures were carried out. To remove dead bodies from the city centre, in 1745 the hospital's new cemetery was erected beyond the city walls at Porta a Pinti. In support of obstetric training, in 1756 Giuseppe Vespa was appointed the city's first Chair of Obstetrics at the hospital, and director of the delivery room.

Professional medical training was an important focus for innovative measures centred on anatomical and practical training. In many cases, Cocchi claimed, Florentines had altogether done away with university studies, and sent their sons directly to the hospital for training in medicine, surgery and pharmacy.[54] Anatomy and the availability of corpses were central for this training. Already in the early eighteenth century the hospital's overseers (the *spedalinghi*) had recognised the importance of anatomical studies for young physicians and surgeons, and had erected within the hospital's main building, an anatomical theatre (in 1726), and a dissection room (in 1732).[55] Anatomy remained a central element of students' work at the hospital throughout the century. In 1760, for instance, surgery student Girolamo Ristorini proudly presented a series of life-sized watercolours of myological structures to his professor. The images imitated poses taken from recent life-sized illustrations by Gautier D'Agoty, but were based, the student stressed, on his own preparations of real corpses.[56]

To make the most of corpses at students' and teachers' disposal, anatomical preparations were a routine part of medical education and anatomical practice.[57] In addition, the Regency government introduced university lectures for trainee surgeons at the hospital to complement their practical instruction. Surgical education at Santa Maria Nuova thus became formally part of the city's Facoltà di arti like other academic subjects. Cocchi applauded these government measures for the promotion of anatomy, which removed 'the stubborn and slanderous obstacles to research into the true causes of disease by means of dissection, for the use and satisfaction of the professors on the bodies of their patients'.[58]

Cocchi himself held weekly anatomy lectures, and public demonstrations at the end of winter. He also took on private students, who followed him on his hospital rounds. In 1751, he was officially charged with anatomy teaching for surgeons, seconded by Angelo Nannoni (1715–90) and Antonio Benevoli (1685–1758) – the beginning of the famous Florence school of surgery, which was imitated throughout Italy. Anatomy teaching was not confined to research

into the causes of diseases, but also included the practice of surgical operations on corpses, including the development of new surgical techniques.[59]
In his records entitled *Adversaria anatomica* (1735–56), Cocchi described
numerous autopsies and the teaching of dissections.[60] As a vocal advocate of
anatomical reform in state service, and of anatomy as a tool for achieving public
happiness, the physician was willing to use himself as an exemplar, performing
the role of good citizen even after his death. True to his convictions, and following Bellini's example, Cocchi himself was dissected a day after his death in
1759, at his home, by surgeon Biozzi and dissector Gosi under the direction of
professors Francesco Tozzetti and Angelo Nannoni; with other professors and
foreign visitors being invited to observe. An extensive description of the event
was published by Cocchi's former student Saverio Manetti.[61] Manetti used the
opportunity to highlight once more his master's conviction of the importance
of anatomical studies for the progress of medical knowledge.

Education was also central to reformers' institutional changes. In addition to
innovations in anatomical and surgical instruction, Cocchi proposed measures
to improve the state of the hospital's teaching materials. He suggested the consolidation of the collections of books, mathematical and surgical instruments,
curiosities and *materia medica*, according to didactic considerations.[62] Again,
progress was patchy, and many of Cocchi's suggestions for turning the hospital
into an educational institution in state service had to wait. In 1775, Cocchi's
son Raimondo, himself an anatomist at Santa Maria Nuova, concluded his
series of lectures with the hopeful appeal that soon there might arise 'a man
who chooses to . . . serve the fatherland, a founder of new schools, a producer
of new conveniences for our studies'.[63]

Pietro Leopoldo's medical reforms

Many of the changes proposed by Antonio Cocchi in the 1740s would finally
be realised and developed further under Grand Duke Pietro Leopoldo, who
shared his Tuscan subjects' view on the importance of medicine for the enlightened state. In particular, he agreed with the tenor of previous debates on the
importance of professional medical education, and on the improvement of
obstetrics through the introduction of anatomical training. However, he went
beyond ideas developed in the preceding decades in a number of ways, both
in the more far-reaching extent of his reforms of medical education, and in the
introduction of comprehensive public health administration. Other measures
drew on more recent debates and discoveries in medicine and natural philosophy. These included, for instance, the introduction of non-punitive treatment
for the insane and the renovation of the Bonifazio mental asylum.

An impressive 600,000 Lire were invested in making the buildings of Santa Maria Nuova more salubrious, following recent scientific studies such as Joseph Priestley's work on air. Pietro Leopoldo also tried to exploit the potential health benefits of Tuscany's natural riches: his public health measures included promoting the benefits of the waters at Montecatini and the erection of public baths at Porta al Prato.

Some of the Grand Duke's measures in the 1770s and 1780s directly adopted Cocchi's suggestions concerning the reforms of medical governance and of hospitals, especially of Santa Maria Nuova. In his observations on the state of his domain, *Relazioni sul governo della Toscana*, the Grand Duke lamented Tuscan hospitals' lack of economy and medical focus. To improve the situation, Pietro Leopoldo followed Cocchi's earlier advice that the 'eye of the physician' should rule over hospitals, and implemented various measures to turn hospitals into places exclusively dedicated to medical treatment rather than undifferentiated charitable institutions. The sole exception to this measure was the continuing practice of taking in foundlings at obstetric wards, a measure that contributed to population growth. Further measures combined the practice and teaching of obstetrics. In agreement with Cocchi's arguments that anatomical knowledge was of central importance for the improvement of medical practice in general, and male obstetricians' claims to superiority based on knowledge of anatomical theory more specifically, practitioners of both sexes would now receive some theoretical foundation to their training. In 1773, for instance, a delivery room for the poor was set up at Santa Maria Nuova to serve the practical instruction of midwives for the Grand Duchy. Ten years later a new clinic of obstetrics replaced the old school located at the Orbatello hospital.

Going beyond Cocchi's suggestions, however, the Grand Duke also implemented major changes in the state- and city-wide administration of public health. In May 1777, superintendents (*commissari*) were put in place for the four quarters of the city of Florence, each aided by a physician and an obstetrician. Their policing duties included ensuring the observance of new public health measures such as new burial regulations, which prohibited the uncovered laying-out of corpses, burial before the end of a 24-hour period, and church burials.[64] During the course of his public health reforms, the sovereign decided not to rely solely on his own observations and those of individual practitioners like Cocchi, but to systematise the collection of relevant information and to give it a comprehensive geographical scope. In 1778 Pietro Leopoldo installed a deputation to investigate the state of Tuscan hospitals and religious institutions in more detail than his own *Relazione* had done. His motivations to reform the provision of medical care and charity received additional fuel on his visit to Austria in 1778/9, where he witnessed his imperial brother's attempts to turn church institutions into instruments of governance. Thus, the Tuscan hospital reforms became part of a centralised system of police, culminating in 1784 in the institution of the *Buongoverno*, effectively a ministry of the interior separate from the judiciary. After the reform of the *Collegio Medico* in 1781 and the abolition of the ancient *Magistrato di Sanità* in 1784, medical supervision was now part of the duties of the city's four *commissari*. With Pietro Leopodo's reforms, medical expertise became closely integrated into the business of state governance.

The reform efforts also established new regulations in 1783.[65] Contemporary observers attested the reforms' success. René Desgenettes (1762–1837), a French military surgeon who had spent a few years in Italy from 1785 to 1789, put forward Santa Maria Nuova as a model for hospital reform in a 1792 report for the French Revolutionary government. His observations indicate that the reforms were largely put into practice.[66] Many of the changes prescribed in the regulations and described by Desgenettes concerned the hospital's teaching. Among the measures originally suggested by Cocchi had been the consolidation and systematisation of teaching materials. In 1783, accordingly, the Magliabechiana Library was ordered to transfer its medical books to Santa Maria Nuova, and publishers were requested to send copies of new medical publications to the hospital. In addition, the hospital received a new botanical garden and lecture room, an improved pharmacy, a new laboratory with a teaching collection of *materia medica* and a herbal, as well as a new anatomical theatre.[67]

Pietro Leopoldo's measures not only aimed to improve the material situation of medical teaching at the hospital, but also improved and formalised the institutionalisation of medical expertise. The reforms of 1783 established eight teaching chairs, in practical medicine, anatomy, *instituzioni chirurgiche*, surgical practice, surgical operations on corpses, obstetrics, botany and *materia medica*, and pharmaceutical chemistry.[68] Systematised by the new regulations, clinical training at Santa Maria Nuova included three levels of practical training, and one of theory. First, students learned at the bedside, assisted by the treating physician, then they visited patients by themselves. Finally, the professor of practical medicine gave lessons at the bedside as well as theoretical lectures.[69] Students who had received their doctorate at a university had to do an additional two-year internship at Santa Maria Nuova in order to receive a licence to practise (*matricola*) from the Florentine *Collegio Medico*.[70] During those internships students were assigned patients to observe, to describe their case histories, and, if necessary, to perform the dissection if the patient died.[71] Trainee surgeons similarly followed the development of individual patients from admission to dissection.[72]

Teachers had ample material at their disposal: the large male and female wards where lecturers and practitioners took their students on rounds, the reorganised botanical garden and collections, as well as a regular supply of corpses from the wards. Corpses, in particular, were much sought-after teaching resources for different groups within the hospital who used dead bodies for demonstrations of anatomical details, surgical techniques, and midwifery to medical students, trainee surgeons, and female midwives.[73] The new regulations recognised this competition and formalised access to dead bodies, requiring decorum and discretion in dissection and transport. Corpses were to be used only by teachers who were members of the hospital, and by the modelling workshop at the new Museum of Physics and Natural History. Thus, medical teaching at Santa Maria Nuova was now conducted by officially recognised and institutionally established experts appointed by the state. The training, both for physicians and surgeons, integrated theoretical and practical instruction, and was based on the study of anatomy, which Cocchi had identified as being crucial for the improvement and security of medical knowledge.

Giuseppe Galletti, Bologna and a model collection for Florence

Arguments for the utility of anatomical knowledge since the early decades of the eighteenth century thus made the bodies of the living and the dead increasingly important for the state, and for the training of a wide range of medical practitioners in Florence, from physicians and surgeons to midwives. While changes in medical teaching were introduced at institutions such as Santa Maria Nuova, local practitioners simultaneously developed schemes to improve anatomical learning in other ways.

The original suggestion to establish a collection of anatomical models in Tuscany had been put forward to court physicist Fontana by local obstetrician Giuseppe Galletti (1738–1819). Galletti was part of a new generation of male obstetricians who were intent on elevating the status of their discipline by basing it on the study of anatomy. Childbirth had long been the prerogative of female midwives, but in the eighteenth century, male practitioners, especially surgeons, increasingly claimed it as their own field of practice. Their claims to superiority were frequently based on their knowledge of human anatomy.

In August 1770, Galletti spent a few weeks in Bologna, a city in the Papal State which, like Florence, at that time assigned an increasingly important role to anatomy. The Bologna Academy of Science had been restructured in 1742, to include a new chair of human anatomy following orders of Pope Benedict XIV.[74] Galletti came to Bologna to learn more about obstetrics from celebrated surgeon Giovanni Antonio Galli, who taught anatomy and midwifery to surgeons and midwives.[75] Galli possessed a collection of anatomical models for teaching purposes, including clay and wax models showing the child in different positions in the womb. These obstetric models were neither the first objects to depict pregnancies in three-dimensional form, nor the first artificial anatomies used for teaching purposes. During the Middle Ages sculptors had developed the genre of the 'pregnant Virgin', statues of Mary with the baby Jesus visible inside the womb.[76] Miniature models in wax, ivory, wood and metal had been known at least since the seventeenth century.[77]

Around 1700, obstetricians began to develop life-sized models for teaching purposes: dummies of pregnant women and foetuses, which could be used for demonstrations and hands-on training.[78] Throughout the eighteenth century, midwives, surgeons and physicians around Europe used such 'phantoms' or 'birth machines' (*macchine de' parti*) in their teaching.[79] Practitioners designed their own versions of these machines to suit their needs: intricately mechanised full-size females, or simple, robust torsos in leather and wood (figure 7). The French Royal midwife Mme du Coudray devised a machine that included wet sponges and bladders to imitate body fluids; she left copies of this phantom in the larger cities she visited on her tour of the French provinces to enhance continuing instruction. Galli's version in Bologna contained a glass uterus to enable students to see inside.[80]

However, Galli's hands-on teaching tools were not the only artificial anatomies on display at the time of Galletti's visit, and the Florentine obstetrician would have seen a wide variety of different forms of anatomical models. The city was home to a number of renowned modellers, especially sculptor Ercole Lelli (1702–66), and the husband-and-wife team of Giovanni Manzolini (1700–55) and Anna Morandi Manzolini (1714–74). Lelli's works, a series of expressive full-sized statues, which presented anatomical details within the aesthetics of the early modern *memento mori* tradition, had been commissioned by the pope for use by artists. Manzolini and Morandi on the other hand produced models primarily for a medical audience, including Galli, and engaged in anatomical teaching themselves. Anna Morandi in particular achieved international fame as a female savant and was widely celebrated in eighteenth-century Europe as an anatomist.[81] Hers were the models that most impressed Galletti in Bologna; they eschewed the aesthetic conventions of Lelli's works, and did not strive to imitate the haptic qualities of obstetric practice. Instead, Morandi's models in delicate wax provided life-like, accurate visual representations of anatomical details in numerous series of organs, senses, and body parts. Thus, Galletti may have assumed that these models, in particular, could be used to underscore obstetricians' claims that their expertise was valuable to the state and its population – claims based on their knowledge of anatomy.

On his return to Florence, Galletti set out to produce a similar collection, motivated by a concern for 'public utility'.[82] The obstetrician aimed to produce models which, like the Bologna collection, would 'reveal in wax in natural size and colouring all parts of the human body in such views and positions as can be of use for anatomical studies'.[83] Finding his own sculpting abilities wanting, the obstetrician went in search of support from sculptors.[84] In Florence, Galletti could draw on an established tradition of wax modelling, that had begun with the production of votive offerings, and the use of wax for anatomical preparations and for preliminary studies of sculptures since the Middle Ages.[85] Wax models were routinely used for the production of bronze and ceramic sculptures, for example locally at the large Tuscan porcelain manufacture in Doccia, which had been founded in 1737.[86] Wax was a popular medium for portraits, miniature scenes such as Zumbo's of death and decay in the *memento mori* tradition, and votives.[87] The Florentine church Santissima Annunziata was famously filled with a vast collection of votives depicting many generations of afflictions and the afflicted. Eventually, Galletti employed the sculptor Giuseppe Ferrini from Livorno, who had learned anatomical modelling in Bologna, to work under his guidance.

Satisfied with the first fruits of the collaboration, Galletti approached Felice Fontana with his ideas, hoping to reach the ear of the Grand Duke through his court physicist. Given Pietro Leopoldo's interest in the reform of medical training and public medical care, Galletti had reason to believe that his suggestions would be well received at court. In his proposal, the obstetrician highlighted the models' use for 'students of medicine and anatomy',[88] if the preparations were to be put up at the university of Pisa 'or in another public place', potentially the emergent Royal Museum.[89] The physician's suggestion was thus intended to contribute primarily to professional medical training in Florence or Pisa.

Fontana's proposal for a model collection in Florence

When Fontana passed on the suggestion to the Grand Duke, the museum director gave it a different spin, thus reinterpreting the value of the anatomical models for the state from a tool for professional medical instruction to an instrument for public enlightenment and, simultaneously, a visible demonstration of Tuscan scientific tradition and the Grand Duke's benevolence.[90] While maintaining Galletti's claim to the models' utility for anatomical studies, Fontana favoured their acquisition for public display at the Museum of Physics and Natural History rather than at an institution devoted exclusively to medical training.[91] In his opinion, the models' utility was in their synoptic function, which was to turn anatomy into an 'aspect of physics' in the sense that the simultaneous visibility of anatomical components and their spatial relationships would enable an enquiry into the body's functional relationships.[92] Like his contemporaries, Fontana used the notion of 'physics' to encompass all areas of natural knowledge, which aimed at providing explanations rather than mere descriptions. In the parlance of early modern naturalists, the models should serve as philosophical instruments. Fontana's idea about the relationship between medicine and natural philosophy was thus not so different from Cocchi's earlier iatromechanics as Fontana usually made it out when he distanced himself from what he saw as a uselessly erudite Florentine tradition. His idea that medicine could only progress through the influence of science was present in contemporary publications such as the local journals.

In Fontana's version of the proposal for anatomical model production and exhibition presented to the sovereign, he combined these new purposes with one already well established: in addition to the models' contribution to public education and to anatomy as an aspect of physics, Fontana stressed that the Bologna models 'render the memory of Benedict XIV, who ordered them, immortal and dear to posterity'. Therefore, Fontana hinted, a new Florentine model collection would similarly contribute to its noble patron's immortality, just as the Medici cabinet of curiosities had done for the previous reigning dynasty as celebrated patrons of science.[93] In addition, he added to the models' utility for professional medical education their potential uses for the anatomical instruction of artists.

Significantly, in Fontana's proposal, the models' projected utility for the Tuscan state was not limited to one clearly defined and circumscribed function. Like other elements in the museum, they should contribute to the institution's main task of turning subjects into citizens: to enlighten the public about the existence and intelligibility of natural laws, and to develop their faculties of reasoning for an active command of knowledge. The artificial anatomies could also serve a more specialised purpose: to convey anatomical knowledge to medical students and artists. The models' multiple roles would thus mirror the multiple envisioned functions of natural knowledge for absolutist Tuscany more generally: to serve legitimatory purposes, and to contribute to material improvement.

This new interpretation was not the only significant change to Galletti's initial initiative. Fontana failed to mention that the plans originated with the obstetrician when he communicated them to the grand-ducal court. In addition to appropriating Galletti's idea, upon royal approval for an anatomical model workshop at the museum the natural philosopher also successfully poached the artist Ferrini. Wax modellers and other artisans now collaborated in the museum with naturalists and anatomists at a new workshop to produce models of normal human anatomy for public display. Tuscan intellectuals applauded the collection of artificial anatomies.[94] Scholars actively engaged in the promotion of the collection in local journals and other publications. Marco Lastri's *Osservatore Fiorentino* – a description of Florence which highlighted the great artistic and natural philosophical tradition of Tuscany – showcased the museum as an outstanding continuation and advancement of this tradition: 'an institution as there are few, orderly, rich, splendid in all subjects'. The anatomical models were praised as evidence for both the scientific and the artisanal talent in Tuscany.[95]

Despite this major setback in his search for support, Galletti continued to pursue his project – motivated, perhaps, by anatomist Raimondo Cocchi's 1775 appeal for a 'producer of new conveniences for [students'] studies'.[96] Throughout the 1770s, Galletti experimented further with different materials. His models in clay and wax of natural and assisted births served for private courses at his house, and he developed a teaching model in wood, which was sent to the University of Pavia.[97] In his quest to improve the study of obstetrics, Galletti also translated into Italian the Göttingen professor Johann Georg Roederer's Latin *Elements of Obstetrics* (*Elementa artis obstetriciae* 1753, first Italian edition 1775). Local scholars like Giuseppe Pelli, Cocchi's successor as director of the Uffizi Gallery, followed and publicised Galletti's efforts, praising him as an 'able surgeon' and his terracotta models as 'exact, elegant, and useful'.[98] Eventually, Galletti's initiatives and public reputation gained official recognition. When the chair of obstetrics at Santa Maria Nuova was divided into separate chairs for theory and practice in 1806, Giuseppe Galletti – now in his late 60s – received the position for obstetric practice, directing the hands-on instruction of surgeons and midwives, and using wax and terracotta models for hospital-based medical education as he had originally proposed.[99] While this elevation of Galletti came too late to be witnessed by Fontana, who had died the year before, the new position, nevertheless, gave Galletti an opportunity for public vindication. In his inaugural lecture, Galletti explained that the Florentine collection of anatomical models had been his idea.[100] However, in the thirty years since the museum's opening to the public the anatomical waxes had earned international fame exclusively for the Royal Museum, its founder Grand Duke Pietro Leopoldo, and its director Felice Fontana.

Conclusion

Knowledge about the body was important to a variety of communities in eighteenth-century Tuscany for different reasons. Government officials were keen to improve public health to increase state revenue; intellectuals argued that self-knowledge was central to the creation of the enlightened citizen; and male obstetricians, a newly emergent professional group, cited anatomical knowledge as the basis for their superiority to traditional midwives. Thus, a variety of arguments in Tuscan public discourse could be used to support the production of anatomical teaching aids.

These arguments also contributed to the development of expertise in state service. For physician Cocchi in the mid-eighteenth century, anatomical expertise consisted of a combination of theoretical understanding and practical experience, and it could be useful to the state in two ways. First, anatomical research produced facts that could be used to improve specific areas of the polity, such as public health or arts and manufacture. Second, anatomists' analytical-deductive method, integrating theory and experience, led to the most reliable knowledge, and could therefore be used to improve other disciplines and areas of investigation. Anatomists, in Cocchi's view, were useful to the state, not only for what they knew about the body, but equally for the way they acquired this knowledge. They could thus serve as exemplars for useful expertise more generally. Medical reformers during the Regency and under Pietro Leopoldo agreed with this view of expertise as constituted by theory and experience, and accordingly supported a combination of practical and theoretical training in anatomical instruction to improve the practice of a wide range of medical professionals: physicians, surgeons, obstetricians and midwives. But, as shown in Chapter 1, Pietro Leopoldo was also intent on exploiting the improving potential of the anatomical method in fields beyond medicine and public health. In new and reformed institutions, such as the Georgofili Agricultural Academy and the Royal Museum of Physics and Natural History, the Grand Duke attempted to institutionalise expertise based on a reliable analytical-deductive method that would deliver true and useful knowledge in state service. However, Pietro Leopoldo soon found that those who possessed this authoritative natural knowledge could use it to claim more political agency for themselves. His experience with these new cadres of experts brought the problem of expert control to the fore, especially at the new Chamber of Commerce where this struggle eventually led to its dissolution. It is not surprising, then, that the sovereign's measures for public health tightly intermeshed the support of medical expertise with administrative surveillance.

Medical practitioners benefited from government support and were happy to collaborate with the state. The Florentine obstetrician Giuseppe Galletti, for example, provided an important early impulse to establish a collection of wax models in Tuscany to improve the training of medical professionals. His subsequent proposal to the Grand Duke's court physicist Fontana reflected recent intellectual, political and institutional developments as well as a long tradition of institutionalised medical care and medical training in Florence.

Communicating Galletti's proposal to his sovereign, however, Fontana reinterpreted the medical practitioner's ideas to tie in more closely with the Grand Duke's concerns. In Fontana's version, the models became tools of public enlightenment as well as testimonies to the benevolence of the ruling dynasty. This interpretive flexibility of the models remained a characteristic feature of the collection.

With his reinterpretation of the anatomical models' uses, Fontana and his museum took on a heavy responsibility for some of the core elements of the Grand Duke's reform projects: for the creation of the enlightened citizen as well as for supporting the legitimacy of Pietro Leopoldo's regime. This responsibility charged everyday practices at the museum. Practices of model production and model display, in particular, became contentious within the museum, and between museum and court. Part II turns to the everyday life of the museum to show how naturalists articulated their roles as experts in state service, investigating conflicts such as the struggle for authority between artisans and naturalists in model production (Chapter 3), and debates about the control of visitor responses at the exhibition (Chapter 4).

Notes

1 For the cultural associations of wax in the early modern period, see Lucia Dacome, 'Women, wax and anatomy in the "century of things"', *Renaissance studies* 21:4 (2007), pp. 522–50.

2 M. Bucci, *Anatomia come arte* (Florence: Edizioni d'Arte Il Fiorino, 1969), p. 197.

3 E. Cochrane, *Florence in the forgotten centuries 1527–1800. A history of Florence and the Florentines in the age of the Grand Dukes* (Chicago and London: University of Chicago Press, 1973), p. 471.

4 For Italian discussions of the role of women in society, see e.g. Luciano Guerci, *La discussione sulla donna nell'Italia del Settecento. Aspetti e problemi* (v. 1 and 2, Torino: Tirrenia Stampatori, 1987–88); L. Guerci, *La sposa obbediente. Donna e matrimonio nella discussione dell'Italia del Settecento* (Torino: Tirrenia Stampatori, 1988); Rebecca Messbarger, *The century of women: representations of women in eighteenth-century Italian public discourse* (Toronto: University of Toronto Press, 2002).

5 For diverging interpretations of the role of mothers in foetal development and childbirth, see e.g. contributions in Lorraine Daston and Gianna Pomata (eds), *The faces of nature in Enlightenment Europe* (Berlin: BWV-Berliner Wissenschafts-Verlag, 2003). For the historiographical debate around images of foetal autonomy see Karen Newman, *Fetal positions: individualism, science, visuality* (Stanford: Stanford University Press, 1996), and critical responses including Rebecca Messbarger, 'Re-membering a body of work: anatomist and anatomical

designer Anna Morandi Manzolini', *Studies in eighteenth-century culture* 32 (2003), pp. 123–54; Lianne McTavish, *Childbirth and the display of authority in early modern France* (Aldershot: Ashgate, 2005); Lyle Massey, 'On waxes and wombs. Eighteenth-century representations of the gravid uterus', in *Ephemeral bodies: wax sculpture and the human figure*, ed. Roberta Panzanelli (Los Angeles: Getty Research Institute, 2008), pp. 83–106.

6 Nadia Maria Filippini, 'Eine neue Vorstellung vom Fötus und vom Mutterleib (Italien, 18. Jahrhundert)', in Barbara Duden, Jürgen Schlumbohm, and Patrice Veit (eds), *Geschichte des Ungeborenen. Zur Erfahrungs- und Wissenschaftsgeschichte der Schwangerschaft, 17. -20. Jahrhundert* (Göttingen: Vandenhoeck & Ruprecht, 2002) , pp. 99–128.

7 For European developments of obstetrics outside of Italy see exemplary Adrian Wilson, *The making of man-midwifery: childbirth in England, 1660-1770* (Cambridge, Mass.: Harvard University Press, 1995); Jean Donnison, *Midwives and medical men: a history of the struggle for the control of childbirth* (New Barnet: Historical Publications, 2nd edn, 1988); Hilary Marland (ed.), *The art of midwifery: early modern midwives in Europe* (London: New York: Routledge, 1993).

8 Messbarger, 'Re-membering'.

9 Nina Rattner Gelbart, *The king's midwife. A history and mystery of Madame du Coudray* (Berkeley, Los Angeles, London: University of California Press, 1998).

10 Ghislaine Lawrence, 'An obstetric phantom', *Lancet* 358:9296 (2001), p. 1916; Gelbart, *King's midwife*, especially pp. 60–5.

11 For medical reforms in eighteenth-century Florence, especially at the general hospital Santa Maria Nuova, see Jacqueline Brau, 'La professionalization de la santé dans la Toscane des Lumières, 1765-1815', *Revue d'histoire moderne et contemporaine* 41:3 (1994), pp. 418–39; Renato Pasta, '"L'Ospedale e la città": riforme settecentesche a Santa Maria Nuova', *Annali di Storia di Firenze* 1 (2006), pp. 83–98.

12 For a comprehensive list of Florentine hospitals see e.g. A. Aleardi, G. Germano, C. Marcetti, and N. Solimano (eds), *L'Ospedale e la città. Dalla fondazione di S. Maria Nuova al sistema ospedaliero del 2000* (Florence: Polistampa, 2000), pp. 92–117.

13 Leon Battista Alberti, *L'Architettura*, ed. G.Orlandi and P. Portoghesi (Milan, 1966), v. 1, 367–8. Translated by John Henderson; quoted in Henderson, *The Renaissance hospital. Healing the body and healing the soul* (New Haven and London: Yale University Press, 2006), p. xxv.

14 Nicolas René Desgenettes, 'Observations sur l'enseignement de la medicine dans les hôpiteaux de la Toscane', *Journal de Médecine, Chirurgie et Pharmacie* 91 (1792), pp. 233–56, p. 237.

15 'Nella medicina ha lo spedale come pubblici maestri, benché senza particolare stipendio, alcuni dei suoi medici ordinari più distinti per la loro dottrina, i quali per un costume introdotto per sola loro cortesia ammettono alla loro scuola nelle lor visite quotidiane tutti gli scolari o dilettanti di quella professione che vogliono,

come si dice, far pratica'. Antonio Cocchi, *Relazione dello Spedale di Santa Maria Nuova di Firenze* (Florence: Casa Editrice Le Lettere, 2000), ed. Maria Mannelli Goggiolo, p. 167.

16 Cocchi, *Relazione*, p. 117.

17 For the life of Antonio Cocchi, see e.g. Saverio Manetti, 'Una lettera con notizie sula [sic] vita del Cocchi, la sua morte e l'autopsia' (1759), reprinted in Weber, *Aspetti poco noti*; Miriam Fileti Mazza and Bruna Tomasello, *Antonio Cocchi: primo antiquario della Galleria fiorentina, 1738-1758* (Modena: F.C. Panini, 1996).

18 '[D]i ottima struttura di corpo, . . . robusto, . . . inclinato agli studj'. Saverio Manetti, 'Una lettera', p. 106.

19 Desgenettes, 'Observations', p. 1.

20 Antonio Cocchi, *Lettera intorno all'educazione e al genere di vita degl'Inglesi* (1724).

21 Jean Boutier, Brigitte Marin, and Antonella Romano (eds), *Naples, Rome, Florence: Une histoire compare des milieux intellectuels italiens (XVIIe–XVIIIe siècles)* (Rome: École française de Rome, 2005), p. 706.

22 Horace Walpole, *Horace Walpole's correspondence with Sir Horace Mann*, ed. W. S. Lewis, Warren Hunting Smith, and George L. Lam (London: Oxford University Press; New Haven: Yale University Press, 1954–71).

23 Walpole, *Correspondence*, v. 1, p. 57, Mann to Walpole, 3 June 1741.

24 '[U]n savant anatomiste, . . . habile médecin, . . . érudit profond, . . . élégant écrivain', René Desgenettes, 'Remarques sur le passage suivant, inséré dans le journal de médecine, chirurgie et pharmacie, cahier de mars 1806, tome XI, page 459; 'La réputation de l'illustre Cocchi n'a pas encore franchi les Alpes'. Par R. Desgenettes, docteur et professeur en médecine, etc.', *Journal de Médecine, Chirurgie et Pharmacie* 11 (1806), insert, p. 2.

25 '[C]he l'anatomia non sia giammai per decadere tra noi dal publico favore', A. Cocchi, *Dell'anatomia discorso* (1745), p. 72.

26 Lorenzo Bellini, *Discorsi di anatomia ora per la prima volta stampati dall'originale esistente nella libreria Pandolfini . . . colla prefazione di Antonio Cocchi . . .* (Florence: Francesco Moücke, 1741–44).

27 Cocchi, 'Prefazione' to Bellini, *Discorsi*, p. viii.

28 '[R]idurre alla dimostrazione esatta i teoremi della fisiologia', Cocchi, 'Prefazione' to Bellini, *Discorsi*, p. ix.

29 '[E]scludendo le cause finali e riducendo gli effetti materiali alla fisica necessità', Cocchi, 'Prefazione' to Bellini, *Discorsi*, p. ix.

30 '[L]'unico che possa promuovere la cognizione umana particolarmente nell'anatomia', 'descrivendone con sincera e piena esatezza le parti e la fabbrica, e quindi deducendo con discorso semplice e sicuro la loro attitudine a produr certi effetti, e la necessità di produrgli in certe circostanze', Cocchi, 'Prefazione' to Bellini, *Discorsi*, p. xxxiii.

31 '[L'anatomia] non altro viene ad essere che istoria naturale, la quale è parte

principalissima della fisica, e nella quale l'intelletto è solamente paziente, consistendo il suo ufficio nel ricevere le imagini di ciò per mezzo dei sensi ci comprende senza veruna aggiunta di propria invenzione', Cocchi, *Dell'anatomia discorso*, pp. 7–8.

32 'Gli usi poi che la cognizione della fabbrica del corpo dell'uomo e degli altri animali può avere per varie arti utilissime alla civil società sono innumerabili, si per misurare le loro forze colla coniettura della similitudine e analogia delle parti, si per rinvenire la sede e la qualità dei liquidi loro o salubri o velenosi all'uomo, e l'artifizio delle loro armi e strumenti'. Cocchi, *Dell'anatomia discorso*, p. 35.

33 Cocchi, *Dell'anatomia discorso*, p. 10 ff.

34 '[H]o procurato di mostrare . . . quanto [l'anatomia] sia facile e certa, e quanto utile per la fisica contemplazione, per la medicina, per la chirurgia, e per la vita civile'. Cocchi, *Dell'anatomia discorso*, p. 71.

35 For a comprehensive inventory of Tuscan journals, see Benvenuto Righini, *I periodici fiorentini (1597–1950). Catalogo ragionato* (Florence: Sansoni antiquariato, 1955). For an exhaustive history of publishing in eighteenth-century Florence see Maria Augusta Morelli Timpanaro, *Autori, stampatori, librai. Per una storia dell'editoria in Firenze nel secolo XVIII* (Florence: Olschki, 1999).

36 Morelli Timpanaro, *Autori*, p. 194. For such celebrations of the social benefits of natural knowledge, see e.g. *Novelle Letterarie* no. 18 (5 May 1780), which reprinted extracts from Giuseppe Lombardo-Buda's poem 'La Necessità, principale origine di ogni bene per la Società, stabilita sù principj interessanti all'Istoria (particolarmente Naturale) e al Commercio' ('Necessity, the principal origin of all benefit to society, established on principles pertaining to History (especially Natural) and Commerce').

37 *Gazzetta Toscana* no. 9 (1776); no. 31 (1777); *Gazzetta Toscana* no. 31 (1798); *Gazzetta Toscana* no. 52 (1777); no. 45 (1797).

38 *Novelle Letterarie* no. 1 (1776): 'Secolo delle scienze', 'dar metodo ai buoni studj, e preferir le utili cognizioni alle oziose ed inconcludenti, . . . a conoscer qualche verità che interessa la pubblica felicità e quella degl'individui. . . . Una sola massima adottata dai Filosofi e dai Principi è capace di far delle variazioni enormissime'.

39 E.g. *Novelle Letterarie* nos. 1, 2, 3 (1781); see also no. 1 (1782).

40 '[I] progressi nella Fisica . . . oggetti . . . interessanti il Fisico, e il Morale dell'uomo, la prosperità, e il ben essere del Corpo Politico, e del Governo Civile', *Novelle Letterarie* no. 1 (1778).

41 Edited by Pagani and Valli, 1769–70. Others included e.g. the *Osservatore italiano, ossia raccolta di discorsi istorici, filosofici, scientifici ecc.* ('Italian observer, or selection of historical, philosophical, scientific debates', eds, Stecchi and Pagani, 1770–73), the *Raccolta di opuscoli medico-pratici* ('Collection of practical medical works'; ed. G.L. Targioni, 1773–85), the *Raccolta di opuscoli fisico-medici* ('Collection of physico-medical works', ed. G.L. Targioni, 1774–82), the *Avvisi sopra la salute umana* ('Advice on human health', ed. G.L. Targioni, 1775–85)

and the *Notizie chirurgiche universali* ('Universal surgical news'; ed. Giuseppe Allegrini, 1775). See also G. Nicoletti (ed.), 'Periodici toscani del Settecento', *Studi italiani* 14 (2002), pp. 363–411.

42 See e.g. *Novelle Letterarie* no. 29 (1783): review of Pietro Moscati, *Osservazioni ed esperienze sul sangue fluido e rappreso . . .* (Milan 1783); no. 40 (1785): review of Gaetano Torraca, *Dissertazione sopra il quesito: Quali difetti ed eccessi debbano evitarsi nello studio della storia naturale* (Mantua 1784); no. 47 (1790): review of Pietro Visconti, *Nosografia, o sia Descizione delle malattie ricevute e curate nel R. Arcispedale di Santa Maria Nuova di Firenze per l'anno 1789* (Florence 1790).

43 *Gazzetta Toscana* nos 3, 6, 12, 13, 15 (1775).

44 'La serie numerosissima d'esperienze, e d'osservazioni', 'una prova assai manifesta', *Novelle Letterarie* no. 2 (1782): column 19; also no. 3 (1782).

45 E.g. *Gazzetta Toscana* no. 28 (1775); *Gazzetta Toscana* no. 17 (1775); no. 31 (1777); *Gazzetta Toscana* no. 50 (1775).

46 David Gentilcore, *Medical Charlatanism in Early Modern Italy* (Oxford: Oxford University Press, 2006).

47 *Novelle Letterarie* no. 1 (1780): 'La Medicina più semplice, è insieme la più vera; ed appunto per essere semplice, può essere messa nelle mani di ognuno. Tissot e Buchan, accreditatissimi medici viventi, anno inteso questa verità, e spogliando di qualunque impostura l'Arte Ippocratica, anno scritto per il Popolo, ed *anno rimesso a ciascuno la cura della propria salute*' (italics A.M.).

48 *Novelle Letterarie* no. 2 (1782): '[A]nno [gli autori] tentato di rendere l'esecuzione di questo progetto così facile e chiaro, che non i Medici soli, ma tutte quante le Persone, purchè *fornite di un discreto talento e di buon senso*, fossero capaci da per loro, di conservarsi la salute, e di condurre a buon fine una cura' (italics A.M.).

49 [Dr Lorenzo Pignotti], *Istruzioni Mediche per le genti di campagna* (Florence: Giuseppe Tofani, 1784), especially pp. 3–8. 'Il nostro progetto è . . . di tirare (s'è possibile) questa linea di divisione tra le malattie facili a conoscere e a curare, e quelle che ricercano la cura d'un abile professore', pp. 7–8.

50 *Gazzetta Toscana* no. 42 (1795): 'È giustizia, e dovere, che il Pubblico resti informato dell'abilità di quei Professori, i quali nelle difficili cure, che gli si presentano danno un vero saggio del loro sapere'. See also, e.g. no. 29 (1779); no. 30 (1794).

51 Walpole, *Correspondence*, v. 6, p. 150, Mann to Walpole, 11 June 1763.

52 Francesca Vannozzi, 'Dall'arte empirica alla sperimentazione sistematica. Il 'nuovo' medico del settecento riformatore', in Enrico Ghidetti and Esther Diana (eds), *La bellezza come terapia: arte e assistenza nell'ospedale di Santa Maria Nuova a Firenze: atti del Convegno internazionale, Firenze, 20–22 maggio 2004* (Florence: Polistampa, 2005): pp. 295–311, p. 303.

53 Othmar Keel, 'La scuola di Santa Maria Nuova modello per l'Europa e nella Francia della Rivoluzione', in Ghidetti and Diana (eds), *Bellezza come terapia*, pp. 313–75, p. 348; Cocchi, *Relazione*, p. 175.

54 Cocchi, *Relazione*, p. 117.

55 Aurora Scotti, 'Malati e strutture ospedaliere dall'età dei Lumi all'Unità', in Franco Della Peruta (ed.), *Storia d'Italia*, v. 7 (Malattia e medicina), pp. 237–96, p. 252.

56 Wellcome Library Archives, London, MS2488, 'Myologia completa del Signore Douverney [*sic*] tradotta dal francese da Girolamo Ristorini studente chirurgia nel Regio Spedale di Santa Maria Nuova', 1760, n.p. See also M. Duverney and Jacques Fabien Gautier D'Agoty (ills), *Myologie complette en couleur et grandeur naturelle: composee de l'Essai et de la Suite de l'Essai d'anatomie, en tableaux imprimes; ouvrage unique, utile et necessaire aux etudians & amateurs de cette science* (Paris 1746).

57 See e.g. Cocchi, *Adversaria anatomica* (1735–36), reproduced in Weber, *Aspetti poco noti*, pp. 120–51, for a recipe for wax injections (p. 124), and trials of different methods to macerate and prepare bones.

58 '[I] pertinaci e calunniosi ostacoli all'indagare le vere cause dei mali col mezzo della sezione anatomica, per uso e soddisfazione de'professori sopra i corpi de loro curati'. Quoted in Elena Brambilla, 'La medicina del Settecento: dal monopolio dogmatico alla professione scientifica', in Franco Della Peruta (ed.), *Storia d'Italia*, v. 7 (Malattia e medicina), pp. 5–147, p. 77.

59 On 1 April 1735, for instance, visiting surgeon John Bedford demonstrated Cheselden's technique for cutting the stone on a corpse: Cocchi, *Adversaria anatomica*, in Weber, *Aspetti poco noti*, pp. 120–51, p. 123. For further examples of the development of new surgical techniques at Santa Maria Nuova see e.g. Angelo Nannoni's *Dissertazioni chirurgiche* (1748).

60 Cocchi, *Adversaria anatomica*, in Weber, *Aspetti poco noti*.

61 Saverio Manetti, 'Una lettera', in Weber, *Aspetti poco noti*.

62 Cocchi, *Relazione*, p. 118.

63 '[U]n uomo . . . che . . . scelga di . . . servire per la Patria, un Fondatore di nuove Scuole, un Fabbricatore di nuovi comodi ai vostri studj'. Raimondo Cocchi, *Lezioni fisico-anatomiche recitate pubblicamente in Firenze nel teatro del Regio Spedale di Santa Maria Nuova dal Dottore Raimondo Cocchi già professore di Anatomìa in detto Spedale* (Livorno: Tommaso Masi, 1775), p. 108.

64 Adam Wandruszka, *Leopold II.* (Vienna and Munich: Herold, 1963), v. 2, p. 312.

65 *Regolamento del Regio Arcispedale di Santa Maria Nuova di Firenze* (Florence: Gaetano Cambiagi, 1783); *Regolamento dei Regi Spedali di Santa Maria Nuova e di Bonifazio* (Florence: Gaetano Cambiagi, 1789).

66 René-Nicolas Dufriche Desgenettes, 'Observations sur l'enseignement de la médecine dans les hôpitaux de la Toscane, lues à la Société royale de médecine dans sa séance du 15 mai 1792', *Journal de Médecine, de Chirurgie et de Pharmacie*, v. 91 (July 1792), pp. 233–57. For Desgenettes' life and publications, see Ange de Saint-Priest (ed.), *Encyclopédie du dix-neuvième siècle: répertoire universel des sciences, des lettres et des arts, avec la biographie de tous les hommes célèbres* (Paris: Bureau de l'Encyclopédie du XIXe siècle, 1836–53), v. 10, p. 56;

Catalogue des livres composant la bibliothèque de feu M. le Baron Desgenettes . . . dont la vente se fera le mardi 6 juin 1837. . . (Paris: Galliot, 1837).

67 Cocchi, *Relazione*, p. 118.

68 *Regolamento* (1783), p. 237.

69 Othmar Keel, 'La scuola di Santa Maria Nuova modello per l'Europa e nella Francia della Rivoluzione', in Ghidetti and Diana (eds), *Bellezza come terapia*, pp. 313-75, p. 329.

70 Keel, 'Scuola', in Ghidetti and Diana (eds), *Bellezza come terapia*, pp. 313-75, p. 330.

71 *Regolamento* (1789), p. 223.

72 Quoted in Keel, 'Scuola', in Ghidetti and Diana (eds), *Bellezza come terapia*, pp. 313-75, p. 341.

73 *Regolamento* (1783), p. 237.

74 For the history of the Bologna Academy and its wax models see e.g. Maurizio Armaroli, *Le cere anatomiche bolognesi del settecento* (Bologna: CLUEB 1981); Lucia Dacome, '"Un certo e quasi incredibile piacere": cera e anatomia nel Settecento', *Intersezioni*, 25:33 (2005), pp. 415-35.

75 Lucia Dacome, 'Women, wax and anatomy in the "century of things"', *Renaissance Studies* 21 (2007), pp. 522-50 (pp. 533-4).

76 Claudia Pancino and Jean d'Yvoire, *Formato nel segreto. Nascituri e feti fra immagini e immaginario dal XVI al XXI secolo* (Rome: Carocci, 2006), pp. 52-3.

77 Gerhard Ritter, 'Das geburtshilfliche Phantom im 18. Jahrhundert', in *Medizinhistorisches Journal* 1 (1966), pp. 127-43, p. 127.

78 Pancino and d'Yvoire, *Formato nel segreto,* especially Ch. 1.6, 'Feti della ceroplastica, Veneri scomponibili, Madonne apribili', pp. 48-63. See also Pancino, *Il bambino e l'acqua sporca; La 'machine' de Coudray ou l'Art des accouchements au XVIIIe siècle* (Rouen: Point de vues, 2005); *Ars ostetricia bononiensis. Catalogo e inventario del museo ostetrico Giovan Antonio Galli* (Bologna: CLUEB, 1988); A. Zanca, *Le cere e le terrecotte del Museo di storia della scienza di Firenze* (Florence: Arnaud, 1981); Georges Didi-Huberman, *L'image ouvrante. 1, Ouvrir Vénus: nudité, rêve, cruauté* ([Paris]: Gallimard, 1999); M.L. Azzaroli Puccetti et al., 'La Venere scomponibile', *Kos* 1 (1984), pp. 65-94; Maurizio Armaroli, *Le cere anatomiche bolognesi del settecento* (Bologna: CLUEB 1981); Gabriella Berti Logan, 'Women and the practice and teaching of medicine in Bologna in the eighteenth and early nineteenth centuries', *Bulletin of the history of medicine* 77:3 (2003), pp. 506-35.

79 Francesca Vannozzi, 'Dall'arte empirica alla sperimentazione sistematica. Il 'nuovo' medico del settecento riformatore', in Ghidetti and Diana (eds), *Bellezza come terapia,* pp. 295-311, p. 299.

80 For Coudray's machine see Gelbart, *King's midwife,* especially pp. 60-5; Ritter, 'Phantom', p. 139; A.M. le Boursier du Coudray, *Abrégé de l'art des accouchemens* (Paris 1759); Jessica Riskin, 'Eighteenth-century wetware', *Representations* 83 (2003), pp. 9-125; for Galli's phantom see Ritter, 'Phantom', p. 134.

81 Rebecca Messbarger, 'Waxing poetic: Anna Morandi Manzolini's anatomical sculptures', *Configurations* 9 (2001), pp. 65–97; Miriam Focaccia (ed.), *Anna Morandi Manzolini: Una donna fra arte e scienza. Immagini, documenti, repertorio anatomico* (Biblioteca di Nuncius n. 65, Florence: Olschki, 2008).

82 '[P]ubblica utilità'; IMSS–ARMU, Negozi 1791, fol. 214v.

83 '[D]i rilevare in Cera al naturale si nella grandezza come nel colorito tutte le parti del Corpo umano in quelle vedute, e situazioni che possono essere d'uso e d'utilità alli studi Anatomici, 'IMSS–ARMU, Filza di negozi dell'anno 1791, fol. 225v.

84 IMSS–ARMU, Filza di negozi dell'anno 1791, fol. 225, testimony of Giovanni dell'Agata, 16 July 1772.

85 For a general history of wax modelling see Reinhard Büll, *Das große Buch vom Wachs. Geschichte, Kultur, Technik* (Munich: Callwey, 1977).

86 Klaus Lankheit, *Die Modellsammlung der Porzellanmanufaktur Doccia. Ein Dokument italienischer Barockplastik* (Munich: Bruckmann, 1982). Italian sculptors also took advantage of business opportunities that came with the influx of foreign travellers: The British traveller Adam Walker for instance reported of Italy that '[t]he sculptors are excellent, and successful in their imitations of the antique: No doubt but some are employed in MAKING *Antiquities for English and other Nobility!*' Adam Walker, *Ideas Suggested on the Spot, in a Late Excursion Through Flanders, Germany, France, and Italy* (London 1790), p. 323; highlights in the original.

87 'Orsini, under the direction of Andrea Verrocchio, modelled three life-size figures in wax of the prince [Lorenzo the Magnificent] for churches'; Virginia W. Johnson, *The lily of the Arno: Or Florence, past and present* (Boston: Estes and Lauriat, 1891), p. 142.

88 '[S]tudenti di Medicina, ed Anatomia'; IMSS–ARMU, Filza di negozi dell'anno 1791, fol. 226.

89 IMSS–ARMU, Filza di negozi dell'anno 1791, fol. 226, 226v.

90 For Fontana's appropriation of Galletti's project see Galletti's defense in IMSS–ARMU, Filza di negozi dell'anno 1791, fol. 211–237; and a brief discussion in Contardi, *Casa di Salomone*, pp. 111–12.

91 IMSS–ARMU, Filza di negozi dell'anno 1791, fol. 211–237, especially fol. 226.

92 Anon., *Saggio del Real Gabinetto di Fisica, e di Storia Naturale di Firenze* (Roma: Giovanni Zempel, 1775), p. 32: 'L'intenzione del Direttore è non solo di fare l'analisi delle parti del corpo umano, come fa l'Anatomico, ma di rappresentare ancora moltissime parti, i di cui usi sono certi nell'atto della loro *operazione*, che è lo scopo del Fisico. Così l'Anatomico, e il Fisiologo troveranno nel tempo stresso di che sodisfarsi, e *l'Anatomia in tal guisa diventerà una delle parti più belle della Fisica moderna*' (italics A.M.) (The *Saggio* was reprinted in *Antologia Romana* 1 (1775), pp. 225–9, 233–7. 241–4, 249–260, 265–9, 273–7, 281–5, 289–91, 297–301.)

93 '[R]endono immortale, e grata ai posteri la memoria di Benedetto XIV che le ordinò', IMSS–ARMU, Filza di negozi dell'anno 1791, fol. 226v.

94 For a positive personal account of the new museum see e.g. BNCF, manuscript collection NA 1050, Giuseppe Pelli, 'Efemeridi', vol. XXXII (2 April 1775), fol. 436v.

95 '[U]no stabilimento, come ve ne son pochi, ordinato, ricco, splendido in ogni genere'; 'bravi artefici', Marco Lastri, *L'Osservatore Fiorentino sugli Edifizi della sua Patria* (Third edition, based on the second edition of 1797, Florence: Gaspero Ricci, 1821), v. 7, p. 126.

96 '[U]n Fabbricatore di nuovi comodi ai vostri studj'. Raimondo Cocchi, *Lezioni fisico-anatomiche recitate pubblicamente in Firenze nel teatro del Regio Spedale di Santa Maria Nuova dal Dottore Raimondo Cocchi già professore di Anatomìa in detto Spedale* (Livorno: Tommaso Masi, 1775), p. 108.

97 Francesco Aglietti (ed.), *Memorie per servire alla storia letteraria e civile* (Venice 1796), p. 63.

98 *Novelle Letterarie* no. 7 (17 February 1775); BNCF, manuscript collection NA 1050, Pelli, 'Efemeridi', Serie II, vol. 3, p. 404v (30 January 1775).

99 Giovanni Prezziner, *Storia del pubblico studio e delle società scientifiche e letterarie di Firenze* (Florence: Carli 1810), vol. 2, p. 256f; Attilio Zanca, *Le cere e le terrecotte ostetriche del Museo di Storia della Scienza di Firenze* (Florence: Arnaud, 1981).

100 Giovanni Prezziner, *Storia del pubblico studio e delle società scientifiche e letterarie di Firenze* (Florence: Carli 1810), vol. 2, p. 257.

Part II

Articulating expertise in everyday practice

3

Accuracy and authority in model production

The models' political significance – as tools for achieving public happiness through public enlightenment, and as evidence for the legitimacy of Pietro Leopoldo's rule – had consequences for everyday practices at the museum, and shaped museum naturalists' roles as experts in state service. Reframing Galletti's proposal of model production for the Tuscan state, Fontana confirmed the Grand Duke's ideas on the function of experts and natural knowledge in state service. In practice, however, their opinions sometimes diverged. How practices of model making and display shaped the relationship between experts, the state, and the public, is the subject of Part II. This chapter investigates the strategies used by museum director Fontana to ensure the models' accuracy, which he considered essential for the museum's mission. An analysis of the museum's 'back stage', the model workshop, highlights that the achievement of accuracy was difficult.

Everyday problems with model production and model display prompted naturalists to articulate their role vis-à-vis the state and the public in ways that, at times, conflicted with the sovereign's expectations. At La Specola, actors had to negotiate their authority in the interplay between artisanal practice and administrative control in the new institutional context of a state museum. Naturalists could draw on a number of frameworks to articulate their position. Some of these were well established, such as the role of client to a noble patron or the distinction between intellectual and manual labour, others emergent, such as the role of the state employee or the notion of the genius. Fontana and his assistant Fabbroni, in particular, articulated their role for the state through negotiations about the problems attendant to model production – such as discipline and accuracy – in very different ways. Ultimately, Fabbroni's understanding of his role as state employee was more acceptable to the court since he adhered to its administrative requirements.

Accuracy

Regarding the production of anatomical models at the museum's workshop, director Fontana stressed that 'the interest of the Royal Museum require[d] that all defects be removed, and that the works be perfect'.[1] In order to fulfil their political functions, the models had to represent perfectly accurate descriptions of the human body. To maintain the museum naturalists' status as reliable sources of natural knowledge, and to preserve the sovereign's reputation, the collection had to reflect the current state of research, and minimise possibilities for criticism. To do so, the models had to incorporate the most recent anatomical discoveries. The museum's mission of public enlightenment also required 'perfect' representations. Fontana's teaching strategy was based on contemporary sensationalist theories of learning which claimed that rational faculties arose from sense perception.[2] The presentation of the collection reflected Fontana's assumption that the laws of nature would become unproblematically accessible to anyone if the objects were presented in a systematic manner, if they could be taken in instantaneously, and if they were aesthetically appealing. Despite his acknowledgement of the importance of the collection's aesthetic appeal for its utility as a teaching device, he did not specify further what constituted such aesthetic appeal, and how it could be achieved. He claimed, however, that the museum's systematic presentation of objects ensured that 'at one glance everything is seen, everything is known'.[3] For the collection, and especially for the anatomical models to fulfil their intended use, it was crucial that they should be perfectly accurate representations of nature: 'they require all perfection which they can attain, and which is absolutely necessary if they are to be used for public education.'[4] Otherwise false relationships between parts would be conveyed to the model user, from which no synthesis of the correct laws of nature could arise.

The anatomical models, in particular, were exhibited in such a way as to underline the universality of natural laws that was central to Pietro Leopoldo's politics. The new museum presented the human body as a constituent of the Creation, continuous with other natural objects and, like those, governed by the same perceptible laws of nature. This continuity was achieved by displaying the models within the microcosm represented by the museum's collection, between rooms filled with taxidermised animals and mechanical tools. For individual models, Fontana explicitly developed ways of representation which were supposed to enable every detail to be immediate visible, depicted by means of a two-dimensional drawing that accompanied each wax model. On a circular or elliptical frame around the drawing, details were pointed out with dotted lines, so as to maintain full visibility of the entirety of the elements (plate

IV).[5] The director aimed to visualise not only the structure of body parts, but also their function, by clarifying the spatial relationship between components. Thus, Fontana maintained, anatomy would become 'one of the most beautiful components of modern physics'.[6]

Physics, in his sense, encompassed all areas of knowledge to do with the explanation, rather than description, of nature.[7] Suitable ways of presenting functional connections between parts, such as the simultaneous representation of heart valves from different well-chosen angles, Fontana claimed, would directly convey these relationships to the audience. Implicitly, this stance contained a central contradiction in assuming the possibility of a form of 'unmediated mediation'. On the one hand, Fontana asserted that the laws of nature were intelligible and accessible to anyone through visual perception. On the other hand, this perception required suitable representations of nature – and, Fontana claimed, it was the naturalist's task to ascertain this suitability. In the case of the heart, for instance, Fontana did not specify in this account what would constitute suitable angles, implying that this was a matter for the naturalist's judgement.[8] Exhibition practice at the museum is discussed in more detail in Chapter 4. What matters here with regard to model production is that, for Fontana, the models' accuracy as descriptions of the body was essential for their prescriptive function as examples of the intelligibility and universality of natural law.

Given the aim of producing immediately accessible, true representations of the living body, the Florentine models had to go beyond both textbook illustrations and real body parts in a number of ways: instead of two dimensions, they had to represent three; instead of a dead body, they had to depict a living one; and instead of representing one specific body, the models had to represent an ideal type, true to nature.[9] Again, Fontana did not specify how a universally valid representation of the normal human body was to be achieved on the basis of individual specimens, but claimed for himself the ability to do so. In order to ascertain the models' accuracy, Fontana drew on a number of validating instances – especially the judgement of his peers – and the simultaneous use of both authoritative illustrations and real bodies in model production. However, in the collaborative enterprise at the workshop these strategies did not sufficiently address all practical and conceptual problems which arose in model production. These practical problems prompted naturalists to articulate their position in state service in order to justify their authority. They did so in different ways, drawing both on established and on newly emergent social roles and personas. A comparison of Fontana's and Fabbroni's different self-images, in particular, shows that some articulations of expertise in state service were more acceptable to the court and its requirements than others.

Model production at the museum's workshop

The control of employees and expenses became a contentious issue in model production where different professional perspectives and different concepts of expertise met, both between naturalists and artisans, and between museum and court. The production of anatomical models had begun under Fontana's direction in the early 1770, a few years before the official opening of the museum in 1775. The first modeller to be employed at La Specola was the artist Giuseppe Ferrini, who had learned techniques of wax sculpting at the anatomical model workshop in Bologna, which had inspired the Florentine surgeon Giuseppe Galetti to put forward his modelling project for Tuscany. In 1773, Ferrini took on an assistant, Clemente Susini (1754–1814), who had trained as a sculptor at the Royal Gallery, and worked at the sculpture workshop of Pompilio Ticciati. In 1782, Susini (plate IIc) succeeded Ferrini as chief modeller, a position which he held until his death.[10] Susini's assistant Francesco Calenzuoli subsequently took over the model workshop.

The artisans mainly produced three types of models: whole body sculptures, sections showing the spatial arrangement of body parts, and detail studies showing isolated elements of the body – a convention adopted from anatomical illustrations in the works of Vesalius and others.[11] In accordance with Fontana's aim of displaying functional relationships, all models depicted the living body: they had rosy skin (where they had any), and were sometimes presented gesturing.

The workshop was occasionally relocated within the museum to accommodate exhibition restructuring and enlargement of the building.[12] It held tools such as kettles to heat wax, balances, instruments such as spatulas and needles, blackboards, wooden tables and marble plates for mounting the models and for blending materials, as well as the materials for model production – from different kinds of wax to turpentine, oils, pigments, wood, and metals (figure 8).

Model production was overseen by Fontana, who drew on two main sources of accuracy: models were designed after the works of renowned anatomists, and Fontana employed real body parts obtained from local hospitals. Visitors with anatomical knowledge approvingly identified perspectives adopted from the works of well-known authors such as Vesalius, Albinus, Haller, Mascagni, Vicq d'Azyr, Loder, Sömmering, and Weitbrecht.[13] Contemporary accounts of the museum's models highlighted both the explicit reference to authoritative images, and the use of real bodies and body parts as support for the models' claim to accuracy. An account of the museum in a contemporary travellers' guide, for instance, explained that the 'vast collection of human anatomy' was 'executed in wax *after nature*, and after the *descriptions of the best*

8 Modellers' tools and journals, La Specola. (Saulo Bambi, Museo di Storia Naturale, Florence)

authors'.[14] Fontana also encouraged knowledgeable visitors to report favourably on his institution and his models. Thus, the French army surgeon Nicolas René Desgenettes and the German physician Engelbert Wichelhausen were privileged with private tours of the museum, with Fontana himself. In their subsequent published accounts they reported approvingly of the models.[15] Parallels between Fontana's own statements on model production and those of Desgenettes and Wichelhausen suggest that both accounts were produced in consultation with the museum's director.[16] In the absence of a detailed account of modelling by Fontana himself, Wichelhausen's description here represents the director's own vision of the modelling process.

Ideally, this process was as follows: a knowledgeable natural philosopher or anatomist, usually Fontana himself, chose an illustration from a renowned publication which in his judgement showed well particular anatomical details, especially with regard to recent discoveries. These illustrations were complemented by similarly positioned preparations, made by a dissector from real cadavers: 'One never models from copper etchings alone, but these only serve as a guide for the dissector'.[17] Subsequently, the artisans would model the prototype after these preparations. A multitude of similar preparations from different corpses was used to ensure accuracy: 'Often a great many cadavers are necessary to achieve the greatest completeness of the parts that one wants to imitate, and to make them clear to the modeller'.[18] Fontana boasted of hundreds of bodies used for a single model, but in reality the museum seems to have received 100–200 body parts per year.[19]

After the preparation of an anatomical specimen, the artisans prepared a plaster mould, either directly from the specimen or by manually creating a freely modelled copy of the object. The modellers and anatomists then corrected the mould before producing the positive copy in wax, adding the molten wax to the mould in thin layers, which were painted on the inside. Small structures such as vessels or membranes were imitated using fine metal or textile threads covered in wax, or painted on the models' surface. The modellers then assembled the complete model piece by piece, and covered the final product in a shining varnish, both to resemble the gloss of moist living tissue and to protect the model from dust.[20] The modellers, the naturalists, or artists hired on a daily basis, also prepared two-dimensional drawings of the finished models for the public exhibition. On these drawings, details were numbered according to lists of details' named. Museum visitors had access to both drawings and lists, which were kept in drawers integrated into the models' showcases.

In Fontana's early statements on model production the director ascribed to the artisans a purely instrumental function. The naturalist claimed to use the artisans like 'tools', as sources of manual labour who were completely dependent on the intellectual guidance of the naturalist.[21] In practice, model production could rarely be carried out in this ideal fashion. As shown below, modellers' resistance to disciplinary measures and their craft knowledge prevented them from being instrumentalised in this way. In addition, practical contingencies such as the limited supply of (suitable) cadavers created interruptions in production. Grand Duke Pietro Leopoldo had granted the museum the privilege of using bodies from local hospitals: adult bodies from Santa Maria Nuova, and children's bodies from the hospital of the local orphanage Istituto degl'Innocenti. Twice daily, the museum's sweeper Giacinto Guidetti made his rounds of the hospitals to fetch available body parts.[22]

The supply of cadavers was a contentious issue, but this was not due to public protest. The only public response to the use of corpses seems to have been the reluctance of coffee shops to admit Guidetti for a break on his tours: 'in times of rain or snow etc. he cannot take a break anywhere, since he carries with him the basket with dead bodies, which task makes him detestable to everyone, and he is treated badly in the coffee houses which he used to frequent'.[23] More contentiously, the supply question put the museum's modelling enterprise in competition with the teachers and students at the hospital Santa Maria Nuova, who considered the bodies of deceased patients indispensable for their medical training. The tension between the two groups was heightened by Fontana's occasional omission in using all the cadavers he received.[24] Upon returning some intact body parts to the cemetery, for instance, Guidetti was attacked by a cemetery employee disgruntled about the waste, since anatomy professor Lorenzo Nannoni could have used the bodies for his teaching at the hospital. Head modeller Susini complained that 'the man from the cemetery called Cintio [Giacinto Guidetti] a fucking vagabond, [and said] 'you return the dead bodies without operating on them, those that are there have to serve for Nannoni'.[25]

In some cases the absence of suitable corpses posed a problem, especially for obstetrical and embryological models. It was particularly difficult to procure specimens for the early stages of gestation, and also in those early stages to tell whether a woman had indeed been pregnant – in many cases the woman herself may not have known, and almost always there was no information as to how much time had passed since fertilisation. For those models, therefore, Fontana and the modellers resorted to illustrations, which, however, in the eyes of naturalists and physicians rendered these models less accurate than those where real body parts were used in production. Visiting physician Wichelhausen, for instance, remarked that the obstetrical models were not as correct (*richtig*) as the others, 'but then they could not be done after nature, but after illustrations'.[26]

In addition to using recognisable illustrations and real body parts, Fontana also resorted to other strategies to support the models' claim to accuracy. In particular, he mobilised a network of supporters among visitors interested in natural philosophy and his scholarly correspondents. As in the cases of Desgenettes and Wichelhausen, Fontana was happy to devote time to private guided tours for knowledgeable visitors who subsequently reported favourably on the collection. Many of the existing accounts of the museum's exhibition in its early years do indeed bear a remarkable similarity; the phrasing almost always resembles closely that used by Fontana himself in his reports to the grand-ducal court. Another way of mobilising support among natural philosophers was Fontana's trade with renowned anatomists, giving wax models of recent anatomical discoveries in return for positive judgements of the models' accuracy, which could be circulated. Antonio Scarpa, professor of anatomy at the University of Pavia, for instance, requested (and received) specific representations of the new discoveries on the lymphatic system made by Paolo Mascagni, and of his own work on the ear.[27] In his letter to Fontana on receipt of the models, Scarpa applauded the perfection both of the modellers' and the anatomists' work. On a statue depicting lymphatic vessels he assured Fontana, and other naturalists who would read his letter in copies, that 'there is nothing in this statue which does not stand up to the most scrupulous examination by an able sculptor or an anatomist'.[28] He, nevertheless, put forward concrete criticism as well with regard to the models' features, and suggested specific tables from the recent publication by Paolo Mascagni as potential sources for the modellers to work with.[29] Subsequently, Fontana cited Scarpa's positive overall judgement to support his position vis-à-vis the grand-ducal court.

However, problems of authority had to be resolved not only with respect to the scholarly community of Fontana's peers, but also *in situ* at the model workshop itself, and between the museum and the court, where different forms of authority were at stake. It was in these negotiations that Fontana's self-perception as a man of letters clashed both with his artisans' conduct, and with the court's expectations of Fontana as an employee of the state.

Status and authority in early modern natural philosophy

On his advancement to Tuscan court physicist in 1766, Fontana proudly declared that he had 'finally succeeded in all [his] aims'.[30] He had obtained the position once held by Galileo, the most celebrated of Italian natural philoso-phers, who was appointed court philosopher to the Medici in 1610. This self-perception was crucial in shaping Fontana's role at the museum. The natural philosopher adopted Galileo as his role model not just for his scientific accom-plishments, but also in his relationship to his royal benefactor. Natural phi-losophers in early modern Italy had frequently been clients to a noble patron.[31] This situation had important ramifications for their ability to make truth claims because a person's cognitive authority, their capacity to speak the truth about nature, was dependent on their social status within the early modern polity.[32] As Mario Biagioli has shown, in the case of Galileo, the assumption of inde-pendence was the basis for cognitive authority in such patronage relationships despite the (unacknowledged) dependency of the client. Early modern patrons did not usually endorse their clients' philosophical positions, since this would have put their own honour in jeopardy by opening it up to challenges, and strong commitment to a particular philosophical system could be seen as con-tradicting a nobleman's independence. Instead, they invited challenge and dis-pute among philosophers, which would not require them to take sides – rather, the debates themselves were valued as performances.

Natural knowledge publicised by the client in honour of the patron could only benefit the patron if it were presented as voluntary and accepted as truth-ful. In the case of Galileo and his Medici patron, both sides therefore took pains to display their relationship as an association between equals that was not based on financial or utilitarian considerations. The client was treated differently from the patron's other dependants. Thus, for instance, Galileo's payment was not accounted for in the same payroll as those of other employees.[33]

Fontana articulated his relationship to his royal patron within these conventions of patronage, similar to his eminent predecessor, and continued to do so even as his status changed when he became director of the new public museum in 1775. However, Pietro Leopoldo's relationship with his court physicist differed from the Medici's treatment of Galileo, in important respects. As museum director, Fontana and his salary were administered in the same way as any other museum employee.[34] Unlike the Medici Grand Dukes of the seventeenth century, Pietro Leopoldo no longer expected his court physicist to stage natural philosophical disputes as performances. On the contrary, as a central source of political legitimacy, the interpretation of nature could *not* be seen to be controversial, and Pietro Leopoldo's Florentine chief of police put a stop to the public dispute between Fontana and Giorgi over their replications of Lavoisier's experiments. Nevertheless, Fontana continued to present his scientific activities as contributions both to the honour of the Grand Duke and to his own, thus claiming for himself the role of a highly visible client on the same level as Galileo. In his correspondence with colleagues, and in reports to the grand-ducal court, he strongly articulated criticism of his work as attacks upon his honour, 'which no man can give up'.[35] The practices involved in model production and the changed institutional context of the museum made this position difficult to maintain, however. Both Fontana and his assistant Fabbroni rearticulated their claims to expertise, and especially to the authority to evaluate and authorise the models, in response to the requirements of a state institution.

Secret knowledge, exhausting attention, and the production of accurate models

A large number of people contributed to the modelling process, and their diverging perspectives on the work were articulated in the ensuing confrontations. The cooperation between natural philosophers, anatomists, and artisans was not the interdisciplinary ideal sometimes evoked by modern analysts of La Specola's anatomical models.[36] Fontana and his assistant Fabbroni oversaw the activities, and occasionally engaged in modelling, drawing and the preparation of body parts themselves. In addition, local anatomists were hired on a daily basis to produce preparations and oversee the modellers' work. Free modelling and moulding were done by the modellers Susini and Calenzuoli; sometimes additional artists were hired to produce more drawings. Guidetti carried corpses from the hospitals and back; as a former kitchen aid to the court he also prepared the corpses by cutting the flesh into pieces and injecting the vessels.[37] Numerous artisans were hired on occasion to make wooden showcases, gild them, produce the silk cushions on which the models rested, sharpen the modellers' tools, and deliver materials.

Initially, Fontana claimed that a comprehensive collection of normal human anatomy could be completed in eight to ten years. However, during the course of the 1780s it became increasingly obvious that the workshop did not meet those expectations. The museum regularly ran over budget by as much as 100 per cent, and projected additions to the anatomical model collection failed to materialise on public display. At this point, the court began to request reports from various museum employees. Those at the museum itself who were involved in model production and museum administration had different explanations for the institution's failure to produce the models on time. These explanations were established through reports of production practices and employees' behaviour from different perspectives within the workshop. The reports provide different accounts of the institution's failings, and indicate that the various actors involved in model production had different perceptions about the modelling work and of their own roles within it. Furthermore, these perceptions did not coexist harmoniously.

The new institutional form, and especially the attempts both on the part of museum management and of court administrators to control the men and materials involved in the modelling process, brought about different articulations of the roles of natural philosophers and modellers. The space for knowledge production was not dedicated for director Fontana's personal use, and the artisans involved in the production of anatomical models were not Fontana's servants. Instead, both artisans and natural philosophers were employees at a state institution. In this context, artisans were perceived to possess special knowledge, and natural philosophers engaged in the manual labour of anatomical preparation. Thus, naturalists had trouble maintaining their difference from, and superiority to technicians on the basis of intellectual versus manual labour. Unlike the early modern client or the independently wealthy gentleman experimentalist, Fontana could no longer refer to his independence and claim cognitive authority as he was now an employee himself, whose duty was to serve the sovereign's interest.

In their reports to the court, different actors revealed divergent attitudes towards the production of models. Fontana attempted to justify his continuing case for cognitive authority despite his status as a state employee by claiming for himself a mental, and possibly physical, difference from and superiority to other employees that made him indispensable in the production and evaluation of accurate models. Fabbroni, on the other hand, made reference to his reliability as demonstrated in his compliance with court procedure and his history of dependable service for the state.

For the artisans employed at the museum, the main issue of contention was not so much cognitive authority as the extent of their autonomy within the institution. While Pietro Leopoldo's abolition of the guilds in 1770 had freed artisans from corporate regulations, the modellers' employment at a state institution brought with it its own, new set of rules, limitations and surveillance. Some of the museum's artisans had previously owned their own workshops, or worked independently in their spare time. Chief modeller Susini, for instance, produced wax portraits for private customers such as Uffizi director Giuseppe Pelli (who found his bust 'a good likeness', but less than flattering in capturing the effects of age).[38] Used to a high degree of autonomy, the artisans were disinclined to submit to the museum's hierarchy, and to the discipline imposed.

Mechanic Felice Carmine at one point expressed this attitude unequivocally. When reminded that he had to ask permission before taking a day off, Carmine responded by saying: 'I don't give a damn, and I will not ask anybody.'[39] This attitude of artisans' insisting on their autonomy vis-à-vis their superiors at the museum was particularly common among the wax modellers: they were the ones who consistently arrived late for work (or not at all); they were the ones about whose lack of discipline, expressed in chatting and the frivolous consumption of hot chocolate at work, director Fontana and custodian Gagli repeatedly reported to the grand-ducal court; they extracted material from the museum to use in the production of wax portraits, toys, and votive offerings at their own workshops.[40]

The issues of cognitive authority and autonomy were not wholly separable in model production. The wax modellers considered themselves as possessing special knowledge which distinguished them from the museum's natural philosophers and administrators, and which guaranteed their degree of autonomy at the museum, first, because artisans' knowledge of material properties made it difficult for natural philosophers and administrators to control modellers' work on a purely quantitative basis, and second, because this special knowledge was not easy to replace. When modeller Cappeletti was suspected of stealing wax from the museum for his own business, for instance, the disciplinary investigation reported that he expressed his sense of invulnerability by saying that 'regarding the wax none of those simpletons of the museum can find him out as turpentine hides everything'.[41] Turpentine and other materials were added to the wax in different proportions in order to change its material properties, thus making it extremely difficult to account for the quantities of wax used.

Cappeletti's knowledge of the properties of turpentine and wax enabled him, quite literally, to cover his tracks by adulterating his materials.

In some reports on artisanal practice, the administrators and natural philosophers at the museum shared the modellers' conviction that owing to their special knowledge, the modellers were difficult to control. In an evaluation for the court of an automatic lens-grinding machine, for instance, Fontana had admitted that it might be impossible in principle to separate artisanal skills from their owners. In his evaluation Fontana expressed doubt that the 'spontaneous movements of the hand' in the hand-crafting of lenses could ever be mechanised, as they might be 'indeterminable by their nature'.[42] Similarly, when chief modeller Ferrini was found to have stolen silver from the museum, the internal investigation came to the conclusion that this theft had been possible because of the trust which the superiors necessarily had to grant to the artist on account of his knowledge. In this case, Ferrini had claimed that only silver leaves of a certain thickness could be used for the imitation of tendons. He then replaced these leaves with some of thinner quality, or a different material altogether, keeping the remaining silver for himself.

In the administration's own interpretation, the theft had been possible because of the trust placed on Ferrini's information about the materials needed, and it had been his 'secret experience to the contrary'[43] that had made the theft possible. The shared perception that artisans possessed special knowledge not only enabled these transgressions, but at the same time secured the modellers' position. Knowing that their artisanal skills were hard to replace, and knowing that the director was fully aware of this fact, the wax modellers made use of their position of security, and continued, for instance, to be late for work.[44]

To maintain their understanding of anatomical modelling as similar to their other sculpting activities, such as the production of toys or portraits, the modellers, for the most part, presented a united front to the naturalists.[45] This concerted performance broke down only once, during the museum's early years, during the investigation against modeller Ferrini. For once, the administrators and naturalists gained insight into the workshop. This insight into Ferrini's practices and his abuse of his claims to special knowledge regarding materials, was only possible because Fontana could convince Ferrini's assistant Susini to testify against his superior under threat of dismissal. At this early stage in his career, Susini may have agreed to testify against Ferrini because he still assumed that Fontana would carry out his threat, or he may have seen this – correctly – as an opportunity for his own advancement. Ferrini was fired and Susini promoted to the position of head modeller. In response to any later charges, however, the artisans presented a united front.[46] While the modellers formed a group that was distinct from, and opposed to, the museum's administrators when they insisted on their autonomy, in other cases the alliances were more fluid. The absence of conflict from visitors' accounts such as those of Desgenettes and Wichelhausen indicate that, in the presence of outsiders, artisans and naturalists teamed up to present an image of harmonious cooperation.

The shared assumption that the modellers possessed indispensable skills that could not be fully articulated and transferred was confirmed repeatedly, for example during the production of copies for Emperor Joseph II in the early 1780s (see Chapter 5), and for the French government in the 1790s (see Chapter 6). For these tasks, Fontana had initially employed artisans from outside the museum's workshop, and had claimed that he would be able to train them in model production himself. However, Fontana's trainees failed to produce models that satisfied his expectations, and he had to ask the museum's modellers for support.

In a private note, deputy director Fabbroni mocked Fontana's failure, and the apparent contradiction between his superior's conviction that the artisans could be used like tools and the admission of the existence of special skills:

> How come that the man who forms artisans from scratch, who uses them like saws and hammers, now confesses that there are tasks which only Susini can perform, and how dare he pronounce this![47]

The court's response to the problem of workspace discipline was to reaffirm Fontana's authority to fire employees, as well as to communicate to the museum a very different kind of model produced at the court itself. These 'models' (*modelli*) were standardised templates of administrative forms, which were developed to streamline administrative practice across state institutions.

However, these measures did not bring about improvement, and the court administration continued to remind Fontana that it expected a complete model collection. His response was to offer a second explanation for the delay in production. This time, instead of reporting on the modellers' practices, he reported his own. Fontana now described production as an iterative process. He argued that since model production was always accompanied by the analysis and preparation of real body parts, during the modelling process itself new anatomical details would be discovered which then had to be incorporated into the model. This phenomenon would create a chain of iterations that would break only when the complete representation of all anatomical details was achieved. In accordance with his previous articulations of his notion of honour, Fontana argued that it was impossible for him to release any models for public viewing that had not yet attained perfect accuracy, thus justifying his delay in putting the artificial anatomies on display.[48]

This explanation did not satisfy the court administrators, whose patience

Fontana continued to try with his apparent refusal or inability to comply with their requests. Financial transparency, economy, and accountability were of central importance for Pietro Leopoldo's enlightened bureaucracy. Fontana, however, repeatedly stressed that he considered economic surveillance 'alien to a man of letters'.[49] He did not draw up reports, receipts and other documents in the manner specified by the central administration's *modelli*, or failed to produce them at all. When asked to account for funds that had gone into model production in terms of the materials and working hours spent, for instance, Fontana's response was an estimate based on what he assumed the market value for such a collection to be. But, of course, that kind of information was useless for keeping track of the state funds spent on the museum.[50]

Museum naturalists developed ways of self-presentation other than the image of the 'man of letters'. Anatomist Matteucci, director Fontana, and deputy director Fabbroni justified their claims to the authorities in different ways, and offered different perspectives on the modelling process and the problem of discipline to the court. Unlike the artists, who did not discursively link their work to their bodies in any way, some of the naturalists explicitly discussed the part played by actors' bodies in the production process. They evoked images of the cooperation at the museum as the work of a 'social organism' where each group had its own tasks. The anatomist Matteucci, a doctor at the hospital Santa Maria Nuovas provided anatomical preparations for modeller Ferrini during the 1770s, and was called upon to evaluate and correct the modeller's work. The physician drew attention specifically to the active and crucial involvement of the anatomist's body both in the process of making the preparations, and in the process of supervising the modeller's subsequent work.[51] It was 'the eye and the hand of the dissector' which 'unveiled' minute details in the anatomical specimen in a process that he described as 'laborious', 'subtle', and 'difficult'.[52]

While thus acknowledging manual labour, the role of the hand, as part of his own work, Matteucci distinguished his activity from that of the modeller by stressing, in addition, the visual and intellectual aspects of his task. The natural philosopher claimed for himself the possession of the 'anatomical eye',[53] a gaze controlled by reason, which allowed Matteucci to discover anatomical details and to prepare the specimen accurately, as long as his surroundings provided peace and quiet to enable him to concentrate – preferably in a room of his own. His tasks in the modelling process were to 'examine', 'observe', 'see'.[54] This special vision enabled Matteucci to produce a representation of the 'true and natural state' of the living body from a preparation of inanimate body parts.[55] His ability to coordinate the specimen, hands, eyes and mind gave the natural philosopher the responsibility for the exactness of Ferrini's work, and authorised him to give orders.[56] Accordingly, the anatomist described the modeller's work as one of unreflective copying, as a work devoid of any exercise of reason: the modeller 'imitated', and was considered unable to reconstruct the 'true and natural state' of the body without the naturalist's contribution.[57]

Natural philosopher Fontana similarly referred to the process of model production in a way that stressed natural philosophers' physical involvement, especially in his reports to the court. With these accounts, the director justified his cognitive authority in a way that did not draw on social status. This justification contributed to Fontana's formulation of disciplinary measures at the workshop. For custodian Gagli, the problem of artisans' behaviour was mainly one of losing working hours.[58] For Fontana, however, as the driving force behind, and final overseer of, model production, the problem of the modellers' discipline was not so much one of speed as of accuracy, on which in his view the very success of modelling depended. In his articulations of the cooperation vis-à-vis the court, Fontana came to contrast the apparent presence of the artisans' special knowledge or abilities with an apparent absence of another faculty. According to the director, it was the 'shameful and guilty lack of attention' which caused the modellers to commit 'a thousand errors of eye and hand', even if the object to be copied was directly before their eyes.[59]

There were two different notions of 'attention' at play in Fontana's statements for the court. The first very generally referred to the director's assiduity, e.g. when Fontana assured the court that he pursued his work 'with the greatest possible zeal and attention'.[60] However, when referring to attention in the specific context of anatomical modelling, Fontana linked it to the physical activities at the workshop, to the eyes and hands of the modellers. In this sense, 'attention' became the connection between preparations of body parts, eyes and hands, which enabled the production of accurate representations.[61] In his early statements on the problem, when Fontana had promised the court that he would train artisans from scratch to become highly skilled modellers, he had voiced the conviction that this attention was a faculty that could be acquired at will by anybody (and thus the modellers could be 'guilty' of not doing so). Only if the modellers wanted to pay attention, and if they focused their gaze well on the object, could these errors be removed.

Fontana introduced two means to achieve this attention: first, he offered financial incentives for work well executed, and second, he explicitly required 'attention' in wax modellers' contracts.[62] However, when confronted with the fact that the modellers continued to chat during their work – which in Fontana's view would inevitably prevent them from exerting the required diligence – he stressed a demarcation between the natural philosophers and the artisans in a way which suggested that the difference between the two was whether or not they were in principle capable of attention.[63] Thus the task of the controlling natural philosopher was to provide this attention, this link between nature, hand, eye and mind that ensured the accuracy of the anatomical representations. His presence was required 'at all times' for the artisans' 'control' and 'guidance'.[64] In this conception of cooperation, the director rhetorically relegated artisans to the status of mindless 'tools' in the hands of the natural philosopher.[65] While Fontana did not explain whether the capacity for attention was a physical or mental attribute, it clearly was for him an ability located in the person of the natural philosopher. It was more than discipline or zeal: as Fontana explicitly argued, it was not enough that just anyone (such as custodian Gagli) was present at the workshop to oversee modellers' activities. Only his own presence could ensure that modelling activity resulted in accurate representations.[66] This articulation of attention as a difference located in the individual enabled Fontana to claim cognitive authority in a way that no longer required recourse to his social status, but to personal attributes: he could thus maintain for himself the ability to evaluate and authorise accurate representations of nature, despite a lack of independence.

The physical localisation of difference was expressed most clearly in Fontana's explicit claims to a strong connection between his work and his body. In reports to the court, he repeatedly implied that over-exertion in his work caused an exhaustion which resulted in physical illness.[67] Fontana stressed that he had 'jeopardised his health' in the service of the museum, in his 'brave' and 'passionate' quest for the models' perfection.[68] While we do not have any explicit statements by the modellers on the notion of attention and its importance in the execution of the work at the wax modelling studio, reports of their continued chatting indicate that the modellers did not share Fontana's opinion. Unlike the director, the modellers, who would view their illnesses as being due to an imbalance in bodily temperature, never connected these imbalances to their work. They continued to chat, invite outsiders, and drink hot chocolate apparently without considering this an impediment to their ability to produce models.

Genius

Confronted with the difficulty of controlling the artisans and upholding his own authority, Fontana increasingly came to contradict his own initial assertion that all knowledge of nature was, in principle, accessible to everyone if presented in a suitable way such as the museum's exhibition. Faced with the apparent impossibility of separating artisans' 'secret experience' from its owners, Fontana similarly postulated for himself a faculty of 'attention'. Like the 'secret experience', 'attention' was inherent in, and inseparable from, its owner. Crucially, this faculty served to justify his claims about the models' accuracy. In its articulation as an inherent, inexplicable quality, rather than a capacity that could be acquired by anyone, this notion of attention was similar to an influential new concept of genius developed during the previous decades by Diderot and his contemporaries.[69] Just as Fontana claimed that the contribution of the attentive natural philosopher was indispensable for achieving accurate, three-dimensional representations of the living body going beyond traditional illustrations and pickled specimens, Diderot put forward the view that only a genius could transcend existing conventions of representation to achieve more truthful depictions of nature. These works could then serve as precedents for further imitation, just as Matteucci's preparations and Fontana's innovative ideas for the design and presentation of the models served for further imitation by the modellers.[70]

Both Diderot and Fontana ultimately left open the question whether these special abilities were caused by physical peculiarities, but stressed their inseparability from their 'owner'. Diderot, like Fontana, increasingly came to regard genius as a personal attribute that could not be fully explained through reasoned principles; it was based on a unique conjunction of faculties similar to the natural philosophers' coordination of manual, visual, and mental activity. Fontana stressed this passionately in communications to the court. His contemporaries also noted his difficult character and his inability to make friends. Uffizi director Pelli, a critical observer of Fontana's activities, considered him 'a man of talent and reputation, but of a harsh and false character'.[71] This image fits well with the new image of the genius as a man of a singular talent, aware of his historical importance and beyond social conventions. According to Diderot, geniuses were 'good at one thing alone: apart from that, nothing; they do not know how to be citizens, fathers, mothers, parents, friends . . . The genius is a hard man, a brutal man; he is without humanity, he is full of avarice' – a description echoed by many of Fontana's acquaintances.[72]

Thus, Fontana drew on a conceptual framework similar to the new late eighteenth-century concept of the genius to reclaim the ability to speak the truth about nature in a new social and institutional context, from a position of diminished independence. His self-presentation, either explicitly as a 'man of letters' who was above administrative tasks, or implicitly as a genius who was beyond social conventions altogether, did not agree too well with his role as employee in state service. Claims to knowledge that were based on unique features of the exceptional individual did not meet the grand-ducal administration's expectation of knowledge that was intelligible to others and could be shared.[73]

Administrative control

Fontana's failing efforts to subject the artisans to stricter discipline increasingly prompted court administrators to apply such disciplinary measures equally to the museum's expert naturalists. A number of measures were introduced at the museum during the 1780s to respond to the problems. 'Most of these ills', Fontana hoped, would 'in future be resolved by separating the two modellers Ferrini and Susini . . . In this manner all gatherings and reciprocal complicities are interrupted, and finally the works of everyone can be judged separately.'[74] In an attempt to enforce attention and in order to make individual artisans more clearly accountable for their work, the materials which artisans used in model production were registered, as well as their late arrivals; workers were separated into different, closed rooms, and conversation during work prohibited. Since these measures were not overwhelmingly successful, even after the sacking of Ferrini, Fontana repeatedly turned to the court for support. However, this alliance backfired owing to the court's different perspectives on model production. The administration's concern was with the quantitative control of funds and the timely completion of models for public display. Thus, court administrators readily reaffirmed Fontana's right, as director of the museum, to hire and fire subordinates at will – a measure which did not address the problem as Fontana saw it, having learnt that the modellers could not easily be replaced. For his superiors at court it was Fontana himself, as director and overseer of model production, who was responsible for the models' accuracy.[75] The articulation introduced by the natural philosophers themselves, which located cognitive authority in their bodies and minds, facilitated a perspective according to which the models' validity was ascertained by a natural philosophers' physical presence.

The administration's concerns regarding the efficient production of models was reflected in the measures imposed on the museum as a whole, which increasingly subjected the naturalists to similar sets of rules as the artisans, especially with respect to incurring expenses.[76] Like the artisans, naturalists had to keep accounts of materials used. In addition, they were to follow the court's instructions regarding the completion of projects, and await the court's permission for the production of new models. The requirement for the modellers to keep a record of their daily work in journals was thus a means of controlling not only the artisans, but also the naturalists, whose orders they carried out.[77]

Whether as a man of letters or a genius, Fontana did not fully comply with the court's *modelli* that were intended to standardise administrative practice among the state's various departments. Court administrators such as the Grand Duke's adviser Francesco Maria Gianni came to express the conviction early in

1789 that: 'Little can be said about the Museum by way of an examination of the finances.'[78] As he pointed out, the sovereign's main means of control under these circumstances was to withdraw funding at will. However, that would have run counter to the Grand Duke's intention of creating a complete collection for public exhibition.

The continuing administrative problems indicated to the court that the museum's experts, like the local medical experts and those at the Chamber of Commerce and the Georgofili Academy, required closer government control. In the late 1780s, the court requested accounts of museum employees and their activities, especially reports of the museum's inner workings from persons other than the director, in order to install a new 'method of economic government'. In the view of the Administrator of Crown Affairs Luigi Bartolini, this knowledge would 'constitute the true knowledge of the quality, power, competencies, and relationships of the subordinate institutions; which is the sole fundamental principle from which any good and exact regulation . . . arises'. He hoped that it was this rational government 'through which any disorder and obscurity is removed, from which the activity of the entries can finally be determined, [and also] the measure of expenses, the capability of the employees, and the secure basis for improving the budget, or for achieving savings'.[79]

Porters, modellers, and Fontana's assistant Fabbroni were asked to report their perspective of the museum's activities and reasons for delay. Not surprisingly, the image of model production that emerged from these reports was very different: modellers and other employees stressed the incompetence of the director in administrative and organisational matters, his erratic behaviour, his inability to keep order, and his volatile temper. Porter Giuseppe Becchini reported in 1789 on the proliferation of useless duplicates and refuse, and described director Fontana's dwelling as a 'room . . . that seems like a jumble due to the large quantity of things in disorder and the many unusable waxes'.[80]

Fabbroni: The naturalist in state service

While Fontana's understanding of his role continued to conflict with the court's expectations, other museum naturalists were more successful at articulating their position as experts in state service, to their benefit. One museum employee who particularly stressed his adherence to the court's requirements was Giovanni Fabbroni, Felice Fontana's student and assistant. In his occasional dealings with the central administration, even before the requested reports, Fabbroni explicitly adopted formats set up by the court. In 1789, head auditor Giulio Piombanti suggested to the sovereign the installation at the museum of a 'head of department, who holds account of the other employees, who examines, and reports their operations'.[81] In response, that year Fabbroni was named deputy director and economic supervisor of La Specola in the course of an administrative reform of the museum which he himself had suggested. He was given full responsibility for all financial aspects of the museum; thus, all projects that involved costs (i.e. any projects) had to be approved by Fabbroni. The annual budget was set at 32,000 Lire to be paid up-front in quarterly instalments replacing previous reimbursement, and the production of new models was subject to the approval of the sovereign.

In general, the completion of works in progress had priority over new projects.[82] The museum's natural philosophers were ordered to obey the same rules as the modellers with regard to the exact and regular registration of the quantity and location of materials, and to present finished products at times specified by court administrators. Thus, the administration, in practice, denied Fontana the authority to determine when a perfectly accurate representation was achieved.[83] While Fontana's reputation and continued involvement in model production justified the models' claims to accuracy vis-à-vis learned visitors and correspondents, his autonomy within the museum had thus been diminished significantly. Decisions concerning models' completion and their transfer to other institutions were now made by the new deputy director. Where Fontana referred to his status as a man of letters in order to refuse compliance with state requirements, Fabbroni identified himself as a trustworthy servant of the state – a true 'model expert' – through explicit adherence to the *modelli*, the required forms, procedures and control measures.[84]

Unlike Fontana, Fabbroni's understanding of honour was based not primarily on his reputation as a natural philosopher, but on fulfilling his duty as a state employee in the service of the sovereign. In contrast to his superior, Fabbroni conceded that pursuing the sovereign's interest at the museum was not necessarily identical with 'the private glory of the director'.[85] Submission to the conventions of state administration was not only a sign of the naturalist's dutifulness, but also, importantly, an indispensable basis for properly doing one's duty in the first place. This 'civil behaviour', or 'deference', Fabbroni asserted, 'contributes to the highest exactness of the work, to the highest economy, and internal harmony'.[86] An individual's trustworthiness in this framework was thus determined not by his social position, but was a temporally emergent feature dependent on a history of reliable service. Unlike Fontana's self-presentation of the naturalist as genius, whose capabilities were tied to the individual, Fabbroni's image of the naturalist in state service was grounded in experience.

This stance fitted much more readily with the requirements of bureaucratic hierarchies since it assumed that, in principle, everybody was capable of taking up any position within the system. It enabled the naturalist to trust his subordinates despite having to answer to the court for their actions – an indispensable requirement for a public institution where the delegation of tasks and the centralisation of responsibility were a necessity.[87] Similarly, in contrast to Fontana, Fabbroni accorded significant agency to the modellers in the production of anatomical waxes, asserting that 'with exact examples before his eyes, and wax in his hands, there is no modeller who cannot and does not know how to imitate them'.[88] This attitude became especially salient in Fabbroni's comments on a report by anatomist Paolo Mascagni, which Fontana had solicited in the early 1790s in his defence.

Mascagni: Fontana's outside support

Fontana's modelling activities came under threat especially after the administrative reform of the museum in 1789, which had made Fabbroni economic supervisor of the museum. Model production slowed down even further when Fontana embarked on a new project: the production of a decomposable model in wood. Wooden models, which enabled hands-on interaction, the director argued, would be superior to the fragile waxes. However, this enterprise strained the museum's resources and occupied its artisans at the expense of wax model production. In 1790, Fontana's patron Pietro Leopoldo left Florence to succeed his brother Joseph II as Austrian emperor Leopold II. A memorandum written by Fontana in his defence reached Pietro Leopoldo in Vienna that same year, but at that point, shortly after the outbreak of the French Revolution, the new head of the Holy Roman Empire had other things on his mind than to respond to his former court physicist's complaints.[89] In 1793, in order to justify his works to Pietro Leopoldo's successor, his second-born son Ferdinando III, La Specola's director attempted once more to gain additional support for model production by asking for the court's permission to call upon the judgement of the Siena anatomist Paolo Mascagni (1755–1815) in a request which he framed as an attempt to secure the museum's reputation.[90]

> For my peace and certainty, and for the benefit of the museum, I do not want to put trust in myself alone, and I ask that those articles be determined together with a person of good judgement, and above any objections, I therefore ask that Professor Mascagni of Siena, who is well known for his works, examine the waxes of the museum, and determine with me what remains to be done to complete the anatomy in wax.[91]

Mascagni had already contributed to the Florentine modelling enterprise in 1785 with preparations displaying the lymphatic system, his field of specialisation. However, as Fontana had remarked then, at that point he had not yet published any work, and was therefore of limited use to the museum.[92] This changed in 1787, when Mascagni issued his first book on his research on the lymphatic system, *Vasorum lymphaticorum corporis humani historia et icono-graphia*.[93] The anatomist's contributions were honoured by foreign academies and the sovereign, and with a premium of 2000 Lire from the Paris Academy of Sciences in 1792.[94] Despite Mascagni's credentials, the court denied Fontana's request, favouring instead the local expertise of Tommaso Bonicoli (1746–1802), a well-respected Florentine anatomist frequently employed by the museum for anatomical preparation.

Nevertheless, Mascagni visited Florence from 6 to 14 March at Fontana's request, and submitted a report to the Grand Duke. As a judge of the collection, the Siena anatomist was not entirely 'above any objections', as Fontana claimed. Fabbroni, in particular, was highly sceptical of the value of Mascagni's 'independent' judgement: Mascagni had collaborated with Fontana before, and was his friend as far as Fontana had any. The deputy director pre-empted Mascagni's judgement in a confidential note of 8 March to the court in which he predicted that Mascagni's suggestions would be identical to Fontana's requests for more resources for the production of the anatomy in wood: the hiring of a permanent dissector, more workers, and more cadavers.[95]

Not surprisingly, Mascagni's account did indeed echo Fontana's own position. The Siena anatomist confirmed that the artificial anatomies could greatly facilitate and speed up learning about human anatomy, especially if additional resources were granted. The models, he assured Grand Duke Ferdinando, were 'carried to the greatest possible perfection', and were thus a 'worthy monument to the Sovereign' as well as doing 'great honour to the one who imagined and directed it', that is, Fontana, whose permanent presence was indispensable for model production.[96] Following Fontana's earlier accounts of workshop practice, Mascagni's report rhetorically diminished the role of the modellers – to the indignation of Fabbroni, who vented his anger in his private remarks: 'see with what humiliating affectation Fontana always calls <u>waxworkers</u> the modellers at whose expense he makes such a good figure'. Mascagni's claim that the artisans could not read and write prompted Fabbroni to call him a 'wicked liar': 'Look at the journals which they keep, and ask God's forgiveness for your perfidious iniquity, or rather for that of the Director who dictated this writing to you'.[97]

In his report to the court on Mascagni's evaluating activity, Fabbroni voiced his discontent in more polite, but no less forceful ways. He, in turn, enrolled other museum employees to support his scepticism: he added to his own report evaluations of the model collection by anatomist Bonicoli and chief modeller

Susini, which confirmed Fabbroni's opinion that wax model collection could soon be completed if artisans were not distracted by Fontana's wood anatomy project.[98] Bonicoli expressed strong doubts concerning the utility of the decomposable model in wood, since the material was too coarse for a reproduction of finer anatomical details, and it distorted easily with changes in temperature or humidity. Fontana's calling on Mascagni's judgement thus served two purposes. Not only did the Siena anatomist confirm the models' accuracy; the necessity of accuracy was furthermore instrumentalised to argue for an increase in government support. However, Fabbroni's negative evaluation and Bonicoli's competing expertise undermined Fontana's efforts, and Mascagni's report did not move the court to grant additional resources.[99]

Conclusion

Museum director Felice Fontana considered accuracy indispensable for the models to fulfil their functions as tools for public enlightenment and demonstrations of grand-ducal legitimacy. In accordance with his image as a man of letters, vis-à-vis the scholarly community and learned museum visitors, he supported the models' claim to accuracy by imitating authoritative images and the publicised use of real body parts. The director enrolled outside members of the 'republic of letters' to report favourably on these validating elements of model production. However, these measures did not solve internal problems with the production practice, which threatened the achievement of accuracy. Modellers resisted the idea of being used like 'tools'. The artisans treated anatomical model production as similar to their production of other wax sculptures. They considered themselves to possess special craft knowledge, which secured their position at the museum and permitted the transgression of rules.

Ironically, Fontana thus encountered similar problems of control and authority on the level of the museum to the ones experienced by the Grand Duke on the level of the Tuscan polity. Different groups who contributed to model production claimed autonomy on the basis of their professional skills, prompting Fontana to suppress these claims to maintain his own authority. Such disciplinary problems led to investigations back-stage at the museum. Subsequent reports on modelling practice established different articulations of naturalists' roles at the new public museum. In Fontana's reports to the court, prompted by the need to justify delays and budget overdrafts, he articulated an image of the interaction between different social groups in model production in such a way as to present the artisans as either unable or unwilling to pay the required attention that was, in his view, indispensable for the production of accurate anatomical models. Concomitantly, Fontana's account defined the role of the naturalist as a necessary presence in model production to ensure the accuracy of the representations. In his accounts, Fontana strongly linked the accuracy of the models to his own honour as a man of letters, a self-understanding which he tried to carry over from his position as the Grand Duke's client to his new situation as museum director and expert in state service. However, the naturalist as state employee could no longer support his claim to cognitive authority on the basis of the early modern principle that 'free action was the condition for speaking truth'.[100] In an effort to ascertain the accuracy of the models and to maintain their own authority within this changed context of knowledge production, director Fontana and anatomist Matteucci drew on personal attributes in their accounts of model production to claim cognitive authority.

Fontana's self-perception, in particular, conflicted with the state's requirements for financial transparency, accountability and economy, both in his resort to the image of the 'man of letters' and his implicit play on the emergent notion of the genius. Throughout the 1780s, the court issued calls for the economic government of the museum, and especially for efficient model production. The museum's initial reports, which had ascribed failures to artisans' lack of discipline, prompted the court to reinforce the directors' authority to fire employees, and to transmit its own 'models' as means for streamlining administrative practice and enabling the evaluation of all employees according to uniform standards. Fontana did not adhere to those *modelli* since he considered this inappropriate for a man of letters. His responses continued to stress the connection between the models' accuracy and his own honour, and his disdain for administrative tasks.

Fontana's refusal to comply with the court's requests in the expected manner prompted court administrators to request reports of the museum's inner workings from sources inside the institution other than Fontana himself. These reports from other employees established a very different image of social interaction and the modelling process: in the accounts of modellers and porters, in particular, delays and other problems in model production were ascribed mainly to Fontana's own erratic behaviour and his contradictory demands of the modellers. These accounts, together with the director's apparent unwillingness or inability to adhere to administrative procedure, informed the court's subsequent response. Just as naturalists were employed to oversee model production for its accuracy, Fontana's former assistant Fabbroni was given the task, as deputy director, of overseeing the museum's finances, especially those of model production. In this process, the previous reports and investigations served as an indicator of trustworthiness. While Fontana continued to refuse compliance, Fabbroni identified himself as a reliable servant of the state through explicit adherence to the required procedures.

Accounts of the museum's 'back-stage', its offices and workshops, thus not only informed administrative practices intended to secure model production. These reports also contributed to the articulation of different images of the naturalist's role as expert in state service. A naturalist in public service as he emerged from the interactions between court and museum over the problem of model production was no longer an autonomous natural philosopher whose notion of honour was tied to his truth claims. The new institutional context of the public museum prompted Fontana to resort to a self-presentation akin to the new image of the genius. In a very different way, Fabbroni presented himself as an employee in state service whose honour depended on a history of reliable service for the state and adherence to its administrative conventions. For the naturalist to be useful as an expert in state service, scientific talent and intellectual capacity were not enough. If scientific expertise was to be useful for the state it had to prioritise the state's interests over personal ones such as Fontana's honour. The naturalist had to conform to standardised procedures, to produce knowledge that was intelligible and accessible to the administration on its own terms.

Notes

1 '[L]'interesse del R. Museo esigge che sieno Levati tali difetti, e che i Lavori sieno perfetti', IMSS–ARMU, Filza di negozi dell'anno 1789 A, fol. 184, 2 October 1785.

2 Renato G. Mazzolini, 'Plastic anatomies and artificial dissections', in Soraya de Chadarevian and Nick Hopwood (eds), *Models: The third dimension of science* (Stanford: Stanford University Press, 2004), pp. 43–70.

3 'Ogni cosa resta ben serrata negli scaffali da maestosi, e grandi cristalli, e *a un colpo d'ochio tutto si vede, tutto si conosce*' (italics A.M.). Anon., *Saggio del Real Gabinetto di Fisica, e di Storia Naturale di Firenze* (Roma: Giovanni Zempel, 1775), pp. 29–30.

4 '[S]i voglia dar Loro tutta quella perfezione, di cui sono suscettibili, e che è affatto necessaria se si voglion far servire p l'Istruzione pubblica'; IMSS–ARMU, Filza di negozi dell'anno 1791, fols 117–21: 'Memoria del Professore Cav.re Fontana sopra Le Cere Anatomiche per L'Università di Pavia', fol. 118r.

5 Anon., *Saggio*, p. 33.

6 '[L]'Anatomia in tal guisa diventerà una delle parti più belle della Fisica moderna'. Anon., *Saggio*, p. 32.

7 For Fontana's distinction between descriptive anatomy and explanatory physics see also his correspondence with Caldani. Renato G. Mazzolini and Giuseppe Ongaro (eds), *Epistolario di Felice Fontana*, vol. 1. Carteggio con Leopoldo Marc'Antonio Caldani (Trento, Società di Studi Trentini di Scienze Storiche, 1980), p. 127, letter of 30 October 1758.

8 Anon., *Saggio*, p. 33.

9 For similar contemporary issues in scientific illustration see Lorraine Daston and Peter Galison, 'The image of objectivity', *Representations* 40 (1992), pp. 81–128.

10 IMSS–ARMU, Filza di negozi dell'anno 1794, fol. 269–287 (doc. 57), 'Copia della Portata fatta dai Soggetti impiegati a Ruolo Stabile nel Real Museo di Fisica rimessa alla Reale Segreteria della Corona, e di Corte il dì 31. Luglio 1794. Portate fatte dai medesimi Soggetti Separatam'. fol. 281.

11 Thomas Schnalke, 'Vom Model zur Moulage. Der neue Blick auf den menschlichen Körper am Beispiel des medizinischen Wachsbildes', in: Gabriele Dürbeck et al. (eds), *Wahrnehmung der Natur, Natur der Wahrnehmung. Studien zur Geschichte visueller Kultur um 1800* (Dresden: Verlag der Kunst, 2001), pp. 55–70.

12 For an architectural reconstruction of La Specola from historical floor plans and administrative documents see Alfredo Forti (ed.), *L'Imperiale e Regio Museo di Fisica e Storia Naturale di Firenze: indicazioni per un metodo di lettura e per una soluzione museografica* (Florence: Angelo Pontecorboli, 1995), especially Rita Vagnarelli, 'Evoluzione e modifiche della fabbrica della Specola attraverso le piante storiche', pp. 29–42 and M. Luciana Zullino, 'L'organizzazione museologica della Specola nelle varie epoche', pp. 43–5.

13 E.g. Engelbert Wichelhausen, *Ideen über die beste Anwendung der Wachsbildnerei, nebst Nachrichten von den anatomischen Wachspräparaten in Florenz und deren Verfertigung, für Künstler, Kunstliebhaber und Anthropologen* (Frankfurt am Main: J.L.E. Zessler, 1798), pp. 36, 41, 42. See also IMSS–ARMU, Fondo Fabbroni II 16, doc. 328, letter from dissector Bonicoli to Fabbroni (5 November 1791).

14 'Apre l'ingresso alla Storia Naturale una vastissima collezione di Anatomìa dell'uomo eseguita in cera *dappresso alla natura*, ed alle *descrizioni dei migliori Autori*'. Vincenzo Follini and Marco Rastrelli, *Firenze antica e moderna illustrata* (Florence: Iacopo Grazioli, 1798–1802), vol. 8, p. 178 (italics A.M.).

15 Nicolas René Desgenettes, 'Réflexions générales sur l'utilité de l'anatomie artificielle; et en particulier sur la collection de Florence, et la nécessité d'en former de semblables en France', *Journal de Médecine, Chirurgie et Pharmacie* 94 (1793), pp. 162–76, 233–52. Wichelhausen, *Wachsbildnerei*.

16 This is corroborated by Fabbroni's account of the origin of Desgenettes' report, and by Wichelhausen. IMSS–ARMU, Fondo Fabbroni II 16, doc. 418. Wichelhausen, *Wachsbildnerei*, pp. xv, 96, 121.

17 'Doch modellirt man nie nach Kupferstichen allein, sondern diese dienen nur dem Zergliederer zur Leitung'. Wichelhausen, *Wachsbildnerei*, p. 117.

18 'Oft sind sehr viele Kadaver erforderlich, um die größte Vollständigkeit der Theile, die man nachbilden will, zu erhalten und dem Modellirer deutlich zu machen'. Wichelhausen, *Wachsbildnerei*, pp. 117–18.

19 Fabbroni's records indicate 151 pieces for 1795 and 139 for 1796 (IMSS–ARMU, fondo Fabbroni II 16, doc. 358–369). For the year 1797 a register indicates a total of 112 body parts. IMSS–ARMU, Negozi 1800, fol. 98–101 (doc.

89): 'Tabella Annuale Dei Pezzi di Cadavere, che sono venuti dal Regio Spedale di S[anta] M[ari]a Nova [sic] al Real Museo, ad Uso p[er] i Lavori Anatomici in Legno, di ordine del Ill[ustrissi]mo Sig[no]re Direttore Felice Fontana, dal Primo Gennaio a tutto Xbre 1797'.

20 An overview of the production process is given in Kleindienst, *Ästhetisierte Anatomie*. For a detailed description of the models' technical features from a restorer's perspective see Rita Furrer, 'Die Restaurierung anatomischer und geburtshilflicher Wachsmodelle im Wiener Josephinum', *Restauratorenblätter* 2:1 (2000), pp. 105–16. For a contemporary description of model production in Florence see Wichelhausen, *Wachsbildnerei*, pp. 97–122.

21 See e.g. Fontana's letter to Caldani, 30 October 1791, in Mazzolini and Ongaro, *Epistolario*, vol. 1, p. 319. For similar contemporary attitudes to artisanal labour see e.g. Simon Schaffer, 'Enlightened automata', in William Clark, Jan Golinski and Simon Schaffer (eds), *The sciences in enlightened Europe* (Chicago and London: University of Chicago Press, 1999), pp. 126–65.

22 IMSS–ARMU, Filza di negozi dell'anno 1791, fol. 7, 'Istruzioni per lo Spazino Giacinto Guidetti' (31 January 1791).

23 '[I]l suo mestiere richiede ancora il trasportare i Cadaveri da S.M. Nova al il R. Museo, p uso dei lavori in Cera, ed in tempo di pioggia di neve ec. non si può fermare, in verun luogo, avendo, appreso di se la sporta dei Morti, Il quale mestiere lo rende odioso a tutti, ed e trattato male nelle cafè ove à abitata' IMSS–ARMU, Filza di negozi dell'anno 1792, fol. 253 (doc. 85), letter in Guidetti's name to the museum's deputy director, 19 October 1792.

24 See e.g. IMSS–ARMU, Fondo Fabbroni II 16, docs 331–332, 'Registro a parte di quei giorni che il Sig.re Direttore si porta al Real Museo, principiando dal dì 8 Marzo 1793 tenuto esatto dai due Guardaportoni'.

25 '[L]'Omo [sic] del Campo Santo, disse a Cintio Baronfottuto, tu riporti i morti senza adoperare, questo, che ci è, deve servire p[er] il Nannoni'. Fondo Fabbroni II 16, docs 350–55: '1794, Ricordo dei Cadaveri portati da Diacinto Guidetti p[er] Istruzione del Sig[no]re Direttore Felice Fontana dagli Spedali di S[anta] Maria Nova, e Innocenti', fol. 350v.

26 'Aber sie haben auch nicht nach der Natur gemacht werden können, sondern nach Abbildungen'. Wichelhausen, *Wachsbildnerei*, p. 35. Representations both two- and three-dimensional of embryo development continued to be problematic throughout the nineteenth century: see e.g. Nick Hopwood, 'Giving body to embryos: Modeling, mechanism, and the microtome in late 19th-century anatomy', *Isis* 90 (1999), pp. 462–96.

27 IMSS–ARMU, Filza di negozi dell'anno 1791, fol. 114–121 (doc. 35); Filza di negozi dell'anno 1790, fol. 228–9 (doc. 54). For the Florentine models for Pavia see Peter K. Knoefel, 'Antonio Scarpa, Felice Fontana, and the wax models for Pavia', *Medicina nei secoli* 16 (1979), pp. 219–34; Francesca Monza, 'Le arti al servizio delle scienze: la ceroplastica', in Angelo Stella and Gianfranco Lavezzi (eds), *Esortazioni alle storie* (Milan: Cisalpino, 2001), pp. 629–42.

28 '[N]on v'è cosa in questa Statua che non regga il più scrupoloso esame d'un abile
    Scultore, e d'un Anatomico', IMSS–ARMU, Fondo Fabbroni II 16, doc. 238,
    copy (by Bicchierai) of Scarpa's letter to the museum, Pavia 19 December 1794.

29 'Let the artists look above all at table XXVII . . .' ('Faccia loro [gli artisti] con-
    siderare sopra tutto la Tav. XXVII fig. 4, no 128.129.199.193 fig.5 R.S.T. Tav.
    XIX 187'). Ibid. For a similar economy of models and judgments see e.g. an
    exchange between Siena anatomist Paolo Mascagni and Jena anatomist Justus
    Christian Loder; in AFS, Fondo Mascagni Fasc. 25, Lett.1–3: Giuseppe Gautieri
    to Mascagni, 30 Pratile an IX (1801).

30 Cited in and translated by Simone Contardi, 'The origins of a scientific institu-
    tion. Felice Fontana and the birth of the Real Museo di Fisica e Storia Naturale di
    Firenze', in *Nuncius* 21/2 (2006), pp. 251–63, p. 252.

31 Mario Biagioli, *Galileo courtier* (Chicago: University of Chicago Press, 1993),
    especially pp. 84–90.

32 Steven Shapin, *A social history of truth* (Chicago and London: University of
    Chicago Press, 1994).

33 See Biagioli, *Galileo*, p. 85.

34 For Fontana's entry in the museum's payroll see e.g. IMSS–ARMU, Negozi
    1790, fol. 15v, 16r: 'Ruolo d'Impiegati, Aggregati, e Pensionati al Servizio del
    Real Museo di Fisica e Istoria Naturale che si propone a Sua Altezza Reale per la
    Sovrana approvazione questo di 19. Novembre 1789'.

35 '[L']onore, che nessun uomo può abbandonare'; ASF, Imperiale e Reale Corte
    Lorenese, 360, no. 284 I, 'Memoria dl Cav. Fontana in sua giustificazione' (n.d.),
    pp. 48–9. See also e.g. a draft of a report on Fontana's plans for the foundation
    of a scientific academy to Pietro Leopoldo by Fontana, n.d. (but before 1789):
    'This vast plan . . . already does much honour to the Great Patron, and will do so
    even more before long'. ('[Q]uesto vastissimo piano . . . fa già al presente tanto
    onore, e trappoco lo farà anche maggiore al Gran Mecenate'. IMSS–ARMU,
    Filza di negozi dell'anno 1789A, fols 433–3.) For Fontana's notion of honour
    as bound up with his truth claims see e.g. the letters to Caldani: Mazzolini and
    Ongaro, *Epistolario*, letters 99 and following. See also the 'Memoria sopra le
    due Collezioni anatomiche del R. Museo di Firenze' (1794), pp. 2, 17, 26, in
    ASF, Imperiale e Reale Corte Lorenese 378, Protocollo LXV, signed by Paolo
    Mascagni, but in a different handwriting, and probably dictated by Fontana (for a
    discussion of the Memoria's authorship see below).

36 E.g. in Kleindienst, who portrays the Florentine anatomy workshop as 'a wax
    manufacture of interdisciplinary working spirit' ('eine Wachsmanufaktur mit
    interdisziplinärem Arbeitsgeist'). Kleindienst, *Ästhetisierte Anatomie*, p. 61. Also
    Irmela Marei Krüger-Fürhoff, *Der versehrte Körper. Revisionen des klassizistischen
    Schönheitsideals* (Göttingen: Wallstein, 2001), p. 85.

37 Guidetti had previously worked for the court as a kitchen aid and for the grand-
    ducal Dragoons (IMSS–ARMU, Filza di negozi dell'anno 1794, fol. 269–87
    (doc. 57), 'Copia della Portata fatta dai Soggetti impiegati a Ruolo Stabile nel

Real Museo di Fisica rimessa alla Reale Segreteria della Corona, e di Corte il dì 31. Luglio 1794'. For his work with corpses see IMSS–ARMU, Filza di negozi dell'anno 1795, fol. 57 (doc. 18). For Guidetti's injecting work see Fondo Fabbroni II 16, docs 350–5, '1794, Ricordo dei Cadaveri portati da Diacinto Guidetti p[er] Istruzione del Sig[no]re Direttore Felice Fontana dagli Spedali di S[anta] Maria Nova [sic], e Innocenti'.

38 Pelli considered his portrait 'too serious, and austere, an effect of the characteristic of age which always makes caricatures in contrast to the heart when it is not yet ulcerated by the years'. ('. . . a me pare di esser troppo serio, e burbero, effetto dl carattere dll'età che fà sempre dlle caricature in contrasto col cuore ancor quando non è ulcerato dagli anni'.) BNCF, manuscript collection NA 1050, Pelli, 'Efemeridi', Serie II, vol. XVII, fol. 3574v, 20 December 1789. For an example of a late eighteenth-century portrait bust in wax see e.g. the portrait of Pietro Leopoldo (plate IIa).

39 '[N]on me ne importa un cazzo [lit.: prick], e non vo chieder nulla a nessuno'. IMSS–ARMU, Filza di negozi dell'anno 1789B, fol. 441.

40 See e.g. reports by Fontana in IMSS–ARMU, Filza di negozi dell'anno 1789A, fol. 218 ff; Gagli in IMSS–ARMU, Filza di negozi dell'anno 1789B, fol. 477 and fols 480 ff.

41 '[E]gli disse, circa alla cera nessuno di quei minchioni del Museo non Lene possono avvedere perchè la Trementina è quella che ricopre ognicosa'. IMSS–ARMU, Filza di negozi dell'anno 1789B, fols 480–90, 'Quaderno In cui sta registrato tutte le mancanze dei lavoranti si in cera, come di Macchine dal di 3. 8bre 1782 a X: il 1786'; fol. 482v.

42 '[Q]esti moti spontanei della mano non sono ancora stati da'nessuno ben determinati, nè sono forse di sua natura determinabili'. ASF, Segreteria di Finanze, Affari prima del 1788, 480. For the problem of automation in early modern lens production see Simon Werrett, 'Wonders never cease: Descartes's Météores and the rainbow fountain', *British journal for the history of science*, 34 (2001), pp. 129–47; Myles Jackson, *Spectrum of belief: Joseph von Fraunhofer and the craft of precision optics* (Cambridge Mass.: MIT Press, 2000).

43 'Segreta esperienza del contrario', IMSS–ARMU, Filza di negozi dell'anno 1789A, fol. 60.

44 References to the problem of latecoming cease after the last attempt to instil punctuality in museum employees, a reformed work schedule by Fabbroni of 1797 in which the deputy director shortened working hours, especially for the heads of the two workshops, Susini and Gori. IMSS–ARMU, Filza di negozi dell'anno 1797, fol. 249 (doc. 18), Fabbroni, 20 May 1797: 'Regolamento in aggiunta agli Ordini di SAR contenuti nel B.R. del dì 19. Luglio 1793'.

45 Erving Goffman, *The presentation of the self in everyday life* (New York: Anchor Books Doubleday, 1959), p. 104.

46 IMSS–ARMU, Filza di negozi dell'anno 1789A, fols 41–2, 'Attestato del Susini', 31 July 1781. Statements by Susini and Gori for their respective workshops of 25

June 1792 (IMSS–ARMU, Filza di negozi dell'anno 1792, fols 142–6, docs 46 and 47).

47 IMSS–ARMU, Fondo Fabbroni II 16, doc. 84, copy of 'Appunti del Dirett.e e Scritti difeso avuti a mano questo dì 31. Gennajo 1793', with Fabbroni's comments in the margins: 'Come mai l'uomo che forma gli artefici dal Nulla; che le adopra come la Sega e il Martello, confessa egli adesso, che vi sono lavori esclusivi p[er] Susini, e come ardisce Egli di pronunziarlo!'

48 IMSS–ARMU, Filza di negozi dell'anno 1789A, fols 441v, 442r (n.d.).

49 '[A]liena ad un'Uomo di Lettere'; ASF, Segreteria di Finanze Affari prima del 1788, 'Casa Reale. Museo di Fisica. Disposizioni particolari', secretary's report to the Grand Duke, n.d. but 1782, p. 479.

50 IMSS–ARMU, Filza di negozi dell'anno 1790, 26r (14 September 1789); Filza di negozi dell'anno 1790, 89r (n.d.).

51 The anatomists working for the museum in the late eighteenth century were well trained, and renowned doctors who had received their training at the large Florentine hospital Santa Maria Nuova. Working as a dissector did not necessarily imply an inferior status to other physicians; thus e.g. Lorenzo Nannoni worked as a dissector before succeeding his father as full professor at the hospital. Anon., *Cariche occupate in Firenze dal Prof. Nannoni* (Florence, s.n. 1809). According to Fabbroni, at the larger hospitals the dissector held at the same time the position of one of the head surgeons (IMSS–ARMU, Filza di negozi dell'anno 1792, fol. 92r, report on dissector Tommaso Bonicoli, 28 June 1792). However, anatomists such as Mascagni considered the routine production of preparations for teaching purposes to be 'mechanical' and detracting from research. AFS, Fondo Mascagni 3, Fasc. 58, letter of 14 December 1795: 'l'ottima sua riuscita [del dissettore], onde vi solleva dal meccanismo delle preparazioni, e vi lascia il tempo di far ricerche nuove, ed osservazioni'.

52 '[L']occhio e la mano del dissetore potesse arrivare a *spogliarle* [le parti anatomiche] di tutte quelle membrane, e cellulari, che vi scorrono sopra'. IMSS–ARMU, Filza di negozi dell'anno 1789 A, fol. 238v (italics A.M.).

53 '[O]cchio anatomico'; IMSS–ARMU, Filza di negozi dell'anno 1789 A, 'Memoria di Antonio Matteucci risguardando il suo obbligo di dissettore delle preparazioni in cera, che si fanno per il servizio di S.A.R'., fol. 228v (n.d., but 1770s).

54 '[E]saminare', 'osservare', 'vedere'; IMSS–ARMU, Filza di negozi dell'anno 1789 A, 238v (n.d.).

55 '[I]l vero stato naturale'; IMSS–ARMU, Filza di negozi dell'anno 1789 A, 'Memoria di Antonio Matteucci risguardando il suo obbligo di dissettore delle preparazioni in cera, che si fanno per il servizio di S.A.R'., fol. 228v–229r (n.d., but 1770s).

56 'Seguendo qualche errore di Anatomia io ne devo essere *responsabile*, ed il Ferrini deve pressarsi a tutto quello che io gli consiglierò di fare per *l'esatezza anatomica*'. IMSS–ARMU, Filza di negozi dell'anno 1789 A, fol. 238v. Italics A.M.

57 '[P]erche fossera *imitate* dall'Artefice'; IMSS–ARMU, Filza di negozi dell'anno 1789 A, fol. 235r (italics A.M.).

58 Gagli's report, 9 September 1786, IMSS–ARMU Filza di negozi dell'anno 1789 B, fol. 477.

59 '[U]na *vergognosa*, e *colpevole* mancanza di attenzione'; 'mille errori di occhio, e di mano'. IMSS–ARMU, Filza di negozi dell'anno 1789 A, fol. 184 (2 October 1785) (italics A.M.).

60 '[C]ol più gran Zelo ed attenzione possibile'. ASF, Imperiale e Reale Corte Lorenese, 360, no. 284III, 'Memoria dl Professore Cav.e Fontana sulle preparazioni anatomiche fatte per Vienna'.

61 His definition of attention thus went beyond the one given e.g. by the abbé Claude Yvon (1714–91) in the *Encyclopédie*: 'a kind of microscope that enlarges objects' ('une espece de microscope qui grossit les objets'), Diderot and d'Alembert (eds), *Encyclopédie ou Dictionnaire Raisonné* (1751–72), vol. 1, 840, 'Attention'. For early modern notions of attention see Lorraine Daston, *Eine kurze Geschichte der wissenschaftlichen Aufmerksamkeit* (Munich: Carl-Friedrich-von-Siemens-Stiftung, 2001). For attention around 1800, see the contribution of Michael Hagner, 'Aufmerksamkeit als Ausnahmezustand', in *Aufmerksamkeit*, eds Norbert Haas, Rainer Nägele, and Hans-Jörg Rheinberger (Eggingen: Isele, 1998), pp. 273–94.

62 IMSS–ARMU, Filza di negozi dell'anno 1789A, fol. 184 (2 October 1785), for Fontana's offer of monetary incentives, and Filza di negozi dell'anno 1789B, fol. 15 (n.d.), for a contract between a modeller and the museum.

63 Fontana's attitude wavers between finding the artisans incapable of attention, and unwilling to do so. His continuing habit of calling them 'rogues' and 'vagabonds' ('monelli', 'birbe') points to the implication of moral failure (i.e. unwillingness) on their part. See e.g. the notes of custodian Luigi Gagli on the modellers' work between 1 March and 23 November 1784, IMSS–ARMU, Filza di negozi dell'anno 1789B, fols 461–2.

64 '[E]ro obbligato ad ogni momento a riprendere, a guidare'; ASF, Imperiale e Reale Corte Lorenese, 360, no. 284 I, 'Memoria dl Cav. Fontana in sua giustificazione'(n.d.), p. 15.

65 ASF, Imperiale e Reale Corte Lorenese 119, 'Memoria presentata in Vienna a S.M. l'Imperatore Leopoldo' (n.d., but 1790). Translated in Peter K. Knoefel, *Felice Fontana. Life and works* (Trento: Società di Studi Trentini di Scienze Storiche, 1984), p. 344.

66 ASF, Imperiale e Reale Corte Lorenese, 360, no. 284I, 'Memoria dl Cav. Fontana in sua giustificazione' (n.d.), p. 15.

67 See e.g. one memorandum submitted by Fontana to the court in 1790, translated and reprinted in: Knoefel, *Felice Fontana*, part III, Documents: ASF, Imperiale e Reale Corte, filza 119, 'Summary protocol of affairs of the Department of the Crown and Court, . . . 1791'. See also another memorandum in ASF, Segreteria di Finanze Affari prima del 1788, pezzo 481, 'Memoria del Direttore del Real Museo F. Fontana' (n.d., but circa 1786).

68 '[A]ver messa in pericolo per tante volte la mia salute'; ASF, Imperiale e Reale Corte Lorenese, 360, no. 284 I, 'Memoria dl Cav. Fontana in sua giustificazione' (n.d.), p. 2 (see also p. 15); 'ardito'; p. 7; '[a]ppassionato'; p. 22.

69 Herbert Dieckmann, 'Diderot's conception of genius', *Journal of the history of ideas* 2:2 (1941), pp. 151–82; Hubert Sommer, *Génie. Zur Bedeutungsgeschichte des Wortes von der Renaissance zur Aufklärung* (Frankfurt: Peter Lang, 1998), especially pp. 118–23, 'Voltaire, Diderot und die Encyclopédie'.

70 'Nature pushes the man of genius, the genius pushes the imitator' ('La nature pousse l'homme de génie, l'homme de génie pousse l'imitateur'. Diderot, *Oeuvres* II, p. 411; quoted from Dieckmann, 'Genius', p. 159).

71 IMSS–ARMU, Pelli, 'Efemeridi', Serie II, vol. VIII (1780): fol. 1v, 27 September 1780: 'L'Ab. Felice Fontana Fisico di S.A.R. [è] Uomo di talento e che hà un nome, ma è di un carattere duro, finto. . .' BNCF, Pelli, 'Efemeridi', Serie II, vol. IX (1781): fol. 1650r, 29 March 1781: Pelli mused on bringing together local 'men of genius', such as painter Tommaso Gherardini, Fontana, and architect Proletti, but came to the conclusion that this project was probably doomed since 'men of genius do not love their equals, and have all a dose of madness' ('gli Uomini di Genio non amano i loro simili, ed hanno tutti una dose di pazzia').

72 '[Les génies] ne sont bons qu'à une chose: passé cela, rien; ils ne savent ce que c'est d'être citoyens, pères, mères, parents, amis. . . [Le génie] est un homme dur, c'est un brutal; il est sans humanité, il est avare'. Denis Diderot, *Le Neveu de Rameau* (1762), cited from Sommer, *Génie*, pp. 120–1.

73 The problem of the articulation of subjective knowledge in science around 1800 is investigated further in Simon Schaffer, 'Self evidence', in *Critical inquiry* 18 (1992), pp. 327–62; Stuart Walker Strickland, 'Reopening the texts of romantic science: the language of experience in J.W. Ritter's *Beweis*', in Kostas Gavroglu et al. (eds) *Trends in the historiography of science* (Dordrecht: Kluwer, 1994), pp. 385–96; Strickland, 'The ideology of self-knowledge and the practice of self-experimentation', *Eighteenth-century studies* 31:4 (1992), pp. 453–71.

74 '[L]a maggior parte di questi mali sarà levata nell'avvenire col separare i due modellatori Ferrini, e Susini . . . In questa maniera . . . si rompe l'unione, e le connivenze reciproche, e si giudichera per l'ultimo del lavoro separato di ciascuno'. ASF, Segreteria di Finanze prima di 1788, pezzo 480, information written by Fontana on modellers, 15 January 1782.

75 See e.g. the letter from Bartolini to Fontana on 29 July 1791 concerning copies of models for Pavia. IMSS–ARMU, Filza di negozi dell'anno 1791, fol. 115 r.

76 See e.g. IMSS–ARMU, Filza di negozi dell'anno 1789A, fol. 256 ff, 'Copia di Biglietto estratto dal Protocollo Particolare dl di 25 Maggio 1782', for the court's insistence that Fontana and Fabbroni obey the same rules as other employees.

77 LS, '1793. Giornale dei Modellatori', '1796. Giornale dei Modellatori', '1797. Giornale dei Modellatori', '1798. Giornale dei Modellatori'.

78 'Del Gabinetto di Fisica poco potrebbesi dire in forma di Esame di Finanze'. ASF, Gianni, pezzo 7, inserto 95, 'Memoria In Ordine al Biglietto de 19. Maggio 1789.

Sul Gabinetto di Fisica, Lavori per il Littorale, e Maremma, Sussidj ordinarj, e Straordinarj, Gratificazioni, Dette per Case Rurale Imprestiti', fol. 1.

79 '[I]l Metodo immaginato di Governo economico'; 'costituire la vera cognizione delle qualità, forza, competenze, e rapporti delle Aziende medesime; Lorchè è il solo fondamentale Principio, d'onde prende vita ogni buono, ed esatto regolamento di questa Specie, d'onde si toglie ogni disordine e occultazione, e d'onde finalmente si distingue l'attività delle Entrate, la misura delle Spese, la capacità degl'Impiegati, ed i fondamenti sicuri per elargir Denaro, o per procurare risparmio'. ASF, Imperiale e Reale Corte Lorenese, 344, no. 77, letter by Bartolini of 28 August 1789.

80 'Lo Stanzone ove sta il Direttore Fontana costi pare un arsenale, p[er] le gran quantita di Robe tutte male in ordine e tanta cera inservibile', ASF, Imperiale e Real Corte Lorenese, 344, No. 79, 'Rapporto del Guardaportone del R. Museo Giuseppe Becchi' (September 1789).

81 '[U]n Capo di Dipartimento, il quale tenga acconto gli altri Ministri, esamini, e risponda delle loro operazioni'. ASF, Imperiale e Real Corte Lorenese, 344, no. 77 (27 Agosto 1789).

82 IMSS–ARMU, Filza di negozi dell'anno 1790, fols 5–14, 'Istruzioni per il sotto direttore e soprintendente economico'; fols 32–6, 'Istruzioni per il gabinetto di fisica'.

83 Mazzolini, 'Dissections', p. 55.

84 Similarly, William Clark in his analysis of visitations of universities in early modern Germany has shown the use of forms and instructions in the disciplining both of the scholars visited and of the bureaucrat who conducted the visit. Clark, 'On the ministerial registers of academic visitations', in Peter Becker and William Clark (eds), *Little tools of knowledge: historical essays on academic and bureaucratic practices*, pp. 95–140 (Ann Arbor: University of Michigan Press, 2001).

85 '[D]eve essere in primo Luogo l'Interesse, e Splendor del Sovrano, che resulta dall'impiegare utilmente ciò che assegna al Museo; e può essere, in secondo Luogo, la privata gloria del Direttore [. . .] l'uno, o l'altro ebbi io stesso in mira egualmente, sempreche compatibil sembrò la loro unione al mio piccolo intendimento'; IMSS–ARMU, Filza di negozi dell'anno 1792, doc. 44, Promemoria of Fabbroni (n.d., but 1792), fol. 136v.

86 '[C]ontegno urbane'; 'quella deferenza che contribuisce alla maggior esatezza del Lavoro, al maggior risparmio di Spesa, ed'alla interna Armonia'; IMSS–ARMU, Filza di negozi dell'anno 1792, doc. 44, Promemoria of Fabbroni (n.d., but 1792), fol. 136v.

87 For Fabbroni's affirmations of trust in his subordinates see e.g. his communication to the court of a report by Zuccagni on a herbarium offered to the museum, in which the deputy director asserted that due to his 'trust' he judged it 'superfluous' to examine the offer himself. ('La fiducia . . . mi fece giudicar superfluo ogni mio personale esame'.) IMSS–ARMU, Filza di negozi dell'anno 1792, fol. 230v, 7 August 1792.

88 'Non vi è Modellatore, che avendo Esemplari esatti sotto gli occhi, e Cera fralle mani non possa e sappia imitarli'; IMSS–ARMU, Filza di negozi dell'anno 1791, fol. 237r, report by Fabbroni on Galletti's priority claims, 26 November 1791.

89 ASF, Imperiale e Real Corte Lorenese, 360, Protocollo XLI, no. 10, 'Memoria del Caval.e Fontana in sua giustificazione'.

90 For Mascagni's involvement in the Florentine model production see also Patrizia Ruffo, 'Paolo Mascagni e il Reale Museo di Fisica e Storia Naturale di Firenze', in Francesca Vannozzi (ed.), *La scienza illuminata: Paolo Mascagni nel suo tempo (1755-1815)* (Siena: Nuova imagine, 1996), pp. 241–51; and Gabriela Schmidt, 'Sul contributo di Paolo Mascagni alla collezione viennese delle cere anatomiche nel Josephinum', *ibid.*, pp. 101–9.

91 'Per mia quiete e sicurezza, e per il vantaggio del Museo medesimo non volendo fidarmi di me solo domando che tali articoli sieno fissati insieme con *persona intendente*, e *Superiore ad ogni eccezione*, domando in conseguenza che il Professor Mascagni di Siena *abbastanza conosciuto per le Sue Opere* esamini le cere del Museo, e fissi con me quel che resta da farsi per render completa l'Anatomia in Cera'. IMSS–ARMU, Filza di negozi dell'anno 1793, fol. 363-4 (doc. 133), Fontana, 25 October 1793, 'Memoria sopra il Real Museo di Storia Naturale', 363v (italics A.M.).

92 ASF, Segreteria di Finanze Affari prima del 1788, pezzo 480: note in Fontana's hand, 3 November 1785, 'Informazione del Memoriale di Paolo Mascagni': 'Il Professor Paolo Mascagni quanto poteva essere utile in passato per le cere di Vienna, altrettanto sarebbe inutile in futuro per i medesimi lavori anatomici. Egli aveva fatto delle ricerche in Siena per piu anni sopra i vasi linfatici, e non aveva ancora pubblicato nulla che potesse servirmi per completare sulle cere il sistema di quei vasi; e fu per questo che supplicai SAR, perchè venisse a Firenze, e assistesse a detti lavori. Tra che si sono finiti egli rimane inutile, e conviene sgravare di una grossa somma mensuale le cere anatomiche, che si fanno per Vienna'.

93 Paolo Mascagni, *Vasorum lymphaticorum corporis humani historia et iconographia* (Siena: Carli, 1787).

94 *Gazzetta Toscana*, no. 22 (2 June 1792).

95 In his own copy of Mascagni's report to the court, Fabbroni noted that it had been written by Fontana's student Giuseppe Mangili (1767-1829) and dictated by Fontana, in Mascagni's presence. IMSS–ARMU, Fondo Imperiale e Regio Museo di Fisica e di Storia Naturale, Fondo Fabbroni II 16, d.173, 'Copia dello scritto del Mascagni ['Memoria sopra le due collezioni anatomiche del R.Museo di Firenze']'. Fabbroni commented in the margins: 'N.B. This was all written in the hand of Mangili who wrote it after Fontana's dictation, in the presence of Mascagni' ('N.B. Era tutto scritto di Mano del Mangili che lo scrisse alla detattura del Fontana, presente il Mascagni'). The copy of Mascagni's report submitted to the court is indeed signed by, but not written in the hand of Mascagni: ASF, Imperiale e Reale Corte Lorenese, 378, Protocollo LXV, 'Memoria sopra de due Collezioni anatomiche del R. Museo di Firenze'.

96 ASF, Imperiale e Reale Corte Lorenese 378, Protocollo LXV: 'Memoria sopra le due Collezioni anatomiche del R. Museo di Firenze', March 1794, fol. 2: '[I]n pochi mesi potrà ciascuno acquistarsi le idee più precise, e più dettagliate di tuttociò che spetta alla fabbrica del corpo umano . . . Questo monumento degno del Sovrano . . . fa dall'altro canto tanto onore a chi seppe immaginarlo e dirigerlo, portato all'ultima perfezione di cui è suscettibile'.

97 IMSS–ARMU, Fondo Fabbroni II 16, fol. 173ff, 'Copia dello scritto del Mascagni': 'Vede con che umiliante affettazione si chiamano sempre dal Fontana <u>Cerajoli</u>, i modellatori del Museo alle cui Spese fa tanta buona figura', fol. 185; 'Bugiardo Maligno! Vedi i Giornaletti tenuti da Loro, e chiedi perdono a Dio della tua perfida iniquità, o piuttosto di quella del Dirett. che ti dettò questo scritto', fol. 187. Emphasis in the original.

98 ASF, Imperiale e Reale Corte Lorenese, 378, Protocollo LXV.

99 Ibid.

100 Shapin, *Truth*, p. 405.

4

Model reception and the display of expertise

The conflicts between naturalists and artisans over questions of authority at La Specola's back-stage, the model workshop, show that the museum's political mission – as a tool for public enlightenment, a locus of natural knowledge, and display of legitimacy – had consequences for everyday life at the new institution. In their interactions with modellers and court administrators, naturalists like Fontana, Fabbroni and Matteucci articulated their position as experts in state service in different ways, claiming for themselves the authority to evaluate the models and the collection, as accurate representations of nature that could serve as educational tools, and which could bear witness to the qualifications of the naturalists. But how did the museum's political mission shape the museum's 'front-stage', the exhibition? Fontana claimed that perfect models would by themselves be sufficient for the museum's task of public enlightenment. Once on display, in theory, the models could be left alone. However, visitors responded to the artificial anatomies in a number of ways, which were shaped by different cultural frameworks, and which often deviated from the museum director's programmatic statements.[1] What, then, should be the naturalists' role to ensure the success of the mission?

The public museum was a new form of institution for the production and exhibition of natural knowledge, and it required the simultaneous creation of a new audience: the museum visitor. Comparing prescriptions for visitors to audience responses, this chapter explores the encounter between visitors and objects and between expert naturalists and the public. Reconstructions of reception are, of course, problematic, since no sources ever give access to an unmediated reality of visitors' experiences.[2] For most visitors only material traces of interactions (such as receipts and complaints) and inferences from the cultural context of late eighteenth-century Florence allow for some degree of speculation. Few visitors, usually well-to-do travellers and local intellectuals, left written (and published) accounts of their visits to the museum. These retrospective accounts follow established narrative conventions and should not be used uncritically as descriptions of actual visitor comportment.[3] However, such sources do indicate that a variety of conceptual frameworks for encounters with museum objects were available to different classes of visitors. Interactions with the Florentine collection of specimens and instruments could thus be framed, for example, as similar to encounters with relics, or with works of art.

This discrepancy between the models' intended purpose and visitors' responses raises issues which were central to the emergence of a new constellation of experts, the state and the public. It highlighted the problems inherent in the claim that suitable representations could by themselves determine desired responses. The persistent interpretive flexibility of the models also drew attention to the limits of expert naturalists' agency, an observation which should caution analysts in museum studies against strongly authoritarian readings of displays. The chapter's final section therefore explores how museum naturalists responded to the failure to enforce specific modes of reception. Once more, as in the case of the problems encountered back-stage in model production, problems of front-stage reception led naturalists to articulate their roles as experts in state service in different ways. They put forward different images of public education and assigned different roles to the expert in this process. Museum director Fontana maintained his conviction that the right kind of representation would enable model users to learn by themselves. His response to the problem of reception was to modify the models' features, experimenting with detachable models in order to enable hands-on interaction. The other suggestion for improvement, put forward by the museum's deputy director Fabbroni, was to supplement the public exhibition of artificial anatomies with the presence of a mediating naturalist, thus turning the staging of nature increasingly into a staging of expertise.

Education for everyone

For the museum to fulfil its intended function as a place of enlightenment and learning for princes and paupers alike, it had to reach all Tuscan subjects. To accomplish this, the museum was widely publicised, and its displays were designed to be intelligible to everyone. Tuscans were alerted to the existence of the museum and its collections, not only through announcements of the museum's opening in local newspapers such as the *Gazzetta Toscana*, but also through calls distributed by local priests for the contribution of specimens. In addition, Florentines may have become aware of the local production of artificial anatomies since they could frequently observe a museum employee carrying body parts across town between the museum and local hospitals in wicker baskets. Internationally, the museum was publicised through Fontana's correspondence, journal articles, and visitors' published accounts. And once a member of the public came to visit the museum, he or she would encounter an institution whose exhibitions and regulations were intended to make it an ideal space for general education.

The collection was (in principle) open to everybody free of charge. This openness was reflected in Fontana's attempts to present the collection, and especially the anatomical models, in a way that was accessible to anyone. The didactic strategy pursued at the museum to enable the acquisition of knowledge about the body was congruent with sensationalist epistemology.[4] The presentation of the collection reflected Fontana's assumption that the laws of nature would become unproblematically accessible to anyone 'at a glance' if the objects were perfect, if they were presented in a systematic manner, and if they could be taken in instantaneously.[5] As shown in Chapter 2, in Fontana's opinion the utility of the anatomical waxes was in their synoptic function and the possibility of combining different media: the simultaneous visibility of different anatomical components and their spatial relationships was supposed to enable the spectator to gain insights into the body's functioning. To facilitate this synoptic vision in practice, each wax model was accompanied by a drawing, and on the drawing each detail was given a separate number (plate IV). A list of those numbered details was provided in a drawer underneath to facilitate identification.[6] In addition, the full-size models of standing human bodies were mounted on rotating pedestals to allow for better visibility. With this synoptic mode of presentation, Fontana asserted, 'knowing how to read [was] sufficient for anyone at the museum to learn about natural history'.[7]

In practice, however, the display of accurate models by itself was not enough to turn visitors into civilised receptacles of natural knowledge. In addition to models inspired by sensationalist epistemology, Fontana and his colleagues also introduced a number of disciplinary measures at the museum to enable the educational encounter with natural objects and the subsequent development of common sense as envisioned by the Grand Duke. These disciplinary measures show that enlightenment theories of education were not the only factor determining the presentation and the reception of the collection at the museum; for an assessment of the models' display and reception it is equally important to take into account the museum's pragmatic concerns and visitors' diverging expectations.

Imposing discipline on model users, the museum retained a mix of egalitarian and elitist features. While the museum was open to everybody from its foundation in 1775, Fontana initially segregated commoners and 'genteel' visitors to ensure that the latter would not be disturbed by the presence of the populace. Lower-class visitors were admitted for the early tour in the morning from 8:30 to 10; the later tour from 10 to 12:30 (later at 1 p.m.) was reserved to 'lords and ladies, or very civilised persons such as physicians and lawyers'.[8] In general, porters were told by Fontana not to admit 'unsuitable, strange persons, and only a few peasants, but not too many'.[9] Entrance was free, and it was explicitly prohibited to tip the museum staff. However, admission was permitted only upon the presentation of admission tickets, which had to be requested at the museum in advance, and which were handed out daily from 4 to 6 in the afternoon by the custodian and the porters.

Fontana and Fabbroni may have encountered a similar ticketing system during their stay in London, which had been employed at the British Museum since its opening in 1759. While tickets for the British Museum were free of charge, the application process seems to have been made intentionally time-consuming so as to exclude all but the leisured classes.[10] At the Florentine museum, tickets were to be handed out in person only, except in the case of 'a respectable, and well-known person' who could send a servant to request them.[11] The names of those who had requested tickets for a given day were registered in a list, which was presented to the director and deputy director in the morning to enable them to decide whether 'it would be important for them to be present' to the group of visitors.[12] The custom of advance tickets was amended in 1788 to accommodate travellers from outside Florence. A total of 25 tickets were issued for each of the two tours in order to limit the size of groups; 18 were handed out in advance and seven were reserved to be handed out at the entrance to 'foreigners' (i.e. non-Tuscans) and 'people from the countryside'.[13] On the printed tickets, visitors were reminded to be punctual: '[Visitors] are advised that four or five minutes after the stipulated hour entry will not be permitted'.[14] In 1789, however, the sovereign abolished both the practice of segregation and the limits imposed on visitor numbers which contradicted his aims of social levelling and the most wide-ranging public education possible. From that point, all visitors were admitted at the same time, and average visitor numbers rose significantly.[15]

The popularity of the museum with all social classes was documented in visitors' books kept by the porters.[16] In addition to their names, in the case of visitors from outside Florence, or of high social standing, entries included profession, title and place or country of origin. The books followed established traditions of private collections that maintained visitors' books as a means of demonstrating the collection's prestige. However, unlike for instance the books kept by Ulisse Aldrovandi in the seventeenth century, which listed only male visitors of high status, in accordance with the museum's political mission of public enlightenment, the books at La Specola did apparently include all visitors regardless of rank, gender, or nationality.[17]

The books were occasionally used by the museum administration to justify additional expenses or demands for support such as requests for additional guards from the grand-ducal court.[18] They list a wide range of social and professional groups: nobility, professionals such as physicians, lawyers and civil servants, members of the court, foreign ambassadors, clerics, members of the Jewish community, especially from the Tuscan port town of Livorno, and travellers from all parts of Europe. The occupations of lower-class visitors, which accounted for more than half of the overall number of visitors, were not taken down. Visitor numbers were considerable: the journal of 1783/84, for example, lists 3351 early visitors and 2588 for the later tour; in 1787/88 the ratio was 12,809 against 9121. Single travellers came as well as various kinds of groups (male, female, and mixed); some repeated their visit. The frequency of families, the considerable percentage of female visitors (between a quarter and half) and the presence of all-female groups suggest that, true to Pietro Leopoldo's vision for the museum, the new institution was reaching wide parts of the population. The exhibition's subjects were evidently considered clean family fun for Florentine locals such as Signore Stefano Ciacchi, his wife Clotilde, and his daughters Teresa and Beatrice, who participated in the early morning tour on 9 June 1784.[19] The Grand Duke's restrictions on public entertainment seemed to succeed in directing his subjects towards educational venues.

Museum regulations further targeted the visual appearance of visitors, thus enforcing the cleanliness and levelling of social distinction which the Grand Duke wished to encourage. Upon entering the museum, visitors were asked not only to give their personal information for entry into the books; they were also required to leave behind items that were not seen fit to be carried into the exhibition, such as greatcoats, sticks, and weapons. Some upper-class visitors objected to this rule, mindful of the danger of theft, and a reluctance to part with objects indicative of social position and political rank.[20] In addition, persons who did not meet certain standards of clothing and cleanliness were turned away regardless of social standing.[21] One visitor, for instance, who claimed to be a Russian nobleman, attempted to enter the exhibition with long boots. Custodian Gagli refused the visitor admission, referring to the museum's rules (admitting, however, that director Fontana did not adhere to those rules himself when receiving visitors in person).[22] Similarly, Gagli admonished a group of courtiers to take off their cloaks, arguing that 'this was a rule which held for everybody'.[23] Visitors' complaints and porters' reports indicate that, by and large, such rules were enforced. The museum's administration did turn away individuals, sometimes permanently, if their appearance and comportment did not conform to the image of the civilised citizen which the museum was supposed to further.[24]

Throughout the late eighteenth century it remained customary for Fontana to be present when fellow naturalists and particularly high-ranking persons visited, or even to give them a personal guided tour outside of the collection's regular opening hours. Visiting practice at the museum could thus reintroduce elements of privilege, and it contributed to growing support among the learned and the powerful for Fontana's modelling enterprise. Only a select few visitors received a hands-on demonstration of the 'Venus', a reclining full-scale model of a pregnant woman whose abdomen could be taken apart to reveal the concealed foetus (plate III), and a demonstration of the rotation of the upright full-size human models on their pedestals.[25] This additional guidance helped elicit the desired responses in museum visitors, and would become Fabbroni's model for the practice of expertise at the museum.

However, Fontana maintained his conviction that visitors' encounters with a systematically presented collection, and especially with accurate anatomical models, was sufficient to enable the process of learning about underlying principles of order and functional relationships. Fontana's idea of intervention-free visits prevailed through the last decades of the eighteenth century, and visitors were given little guidance during their tours of the collection. They were initially shepherded through the collection by custodian Luigi Gagli, who lacked natural historical knowledge and was, therefore, unable to provide any explanations. In particular, visiting naturalists who did not receive the honour of a private tour with Fontana after hours complained about the impossibility of pacing their visit according to their own interests.[26] In response to this problem, in 1789 the Grand Duke ordered that visitors be allowed to wander freely among the specimens – to the concern of the administrators who fearing for the collections' integrity, requested additional guards, arguing that since the practice of handing out tickets in advance had been abolished the number of visitors per day had increased to an average of 100.[27]

Like the disciplinary measures, museum layout and display were shaped by a mix of ideological aims and pragmatic concerns. The exhibition was designed to support Fontana's and the Grand Duke's aims to make the exhibition easily intelligible by grouping specimens systematically in different rooms.[28] However, in some places this aim had to be reconciled with practical considerations of space and light. In 1783, the ground floor contained mostly administrative offices, and three particularly large rooms, which held the chemical laboratory, a room for the large quadrupeds, and the room devoted to Tuscan natural products, which was central to the museum's patriotic mission.[29] On the first floor, the physical instruments were displayed in smaller rooms sorted by subject such as mechanics, hydraulics, and optics. Sixteen smallish successive rooms on the second floor were destined for the anatomical waxes. The artificial anatomies were arranged according to conventions adopted from anatomy textbooks, which presented body parts classed by functions, such as muscles, nerves, and the lymphatic system. Each room contained a full-sized, full-body model at its centre providing an overview of the system in question. This overview was complemented by a wide range of models depicting smaller details, arranged around the walls of the room with corresponding drawings and tables (figure 6). The models devoted to the relationship between muscles and bones, for instance, began with a set of four skeletons in poses customarily used to demonstrate the function of ligaments. They were complemented by a further 150 detailed models which displayed the connections between smaller sets of muscles and bones.[30] Similarly, the myological collection centred around four rotating full-body statues, supported by 150 smaller models which followed the work of Albinus, presenting the muscles first in analytical order from outer to inner layers, and subsequently in synthetic order, representing their composition.[31] Thus, as Thomas Schnalke has argued, the anatomical collection at La Specola provided a hybrid between eighteenth-century private cabinets and dissection theatres, presenting the elements of the normal human body systematically and in three dimensions.[32]

Other rooms contained fishes, reptiles, birds, plants, and mineral and wood samples. Like the anatomical collection, the botanical and zoological sections took care to display the most up-to-date knowledge, drawing especially on the Linnaean system of classification.[33] The plant specimens were of different kinds: in addition to living plants preserved at the botanical garden, dried plants were presented sewn onto paper.[34] Other types of plants which could not be dried easily, such as succulents and fragile blossoms, were copied in wax.[35] Entire plants were accompanied by detached blossoms 'for the use of botanists' who were presumably familiar with Linnaeus' system of plant classification.[36] Like the anatomical models, animal and plant specimens were accompanied by labels; in the botanical garden those were made of lead so as to be weather-resistant.[37] Drawings of plants and animals were also made, and schematic tables mounted on the walls highlighted the exhibition's systematic character by showing for each room the order of the branch of natural history presented.[38] Animals were usually taxidermised, and occasionally touched up by the modellers with waxen details. Bird specimens were displayed on branches of trees.[39] Animal models made entirely from wax were rarely produced until the introduction of comparative anatomy at the museum in the early 1800s, investigated further in Chapter 6.[40]

From October 1793, the showrooms were labelled with Roman numerals to enable visitors touring the exhibition on their own to follow the appropriate order of collections.[41] The Grand Duke continued to take an active interest in shaping the museum visitor's experience, suggesting, in 1783, that the museum should have a room for the reception of foreigners on the second floor, by the entrance to the anatomical model collection – recognising that the anatomical waxes were the most popular of the museum's exhibits.

The museum's intention of giving equal access to all visitors was mirrored in the style in which the collection was presented, and which was markedly different from previous early modern cabinets of curiosities. In the sixteenth and seventeenth centuries, noble collectors in Florence had practised a form of subtle concealment: the furniture in which artefacts were stored was often adorned with allegorical or symbolic images which, for erudite observers, hinted at the hidden content, although only privileged visitors were given access to the inside. The furniture was therefore designed for specific objects and a specific order of display: they were not interchangeable.[42] At the Medici residences, the display of *naturalia* and *mirabilia* became in this way integrated into absolutist court ceremony.[43] At the royal villa Poggio Reale in Florence, for instance, in the mid-seventeenth to early eighteenth century, the furniture along the visitor's path towards the audience hall was presented in order of increasing splendour.[44] At La Specola, however, administrators made efforts to produce perfectly uniform showcases for all objects. All showcases were enclosed by glass, thus affording full visibility. Their design was of equal magnificence for all types of specimens: minerals, wax models and animals alike were enclosed in cases made from valuable woods.[45] Except for their size, which was adapted to the objects inside, all showcases were therefore interchangeable.[46]

At the same time, an investigation into their reception indicates that despite the attempted homogeneity some objects drew more attention than others. The administration's efforts to elicit specific, civilised modes of reception notwithstanding, museum visitors reacted to the exhibition and the anatomical waxes in a variety of ways that were shaped by different frames of reference, and which frequently differed from the administration's aims.

Visitors' frames of reference

As shown, the Grand Duke restricted public entertainment in order to prevent 'useless dissipation', but Tuscans still had a range of visually appealing spectacles available to them, some centred around the display of bodies. Forms of public spectacle in Florence, which museum visitors may have used as frames of reference for making sense of La Specola, included courtly celebrations, religious and civil processions, the carnival, athletic games, and plays by local and itinerant troupes. The court celebrated events such as the visits of foreign monarchs, royal births, and coronations. These celebrations were open to all members of the public, 'if decently dressed'.[47] They were highly organised and included dance, theatrical machines and illuminations, as well as enrolling the local clergy for processions and donations to the poor. Descriptions of these celebrations were published soon afterwards.

While commoners probably did not attend the public anatomy lectures held at the hospital Santa Maria Nuova, they would have been familiar with the sight of dead bodies or body parts, which were frequently displayed during civil or religious processions. The funeral of the last Medici Grand Duke, for instance, was preceded by a public viewing of his corpse.[48] Religious processions in particular displayed human bodies in events which, according to Pelli, had devolved into popular entertainment.[49] Florence owned the relics of sixteen saints and martyrs, especially of the city's patron saint John the Baptist, which were displayed in public on high holidays and touched or kissed for their supposedly beneficial powers.[50]

The tradition of votive images and effigies afforded a more permanent display of images of bodies and body parts in a religious and civic context. Wax effigies of officeholders and saints were central elements of Florentine processions and church displays.[51] Votive offerings, images of afflicted body parts in coloured wax and other materials bore witness to miracle cures and saints' responses to prayers.[52] The largest of these collections in Florence was held at the church Santissima Annunziata. In 1785, the ever practical-minded Pietro Leopoldo ordered its destruction, since 'the votives obstruct the beautiful pictures there, and are a nest for dust'.[53] The Prior of SS. Annunziata, Giuliano Piermei, shared the Grand Duke's enlightened zeal and, according to a contemporary report, promptly carried out 'a massacre of all those votives', which met with the 'displeasure of many'.[54]

Other images of bodies in wax were portrait busts, which sculptors produced for the nobility and affluent commoners.[55] In addition to models of bodies and body parts such as votives, there were some occasions to see real human and animal bodies. Educated Tuscans were familiar with natural historical specimens through private cabinets.[56] Less privileged Florentines had to be content with travelling shows in order to encounter marvels such as exotic animals and monsters.[57] On Pietro Leopoldo's departure and accession to the imperial throne in Vienna in 1790, discipline in enforcing his anti-spectacular legislation lapsed. Popular religious practices were reinstated,[58] and travelling showmen readmitted.[59] The latter group included travelling lecturers such as French experimental philosopher François Bienvenu, who gave public demonstration courses in Florence in 1792 for subscribers by permission of Grand Duke Ferdinando III. Bienvenu's course in twelve sessions was in line with the mainstream of experimental lecture classes in the late eighteenth century; it included demonstrations of electrical phenomena from Leyden jar experiments to artificial lightning destroying a model palace, the beneficial effects of the new lightning rod, galvanism, and magnetism among others.[60] Apparently, Bienvenu did not have much competition in Florence for his kind of educational entertainment – Pelli lamented this scarcity as a 'dishonour to Florentine culture'.[61] Bienvenu's class was a commercial success, and he returned in 1795.[62] This local response suggests that La Specola with its lack of public lectures and demonstrations apparently did not by itself exhaust public interest in natural knowledge, although it seems to have whetted public appetite for natural knowledge as Pietro Leopoldo had intended.

Visitors' experiences were shaped in part by their knowledge of alternative forms of spectacle, but were equally coloured by the purpose of their visit, especially in the case of visitors from outside the city. Tuscany was an important destination for eighteenth-century travellers for a number of reasons. To scholars of history, literature and art it offered rich remains of antiquity and renaissance. The Grand Duchy's new status as a model state since Pietro Leopoldo's accession also made it interesting to travellers who were more interested in current affairs: young noblemen preparing for their future responsibilities, administrators, entrepreneurs, and political and economic theorists who wished to observe Pietro Leopoldo's 'laboratory' of reform at first hand.[63] The Russian crown prince Paul Petrovich, for instance, visited the Tuscan capital in March 1782; he was guided not only to places of architectural or historical interest, but especially to sites of enlightened reforms, such as the Royal Museum of Physics and Natural History, the orphanage, and the hospital Santa Maria Nuova.[64] Just as European travel could serve different means, so the encounter with the artificial anatomies was framed within these different perspectives, and to different outcomes.

Visitors' responses

Various measures including the imposition of discipline, and model features like the accompanying schematic drawings were intended to shape visitors' experiences of the artificial anatomies and to elicit the desired responses. Visitors' accounts of their encounters with La Specola's waxes indicate that the museum's measures were not always successful. Not surprisingly, perhaps, some visitors who benefitted from a personal guided tour with Fontana adopted his view of the model collection when the director interpreted the museum experience for them on the spot. This is reflected clearly in enthusiastic descriptions that echoed Fontana's intentions. In contrast, other visitors produced accounts of their experiences which deviated significantly from the directors, and the Grand Duke's, visions for public enlightenment. Pietro Leopoldo's mission for the museum and Fontana's concept of learning with perfect models were supported most vocally by two medical practitioners, the French surgeon René Desgenettes (1762–1837) and the German physician Engelbert Wichelhausen (1760–1814). Both received the privilege of guided tours with Fontana, Desgenettes in 1789 and Wichelhausen in 1794, and their published accounts of La Specola illustrated how the 'ideal visitor' should respond to the collection. Both visitors extolled the virtues of La Specola as a model institution in every sense: they praised the anatomical models as beautiful and accurate, ascribed the achievement to the genius and tireless effort of director Fontana, and hailed the artificial anatomies as excellent tools both for professional education and public enlightenment.

La Specola's 'ideal visitors' celebrated the anatomical models' 'accuracy' and their mode of presentation which, in combination, made the models ideal tools of public education.[65] Desgenettes and Wichelhausen claimed that at the Florentine museum anatomical modelling had achieved perfection, representing 'with scrupulous exactness the immense number of details', combining the highest degree of 'elegance, precision and truth'.[66] The Grand Duke had shown 'true sovereign grandeur' in giving the museum 'unrestricted freedom'. However, it was the 'universally celebrated' savant Fontana, a 'great scholar and artist' of 'immortal reputation', of 'noble character' and 'unforced humility', who had made the museum 'the first in Europe'.[67] The models' perfection was due to Fontana's 'deep natural knowledge, plentiful artistry, iron patience, and felicitous genius'.[68] To make accurate models, the producers had to combine anatomical and artisanal knowledge, as well as 'the art of the genius, to make the results of comparisons between multiple preparations vivid in the most intelligible and natural manner'.[69] Both Desgenettes and Wichelhausen echoed Fontana's view of model production and his own role in it, asserting that the anatomist's surveillance of modellers' work was indispensable for their accuracy: 'without this surveillance, the most excellent sculptors would never copy nature with exactness'.[70] Fontana, then, was the true creator of the models, owing to his 'genius', his 'profound knowledge', and his 'tireless efforts'.[71]

The two visitors further confirmed Fontana's view of how the models should be designed and presented to their users. Unlike preparations of real body parts, the wax models represented body parts in their correct position, volume, and colour.[72] They displayed the living, healthy body rather than the corrupted one.[73] The presentation of the artificial anatomies in their wooden shrines was 'opulent, tasteful' and 'appropriate'.[74] They were displayed in such a way that model users could 'commit them to memory in their position and connection much more easily than on a real corpse'.[75] Desgenettes' positive description of the director's combination of models with schematic drawings and lists of details, in particular, echoed the description in the 1775 *Saggio*, down to the assertion that this new method of presentation would 'facilitate and accelerate study in a singular manner', since it allowed model users to 'grasp clearly and quickly very complicated matters'.[76]

Both French and German model user singled out the synoptic vision afforded through measures such as the rotating pedestals of upright full-body statues.[77] This was also reflected in the decision to adhere to the convention of presenting arteries in red and veins in blue.[78] The medical practitioners applauded the fact that the models represented 'the most interesting new discoveries', and drew on the authoritative images of renowned anatomists from Albinus to Winslow.[79] Desgenettes declared that the anatomical knowledge on display, especially the models produced with Mascagni's help, had enlightened his own ideas about the lymphatic system. He professed to regret that he could not revise his own publication on the subject, *Analyse du système absorbent ou lymphatique*.[80]

Importantly, the two medical practitioners celebrated the models' political uses. They hailed the museum as a continuation and apogee of earlier Tuscan politics of supporting the sciences, begun under the Medici and continued under the 'popular' Pietro Leopoldo.[81] The modelling enterprise, in particular, was of the highest public utility for a number of reasons. Anatomy was 'the fundamental basis of the art of healing', and the models could be particularly useful to surgery and obstetrics.[82] However, the models could benefit a wide range of users, from medical practitioners to anthropologists, artists, and even ladies, who could thus study anatomy without disgust.[83] Desgenettes suggested that similar collections should be adopted by governments elsewhere to become part of 'all collections devoted to culture and the advancement of the natural sciences', for 'the contemplation and meditation of philosophers and physicians' alike.[84] Wichelhausen urged 'humane sovereigns' to adopt the Florentine idea 'for the instruction and utility of the people'.[85] The models would be particularly suitable for the instruction of 'untutored classes of people' as 'the coarse mob is sensual'.[86]

Despite these affirmations of Fontana's vision, visitors' responses differed widely when they were not personally guided around the exhibition as Wichelhausen and Desgenettes had been. The museum's visitors' books indicate a wide range of social groups who came to see the collection, from the high nobility to Grand Tour travellers, local intellectuals and Wichelhausen's 'coarse mob'. Apparently, the wax anatomies were the most popular part of the exhibition: they were singled out in travellers' written accounts, and floor repairs in the model section indicate higher visitor traffic there than elsewhere in the building.[87] From the perspective of museum visitors, the function of

the collections, and particularly of the anatomical models, was not fully determined by their form of presentation. In the absence of verbal instructions or
printed guides, visitors appropriated the collections in their own ways.[88] In
museum studies, this phenomenon has recently attracted attention as an argument against the field's initial interpretation of the museum as a disciplinary
institution based on a 'totalitarian' reading of Foucault. To highlight the
fact that visitors could, and did, resist attempts at coercion, museum historians have begun to reconstruct historical museum visitors' responses. Only
relatively recently, however, have analysts highlighted that this interpretive
flexibility is not tantamount to arbitrariness.[89] This section contributes to
these new historical studies of museums by reconstructing the wide range
of responses from La Specola's audiences. Visitors perceived the artificial
anatomies, for example, as tools for the study of medicine, as displays of
artisanal and scientific accomplishment, or as occasions for moral or religious
contemplation.

Visitors with no profound knowledge of natural history and natural philosophy tended to praise the collection, and especially the anatomical models,
for both their quality and quantity. Depending on visitors' primary interests,
'quality' in their accounts could mean very different things such as aesthetic
appeal, accuracy, or value. The British merchant Brooke, for instance, whose
Observations on the Manners and Customs of Italy of 1798 were intended to
benefit British trade with Italy, praised the museum's collection for its 'quantity
and rarity'. The main selection criterion, according to Brooke, was whether
Fontana found an object 'valuable'; he did not specify what this value would
consist of.[90] In the case of visitors without a medical or natural philosophical
background the Grand Duke's strategy of putting a celebrated naturalist in
charge of the museum paid off. Non-specialists did not question the models'
accuracy, but relied on Fontana's reputation to guarantee it, where they
commented on it at all.

The Reverend John Chetwood Eustace, for instance, who travelled to
Florence in 1802 with his tutees, conceived of his journey to Italy as a means to
elevate the educated over mechanics and labourers, mainly by tracing similarities and differences between ancient and modern Italy. Without further explanation, he mentioned 'the cabinet of anatomical preparations in wax, made
under the inspection of Cav. Fontana, the first in number, beauty, and exact
conformity to the human frame, in Europe'.[91] The Marquis Malaspina, who
had served in the Spanish army and at the court of the King of Naples, was an
experienced courtier who realised the value of the collection for the sovereign's
public image, and singled out the museum's function as a monument to the
Tuscan sovereign. For him, the collection of anatomical waxes was 'the most

rare and surprising part of the Cabinet' due both to 'the excellent quality of the works and for the diffuse quantity of pieces', without, however, elaborating how he assessed the models' quality.[92]

The French magistrate Charles Dupaty in his *Sentimental Letters on Italy* of 1789 considered travel an opportunity to study human nature through empathetic observation. He praised the museum's collection for its 'elegance', 'order', and 'distribution'. Dupaty agreed with Pietro Leopoldo and Fontana in ascribing to the artificial anatomies the power to reveal natural phenomena and convey strong messages. For the French visitor, however, the museum's central purpose was to present 'the brilliant phenomenon of life' in all its forms: 'wandering from kingdom to kingdom' in the exhibition was for him a way of 'following nature distributing motion to all organised forms'.[93] The collection of anatomical models provided 'a complete image of [man]', an understanding of the organic functions which give rise to life, but ultimately an opportunity for moral contemplation:

> You see the most secret pieces of so complicated a machine; some loosen and separate at first, then assemble and re-unite, quite ready to perform, in concert with the general economy of the human body, in their turn, and in their places, the function that concerns them: they are quite ready for life. . . .
>
> The examining a few minutes the neurologic system [sic], made me discover several secrets. Philosophy has been wrong, in not examining still deeper the physical parts of man; it is there the moral man is hidden. The outward man is but the type of the inward one.[94]

The French painter Elisabeth Vigée-Lebrun[95] reported a similar feeling of awe on her visit to the anatomical model collection in 1792. However, the artist was overwhelmed not, as the Grand Duke would have it, by the realisation of the law-like character of nature and its potential to further public happiness, or by the revelation of 'moral man' like her fellow countryman Dupaty. Her revelation was a religious one: the anatomical models were evidence of the existence of a deity; they thus refuted current materialistic philosophies.

> It is not possible to contemplate the structure of the human body without feeling convinced of some divine power. Despite what a few miserable philosophers have dared to say, in M. Fontana's laboratory one kneels and believes.[96]

As in other cases, though, one should not take this description as an unmediated report of her response, but rather as an account framed by the circumstances of its emergence. As Mary Sheriff has argued, Vigée-Lebrun's description of her intense emotional reaction to the artificial human bodies served to highlight her sensibilities, and thus to justify her claims to be an artist, which was challenged by contemporaries on account of her gender.[97]

For visitors of a more natural historical bent, the models' accuracy was of more concern than their moral, philosophical, or religious implications, and they were less inclined to accept the models at face value on the basis of Fontana's reputation. James Edward ('Botany') Smith,[98] first president of the Linnaean Society in London, in his *Sketch of a Tour on the Continent* (1807) promoted natural historical observations while on travels as providing 'a most commendable, disinterested, and delightful tie' to transcend religious and national boundaries. For this same purpose, he included 'an account of various cultivators and teachers of that study'. He praised the models' use for preserving myological structures: 'The muscles are imitated better than the rest, and are very useful; as those parts cannot be well preserved by injections nor any other means.' Smith compared the Florentine models favourably to other anatomical imitations, such as those at the Bologna Institute of Science, which he considered to be 'very good, though less beautiful than the anatomical models at Florence'.[99]

Adam Walker, a lecturer in experimental philosophy, shared James Smith's interest in the accuracy of the artificial anatomies.[100] Like Smith, he stressed that his judgement was based on his knowledge of and comparison with other collections: 'the anatomical imitations in wax, exceed in correctness, number, and elegance all the collections I have seen in England or France'. Walker was one of the few visitors to take notice of, and comment on, the way the collection was 'classed, according to the Linean [sic] system, with great learning and taste; with a manuscript description in a drawer under each class'.[101] However, apart from Wichelhausen and Desgenettes none of the visitors commented on the anatomical models' special synoptic mode of presentation in which director Fontana took such pride.

Little information is available concerning the comportment of the many visitors who did not leave written accounts. However, receipts and other documents pertaining to collection maintenance show that the carefully developed mode of presentation did not always shape public behaviour in the way intended. Rules for civilised comportment had to be reinforced by technical means: in response to damages and thefts, locks were applied to display cases of fragile objects like corals, and those that appealed to roving hands, such as wet specimens of monstrous foetuses and wax models of genitals.[102] Such behaviour can be explained in a number of ways: visitors may have perceived of their visits as similar to other encounters with artificial or preserved bodies in the form of votives and relics, which were frequently touched at religious processions and in churches. Similarly, at art exhibitions displays of sculptures may have been touched since some contemporary theories of aesthetic perception considered touch necessary for the full appreciation of such works of art.[103] The public exhibition of body parts, including both male and female genitals, apparently did not create any public outcry, and families and mixed groups continued to visit. A Scottish visitor in Florence speculated that the lack of indignation among locals was due to their regular exposure to public representations of naked bodies: the 'statues which ornament the streets and squares of Florence . . . without any drapery, continually exposed to the public eye . . . have produced, in both sexes, the most perfect insensibility to nudities'. [104]

Thus, the museum visit was shaped by a number of factors. Ideas about public education held by the sovereign and the museum's administration were important, but not the only influences constitutive of the collections' public exposure. Other factors contributing to the way in which the collection was presented and perceived include pragmatic concerns, especially for damage, new practices of specimen acquisition, and expectations and experiences brought by museum visitors.

Museum naturalists' responses: Fontana's wood anatomy and Fabbroni's performance of expertise

Visitors' divergent responses posed a problem for the museum's teaching strategy, based on the assumption that perfect models would by themselves produce the desired public enlightenment in the audience. Fontana and Fabbroni accounted for this discrepancy is two ways: either the wax models were not as suitable as initially believed, or the very assumption that suitable models were sufficient was false. Accordingly, the two naturalists acted on this observation in different ways.

Fontana continued to insist that suitable representations would suffice. From the late 1780s, the director began to develop new teaching aids, experimenting with wood to create detachable anatomical models. Contrary to his earlier arguments that functional relationships between body parts might be apprehended through synoptic presentation, Fontana now argued that

> the anatomical waxes made by me . . . are of the greatest utility for anatomy, but the waxes are many separated parts, or members of the body, which do not form a whole; neither can they. They do not give an idea of the entirety, they do not demonstrate the relationships, the sites, the positions, the connections between them and to the body as a whole.[105]

Accordingly, Fontana moved from the fragile wax to a more robust material (figure 9).

He employed a carpenter to begin the production of a full-scale, decomposable wooden model of a man, claiming that

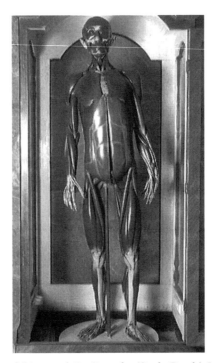

9 Fontana's model in wood, La Specola. (Saulo Bambi, Museo di Storia
Naturale, Florence)

Decomposing man piece by piece and putting him back together as he was
before, is certainly the easiest, and the most useful study for the understanding
of the very composite machine of the human body, and all of this can be done in
hours with the anatomy in wood.[106]

Fontana did not specify how the wooden model should be used, who should
have access, and how. Importantly, however, he suggested that the process of
taking apart and reassembling was indispensable for an understanding of spatial relationships. Fontana stressed that the wooden model enabled the user to
perform an 'analysis and synthesis', a 'decomposition and composition' of the
body.[107] Visitors who were given access to the wooden anatomy's prototype
did not handle the models themselves; 'dissection' was carried out by a servant.[108] Describing the potential use of the models by medical students in a letter
to his friend Caldani, Fontana highlighted that students should 'handle' the
models physically – the hands-off nature of the demonstrations for privileged
visitors thus may have been due to their high status.[109]

As for the earlier wax models, for the wooden model Fontana repeatedly stressed that only those knowledgeable in anatomy could evaluate the artificial anatomies. At the same time, he also claimed that once ascertained of their accuracy, the same models could by themselves, without the aid of a teacher or textbook, turn a student into 'a great naturalist, a great anatomist with the greatest ease, and in very little time'.[110] Fontana thus remained convinced that the expert's role in the project of using anatomical models for public enlightenment was in model production to ensure their accuracy, but not in the subsequent process of model use.

The director pursued the wood model for years despite repeated failures. While he had initially been convinced that he would need only the help of a carpenter but not the modellers for this project, once more, as in the case of the wax models, he ultimately had to request their support, thus distracting them from completing the anatomical waxes. It turned out, however, that wood was not well suited to illustrate minute details, and the material was unstable. Changes in temperature and humidity distorted the wooden models to the point where they were no longer detachable, and according to a report by anatomist Bonicoli the first prototype was reworked many times without success.[111] To support his project against the criticism of his colleagues at the museum, who considered it useless and wasteful, Fontana once more cited the judgement of his peers, which he had already invoked with regard to the wax models' accuracy:

> This [the superiority of wooden models] is not just my opinion, but that of all those who have visited Florence in previous years, and who are in a position to judge, because they are knowledgeable in anatomy and have no interest in slander.[112]

Despite Fontana's relentless efforts, the wooden anatomy remained a work in progress until his death in 1805.

Fontana's admission of the wax models' insufficiency for public education, and his fruitless efforts to develop alternative, decomposable models, were grist to the mill of his former student, current deputy director, and eventual rival, Giovanni Fabbroni. Fabbroni opposed Fontana's project of modelling in wood as a waste of time and public resources, and used it as an opportunity to articulate his own view on the staging of expertise. For him, the explanation for the wax models' failure was not their lack of perfection. Instead, he claimed, the very assumption that artificial anatomies could produce public enlightenment by themselves was incorrect. As Fontana's assistant, Fabbroni had initially contributed to model production himself, but over the course of the 1780s and 1790s he became increasingly vocal about his scepticism concerning the models' utility in their current mode of presentation. While Fontana had for a long time maintained that the models' synoptic presentation was sufficient to enable any visitor to acquire knowledge of the human body, and continued to insist that suitable models would enable model users to learn about functional relationships by themselves, Fabbroni took a position which insisted on the indispensable presence of a knowledgeable teacher not only in model production, but in model reception as well. He claimed that without an expert's instruction and explanation neither the anatomical waxes nor the new wood anatomies could be of use for general public education. After the death of Luigi Gagli in 1795, Fabbroni recommended that the court hire a naturalist for the post of museum custodian rather than another administrator. In his report to the court, Fabbroni stressed that

> the live voice of someone knowledgeable in the matter renders much more useful those magnificent rarities, creates true instruction in the studious, and more delight in simple observers. And it is never the case, or it should never be the case that Nations, and Sovereigns, amass treasures by collecting and preserving productions of nature and of the human spirit only for a sterile and odious display.[113]

He stressed repeatedly that a person highly qualified in anatomy would be able to present the models together with instruction such as public lectures. Without such instruction by an expert, Fabbroni insisted, the collection would remain fruitless.[114] He compared the situation in Florence to public collections elsewhere, which were presided over by knowledgeable 'men of letters', such as the British Museum and the Paris Muséum d'histoire naturelle that was headed by the anatomist Daubenton.[115] The French museum's success, he implied, was due to the presence of the renowned anatomical expert in the public exhibition, which should be emulated at La Specola 'to render the anatomical model collection useful for public education one day'.[116] The repeated success of the public lecture courses of François Bienvenu in 1792 and 1795 may have contributed to Fabbroni's conviction that a teacher's presence and explanations were superior to unaccompanied encounters with natural, or natural philosophical objects. The election of an accomplished naturalist to the position of curator, he pointed out, was not only necessary for turning the exhibition into an effective tool for public education. The election of a layperson would also endanger the public esteem of the museum. On a more pragmatic level, in line with his general stance on expertise in state service, Fabbroni argued that an expert naturalist would also be a better civil servant in the position as a curator, since only a knowledgeable individual would be aware of the requirements for the collection's maintenance, and therefore could be held responsible by his superiors.[117]

Despite Fabbroni's suggestion to supplement the collection with lectures, changes in instructional methods practised at the Royal Museum had to wait until Fontana's demise in 1805. His absence, and the changing political situation under different regimes, gave the museum's new administration, under Fabbroni and Girolamo de' Bardi, opportunities to modify the collection's public presentation – including the introduction of taught courses, which is pursued further in Chapter 6.

Conclusion

The museum director's strategies for public education were informed by contemporary sensationalist theories of learning. Director Fontana in particular tried to incorporate these ideas in the display of objects and in the design of the anatomical models through the combination of different media (models, images, text) for a synoptic mode of presentation.[118] Such a mode of presentation, he claimed, would allow users to grasp immediately the underlying functional relationships between body parts. At the same time, the museum's naturalists attempted to control not only the collection on display, but also the visitors themselves, in order to bring about educational encounters. Prescriptions for visitor behaviour and appearance aimed at creating a civilised audience that was receptive to the museum's enlightenment mission. However, not surprisingly, travellers' accounts and administrative sources indicate that these attempts at control did not fully preclude visitors from appropriating the collection in different ways, be it as occasions for moral contemplation, for natural historical study, or entertainment. A number of measures taken in museum display, such as the introduction of locks to showcases, were a direct response to visitor behaviour – these practical contingencies shaped the exhibition as well as theories of learning or enlightened reform policies.

A comparison between intended purposes for the collection and its public reception highlights the limits of expert naturalists' agency. As producers and evaluators of models and preparations, the museum naturalists had the authority to determine what the normal human body looked like. However, such normative power fell flat when museum visitors appropriated the anatomical models and zoological specimens, not as representations of natural law, but as curiosities, works of art, or objects of moral contemplation. In support of recent historical studies of museum reception, the example of La Specola shows that everyday practices of museum visiting and its regulation strike a balance between coercion and flexibility. The study thus highlights the importance, in historical studies of collections and exhibitions, of supplementing normative documents pertaining to exhibition management with sources which can serve to reconstruct practice as it differs from prescription.

The models' meanings and functions were reinterpreted both by their audience and by the naturalists themselves.[119] Fontana and Fabbroni agreed that the models were part of a civilising mission, but disagreed as to what should be the models' place in this mission, and their own role as experts. In his accounts of the back-stage process of model production, Fontana had maintained that the presence of a knowledgeable naturalist was indispensable in creating accurate representations, but not necessary for the visitor's front-stage encounter with the artificial anatomies. In his view, the exhibition of accurate and suitable models would by itself enable the visitor to see the underlying laws of nature for him- or herself. The director maintained this position even when faced with discrepancies between his own expectations and visitors' comportment. Fontana's response was to change the models' features in a way which would leave the naturalist's role apparently unchanged. With the wood anatomies, as with the waxen ones, Fontana maintained that the naturalist's job was to guarantee the representations' accuracy, submitted only to the judgement of his peers.

Unlike him, Fabbroni turned to the envisioned general public.[120] In response to the lack of success in the museum's educational mission, the museum's second-in-command created a different image of knowledge production at the museum and the naturalist's role vis-à-vis the models. Fabbroni pushed the argument for the expert naturalist further, claiming that the naturalist's presence was necessary not only back-stage in model production to ensure the validity and efficacy of the objects, but also front-stage, mediating visitors' encounters with the artificial anatomies. This mediating presence, Fabbroni insisted, was indispensable for turning the encounter to pedagogical account. Thus, the audience for natural laws would become an audience for expertise. The naturalist's position was defined both in model production and in model use.

The context-dependency of model use is pursued further in the following two chapters. Chapter 5 investigates the reception of a set of Florentine models sent to the Vienna military medico-surgical academy Josephinum in the 1780s to highlight the fragile status of the artificial anatomies as tools of enlightenment. Once more, the tension between education and entertainment became salient in the Vienna case. The final chapter then returns to Florence to investigate the model collection's fate under changing political regimes.

Notes

1 For the framing of museum reception, see e.g. Sharon Macdonald, *Behind the scenes at the Science Museum* (Oxford: Berg, 2002), esp. ch. 8, 'The active audience and the politics of appropriation'.

2 For the problem of reconstructing museum reception given the nature of the available documentation and the historical specificity of visitors' experiences see e.g. Samuel Alberti, 'The museum affect: visiting collections of anatomy and natural history', in Bernard Lightman and Aileen Fyfe (eds), *Science in the marketplace: nineteenth-century sites and experiences* (Chicago: Chicago University Press, 2007), pp. 371-403. A 'reconstruction' of visitors' experiences and Fontana's didactic intentions by art historian Gabriele Dürbeck is based on her impressions of the exhibition itself; a problematic approach, given that the variety of visitor responses highlight the impossibility to ascribe a single meaning to the models, and to discover this meaning by letting the artifacts 'speak for themselves' (even though this was what Fontana claimed). Gabriele Dürbeck, 'Empirischer und ästhetischer Sinn: Strategien der Vermittlung von Wissen in der anatomischen Wachsplastik um 1800', in Gabriele Dürbeck et al. (eds), *Wahrnehmung der Natur, Natur der Wahrnehmung. Studien zur Geschichte visueller Kultur um 1800* (Dresden: Verlag der Kunst, 2001), pp. 35-54.

3 For different ways of framing travel narratives in the eighteenth century see Charles Batten, *Pleasurable instruction: form and convention in eighteenth-century travel literature* (Berkeley: University of California Press, 1978).

4 For Condillac as the likely source for Fontana's ideas about learning see Renato G. Mazzolini, 'Plastic anatomies and artificial dissections', in Soraya de Chadarevian and Nick Hopwood (eds), *Models: the third dimension of science* (Stanford: Stanford University Press, 2004), pp. 43-70, p. 56.

5 See e.g. Anon., *Saggio del Real Gabinetto di Fisica, e di Storia Naturale di Firenze* (Roma: Giovanni Zempel, 1775), pp. 29-30: 'Everything remains well enclosed on the shelves by majestic and great glass panes, and at *one glance everything is seen, everything is known.* The symmetry that reigns within and without the shelves, the order and regularity of the pieces is such that it captivates the observer, and at the same time it instructs and delights him.' ('Ogni cosa resta ben serrata negli scaffali da maestosi, e grandi cristalli, e *a un colpo d'ochio tutto si vede, tutto si conosce.* La simetria, che regna dentro e furi degli scaffali, l'ordine, e la regolarità dei pezzi, è tale, e sì nuova, che rapisce l'osservatore, e nel tempo medesimo lo istruisce, e diletta'.) (Italics A.M.).

6 Fontana claimed that 'this new method is excellent for knowing at once the anatomical parts in relationship to their place both on the model and on the drawing'. ('Certo è, che questo nuovo metodo è eccellente per conoscere ad un tratto le parti anatomiche relativamente al sito sulla figura, o disegno'.) Anon., *Saggio*, p. 33.

7 '[B]asta saper leggere per imparare di presente la storia naturale da chicchessia dentro il Real Museo.' Biblioteca Rosminiana, Rovereto, manoscritti di Felice Fontana, faldone 28.B.110, fol. 8r-8v. Quoted from Simone Contardi, *La Casa di Salomone a Firenze. L'Imperiale e Reale Museo di Fisica e Storia Naturale (1775-1801)* (Florence: Olschki, 2002), p. 167.

8 IMSS–ARMU, Filza di negozi dell'anno 1789A, fol. 220; 'Cavalieri, Dame, o persone molto civili, come medici, Avvocati, e Simili', *ibid.*, fol. 279.

9 '[P]ersone mal proprie, straniate, e solo qualche contadino, ma non . . . troppo', ibid., fol. 278v, 279.

10 Edward Miller, *That noble cabinet. A history of the British Museum* (London: Andre Deutsch, 1973), pp. 62–3.

11 '[P]ersona civile, e conosciuta'; IMSS–ARMU, Filza di negozi dell'anno 1789A, fol. 218 v (n.d.).

12 'Fatta dal custode La Lista di quei, che avranno domandate di vedere il Museo, dovrà egli mandarla al direttore La mattina alle otto, perché il Fabbroni, o il direttore conoscano se importi, o nò di trovarsi anch'essi presenti'. IMSS–ARMU, Filza di negozi dell'anno 1789A, fol. 219.

13 '[F]orestieri', 'gente di Campagna', IMSS–ARMU, Filza di negozi dell'anno 1789A, fol. 279 (doc. 63), 'Regolamento per La Gente del basso servizio del Real Museo' (probably 21 June 1788).

14 '[P]assato quattro, o cinque minuti dopo l'ora prefissa non sarà altrimenti permesso l'ingresso nella Sopraindicata mattina'. IMSS–ARMU, Filza di negozi dell'anno 1789B, fol. 90, 92 (doc. 144).

15 IMSS–ARMU, Filza di negozi dell'anno 1790, fol. 57r, Fontana's report to the Grand Duke (probably 12 December 1789).

16 IMSS–ARMU, 'Giornale del Reale Museo dal 1783 al tutto il 1784 nel 7bre'; 'Segue il Giornale dal di 24. 8bre 1785 fino al di 18. Maggio 1787'; 'Libro in cui vien registrato tutte le persone che vengono a vedere il R. Museo del 21. Maggio del 1787 al 1788 fino al di 12 Luglio 1788'. For a quantitative analysis of one of the visitor books, see also Renato G. Mazzolini, 'Visitors to Florence's R. Museum of Physics and Natural History from September 1784 to October 1785', *Nuncius* 21:2 (2006), pp. 337–48. For changing uses of visitors' books, see e.g. Sharon Macdonald, 'Accessing audiences: visiting visitor books', *Museum and society 3* (2006), pp. 119–36; Liesbet Nys, 'The public's signatures: visitors' books in nineteenth-century museums', *Museum history journal* 2:2 (2009), pp. 143–61.

17 Paula Findlen, *Possessing nature: museums, collecting, and scientific culture in early modern Italy* (Berkeley: University of California Press, 1994), pp. 136–46.

18 IMSS–ARMU, Filza di negozi dell'anno 1790, fol. 57r, Fontana's report to the Grand Duke (probably 12 December 1789).

19 IMSS–ARMU, 'Giornale del Reale Museo dal 1783 al tutto il 1784 nel 7bre' (9 June 1784).

20 IMSS–ARMU, Filza di negozi dell'anno 1799, fol. 39 (doc. 27), 'Istruzioni Per Le Guardie destinate alle pubbliche Ostensioni del Museo di Fisica, e Storia Naturale': 'Una di esse Guardie starà sul Portone d'ingresso, ed'altra nel Vestibolo a Capo Scala p[er] far deporre il Ferrajuolo, Pastrano, o Pelliccia, Spada, Sciabla, e Bastone, e permettere l'ingresso alle Persone decentemente vestite'. IMSS–ARMU, Filza di negozi dell'anno 1793, fol. 98-103 (doc. 30), contains examples

for high-ranking visitors'complaints regarding weapons etc. In Filza di negozi dell'anno 1800, fol. 87 (doc. 81), custodian Raddi reported the thefts of visitors' walking sticks and overcoats (28 April 1800).

21 For problems of discipline and class identity in museums see also Kate Hill, '"Roughs of both sexes": the working class in Victorian museums and art galleries', in Simon Gunn and Robert J. Morris (eds), *Identities in space: contested terrains in the Western city since 1850* (Aldershot: Ashgate, 2001), pp. 190–203; Hill, *Culture and class in English public museums, 1850–1914* (Aldershot: Ashgate, 2005).

22 IMSS–ARMU, Filza di negozi dell'anno 1790, fol. 285–9, December 1790.

23 '[Q]uello era costume che teneva con tutti', IMSS–ARMU, Filza di negozi dell'anno 1791, fol. 2–3 (no doc. no.).

24 IMSS–ARMU, Filza di negozi dell'anno 1792, fol. 29 (doc. 6): complaint by Francesco Bartolozzi concerning his permanent expulsion from the museum, 2 March 1792 (the reasons are not specified). IMSS–ARMU, Filza di negozi dell'anno 1793, fol. 98–103 (doc. 30), contains notes by porters on the expulsion of visitors due to clothing or touching of specimens for the period 1790-93.

25 See e.g. IMSS–ARMU, Filza di negozi dell'anno 1793, fol. 102, 'Ricordi presi dal Custode . . .' (February 1791).

26 See e.g. IMSS–ARMU; Filza di negozi dell'anno 1789A, fol. 427v (n.d.).

27 IMSS–ARMU, Filza di negozi dell'anno 1790, fol. 12. Sometimes, however, it was the guards themselves who posed a problem for collection maintenance: see e.g. IMSS–ARMU, Filza di negozi dell'anno 1793, fol. 130 (doc. 40), report by Gagli of 4 March 1793, for the case of a guard who was caught opening one of the specimen jars filled with brandy. (The jar contained wood samples.)

28 The contemporaneous reorganisation of the art gallery Uffizi under the direction of Giuseppe Pelli since 1775 followed similar principles of systematisation by displaying historical progress in the arts, a change from early modern conventions of presentation which not all visitors appreciated. See e.g. the account of British traveller Eustace, who complained that '[t]he arrangement, it must be admitted, is simple and methodical, but the objects press too close upon each other, and leave no time for discrimination'. Rev. John Chetwood Eustace, *A Classical Tour through Italy An. MDCCCII*, 4th edn (Leghorn: Glaucus Masi 1817), vol. III, p. 426.

29 ASF, Segreteria di Gabinetto pezzo 59, 'Osservazioni di S.A.R. sopra lo stato del Gabinetto di Fisica, ed ordini dati in consequenza delle medesime nell'Agosto 1783'.

30 Engelbert Wichelhausen, *Ideen über die beste Anwendung der Wachsbildnerei, nebst Nachrichten von den anatomischen Wachspräparaten in Florenz und deren Verfertigung, für Künstler, Kunstliebhaber und Anthropologen* (Frankfurt am Main: J.L.E. Zessler, 1798), pp. 41–2.

31 Nicolas René Desgenettes, 'Réflexions générales sur l'utilité de l'anatomie artificielle; et en particulier sur la collection de Florence, et la necessité d'en former de

semblables en France', *Observations sur la physique, sur l'histoire naturelle et sur les arts* 43 (1793), pp. 81–94, here pp. 88–9.

32 For the relationship of La Specola's displays to other anatomical collections in the eighteenth century see Thomas Schnalke, 'Der expandierende Mensch – Zur Konstitution von Körperbildern in anatomischen Sammlungen des 18. Jahrhunderts', in *Medizin, Geschichte und Geschlecht. Körperhistorische Rekonstruktionen von Identitäten und Differenzen*, eds. Frank Stahnisch, Florian Steger (Stuttgart: Franz Steiner, 2005), pp. 63–82, esp. pp. 77–81. For different genres of anatomical representation in the eighteenth century see also e.g. Reinhard Hildebrand, 'Der menschliche Körper als stilisiertes Objekt. Anatomische Präparate, Modelle und Abbildungen im 18. Jahrhundert', in Rüdiger Schultka and Josef N. Neumann (eds), *Anatomie und anatomische Sammlungen im 18. Jahrhundert* (2007), pp. 197–222.

33 Simone Contardi, 'Linnaeus institutionalized: Felice Fontana, Giovanni Fabbroni, and the natural history collections of the Royal Museum of Physics and Natural History of Florence', in Marco Beretta and Alessandro Tosi (eds), *Linnaeus in Italy: The spread of a revolution in science*. Uppsala studies in history of science, 34 (Sagamore Beach, MA: Watson Pub. International LLC, 2007), pp. 113–28.

34 E.g. IMSS–ARMU, filza Conti, doc. 61, bill by Caterina Picciuoli for sewing work, 28 July 1798.

35 See e.g. for a wax model of the rare flower *Dracena* in bloom IMSS–ARMU, fondo Fabboni II/16, doc. 432.

36 '[P]er uso de'Bottanici'; ASF, Imperiale e Reale Corte Lorenese, 360, no. 284I, 'Memoria dl Cav. Fontana in sua giustificazione' (n.d.), 34. For the use of Linnaean classification at the museum, see also Simone Contardi, 'Linnaeus in Italy: the spread of a revolution in science', in Beretta and Tosi (eds), *Linnaeus in Italy*.

37 E.g. IMSS–ARMU, filza Conti, folder 'Scrittoio delle Reali Possessioni', doc. 38, bill by Giuseppe Tofani, 31 December 1799.

38 ASF, Imperiale e Reale Corte Lorenese, 360, no. 284I, 'Memoria dl Cav. Fontana in sua giustificazione' (n.d.), 36. In 1797, the museum also introduced a series of drawings of local mushrooms with the explicit aim to prevent accidental poisoning among the poor. IMSS–ARMU, Filza di negozi dell'anno 1797, fol. 21–3 (14 January, 9 February 1797).

39 ASF, Imperiale e Reale Corte Lorenese, 360, no. 284 I, 'Memoria dl Cav. Fontana in sua giustificazione' (n.d.), 33.

40 Those wax models of animals which were produced earlier seem to pertain to the subjects of Fontana's research, e.g. a viper (IMSS–ARMU, Filza di negozi dell'anno 1798, fol. 36, Gagli's notes of March 1794).

41 IMSS–ARMU, Filza di negozi dell'anno 1793, fol. 387.

42 Michael Bohr, *Die Entwicklung der Kabinettschränke in Florenz* (Frankfurt am Main: Peter Lang, 1993), p. 116.

43 Bohr, *Kabinettschränke*, pp. 88–9.

44 Ibid., p. 117.

45 On efforts to produce uniform showcases see e.g. ASF, Segreteria di Finanze Affari prima del 1788, 479, folder 1779, letter from Pigri to the Grand Duke, 7 April 1779; and ASF, Imperiale e Reale Corte, 5251, 'R. Museo, Affari e Conti 1777-1780', letter by carpenter Spichi of 4 January 1780.

46 For a similar contemporary decision to present anatomical specimens in a uniform manner to draw attention to the anatomist's skill see the case of John Hunter, in Simon Chaplin, 'Nature dissected, or dissection naturalized? The case of John Hunter's museum', *Museum and society* 6:2 (2008), pp. 135–51, p. 144. For contrasting displays of curiosities, see e.g. Clare Haynes, 'A 'natural' exhibitioner: Sir Ashton Lever and his holophusikon', *British journal for eighteenth-century studies* 24 (2001), pp. 1–14.

47 Luigi Zangheri, *Feste e apparati nella Toscana dei Lorena, 1737-1859* (Florence: Olschki, 1996), p. 43.

48 Ibid., pp. 30–1.

49 BNCF, manuscript collection NA 1050, Pelli, 'Efemeridi', 1764, fol. 13: 'people flock to religious solemnities like they flock to profane spectacles' ('alle sacre funzioni vi concorra la gente, come concorre ai profani spettacoli').

50 Pietro Gori, *Le feste fiorentine attraverso i secoli* (Florence: Bemporad, 1926), pp. 351–2. Luciano Artusi and Silvano Gabbrielli, *Feste e giochi a Firenze* (Florence: Becocci, 1976), p. 97.

51 For the tradition of wax effigies in Florence see Roberta Panzanelli, 'Compelling presence. Wax effigies in Renaissance Florence', in Roberta Panzanelli (ed.), *Ephemeral bodies: wax sculpture and the human figure* (Los Angeles: Getty Research Institute, 2008), pp. 13–40.

52 The contemporary account of Marco Lastri in his *Osservatore*, for instance, characterised the production of coloured wax votives of 'eyes, legs, heads, hands, and finally tools, animals and other things' as a typically Florentine tradition (Lastri, *Osservatore*, vol. 2, pp. 153–7, here p. 155).

53 '[I] voti . . . imbarazzano le belle pitture che vi sono, e . . . servono di nido alla polvere', letter from Pietro Leopoldo to Raimondo Adami, 9 September 1785 (ASF, conv.soppr. 119, v. 1010). Quoted from Eugenio Casalini, *La SS. Annunziata di Firenze. Studi e documenti sulla chiesa e il convento* (Florence: Convento della SS. Annunziata, 1971), p. 64.

54 '[U]n massacro di tutti questi voti', 'dispiacere di molti', Costantino Battini, *Atti del Convento SS. Annunziata*, quoted from Casalini, *SS. Annunziata*, p. 65.

55 The museum's chief modeller Susini for example made a portrait bust of Giuseppe Pelli (BNCF, manuscript collection NA 1050, Pelli, 'Efemeridi', Serie II, vol. XVII, fol. 3574v, 20 December 1789). See also e.g. the report of a portrait statue in wax of Antonio Frilli by Giovanni Canardi which was publicly exhibited (*Gazzetta Toscana*, no. 4, 1803). For artistic production that was not restricted to the high nobility see Fabia Borroni Salvadori, 'Committenti scontenti, artisti litigiosi nella Firenze del Settecento', *Mitteilungen des Kunsthistorischen Institutes in Florenz* 39:1 (1985), pp. 129–58, especially p. 157.

56 See e.g. BNCF, manuscript collection NA 1050, Pelli, 'Efemeridi', Serie I, vol. XXVIII, fol. 54, 12 September 1771, for Pelli's visit to the private cabinet of Antonio Fabbrini.

57 Pelli, 'Efemeridi', Serie II, vol. 3 (1775), mentions the public display of an elephant in Florence.

58 Ravenni, *Settecento*, p. 102. For a contemporary account see IMSS–ARMU, Documenti III (2), Pelli, 'Efemeridi', Serie II, vol. XVIII (1790), fol. 3829v, day of Santa Lucia.

59 See e.g. Pelli, 'Efemeridi', Serie II, vol. XX (1792), fol. 4516bis: broadsheet announcing 'il Virtuoso Americano FRANCESCO ADELENTES', an armless man who demonstrated his skill of painting with his feet. See e.g. 'Efemeridi', Serie II, vol. XX (1792), fol. 4598 bis, Agosto 1792, for a public show of automata.

60 Pelli, 'Efemeridi', Serie II, vol. XX (1792), fol. 4717a–m: François Bienvenu, *Prospetto di un corso familiare di fisica sperimentale da dimostrarsi in 21. Lezione. Adattato all'intendimento di qualunque persona. . .* (Florence: Gaetano Cambiagi, 1792); and ibid., fol. 4627a–d. For itinerant lecturers of experimental philosophy in the eighteenth century see Simon Schaffer, 'Natural philosophy and public spectacle in the eighteenth century', *History of science* 21:1 (1983), pp. 1–43; Barbara Maria Stafford, *Artful science: enlightenment, entertainment, and the eclipse of visual education* (Cambridge, Mass.: MIT Press, 1994); Oliver Hochadel, *Öffentliche Wissenschaft. Elektrizität in der deutschen Aufklärung* (Göttingen: Wallstein, 2003).

61 'Egli hà un concorso ben scarso a disonore dlla cultura fiorentina', Pelli, 'Efemeridi', Serie II, vol. XX (1792), fol. 4717r.

62 Pelli, 'Efemeridi', Serie II, vol. XX (1792), fol. 4627. In his later added remark in the margins Pelli dates Bienvenu's return to 1794, but the *Gazzetta Toscana* covered his second course in 1795 (*Gazzetta Toscana*, no. 27, 1795).

63 For travellers who reported on Tuscany as a model state see e.g. Dupaty, *Sentimental Letters*, Sismondi, *Tableau de l'agriculture toscane* (1801), N. Brooke, *Observations on the Manners and Customs of Italy, with Remarks on the Vast Importance of British Commerce on that Continent. . .* (1798). See also Anon., *Il Governo della Toscana sotto il Regno del Granduca Pietro Leopoldo, proposto per modello agli altri Governi* (Cremona 1787).

64 Zangheri, *Feste e apparati*, p. 142.

65 'Genauigkeit', 'Vollkommenheit', Wichelhausen, *Wachsbildnerei*, pp. 18, 21.

66 Desgenettes, 'Réflexions générales', p. 84, 'représentent également avec une scrupuleuse exactitude les immenses details', p. 86; 'élégance, . . . precision, . . . vérité', p. 93.

67 '[G]rosse Gelehrte und Künstler', 'unsterblichen Namen', 'edler Karakter [*sic*]', 'ungezwungene Bescheidenheit', Wichelhausen, *Wachsbildnerei*, p. 93; 'universellement célèbre', 'le premier de l'Europe', Desgenettes, 'Réflexions générales', pp. 84, 87.

68 '[T]iefe Naturwissenschaft, mannichfaltige Kunstkenntnisse, eiserne Geduld, . . . glückliche[s] Genie', Wichelhausen, *Wachsbildnerei*, p. 95.

69 '[D]ie genialische Kunst, die Resultate der Vergleichungen mehrerer präparirter Kadaver auf das deutlichste und naturähnlichste anschaulich zu machen', Wichelhausen, *Wachsbildnerei*, p. 97.

70 '[S]ans cette surveillance les sculpteurs les plus excellens ne copient jamais la nature avec exactitude', Desgenettes, 'Réflexions générales', p. 92. Also Wichelhausen, *Wachsbildnerei*, pp. 116, 118.

71 '[G]énie . . . connoissances profondes . . . soins infatigables de Fontana', Desgenettes, 'Réflexions générales', p. 93.

72 Desgenettes, 'Réflexions générales', p. 89. Wichelhausen, *Wachsbildnerei*, p. 25.

73 Wichelhausen, *Wachsbildnerei*, p. 25.

74 Ibid., p. 30.

75 '[S]o dass man sie in ihrer Lage und Verbindung leichter dem Gedächtnisse einprägen kann, als im wirklichen Kadaver', Wichelhausen, *Wachsbildnerei*, p. 43.

76 'Cette nouvelle méthode facilite & abrège singulièrement l'étude; elle fait saisir nettement & avec promptitude des objets très compliqués', Desgenettes, 'Réflexions générales', p. 91. See also Wichelhausen, *Wachsbildnerei*, p. 50.

77 Desgenettes, 'Réflexions générales', p. 88; Wichelhausen, *Wachsbildnerei*, p. 32.

78 E.g. Wichelhausen, *Wachsbildnerei*, p. 44.

79 Ibid., p. 36.

80 Desgenettes, 'Réflexions générales', p. 89.

81 Wichelhausen, *Wachsbildnerei*, p. 28.

82 '[L]a base fundamentale de l'art de guérir', Desgenettes, 'Réflexions générales', p. 85; Wichelhausen, *Wachsbildnerei*, pp. 26–8.

83 Wichelhausen, *Wachsbildnerei*, p. 26.

84 '[T]outes les collections consacrées à la culture & à l'avancement des sciences naturelles', 'à la contemplation & aux méditations des philosophers & des médecins', Desgenettes, 'Réflexions générales', p. 86.

85 '[H]umane Regenten', 'zum Unterrichte und Nutzen des Volks', Wichelhausen, *Wachsbildnerei*, p. 54.

86 '[U]ngebildete Menschenklassen', '[d]er rohe Haufe ist sinnlich', Wichelhausen, *Wachsbildnerei*, pp. 96, 56.

87 IMSS–ARMU, Filza di negozi dell'anno 1800, fol. 51 (doc. 47), 'Rivista del Real Museo del Mese di Settembre 1795'.

88 For visitors' responses see also Francesco De Ceglia, 'Rotten corpses, a disembowelled woman, a flayed man. Images of the body from the end of the 17th to the beginning of the 19th century. Florentine wax models in the first-hand accounts of visitors', *Perspectives on science* 14:4 (2006), pp. 417–56; Giuseppe Olmi, '"A wonderful collection indeed!" The Royal Museum of Florence in the testimony of two travellers', *Nuncius* 21:2 (2006), pp. 349–68.

89 For an influential early example of a study which highlights the authoritarian nature of museums see Eilean Hooper-Greenhill, *Museums and the shaping of*

knowledge (London: Routledge, 1992). For an overview and critique of the 'new museology' see Randolph Starn, 'A historian's brief guide to new museum studies', in *The American historical review* 110:1 (2005), pp. 68–98. Recent nuanced reconstructions of patterns in visitors' interpretations include Macdonald, *Science museum*; Alberti, 'Museum affect'.

90 N. Brooke, *Observations on the Manners and Customs of Italy, with Remarks on the Vast Importance of British Commerce on that Continent. . .* (London: T. Cadell and W. Davies, 1798), p. 125.

91 Rev. John Chetwood Eustace, *A Classical Tour through Italy An. MDCCCII*. Fourth edition, revised and enlarged (Leghorn: Glaucus Masi, 1817), vol. 1, pp. vi, xiii, 479.

92 'Egli è stato di pianta formato dall'Attuale Sovrano, ed è cosa sommamente onorevole al suo nome', 'un assortimento di pezzi lavorati in cera per lo studio anatomico, i quali, e per l'eccelente qualità del lavoro e per la diffusa quantità dei pezzi; formano a mio giudizio la parte più rara e sorprendente del Gabinetto'. *Miscellanea Fiorentina di Erudizione e Storia. Pubblicata da Iodoco Del Badia*, Anno I, no. 6, June 1886: extract from 'Descrizione del viaggio di Giovan Battista Malaspina nell'anno 1785 ed 86', here p. 86.

93 Dupaty, *Sentimental Letters*, pp. 127, 126.

94 Ibid., p. 128.

95 For the life and works of Vigée-Lebrun see Mary Sheriff, *The exceptional woman. Elisabeth Vigée-Lebrun and the cultural politics of art* (Chicago: University of Chicago Press, 1996).

96 *The memoirs of Elisabeth Vigée-Lebrun*, trans. Siân Evans (Bloomington: Indiana University Press, 1989), p. 123.

97 Sheriff, *Exceptional woman*, pp. 13–19.

98 For James Smith see Margot Walker, *Sir James Edward Smith, 1759–1828* (London: Linnean Society of London, 1988).

99 Dupaty, *Sentimental Letters*, 128. James Edward Smith, *A Sketch of a Tour on the Continent*, vol. I (2nd edn, London 1807), pp. xxvi, 328, 347.

100 For some biographical information on Walker see Stafford, *Artful science*, p. 188.

101 Adam Walker, *Ideas Suggested on the Spot, in a Late Excursion through Flanders, Germany, France, and Italy* (London 1790), pp. 349–50.

102 See e.g. IMSS–ARMU, Filza di negozi dell'anno 1801, fol. 81 (doc. 56): 'Rivista del R.Museo p[er] il Mese di Ap[ri]le 1801': 'Sarebbe altresi necessario far mettere due Serrature alla Custodia Grande nella Galleria dei Parti etc ove sono Le Preparazioni Rappresentanti La Vergine, e La Deflorata'. IMSS–ARMU, filza Mandati 1795, receipt no. 86 of 17 April 1795, to Gio[vanni] Batt[ista] Calvetti, for 'Ferramenti, e Serrature fatte agli Sportelli delli Scaffali della Stanza dei Feti Umani mostruosi'.

103 For an example of this comportment see also Anna Maerker, 'The tale of the hermaphrodite monkey: classification, state interests and natural historical expertise between museum and court, 1791–4', *British journal for the history of science*

39:1 (2006), pp. 29–47. However, at the same time eighteenth-century analyses of the appropriation of sculpture rejected the touching of representations of mutilated, dead, or sick bodies. See e.g. Herder's theory of aesthetic perception of sculpture (J.G. Herder, *Plastik* (1778) and other works), and its analysis by Irmela Marei Krüger-Fürhoff, *Der versehrte Körper. Revisionen des klassizistischen Schönheitsideals* (Göttingen: Wallstein, 2001), especially pp. 61–76. For a more general analysis of eighteenth-century theories of sculpture see Inka Mülder-Bach, *Im Zeichen Pygmalions. Das Modell der Statue und die Entdeckung der 'Darstellung'im achtzehnten Jahrhundert* (Munich: W. Fink, 1998).

104 John Moore, *View of Society and Manners in Italy: with Anecdotes Relating to Some Eminent Characters* (London: Strahan and Cadell, 1781), p. 424.

105 'Le cere da me fatte, nol nego, sono della piu grande importanza per la scienza anatomica, ma le cere sono tante parti, o membri slegati del corpo umano, che non formano un tutto, nè il posson formare, che non danno l'idea dell'insieme, che non mostrano i rapporti, i siti, le posizioni, gli attacchi nè fra di loro, nè col corpo intiero'. ASF, Imperiale e Reale Corte Lorenese, 360, no. 284/I, 'Memoria del Cav. Fontana in sua giustificazione', fol. 25.

106 'Il decompor tutto l'uomo di pezzo in pezzo, e il ricomporlo di poi, come era di prima, è lo studio piu facile, e il piu utile sicuramente per intender la macchina compostissima del corpo umano, e tutto questo si potrà fare in ore coll'anatomia di legno'; *ibid.*, fol. 26.

107 '[A]nalisi, e . . . sintesi, cioè . . . decomposizione, e . . . composizione', IMSS–ARMU, Filza di negozi dell'anno 1789A, fol. 431r, 10 October 1789.

108 Luigi Gelati reports handling the wood anatomy in demonstrations for 'illustrious foreigners' such as Napoleon (IMSS–ARMU, Filza di negozi dell'anno 1797, fols 289–90), as does Parlini (IMSS–ARMU, Filza di negozi dell'anno 1798, fol. 71).

109 Fontana, letter to Caldani, 24 May 1794, in Renato G. Mazzolini and Giuseppe Ongaro (eds), *Epistolario di Felice Fontana*, vol. 1. Carteggio con Leopoldo Marc'Antonio Caldani (Trento, Società di Studi Trentini di Scienze Storiche, 1980), p. 365. I would like to thank Renato Mazzolini for drawing my attention to this reference.

110 '[U]no studioso senza bisogno di Professore, nè di libro può da se solo diventare un gran naturalista, un grand anatomico colla maggior facilità, ed in pochissimo tempo'; ibid., fol. 30.

111 IMSS–ARMU, Negozi 1794, fol. 68–70, doc. 24: 'Copia di Biglietto Scritto dal Sig.re Tommaso Bonicoli Dissettore Anatomico del R.Museo al Sig.re Giovanni Fabbroni Sotto Direttore etc di d.o R.Museo in dì 2. Maggio 1794'.

112 'Questo no è solo il mio sentimento, ma lo è di tutti coloro, che sono passati nell'anno passato, e in quest'anno per Firenze, e che sono in stato di giudicare, perchè intendenti dell'anatomia, ma che non hanno interesse alcuno per calumniare'. ASF, Imperiale e Reale Corte Lorenese, 360, no. 284/I, 'Memoria del Cav. Fontana in sua giustificazione', fol. 26.

113 'La viva voce di un cognitore della materia rende assai più utili questi grandiosi

cimmelj, spargendo vera istruzione negli studiosi, e maggior diletto nei semplici osservatori. E non fu giammai, o esser non deve che le Nazioni, e i Sovrani, p uno sterile ed ozioso fasto soltanto, eroghino tesori nella riunione, e conservazione delle Produzioni della Natura, e dello Spirito umano'. IMSS–ARMU, Filza di negozi dell'anno 1797, fol. 193-204, Fabbroni's comments on applicants for the position of custodian (17 March 1795), fol. 193v.

114 'Può anco dimostrare con cognizione scientifica le preparazioni anatomiche e rendere una volta utili le imitazioni in cera, o con le regolari ostensioni, o dando dei Corsi pubblici . . . ai Giovani studenti nelle vacanze estive; tempo in cui nè si insegna anatomìa nelle Scuole, nè è prudente cosa il dissecare i Cadaveri'; ibid., fol. 202v.

115 'La RAV, anco allorche siano terminate le Anatomie in Cera etc., vedrà che questo ramo del Suo R.Museo avrà sempre bisogno, di tempo in tempo, dell'opra di un Dissettore, e per emendare i difetti, che occhi più sagaci ravvissino nelle Cere Anatomiche già fatte; o per imitare le scoperte, che ci promette il Secolo attivissimo in cui viviamo. VAR sa bene quanto costoso Le sia questo articolo attualmente; nè potrebbe dispiacerLe di vederlo effettuato, alla fine, coll'ordinario Stipendio attribuito al Custode, come, p la illustrazione del Museo di Parigi, Lo fece il Custode e Anatomico Daubenton'; ibid., fol. 201v.

116 '[R]endere una volta utili le imitazioni in cera'; ibid., fol. 202v.

117 '[He] knows how to take care of [the anatomical models'] conservation, and cannot claim ignorance in his defense in the case of negligence, or disaster . . . The choice of a successor devoid of knowledge may now diminish the Royal Museum in the eyes of the public'. ('[S]a provvedere, come conviene, alla loro conservazione, nè può allegare ignoranza in sua discolpa, nel caso di vertenza, o disastro . . . La Scelta di un Successore digiuno affatto di cognizioni, forse degraderebbe adesso agli occhi del Pubblico il Real Museo'; ibid., fol. 193v–194r.

118 For the persistence of such combinations of media and materials in anatomical teaching see Elizabeth Hallam, *Anatomy museum. Death and the body displayed* (London: Reaktion, forthcoming 2011), especially chapter 7, 'Paper, wax and plastic'.

119 For the reinterpretation of models by audiences and practitioners see e.g. James A. Secord, 'Monsters at the Crystal Palace', in Soraya de Chadarevian and Nick Hopwood (eds), *Models: the third dimension of science* (Stanford: Stanford University Press, 2004), pp. 138-69; Christoph Meinel, 'Molecules and croquet balls'; ibid., pp. 242-75.

120 For models' roles in the articulation of scientists' authority and disciplines, see e.g. Meinel, 'Molecules', Simon Schaffer, 'Fish and ships: models in the age of reason', in de Chadarevian and Hopwood (eds), *Models: the third dimension of science*, pp. 71-105; Soraya de Chadarevian, 'Models and the making of molecular biology', ibid., pp. 339-68.

I Tanya Marcuse, Wax Bodies No. 49, 'La Specola', Florence.
(www.tanyamarcuse.com)

IIa Wax bust of Emperor Leopold II of Austria (1747–92), formerly Grand Duke Pietro Leopoldo of Tuscany. (PK.S.I. 136, ÖNB/ Austrian National Library, Vienna)

IIc Painted plaster bust of Clemente Susini (1754–1814). (Saulo Bambi, Museo di Storia Naturale, Florence)

IIb Plaster bust of Felice Fontana (1730–1805). (Saulo Bambi, Museo di Storia Naturale, Florence)

III 'Anatomical Venus', La Specola. (Saulo Bambi, Museo di Storia
Naturale, Florence)

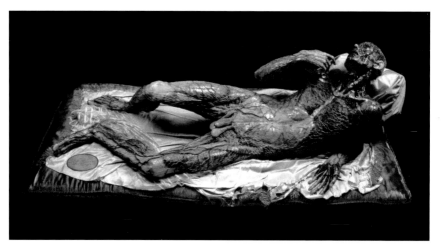

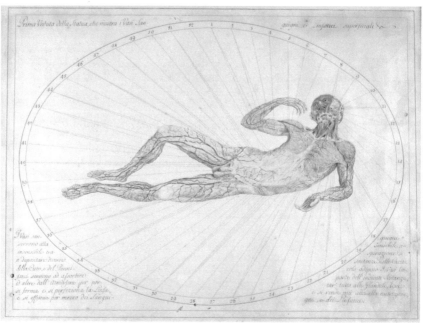

IV 'Lo scorticato' (The flayed man). Anatomical wax model and drawing, La Specola. (Saulo Bambi, Museo di Storia Naturale, Florence)

Part III

Changing model contexts and interpretations

5

The rejection of the Florentine anatomical models in Vienna

In the mid-1780s, at the Austrian emperor's instigation, a set of models from La Specola was sent to the newly founded medico-surgical academy Josephinum in Vienna to serve for the recently reformed training of military surgeons. Like its Tuscan counterpart, the expensive Viennese model collection, displayed on silk cushions in decorated showcases, raised considerable public interest. Transferred into the different disciplinary and institutional context of the Austrian military medical academy, however, the Florentine models were ultimately rejected as useless toys by medical professionals and middle-class commentators, despite being largely accepted as accurate representations of human anatomy. Educated Viennese commentators did not share Pietro Leopoldo's conviction that exhibitions of artificial anatomies would further public happiness and the politics of nature. This chapter investigates the disciplinary, institutional and cultural context into which the models came in late-eighteenth-century Vienna.

The Viennese middle classes were increasingly disillusioned with the possibility of public enlightenment, and highly critical of the emperor's reform measures. This chapter investigates local public spectacle and satirical publications to explain why critics highlighted the similarities of the anatomical waxes to popular entertainment, thus denigrating their value as tools of enlightenment. This depreciation was confirmed in a conflict between physicians and surgeons. Joseph II elevated surgeons' status and reformed their training in an attempt to make them more useful for the state. Some local physicians, educated members of the middle class, perceived this royal support as a threat to their own professional status. They attacked the new Josephinum and its models, which they branded as mere toys and artificial luxuries. Viennese responses to the models thus shaped the debate on what kind of expert was most useful for the state.

Emperor Joseph II and his adviser, the surgeon Brambilla, believed that surgeons were the most useful medical practitioners in state service, saving soldiers on the battlefield, mothers and their newborn babies. Physicians, on the other hand, maintained that specific skills were not enough to constitute useful expertise. Instead, these skills had to be combined with erudition and civilised manners in order to contribute to public happiness. Ultimately, a new generation of surgeons sided with the physicians in rejecting the models in order to distance themselves from the old image of the coarse, uncivilised barber-surgeon.

On a visit to Florence in 1780, Grand-Duke Pietro Leopoldo's brother, the Austrian emperor Joseph II, visited La Specola accompanied by Giovanni Alessandro Brambilla, a military surgeon who had become the emperor's personal surgeon and adviser.[1] The emperor was particularly taken with the museum's spectacular collection of wax models of normal human anatomy. Encouraged perhaps by his surgeon, who increasingly acted as Joseph's adviser on public health reforms, the Austrian sovereign requested copies for Vienna, to be funded from his private coffers. Between 1784 and 1786, a total of 1192 wax preparations arrived in the Austrian capital via the Alps on the backs of mules and men. The models were updated copies of existing Florentine models and new obstetrical preparations produced by La Specola's artisans under the surveillance of its director Felice Fontana. They were put on display at the military surgico-medical Josephsakademie (Josephinum) that was opened in November 1785 under the direction of Brambilla. On 27 August 1786, the final delivery reached Vienna largely undamaged, and the royal surgeon reported to his sovereign with apparent relief: 'Gloria in excelsis Deo. The preparations have happily arrived'.[2]

Despite Brambilla's joy at the models' arrival, and considerable public interest, the Florentine models were ultimately rejected by medical professionals in Vienna, despite their continuing claim to accuracy. Brambilla's instructions for the new academy stipulated that the Florentine models be used for the teaching of surgeons. However, other printed sources point to the possibility that the wax anatomies were not used much in teaching practice, at least during the early years of the military medical academy; and none of the early Josephinum teachers incorporated the models in their textbooks. In his surgery textbook, for instance, Professor Johann Hunczovsky drew on some of the existing material resources at the Josephinum such as the collection of surgical instruments. He also explicitly attempted to coordinate his own teaching with parallel courses, such as the dissector's anatomy class. However, when he enlarged later editions, published after the wax models' arrival, he made no reference to the new model collection.[3]

An anonymous description of teaching at the Josephinum in 1794 mentioned the use of natural preparations in the lectures of Böcking, professor of anatomy and physiology, and dissector Schmidt, but not the waxes.[4] At the same time, the models' utility as teaching aids for the training of surgeons was contested in print, especially by physicians who criticised the new teaching institution as a whole.[5] The Florentine models entered the Viennese public sphere at a time of professional conflicts between physicians and surgeons, and between midwives and obstetricians. The rival factions used models to articulate their expertise and demarcate their professional authority.

In the case of Vienna, then, evaluations of the models have to be understood in the context of redefinitions of the character of surgery and the changing image of the surgeon/obstetrician. The anatomical model collection's appeal to a general public and its association with non-middle-class entertainment ultimately led to the model collection's rejection among medical professionals across the disciplines in their attempt to articulate the utility of their expertise for the state. A number of factors shaped this articulation, such as bourgeois attitudes towards the virtues of the citizen and public education, and critique of the emperor's reforms. The notion of the 'toy' either as an item of useless upper-class luxury or an element of lower-class entertainment lacking in educational value provided a discursive link for these factors in evaluations of the artificial anatomies. The shared rejection of the models by both surgeons and physicians provided a conceptual common ground which enabled a rapprochement of the two disciplines.

Middle-class values and critique of Joseph's reforms

Middle-class satirists and physicians were the most vocal critics of the Florentine models. Their values and their ideas about professional authority and public education determined the models' fate in Vienna. In late eighteenth-century Austria, as elsewhere in Europe, the newly emerging middle class developed its identity by demarcating itself from both noble and lower-class characteristics. Among the elements of middle-class identity were civility, education, rationality, patriotism, self-control, professional competence, and economy, as well as a rejection of courtly artificiality in favour of natural simplicity.[6] The new bourgeoisie perceived of itself as the social group contributing the most to the stability and functioning of the state. Such self-understanding increasingly went hand in hand with a critical attitude towards certain forms of entertainment as idle and uncivilised. When associated with luxury and idleness, such entertainment was considered a pastime of the nobility; when considered as lacking educational value, it was perceived as a lower-class activity.[7]

Commoners, in particular, met with increasing bourgeois scepticism concerning the possibility of public enlightenment. Despite the self-proclaimed enlighteners' best efforts, they complained, the lower classes continued to fall prey to religious superstition and to delight in obscene displays. One contemporary commentator, for instance, chastised the lower classes for the persisting custom of votive offerings – a gaudy exhibition of body parts, and a waste of expensive candle wax.[8] Equally uncouth, another author remarked, was the public display of the body of a presumed saint, which had been found well preserved during the dissolution of a monastery's cemetery in Vienna. The author reported with disgust that this event had prompted the populace to small-scale dismemberment of the body in order to gain relics endowed with supernatural powers.[9] Unlike in Florence, in Vienna the optimistic belief in the power of public education to create the reasonable citizen was increasingly replaced by a sceptical attitude towards the possibility of general public enlightenment.

Initially, the middle class had hailed Joseph's attempts at economic, social, and legal reform as measures that would improve the state in the emerging bourgeois spirit; reform measures such as the introduction of freedom of the press met with much acclaim. However, during the 1780s, the Viennese *Bürger* became increasingly disappointed with the sovereign's actions, which were perceived to be erratic and out of touch with public opinion. Joseph's attempt in 1784 to introduce reusable coffins for instance met with strong public resistance and had to be retracted.[10] Contemporary satire ridiculed Joseph as 'a great poltroon', and explained that

> In first heat [he] felt capable of Herculean deeds; but once that heat had evaporated and mere one-headed snakes obstructed the crowned Hercules's path, he threw away his giant club, and fearful and shaking, like a dwarf, he gave up on all his great plans.[11]

Especially by the end of the decade, harsh satirical or openly critical publications proliferated.[12] The emergent self-image of the new middle class and their critique of Joseph's reforms would come to play a central role for physicians' articulation of the value of their expertise for the state, for their attack on surgery, and for their rejection of the Florentine models.

Joseph's public health policies and the foundation of the medico-surgical academy 'Josephinum'

When the first transport of models arrived from Florence in November 1784, Joseph explained in a letter to his brother Pietro Leopoldo in Tuscany that they would be used at his new surgical academy, the 'Medicinisch-chirurgische Josephs-Akademie', thus contributing to his ongoing reform of surgery and surgical training:

> The anatomical preparations have arrived in perfect condition, and every time I
> thank you anew for having given me permission to have them copied; they will be
> the ornament of the Academy of Surgery, which is already in place.[13]

Joseph's acquisition reflected a long-standing interest in health care which,
as Sonia Horn has argued recently, was an integral part of his politics of centralisation and surveillance.[14] Already, before his accession, medical care was
widely available in the Austrian provinces. Recent analyses show that in most
parts of the empire customers could reach a barber-surgeon's shop within a
45-minute walk.[15] However, public health care was administered by a patchwork of authorities, including the universities' medical faculties, local charities
and communities. Following the suggestions of his political adviser Joseph
von Sonnenfels (1733–1814), the emperor introduced an array of measures to
integrate and centralise public health administration under state supervision,
culminating in the 'Sanitäts- und Kontumazordnung' of 1770.[16] These administrative reforms went hand in hand with the introduction of new, comprehensive means of surveillance which applied to the empire as a whole.

The medical faculties eyed Joseph's measures with suspicion, and eventually
resisted them. In principle, the medical professorate agreed with Joseph on the
importance of public health care for the state. The director of medical studies
at the University of Vienna, Anton von Störck (1731–1803), stressed that the
preservation of the population was paramount for good government since 'the
state's power waxes and wanes with the growth and decline of its members'.[17]
However, the medical faculties disagreed with Joseph when he curbed their
responsibilities and even planned to reduce the number of employees. In 1780,
Joseph asked the medical faculties to shorten the medical degree, to reduce the
number of lectureships, and to restructure the medical curriculum. The universities' resistance to Joseph's plans may have prompted him to found his own
academy in order to realise his plans: the military surgico-medical academy
Josephinum.

Already, in 1775, the Emperor had founded a new teaching institution for
military medical practitioners on the outskirts of Vienna in Gumpendorf – the
School for Interior Medicine and for Training in Military Physic ('Lehranstalt
für die Behandlung der inneren Krankheiten und zur Erlernung der Militär-
Arzneimittellehre'). During his frequent visits to the army during the Bavarian
War of Succession in 1779 the sovereign had witnessed the desperate state
of military medical care. To improve the situation, in 1781, the Gumpendorf
school was ordered to give surgeons a thorough grounding in medical knowledge, which would supplement the artisanal training they had received during
their apprenticeships to barber-surgeons. The sovereign stressed that military

surgeons should not 'be treated to superficial knowledge of the indicated disciplines, to a mere knowledge of jargon and hurried and vague teachings. I want them instead to obtain a firm grasp of their knowledge, and thus endowed to return to their regiments.'[18]

Joseph's personal surgeon Giovanni Alessandro Brambilla acted as his adviser on these reform measures. Both shared the conviction that anatomical knowledge, in particular, was indispensable for surgery; already in 1776 Joseph had ordered that every field surgeon had to study anatomy 'as the foundational science of his profession'.[19] To achieve this knowledge, the Gumpendorf institute was enlarged, and equipped with a collection of surgical instruments, and a library was added in the same year.

The emperor's initiative to improve health care for soldiers and the rural population addressed two main concerns: the improvement of the legal status of surgeons, and the improvement of surgical training. Joseph's decree of 1784 elevated surgery to the same legal status as medicine, which as a liberal art liberated it from the guild system. Examined surgeons were now permitted to practise freely without having to procure a barber-shop. Surgeons' training was targeted as well. In charge of military health care since 1778, royal surgeon Brambilla sent some of the most promising field surgeons abroad, especially to Paris, for advanced studies. On their return, these surgeons received teaching positions at the Gumpendorf institute, soon to be superseded by the new surgico-medical academy.[20]

Faced with continuing resistance from the medical faculties, Joseph finally founded a new institution, independent from the universities but endowed with similar privileges, where he could realise his plans for the improvement of medical and surgical training. This new foundation, which proudly bore the name of the sovereign as a visible sign of his support, created a rift between Austrian physicians and surgeons. Up to that point, there had been strong ties between the two disciplines in Austria, and especially in Vienna. Surgeons customarily shared parts of their education with medical students, in courses held at the universities and public hospitals. Since 1517, master surgeons had to pass an examination at the University of Vienna as well as the guild examination, and the medical faculty was in control of investigating and prosecuting cases of surgical quackery. In the eighteenth century, the university even awarded doctorates in surgery. The close relationship between medicine and surgery had only recently been reiterated during the reforms by Gerard van Swieten (1700–72), Empress Maria Theresa's personal physician, who introduced courses for surgeons and midwives taught by teachers from the university's medical faculty.

Given the difference in opinion between Joseph and the medical faculties, the emperor's support of surgery was likely to be perceived as a threat by physicians, despite the established common ground between the two professions in training and examination. This was especially the case with the creation of the Josephinum. When the new academy was founded, it was directly subordinate to, and funded by, the directorate of the aulic war council (*Hofkriegsrat*), the highest military administration in the Austrian empire. Brambilla, as director of the academy, was simultaneously the head of military medical care. The emperor's high esteem of his new institution was reflected in its direct subordination to the aulic war council and its eponymy with the sovereign. To prove itself worthy of its royal support, the Josephinum demonstrated its position at the forefront of medical research with the publication of its proceedings, which discussed new works of medical or surgical content as well as cases and methods encountered at local hospitals or in physicians' reports.[21]

The institution's generous endowment was well suited to fuel the envy of physicians. The new buildings of the academy consisted of housing for the lecturers and employees as well as room for the various collections, which reflected the emperor's and his adviser's esteem of empiricism – the collection of medical instruments, the library, a collection of pathological preparations bought from German physician Samuel Thomas Sömmering, obstetrics professor Hunczovsky's wax preparations of skin and venereal diseases, and the growing number of wax models of normal human anatomy arriving from Florence. In Vienna, the models were thus isolated from their original context as part of the microcosm of creation. Their envisioned function in the new environment of the Josephinum was far more narrow: instead of proofs for the existence and intelligibility of natural laws, the artificial anatomies should now serve for the professional training of (military) surgeons to help preserve the lives of soldiers and peasants.

Despite the established ties between medicine and surgery, physicians probably perceived Joseph's reforms as a threat to their professional authority. In their responses, some physicians resorted to old stereotypes of the coarse barber-surgeon in their counter-attacks, an image that was well suited to aggravate Austrian surgeons, who usually enjoyed high social standing, and were held to good conduct by their guild.[22]

Brambilla's challenge to medicine

Surgeons' ability to save lives was a central claim in Josephinum director Brambilla's provocative inaugural speech, which argued that surgery was superior to medicine in its utility for the state. The new surgico-medical academy opened with a solemn celebration on 7 November 1785. The importance which the emperor accorded to his new institution was reflected in the list of eminent guests, including the aulic war council, other high military and civil officials as well as local doctors, professors of the university's medical faculty, and the 300 students of the institute, dressed in their military uniforms of blue, black and red.[23]

Surgery, the director claimed in his speech, was the most useful medical art for a number of reasons – it was most effective at saving lives, it was based on the most secure foundations, and historically preceded the practice of medicine. He stressed its importance for the state as the means to preserve soldiers' health, and as a means to convince the population to join the army willingly:

> Who among you, most highly esteemed audience! will not acknowledge with a grateful heart the overwhelming grace of the sovereign towards the miserable? What head of house will not with courage send his sons into the battlefield to fight for the fatherland, and for the country's father, since he is certain that if his sons carry away honourable injuries from the fight they will be attended to swiftly, with love, and the necessary aids? In addition to the advantages derived by everybody from such institutions, the state as well benefits considerably, as the annual count of cripples and deaths will be diminished.[24]

In addition, while being most 'difficult to learn', owing to its vast scope, surgery was also the one medical field based on the 'surest foundations'.[25] Brambilla stressed the need both for surgeons and physicians to be well grounded in surgery and inner medicine, which would enable the practitioner to make the appropriate choice regarding cures.[26] In accordance with his view that anatomy was the primary basis of medical practice, Brambilla's image of the surgeon rested mainly on a thorough knowledge of anatomy. He implied that the mastery of hands and instruments emerged from the surgeon's perfect mental image of the body's interior:

> The surgeon must be the master of his hand and of his instruments in such a way, and perform his operation with such accuracy, as if he had the hidden parts of the human body before his eyes, or could observe them through a glass, somewhat like one can clearly discern the little animals enclosed in a crystal or amber.[27]

Despite his admonition addressed at both disciplines, throughout his speech Brambilla challenged the physicians' claim to superiority by reversing claims for priority. He asserted that historically 'dietetic healing is a daughter of surgery', that 'humanity can live without internal medicine, but without surgery it cannot persevere', and that internal medicine 'by its nature is based mostly in conjectures, such that even the most skilful physician often deceives himself, and can be betrayed'. His historical account, Brambilla concluded, had 'shown that surgery is in many ways to be preferred over internal medicine', and he claimed, in the presence of the medical elite of Vienna, that 'without surgery the latter was almost useless'.[28]

His provocative claim quickly circulated beyond the walls of the auditorium; printed copies of the speech were distributed to the audience, and subsequently sold in Latin, German, and Italian to medical practitioners around Europe, who followed the fate of the new surgico-medical academy with great interest. In Vienna, in particular, Brambilla's inaugural speech outraged local physicians, and provided ample fuel for the conflict between surgeons and physicians that lasted well into the 1790s.

In the light of this conflict, the emperor repeatedly reaffirmed his support for the new academy. In a decree of 1786, it was given the right to confer masters and doctoral titles in the field of surgery equal to those of the university; those titles were valid in civil practice as well as in the military. The explicit purpose of this measure was 'to give to this established institution a *visible sign of Our protection*, and simultaneously to enlarge the range of its utility to the entirety of Our subjects', as well as, once more, 'to convey Our special respect to the part of the nation which risks its life for the defence of the shared fatherland, for the rights of Our throne and the safety of its compatriots, and in order to bring relief to its honourable, but heavy duty'.[29] This affirmation was timely given the strong criticism which the new academy met with from its foundation.

A satirical attack on the Josephinum: Joseph Richter's *Monkeyland*

Physicians and their middle-class supporters in Vienna soon rose to Brambilla's challenge of medicine's utility and pre-eminence, drawing on a long established stereotype of the surgeon as a callous, primitive butcher. Although the sceptical Viennese denied any link between scientific education and political reform as stipulated by Pietro Leopoldo in Florence, they too linked comportment, knowledge and public utility in their critique of the Josephinum. One of the earliest critical comments in print was the 1787 satire *Das Affenland oder der Doktor Fanfarone* (*Monkeyland or the Doctor Braggadocian*).[30] The work was published anonymously by the successful Viennese author and satirist Joseph Richter. It is likely that Richter's satire was widely read by his primary audience – the educated middle class. Not only was he commercially the most successful Viennese writer of the time (being the only one who could live on his income from his publications), but *Monkeyland* was taken up both by contemporary literary criticism and in subsequent publications.[31] The satire established many important elements of the debate, such as the conflict between physicians and surgeons, criticism of the sovereign and his reform measures, and a denunciation of the wax models as mere 'toys' not fit for use by the truly enlightened, and not ultimately useful to the state. Richter's satirical account and subsequent attacks on the Josephinum and its anatomical models claimed that Joseph and his supporters overestimated the public's potential for enlightenment and rationality. They also implied that special skills and knowledge without appropriate civilised comportment were not enough to make a medical practitioner such as a surgeon a useful expert in state service.

In the satire, Austria is portrayed as Monkeyland, a country rich in resources, blessed with women of 'full bosoms and bouncy backsides',[32] but with a credulous population, prone to ape all things foreign. Fanfarone (i.e. Brambilla), appears as a dextrous but uneducated surgeon, whose talent for the administration of bleedings, clysters, and cures for venereal diseases gives him access to Monkeyland's high society, and, ultimately, to its king after the successful removal of a royal boil. Fanfarone's pretensions lead him to consider himself the equal, at least, of the physicians, and prompt him to convince the king to found a new 'surgico-medical greenhouse'.[33] In his account of the institution, Richter implied a very different image of the medical expert from Brambilla. Siding with physicians, the satirist claimed that a consolidation of the surgeon and the physician in the same person was not feasible:

> the pupils of this medico-surgical greenhouse could not possibly practise medicine, as they did not have the opportunity to become acquainted with all diseases . . . it was difficult anyway to rise in two completely different arts, as even the learning of one required a whole lifetime.

In effect, 'the plants of this greenhouse would be hermaphrodites, and thus neither complete physicians nor surgeons'.[34] This gendering language was supported by a depiction of the institution's students as 'beardless boys'. Importantly, the lack of physical maturity was linked to immature behaviour such as the lack of respect for the learned physicians:

> Most preposterous was the comportment of the teachers and pupils of the medico-surgical greenhouse. The former with a content smile gazed at their trimmed bellies and their porte epée [military insignia] while walking about, and they cursed the medical faculty like butcher's hands. The others (although being mostly beardless boys) spat out, whenever they met a physician.[35]

The new medico-surgeons thus lacked civilisation – one of the central values of the Viennese middle class. This lack called into question their suitability as providers of health care, and their utility for the state in increasing public happiness:

> Now that Fanfarone had installed his young sprouts in the rights of real physicians, he sent them out into the world as Christ had sent his apostles. They appeared at the sick-bed, but not with the compassionate demeanour that is so uplifting for the patient, so instilling of consolation and hope. Their tone was

coarse and imperious, their expression dark and proud, and everywhere the callous **field-surgeon** shone through the travestied physician. This did not give them a good reputation, and he who was not entirely desperate called for a real physician. The physicians smiled at this small victory which they had won without fight and bloodshed over the great Fanfarone; but Fanfarone was angry with the people of Monkeyland, who demanded from a physician a compassionate demeanour, empathy, and **civility**.[36]

By contrast, the enlightened physician was characterised by his learning, his compassion and civility towards his patients, and not least his aloofness vis-à-vis the preposterous comportment of Fanfarone and the members of his institute. The satirist's mockery of the immature medico-surgeons was tied up with a (moderate) critique of the sovereign for his erratic reforms, his indecision, his misguided frugality, and inappropriate spending. Thus, in his final rant against Brambilla and the new institute, Richter discursively linked the immature surgeons and their lack of education and civilisation to the Florentine models as mere pretty toys, as symbols of the institute's lack of enlightenment.

And still the physicians smiled at the Doctor Fanfarone, [. . .] his beardless pupils who spit out before every physician, at the barbers in doctors' hats, at the pretty curiosity, [the] pretty toy of his anatomical preparations [i.e. models], at the trimmed bellies of untheoretical teachers, at his authorship, his Latinity without Latin, his medical quackery, . . . his hatred of all physicians, and finally at the entire medico-surgical greenhouse, by which he hopes to banish all physicians from this world.[37]

Affenland thus spearheaded the development of a discursive context which questioned the public utility of anatomical models and their medico-surgical users, and which articulated a competing image of expertise in state service. Ultimately, factors such as the portrayal of surgeons as coarse and uneducated, lacking in civilisation as well as in theoretical knowledge, the gendering or charge of immaturity related to the models' designation as toys, and middle-class criticism of Joseph's reforms, combined to form a cultural and disciplinary context in which physicians supported their claims to expertise and professional authority by rejecting the Florentine waxes. This rejection was adopted by a new generation of surgeons intent on demonstrating their utility by highlighting their commonalities with 'civilised' physicians.

Models as toys: public entertainment in late eighteenth-century Vienna

Contemporary witnesses of the debate could have interpreted the labelling of the anatomical wax models as toys in two ways. First, some observers saw the

Josephinum's anatomical models and preparations as similar to other forms of public entertainment available in Vienna in the late eighteenth century. Second, referring to the models as costly toys branded them as items of luxury, as highly priced objects of no apparent practical use.[38] In either case, the notion of the toy implicitly served to characterise its users as immature and lacking in judgement, and thus threatened their status as tools for the establishment and mediation of expertise.

Popular entertainment in Vienna was free from the strict anti-spectacular legislation imposed by Pietro Leopoldo in Tuscany, and there was a wide variety of spectacles which could serve as frames of reference for audiences of the artificial anatomies at the Josephinum. Among the forms of entertainment offered to the Viennese public of the late eighteenth and early nineteenth centuries were not only various theatres, merry-go-rounds, fireworks, and the popular animal pit fights (*Hetz*), but also events and institutions loosely pertaining to experimental natural philosophy, natural history, and medicine.[39] The balloon craze hit Vienna, like most larger European cities, and travelling 'electrical showmen', 'magnetisers', and 'mechanics' exhibited mind-boggling 'magical experiments' such as the baking of a pie 'filled with living guinea-pigs' and the 'transformation of a pocket-watch into a sixteen-year-old girl'.[40]

It was not unreasonable for Viennese commentators to liken the anatomical waxes to toys, since artificial and real bodies of humans and animals were regularly put on display in various spaces accessible to the lower and middle classes. Mechanical theatres and wax cabinets competed with freak shows and venues such as the lunatics' asylum Narrenturm (Fools' Tower), where visitors enjoyed playing jokes on the insane inmates.[41] Wax images of humans, in particular, were ubiquitous in the city for a while. Around the turn of the century, a female wax doll called the 'schöne Wienerin' ('beautiful Viennese') displayed the latest fashion in the city centre. In the late eighteenth century, Joseph Müller's wax museum at Stock-im-Eisen-Platz (later in Leopoldstadt) exhibited images of famous historical figures, from Lucretia of Roman antiquity to the very recent French revolutionaries – lampooned, like the Josephinum collection, by the indefatigable Joseph Richter.[42] Müller also advertised a detachable life-sized figure of a pregnant woman as one of the collection's highlights, for which he charged extra.[43]

Despite the educational pretensions of some of those collections, the demarcation of education and entertainment was blurred. The experimental show 'Phylidor's natural apparitions' ('Phylidors natürliche Geistererscheinungen') of 1791, for instance, promised 'to show spectral apparitions in the hope that connoisseurs and amateurs will become convinced how some people used to be fooled in the most deceiving manner',[44] thereby offering all the thrills of spectral apparitions while maintaining that this display was enlightening. Similarly, a travelling show of wax figures promised depictions of historical scenes for public edification, but in the very same announcement wax figures of female dancers in 'well-chosen positions' were offered for sale to 'connoisseurs'.[45] Apparently, some of the wax figures produced in Vienna in these years were of a pornographic nature. A police raid of Müller's cabinet in 1791 discovered a clandestine production for private collectors which displayed 'quite a few attitudes the sight of which would in most Christian contemporaries have overturned the good teachings of their preachers'. Thus the police decided 'that it was against all propriety to let anyone see this', and destroyed the figures.[46]

Advertisements for wax models of persons stressed not only their verisimilitude, but also their supposed ability to elicit emotional responses in the spectator:

> In the characters of this gallery one will find no grounds to complain with respect to their colour, eyes, hair, postures, and dress . . . and involuntarily we will be moved to those moods, which the lively character-expression of their wittily contrasting physiognomies would elicit in the real world, we will laugh with the laughing, with the yawning one we will not be able to stifle a little yawn.[47]

Precisely this emotional response to three-dimensional representations of humans would also characterise the popular response to the Josephinum's collection, and thereby contribute to the anatomical waxes' devaluation by medical practitioners.

As in *Monkeyland*, Joseph Richter once more provided a critical middle-class commentary – a sceptical perspective on the impossibility of public enlightenment, with an (albeit fictional) account of the public's response to wax shows and anatomical specimens. In his most successful work, the serialised *Eipeldauer Briefe* (*Letters of the Eipeldauer,* 1785–1813), Richter satirised everyday life in Vienna using the fictional voice of an Austrian provincial from Eipeldau, whose letters home described his new life as a lowly clerk in the big city. The provincial perspective of the Eipeldauer was supplemented with annotations by an equally fictional Viennese voice, that of an editor who considered himself vastly more sophisticated than the Eipeldauer (but usually was not). In his account of the Eipeldauer's visit to Müller's wax cabinet, Richter likened the activity to looking at 'wild beasts', 'giants and dwarfs', and 'monsters' and ascribed to these forms of entertainment a predominantly female audience who satisfy their curiosity by gazing at sensational objects.[48] The provincial Eipeldauer's lack of sophistication in dealing with such displays was indicated by his inability to see through the illusion of living bodies: on visiting the Müller cabinet, he attempted to kiss the hand of one of the waxen figures, taking it to be 'the lady of the house'.[49]

Similarly, Richter's account of the Josephinum's collection elsewhere in the *Eipeldauer Briefe* presented it as just another form of vulgar spectacle. In his fictional description of audience response, he chimed in with middle-class scepticism regarding public education at the Josephinum. He suggested that the lower classes did not learn what they were supposed to learn, but appropriated the collection on a purely entertaining level – a suggestion which supported the physicians' arguments for the necessity of medical expertise and professional authority.

> Recently my wife took me to Währingergasse, where the Josephs-Academy is, and there were a great many beautiful things to see, and there were many thousands of people there, they even ran over the guards. There stood many glass bottles filled with brandy, and there were marvellous things hanging inside, and the women could not be moved away from some of the bottles. In one of those bottles hung a six-week-child, but it was not as big as the six-week-child of my wife.

The fictional editor interpreted the Eipeldauer's puzzlement as a sign of provincial lack of sophistication: 'This will have been something other than a six-week-child; but a simpleton from Eipeldau may be forgiven for taking black for white.'[50]

Avid followers of Richter's serial publication would probably have come to a different conclusion – they knew from previous instalments that the Eipeldauer's marriage had been arranged by his superior, who was rather intimately familiar with the bride, and that Mrs Eipeldauer had given birth six weeks after the wedding.

In the *Eipeldauer Briefe*, the Josephinum collection is only one of many forms of entertainment that display bodies and curiosities, and was apparently considered to be of a similarly popular nature to the other public collections. Again, the public is largely female, and fascinated to the point of standing transfixed. Once more, Richter stresses that the objects on display can easily be misinterpreted: just as the Eipeldauer took the wax figure of a woman in Müller's cabinet to be alive, so here neither the provincial nor the fictional Viennese editor can grasp the meaning of 'six-week-child' by the accompanying description alone (though, presumably, the well-educated bourgeois reader would). While the inscription probably referred to an embryo after a gestation period of six weeks, the Eipeldauer's comparison of this embryo to the child born to his wife six weeks after their wedding does not lead him (or the supposedly more sophisticated fictional editor) to any further conclusions regarding the process of pregnancy and child development (or, for that matter, Mrs Eipeldauer's past activities).

Richter's satirical accounts of public entertainment in late eighteenth-century Vienna cannot be taken at face value as descriptions of audience behaviour. However, his commercial success and exposed position as one of Vienna's foremost enlighteners indicate that Richter's readers, the educated middle class, shared his perception of the Josephinum collection as a form of popular entertainment that was largely devoid of educational value. The public interested in such collections was portrayed as lower class, largely female, and lacking in sophistication. This perception contributed to the models' rejection by physicians and surgeons alike; it was in line with general bourgeois attitudes towards popular enlightenment and public education, as well as with prevalent criticism of Joseph's reforms.

Those elements of bourgeois self-image, and the points of contention with Joseph's reforms, played a central role in critique of the Josephinum and of Brambilla. Physicians resorted to the early modern stereotype of the brute barber-surgeon in their attacks – an image well suited to irritate Austrian surgeons, who usually enjoyed high social standing and were traditionally held to good conduct by their guild.[51] To avoid critics' renewed charges of callousness and brutality, a new generation of surgeons distanced themselves from vulgar behaviour and vulgar objects, stressing instead their commonalities with physicians. In the debate on the utility of the Josephinum and the models, both physicians and surgeons articulated the utility of their profession for the state, and characterised the persona of the ideal healer who claimed special knowledge and skills.

Surgery versus medicine

Brambilla's image of surgery as practised at the Josephinum combined empirical and theoretical approaches, to the exclusion of authors of classical antiquity. Among the disciplines necessary for the formation of reliable surgical knowledge Brambilla listed 'anatomy, physiology, pathology and therapy', and, to a lesser degree, botany, chemistry and comparative anatomy.[52] His demand for students of surgery to learn foreign languages was restricted to those necessary to read the most important contemporary authors: while French, Italian, and Latin were included, Greek was not. Observation and practice in hospitals were necessary for the successful application of theoretical knowledge to surgical practice. As Brambilla had stressed in his opening speech in 1785, only an all embracing knowledge of medicine and surgery could make an accomplished healer. Ultimately, however, Brambilla presented surgery as the most useful of the healing disciplines, owing to its secure empirical foundations.

Brambilla's claims put local physicians, intent on maintaining their professional superiority, into a quandary. As Thomas Broman has pointed out, physicians' proclaimed adherence to Enlightenment ideals of utility, expertise and merit put their own claim to superiority over other healing professions into question. 'Most physicians rallied enthusiastically around the Enlightenment because it represented progress and efficiency', Broman states,

> but the tensions that resulted from their association with the new ideology were never too far from the surface of their rhetoric. Just as a rational, enlightened social order based on 'merit' and expert knowledge threatened to subvert the traditional estates of birth and strip the aristocracy of its claim to social preeminence, so too did the emphasis on useful knowledge and its applications in work undermine one of the profession's key sources of status.[53]

The tension between physicians' meritocratic rhetoric and their attempts to preserve their privileges did not go unnoticed in the debate: In *Drey interessante Fragen als ein Aufschluß zu den neuern Anstalten in den österreichischen Staaten. Die Medizin und Chirurgie betreffend* (1788), the anonymous author, who claimed to be a Viennese physician, countered accusations of Jena professor of medicine Gruner (in his journal *Almanach fuer Aertze und Nichtärzte* of 1788) against Brambilla. Brambilla's defender accused physicians of thinly veiled self-interest:

> The true meaning [of physicians' protest] is roughly this: 'If we doctors want to be honest with ourselves, we cannot deny that we have transgressed upon surgery a little bit in every respect. Of course medicine is not superior to surgery, we recognise this, but our own interest required not to let people know this. It has cost us enough efforts to teach them that surgery was but a subordinate handmaiden of Madame Medicine. Would our annual incomes have been as high if we had committed the foolish mistake to free surgery from its shackles? No, no! The surgeons remain barbers, and we, the physicians, preserve our splendour and our reputation, which we have acquired at the expense of surgery.'[54]

In their attacks on the Josephinum, Viennese observers such as Richter, but also physicians themselves, countered such cynical interpretations by presenting doctors as prime examples of bourgeois virtues who were civilised, empathetic and honest.[55] Richter had presented the doctors of Monkeyland as sophisticated scholarly men, civil and ready to respond to the surgeons' coarse and insulting behaviour with an aloof smile. However, the real doctors of Vienna did not restrict their response to smiles alone. In 1794, following the deaths both of Brambilla's protector Joseph II in 1790 and Fontana's patron Pietro Leopoldo as Emperor Leopold II in 1792, the Viennese physician Johann Peter Fauken published two attacks on the Josephinum. One of them was dedicated to the new emperor, Francis II.[56] The learned Fauken, who served at Viennese public hospitals, presented himself as a dutiful citizen motivated 'to further the economy and the advantages of the state'.[57] As in Richter's satire, Fauken's critique presented Brambilla and the surgeons siding with him in the conflict as immature and even unmanly: the physician insisted that Brambilla's claim for surgery's precedence was 'a childish quarrel, indecent to erudite manly-thinking men; a true scholar and sage regards such airy sweeps as an adult regards children's soap bubbles'.[58]

In neither publication did he discuss Brambilla's claim that, owing to the universality of nature, a healer necessarily had to study both medicine and surgery for a full understanding of the body. Fauken indirectly refuted this assumption, however, stating that it was beyond human mental capacities to acquire an in-depth knowledge of both fields within a lifetime and – according to the physician – this humble insight was the sign of the truly enlightened, as opposed to the hubris of those who presumed the possibility of a surgico-medical 'demigod'.[59]

> The enlightened know that it is very difficult to acquire the knowledge necessary for a dignified practice of medicine.[60]
>
> The ancient physicians, all of whom were great philosophers, have recognised how difficult it is for a single man to study Medicine in its entirety, and this is why they have separated [from it] the part that heals through the operations of the hand, which is called Surgery; judging that the Physician and the Surgeon already had enough difficulties acquiring the skills that one or the other needed to have.[61]

Having thus ruled out the possibility of uniting the professions, Fauken proceeded to the argument that was most likely to catch the sovereign's attention: the Josephinum's utility for the state (or lack thereof). The physician's argument in the publication addressed to Emperor Francis II was based on numerical comparisons. Fauken compared the numbers of soldiers' deaths before and after the foundation of the Josephinum to show that its foundation had not made any positive impact on soldiers' mortality, or even made it worse. Thus, he claimed, all funds going into the existence of the institution should be seen as financial loss. Most vitriolic was his attack on the wax model collection from Florence, which he branded as one of the most expensive and least useful of all investments. Echoing Richter's *Monkeyland*, he denounced the artificial anatomies as 'but a *toy* for children and for persons who have no notion of science whatsoever, who regard such things as the child sees the doll'.[62] Fauken was careful in his critique to place the entire responsibility for the models' expensive and useless acquisition on Brambilla alone, not to the present sovereign's uncle and predecessor Joseph II. He did not discuss the models' features in connection with the demands of surgical training.

With this renewed accusations levelled against the Josephinum and its direc-tor Brambilla,[63] Francis II ordered an investigation into its situation. A commis-sion, composed of physicians and surgeons both within the Josephinum and from outside,[64] took a conciliatory stance, while maintaining the institution's claim to usefulness. In their report, the commission reiterated Brambilla's claim to the uniformity of nature's laws, and his conclusion that, owing to this uniformity, there should be no fundamental distinction between, or separation of, surgery and medicine:

> Medicine and surgery are based on the same principles; they are not only related, but rather an inseparable whole.
>
> There always was but one art of healing, just as from the very beginning there was only one nature, organised and operating according to ever the same laws.[65]

The commission refrained, probably wisely, from responding to Fauken's dis-cussion of mortality rates. Instead, they mentioned the institutional advantages of medico-surgeons for the military, such as clearer hierarchies and an avoid-ance of competency conflicts, both contributing to a smoother running of the military, as well as increased mobility of practitioners within it.

To account for the Josephinum's failure up to now, they pointed to a lack of training with corpses, indirectly implying that this omission was due to the presence of models: 'Ongoing anatomical and surgical practice with dead bodies is so indispensable for the training of military surgeons, that the shortage of those exercises was one reason why no dextrous and courageous operating physicians could be formed [at the Josephinum]'.[66] After all, clini-cal practice became increasingly an integral part of physicians' education, and it was established practice at the University of Vienna to use corpses from the General Hospital for the training of medical students despite 'the public's disgust and dismay' when 'arms and feet of dead bodies were lost during the transport'.[67] The Josephinum was situated next to the new General Hospital – a large institution which could supply surgeons both with dead bodies and with opportunities to study living ones.

Crucially, with this critique the 'new' generation of surgeons at the Josephinum sided more closely with the physicians, at the expense of Brambilla, his teaching regime and, implicitly, the Italian models that were perceived to have been his idea. Nature, not art, was the best instructor. Even contemporaries supportive of the Josephinum had remarked from the very beginning on the wax collection's artistic ingenuity, its splendour and the high costs involved, albeit as evidence of the Emperor's benevolence and his support of surgery.[68] Critics of Brambilla and his institution now reinterpreted these features as evidence of failure. In 1794, an anonymous critic lamented that, 'Unfortunately the Emperor put his trust in a man, who is undoubtedly among the most confused, and most confusing heads of the eighteenth century.' He pointed out that, 'This glorious academy has no anatomical practice facility, neither a surgical, nor a medical clinic' because Brambilla had 'sacrificed the indispensable for voluptuous luxury.' The anonymous observer considered Brambilla's claim to broad foundations in other disciplines to be but lip-service, since actual teaching showed 'as clear as day that he [Brambilla] in practice assumed that in order to study and practice surgery, the student needed no previous knowledge other than anatomy'.[69]

This criticism was subsequently echoed, in a somewhat milder form, by the influential professor of medicine Johann Peter Frank (1745–1821), director of Vienna's General Hospital, and reformer of the Austrian medical system. In a report of 1798 on the present situation of medical and surgical training, Frank too distinguished the models' 'luxury' from 'true riches', but allowed that they could 'usefully serve as an overview'.[70]

With these developments Brambilla resigned in 1796, firing off a last moot attempt at self-defence from his retirement home in Italy in a publication which claimed once more that '[T]hese preparations are of great utility, as the School's Surgeons have a continuing exercise even in the most minute Anatomy, and as in Summer fresh dissection is impossible, in that season the Professor of Anatomy must explain it using the figures in Wax which are put on the table of the Amphitheatre'.[71]

His position of *Protochirurgus* (royal surgeon) was replaced by three separate positions: the direction of the Josephinum, of field apothecaries, and of field medical personnel. The directorate of the academy was converted from a permanent position into an annually elected one among the academy's professors; the professor of obstetrics Johann Hunczovsky was the first to succeed Brambilla in this position. Already in the 1780s, presumably in response to physicians' accusations, Hunczovsky had publicly stressed the new surgeons' departure from the ways of the old 'empirics' in the military. In a speech for the Josephinum's second anniversary in 1787, Hunczovsky agreed that most military surgeons of old had 'by their coarse comportment forever nipped any scientific leanings in the bud', although through no faults of their own.[72] He stressed that the Josephinum's new students were formed in a different, more civilised mould:

> In admitting these students we consider the characteristics both of their bodies and of their souls, and we are as attentive to their moral comportment as subsequently we are to the progress they make in the sciences.[73]

The subsequent publication of the speech further signalled Hunczovsky's attempt to placate the sparring disciplines with a vignette which showed the conciliatory handshake between medicine and surgery, signalling a future of fruitful collaboration (figure 10).

Obstetrics

In a similar move, a new generation of obstetricians distanced itself from the supposedly coarse barber-surgeons by rejecting artificial anatomies, criticising the training with inanimate objects as leading to coarseness, and to a lack of empathy and civility.[74] Like surgery, obstetrics was accorded a central position in Joseph's medical reforms for its ability to preserve lives. The ties between university medicine and midwifery had traditionally been close: like surgeons, Viennese midwives received part of their training at the university. Since the seventeenth century, midwives were inscribed and examined at the university's

10 The reconciliation of medicine and surgery. From Johann Hunczovsky, *Ueber die neuere Geschichte der Chirurgie in den k.k. Staaten* (Vienna, 1787). (Sammlungen der Medizinischen Universität Wien/Collections of the Medical University Vienna)

medical faculty; in the eighteenth century, midwives received instruction together with medical students and surgeons at so-called 'collegia publica' at a Vienna hospital.[75] Nevertheless, the emergence of a new medical practitioner, the male obstetrician, prompted debates in Austria as elsewhere in Europe concerning the importance of theoretical knowledge for midwifery, and the effect of supposedly male or female traits on obstetric practice. Obstetrics in the eighteenth century was thus characterised by conflicts between male obstetricians and female midwives, and by fundamental discussions among practitioners concerning the nature of academic obstetrics and obstetrical practice.[76] Contemporary observers were well aware of the conflict between obstetricians and midwives. In 1786, satirist Franz Xaver Huber fiercely lampooned the conflict, suggesting that it caused suffering to the patients:

> The midwives wanted to deliver the child in their way; the obstetricians claimed that this way was not methodical; the midwives called the obstetricians methodical fools; the obstetricians proved very methodically that they were not; finally the midwives began a fight; the obstetricians threw them to the floor; the [female] assistants helped the midwives. [. . .] The midwives had torn the obstetricians' wigs and hair; those in turn held in their hands the midwives' bonnets and pieces of their clothing; the assistants had black eyes and bumpy heads [. . .] Everybody caught their breath to recover, and meanwhile Miss Ass – died most methodically.[77]

Within obstetrics as an academic discipline, the two main opposing views entailed different degrees of reliance on the powers of nature to help herself and, in this context, different opinions regarding the role of instruments. In Vienna as elsewhere in the German-speaking lands, obstetricians differed in their emphasis on natural versus instrument-assisted birth. However, both pro- and anti-instrument factions were eager to stress their utility to the state as preservers of populations, and their difference from the old 'butchers' and from midwives. The influential Viennese obstetrician Steidele, for instance, whose textbook was taught at the university, claimed that obstetricians' utility as life-savers was dependent on their civilisation and their good judgement, which supposedly would distinguish them from both the old generation of barber-surgeons and from female midwives:

> By their benevolent comportment, their wise orders and dexterity [the obstetrician-surgeons] saved many a dear wife, they preserved mothers for their children, they gave mothers the reward for their hard labour. They preserved successors to the Throne for the benefit of the state.[78]

Given this characterisation of the new discipline, Steidele and many of his colleagues explicitly rejected the use of artificial human anatomies for obstetricians' training as not suitable to develop civilised practitioners.[79] They thus sided with physicians who, in their claims to utility for the state, had argued that manual skill and even theoretical knowledge had to be supplemented by civilised, empathetic comportment to constitute truly useful expertise. Physician and medical reformer Johann Peter Frank, for instance, stressed in a report on medical training of 1798 that 'the instructor must take care to use multiple cadavers of women and unborn children, and to avoid that with the artificial dummy the students get used to such handling as they would only allow themselves on a living patient with danger for her, or for her child'.[80] No matter how accurately they represented spatial or haptic features, dummies could not provide the immediate response of living patients. Training with artificial bodies would, therefore, perpetuate the existence of a group of practitioners who were not attuned to their patients' pain, or in any other way able to interact with their patients in a humane manner – a consideration of no small importance in the days before anaesthetics. As Steidele put it unambiguously,

> All machines [i.e. artificial or dead bodies] mean nothing; they are rather more harmful than useful for the apprentice, as those involuntarily get used to the most coarse practice.[81]

While Steidele did not refer to the Josephinum's models in particular, the obstetrician-surgeon, like some of the general surgeons, discursively linked artificial anatomies to the 'coarse practice' which he considered characteristic of the old barber-surgeons. The new generation of practitioners, he argued, had successfully overcome this lack of civility. However, his criticism went beyond that of the physicians and 'new' surgeons. The physicians' initial criticism of the wax models had been based mainly on their similarity to forms of popular entertainment, not on their features in relationship to the requirements of surgical training, for example their lack of haptic qualities as compared to those of real cadavers. Physicians may have been reluctant to make explicit claims about the requirements of surgical practice since surgeons could have contested those outsiders' descriptions of their work with reference to their unique skills and experience. The obstetrician, however, was himself a practitioner whose activity was largely tactile, and he carried this line of criticism further: both models and corpses, he argued, were insufficient because they lacked the responsiveness of the living patient, which provided indispensable feedback for medical practice.[82] Thus, in his articulation of obstetric expertise, manual skills, knowledge and comportment were mutually supportive. They formed an inseparable array of features, which were indispensable if obstetrics was to be of service to the state and its population.

Conclusion

Critical assessments of the Florentine models of normal human anatomy at the Josephinum persisted in the German-speaking lands through the early nineteenth century.[83] Later attempts to make the models useful as the basis for anatomical tables, and as visual references for an anatomy textbook, suggest that Joseph II's statement that the Florentine wax models 'will be the *ornament* of the Academy of Surgery' turned out to be true in a literal sense.[84] In moments of institutional crisis, such as the years leading up to the Josephinum's temporary closure in 1820, the models were used to demonstrate a previous Emperor's support for the new institution. This strategy, however, depended on the (changing) esteem in which Joseph himself was held by later generations.

A number of factors contributed to the medical community's rejection, or at least lack of public endorsement, of the models on their arrival in Vienna, including middle-class attitudes towards virtues of the citizen and public education, and critique of Joseph's reforms. Physicians criticised the models to highlight the impossibility of general public enlightenment, and thus to underline the necessity of experts for the polity. Medical practitioners' discussions of artificial anatomies also helped articulate their claims to expertise and authority by explaining why they, in particular, were well suited to be those caretakers of public health.

Labelling the models as toys branded them as uneducational, artificial luxuries created by an over-zealous and erratic sovereign. These toys, critics argued, could appeal only to an ignorant public in thrall of the artificial, more interested in entertainment than in education, and to the equally ignorant and uncivilised barber-surgeons. As such, the waxes were not acceptable to enlightened physicians, or to the new generation of surgeons who aligned themselves with physicians by stressing their civilisation, their compassion, and their utility for the state. The agreement among the two professional groups that the models did not meet the relevant criteria such as economy, naturalism and civility provided (at least temporary) closure to the debate by a shared rejection both of a certain image of surgery associated with Brambilla, and of the models that were perceived as his acquisition. Their popularity in one community, the general public, was used to put into question their value in another, the medical profession.[85] Thus, it became opportune for the self-proclaimed new surgeons to publicly renounce the waxes' utility in their attempts to establish their expertise as indispensable to the state.[86] As in the case of La Specola naturalists' interactions with the Tuscan court, in Austria too knowledge and skills had to be matched by suitable comportment to constitute expertise that was useful for the polity.

The last chapter returns to Florence to address similar issues concerning the interpretive flexibility and context-dependency of model reception and model use. Chapter 4 showed that, in the case of La Specola, model use could be envisioned differently even within the same institution, and that these different uses were related to how the museum's experts and its models were supposed to contribute to the improvement of the polity. The period from 1799 to 1814 was characterised by numerous regime changes in Tuscany. These changes of government posed both a threat and an opportunity for the museum: on the one hand, the museum's direction had to justify the continuing existence of the costly institution, and especially the very expensive production of anatomical waxes. On the other hand, such justifications to the new government could be instrumentalised by the museum's administration to push for institutional changes according to their own agenda, which previous regimes had not agreed to.

Notes

1 Giovanni Alessandro Brambilla (1728–1800) worked as a military surgeon in the Austrian army before he became Joseph's personal surgeon in 1764. In this position, Brambilla acted not only on behalf of the sovereign's personal health, but increasingly as Joseph's adviser on the reform of the medical system, to which Joseph turned after his coronation as Holy Roman Emperor in 1764 and his elevation to co-regent at the side of his mother Maria Theresa. In 1778 Brambilla was charged with the direction of military medical care. For the life of Brambilla see e.g. the contributions in *Giovanni Alessandro Brambilla nella cultura medica del Settecento Europeo*, Centro per la storia dell'Università di Pavia (Milan: La Goliardica, 1980).

2 'I Preparati sono arrivati felicamente'; ASCP, Legato Orlandi, Cartella 237, no. 16.

3 Johann Hunczovsky, *Anweisung zu chirurgischen Operationen. Für seine Vorlesungen bestimmt* (Vienna: Rudolph Graeffer, 1785) After his death, further editions were prepared by an anonymous editor, possibly Hunczovsky's successor to the chair of surgery Anton Beinl. They did not mention the models either.

4 *Medicinisch Chirurgische Zeitschrift* (1794), vol. 2, pp. 325ff; vol. 3, pp. 49ff.

5 Helmut Gröger has recently pointed out that neither critics of the institution nor its teachers seemed to have accorded much utility to the models as teaching aids. Nevertheless, he insists that the models' accuracy and availability ensured their being used in practice: 'it can be taken for granted that the anatomical wax preparations will have served as a replacement [of cadavers] not only during the summer months or to replace specific [wet] preparations, as is revealed in [Brambilla's] *Instructions*, but by their permanent availability they will certainly have served as tools for instruction, be it for the recapitulation of demonstrations on corpses, or for a general acquisition of knowledge'. ('Man kann aber auch mit

Sicherheit davon ausgehen, daß die anatomischen Wachspräparate nicht nur in den Sommermonaten oder in Ermangelung eines bestimmten Präparates als Ersatz gedient haben, wie aus den "Instruktionen" hervorgeht, sondern durch ständige Verfügbarkeit sicher als Lehrmittel Verwendung gefunden haben, sei es zur Rekapitulation des an der Leiche Demonstrierten oder zu allgemeinem Wissenserwerb.') Helmut Gröger, 'Die Sammlung anatomischer und geburtshilflicher Wachsmodelle als Lehrmittel', in Manfred Skopec and Helmut Gröger (eds), *Anatomie als Kunst* (Vienna: Brandstätter, 2002), pp. 125–49, on pp. 142–4.

6 Hannes Stekl, 'Ambivalenzen von Bürgerlichkeit', in Gerhard Ammerer and Hanns Haas (eds), *Ambivalenz der Aufklärung. Festschrift für Ernst Wangermann* (Munich: Oldenbourg, 1997), pp. 33–48, on p. 35.

7 Ibid., p. 42.

8 Meisel, *Herr und Frau von Wachs oder ein lustiges Gespräch zwischen zwey wächsernen Opfermännln* (Vienna: von Kurzbeck, 1782).

9 'Manche rissen ihr einen Zahn, oder ein Büschchen Haare aus, und trugen es als ein Heiligthum nach Hause, wo sie es unter den übrigen Reliquien sorgfältig verwahren, oder sie nähen das geraubte heilige Uiberbleibsel in ein Amulette – und tragen es, als ein Mittel wider alles Uibel, bei sich, und ihr Glaube an Heilige und Wunderwerke . . . ist nun wieder . . . so stark, als er es nur immer sein konnte'. 'So nachtheilig als sie für die Vernunft war, eben so nachtheilig was sie für die guten Sitten'. Hieronimus Weiskopf, *Kritische Bemerkung über den bei den Jakoberinnen zu Wien öffentlich zur Schaugestellten unverwesten Körper der Nonne Magdalena, Baronin von Walterskirchen* (Augsburg, 1786), pp. 8–9, 11–12, 14.

10 H.M. Scott, 'Reform in the Habsburg Monarchy, 1740–90', in H.M. Scott (ed.), *Enlightened absolutism. Reform and reformers in later eighteenth-century Europe* (Ann Arbor: University of Michigan Press, 1990), pp. 145–87, p. 147.

11 'Seine Majestät waren ein gewaltiger Poltron. In der ersten Hitze fühlten Sie die Kraft zu Herkulischen Thaten; aber war diese verflogen, und stellten sich dem bediademten Herkules nur einköpfige Schlangen in den Weg, so warf er seine Riesenkeule weg, und gab furchtsam und zitternd, wie ein Zwerge, alle seine großen Entwürfe auf.' Huber, *Der Blaue Esel* (Vienna, 1786), vol. 2, pp. 213–14.

12 Leslie Bodi considers the years 1787–90 the crisis years of Joseph's reforms ('Krisenzeit des Josephinismus'). Leslie Bodi, *Tauwetter in Wien: zur Prosa der österreichischen Aufklärung 1781–1795* (Frankfurt am Main: S.Fischer, 1977), p. 227.

13 'Les préparations anatomiques sont parfaitement bien arrivées, et je vous rends à chaque fois de nouvelles grâces de ce que vous avez voulu permettre que je les fasse imiter; elles feront l'ornement de l'Académie de chirurgie, que est déjà sous toit'. Alfred von Arneth, *Joseph II. und Leopold von Toscana. Ihr Briefwechsel von 1781 bis 1790* (Vienna: Wilhelm Braumüller, 1872), p. 229.

14 Sonia Horn, '"eine Akademie in Absicht der Erweiterung der medizinisch-chirurgischen Wissenschaft . . .": Hintergründe für die Entstehung der medizinisch-chirurgischen Akademie "Josephinum"', in Wolfgang Schmale,

Renate Zedinger and Jean Mondot (eds), *Josephinismus – eine Bilanz/Échecs et réussites du Joséphisme* (= Das Achtzehnte Jahrhundert und Österreich, vol. 22) (Bochum: Winkler, 2008), pp. 215–44.

15 Ibid, p. 220.

16 Joseph von Sonnenfels, *Grundsätze der Polizey, Handlung und Finanz* (3 vols, Vienna 1769–76).

17 '[Des Staates] Macht wächst und fällt nach dem Masse des Wachstums oder der Abnahme seiner Glieder'.; ÖStA; AVA, Akten der StHK Karton 4; fol. 72r, 'Vortrag der Studienhofkommission, die Zahl der bey hiesiger Universität angestellten Lehrern betreffend; Votum des Hofrats Freyherr v. Störck; facult. Med'., 30 November 1782. Quoted from Horn, 'eine Akademie in Absicht der Erweiterung', p. 218.

18 'Meine Absicht geht keineswegs dahin, dass den Chirurgen, die hier formiert werden sollen, nur die Oberfläche von einer jeden der angegebenen Wissenschaften beigebracht und sie bloss mit der Kenntnis der Kunstwörter und einer übereilten und seichten Lehr von hier abgefertigt werden. Ich will vielmehr, dass sie ihre Kenntnisse gründlich fassen und mit solchen versehen zu den Regimentern zurück-kehren'. Imperial decree of 3 April 1781, quoted from Manfred Skopec, 'Anatomie in Wachs', in Skopec and Gröger, *Anatomie*, pp. 31–73, on p. 34.

19 '[A]ls Fundamentalwissenschaft seines Berufes', quoted from Gabriela Schmidt, *Geburtshilfliche Wachpräparate des Josephinums* (Vienna: Wilhelm Maudrich, 1997), p. 13.

20 Johann Hunczovsky (anatomy, physiology, general pathology and therapy, surgery); Gabriel von Gabriely (internal medicine); Wilhelm Böcking (anatomy and physiology); Heinrich Streit (general pathology, therapy and materia medica); Joseph Jakob von Plenk (chemistry and botany); Anton Beinl (prosector and instructor).

21 *Abhandlungen der Kais. Königl. Medicinisch-Chirurgischen Josephs-Academie zu Wien* (Vienna: Albert Camesina), vol. 1 (1787), vol. 2 (1801).

22 Horn, 'eine Akademie in Absicht der Erweiterung', pp. 216–17.

23 *Wiener Zeitung*, no. 90, 9 November 1785.

24 'Wer von ihnen, hochansehnliche Zuhörer! wird nicht die überschwengliche Huld des Monarchen gegen elende Menschen mit dankbarem Herzen anerkennen? Welcher Hausvater wird nicht mit frohem Mute seine Söhne ins Feld schicken, um dort für das Vaterland, und für den Vater des Vaterlandes zu streiten, indem er gewiß weis, daß man seine Söhne, wenn sie im Gefecht ehrenvolle Wunden davon tragen, mit Liebe und den nöthigen Hilfsmitteln auf das schleunigste besorgen werde. Nebst dem Vortheil, den jeder ins besondere von solchen Anstalten zieht, so fließt auch dem ganzen Staat dadurch kein geringer zu, daß man jährlich in demselben nicht mehr so viele Krüppel, und weniger Todte zählen wird'. Giovanni Alessandro Brambilla, *Rede, die er bey der Eröfnung der neuen k.k. medizinisch-chirurgischen Akademie 1785 gehalten hat* (Vienna: Gräffer, 1785), pp. 45–6.

25 '[S]icherste Gründe'; Brambilla, *Rede*, p. 7.

26 'Will also jemand ein Arzt oder Chirurgus werden, so muß er sich in beyden Fällen
die Heilkunde in ihrem ganzen Umfange bekannt machen; denn so wie keiner ein
Arzt seyn kann, der nicht die Chirurgie versteht, so verdient auch im Gegentheil
kein Wundarzt diesen Namen, wenn er nicht die Medizin aus dem Grunde studiert
hat'; Brambilla, *Rede*, p. 22.

27 '[D]er Chirurg muß so Meister von seiner Hand und von seinen Instrumenten
seyn, auch seine Operation mit einer solchen Zuverläßigkeit verrichten, als wenn
er die in dem menschlichen Körper verborgen liegende Theile vor seinen Augen
liegen hätte, oder wie durch ein Glas betrachten könnte, so ungefähr, wie man die
in einem Krystall oder Bernstein eingeschlossenen Thierchen ganz klar unterschei-
den kann'. Brambilla, *Rede*, p. 23.

28 '[D]aß die dietätische Heilkunst eine Tochter der chirurgischen sey'; 'Die
Erdbürger können zwar ohne die dietätische Heilkunst leben; aber ohne die
Chirurgie können sie nicht bestehen'; 'daß sie ihrer Natur nach meistens nur auf
Muthmasungen beruth, so, daß auch der geschickteste Arzt sehr oft sich selbst
betrügt, und auch betrogen werden kann'; 'dargethan, daß die Chirurgie in vielen
Stücken vor der innerlichen Heilkunst einen Vorzug habe . . . daß letztere ohne die
Chirurgie beynahe unnütz sey'. Brambilla, *Rede*, pp. 14, 19, 22, 29.

29 '[E]in *offenbares Merkmal unsers Schutzes*'; 'den Umfang seiner Nutzbarkeit auf
unsere sämmtlichen Unterthanen zu erweitern'. '[U]m dem Theile der Nation,
welcher zur Vertheidigung des gemeinschaftlichen Vaterlandes, für die Rechte
unsers Thrones und die Sicherheit seiner Mitbürger sein Leben jeder Gefahr preis
zu stellen, über sich nimmt, unsere besondere Achtung zu erkennen zu geben, und
zur Erleichterung seiner ehrenvollen, aber beschwerlichen Pflicht beizutragen,
haben Wir in unserer Hauptstadt eine eigne vollständige militar-medicinisch chirurgische Lehranstalt . . . errichtet'. Quoted from Helmut Wyklicky, *Das Josephinum:
Biographie eines Hauses. Die medicinisch-chirurgische Josephs-Akademie seit 1785
das Institut für Geschichte der Medizin seit 1920* (Vienna: Brandstätter, 1985), p.
69 (italics A.M.).

30 N.N. [Joseph Richter], *Das Affenland oder der Doktor Fanfarone* (s.l. 1787).
For an early critique by a physician of Brambilla's (and the Josephinum's) perceived attempt to deprive medicine of its privileges, see Göttingen professor of
medicine Christian Gottfried Gruner's contribution in his *Almanach für Aerzte
und Nichtaerzte* of 1788 (Jena), pp. 203–16, and the anonymous defensive
response, 'Almanacum perpetuum für Aerzte und Nichtärzte; ad aeternam rei
memoriam dem Herrn Doktor Chr. G. Gruner in Jena zugeeignet'. Cited in
Kirchenberger, 'Chronologie der Josefs-Akademie', in *Dr. Wittelshöfer's 'Der
Militärarzt'*, Separatabdruck or. 4 and ff., 1885; reviewed in *Allgemeine deutsche Bibliothek* 85/1 (1789), pp. 426–7. Other anonymous or pseudonymous
contributions to the debate include Anon., *Onuphrius Polykarpus Strieglers
Episteln über die kritische Perturbation des heutigen Arztenthums* (1786);
*Einhundert Paragraphen über medicinische Dissonanzen auf der großen poli-
tischen Baßgeige* (1786).

31 See e.g. the anonymous review in the *Allgemeine Deutsche Bibliothek*, no. 84:2 (1788), p. 607: 'A satire in the Voltairian manner, not lacking in wit, in foolish and droll inspirations' ('Eine Persiflage in der Voltairischen Manier, der es nicht an Witz, an närrischen und drolligen Einfällen fehlt..'.). Quoted from Bodi, *Tauwetter*, p. 338. The trope of the monkey-land is taken up again in Johann Friedrich Ernst Albrecht's *Die Affenkönige oder die Reformation des Affenlandes* [*The monkey kings or the reformation of Monkeyland*] (Vienna: Wucherer 1788), a critique of Joseph's reforms.

32 '[E]inen vollen Busen und einen elastischen Hintern', Richter, *Affenland*, p. 2.

33 '[C]hirurgisch-medicinisches Treibhaus'; Richter, *Affenland*, p. 37.

34 'Die wirklichen Aerzte hätten freilich gern dem König vorgestellt, daß die Zöglinge dieses medicinisch-chirurgischen Treibhauses unmöglich die Arzneikunst ausüben könten, weil sie nicht Gelegenheit hätten, sich mit allen Krankheiten bekannt zu machen: daß es überhaupt schwer sei, in zwei ganz verschiedenen Künsten groß zu werden, da die Erlernung einer einzigen die ganze Lebenszeit erfordert: daß hier sicher das: ex omnibus aliquid, ex toto nihil zutreffen würde, und daß die Pflanzen dieses Treibhauses **Hermaphroditen**, und also weder vollkommene **Aerzte** noch **Wundärzte** sein würden; allein die Aerzte erinnerten sich, daß der König nicht gern nein sagte, wenn er einmal ja gesagt hatte: das Treibhaus wurde also errichtet; Fanfarone hielt eine Rede alla Fanfarone, worin er die Wundärzte und Feldscherer den wirklichen Aerzten auf den Kopf stelte, und die Aerzte begnügten sich, daß sie über diese Rede und das chirurgisch-medicinische Treibhaus lächelten'. Richter, *Affenland*, pp. 38–9 (boldface in the original). 'Treibhaus' (greenhouse) mockingly refers to the frequent non-satirical use of the word 'Pflanzschule' (plant nursery) in similar contexts.

35 'Am lächerlichsten betrugen sich die Lehrer und Zöglinge des medizinisch-chirurgischen Treibhauses. Die Erstern sahen im Gehen mit selbst wolgefälligem Lächeln auf ihren galonirten Bauch, und das porte epée und schimpften, troz Fleischerknechten, auf die medizinische Fakultät. Die andern aber, (wenn die gleich größtenteils unbärtige Buben waren,) spukten aus, so oft sie einem Arzt begegneten'. Richter, *Affenland*, pp. 53–4. The surgeons' new uniforms were trimmed with braids ('galoniert') to indicate their rank; similarly the *porte epée*, a decorative tassle worn on the sable as insignia of officer's status.

36 'Fanfarone schikte nun seine jungen Sprossen, da er sie einmal in alle Gerechtsame der wirklichen Aerzte eingesezt hatte, wie Christus einst die Apostel, in die ganze Welt aus. Sie erschienen vor dem Krankenbett; aber nicht mit der menschenfreundlichen den leidenden Kranken so aufrichtenden, so Trost und Hofnung einflößenden Miene. Ihr Ton war rauh und gebieterisch, ihr Blick finster, und stolz, und der gefüllose **Feldscherer** gukte auf allen Seiten durch den travestirten Arzt durch. Das brachte sie nicht in den besten Ruf, und wen nicht die Not drükte, ließ einen wirklichen Arzt rufen. Die Aerzte lächelten über diesen kleinen Sieg, den sie ohne Streit und Blutvergiessen über den grossen Fanfarone davon trugen; Fanfarone aber ärgerte sich über die Einwohner des Affenlandes, die von einem

Arzt eine menschenfreundliche Miene, Teilnehmung und **Höflichkeit** fordern'.
Richter, *Affenland*, pp. 59–60 (boldface in the original).

37 'Die Aerzte lächeln also noch immer über den Doktor Fanfarone, . . . seine unbärtige Zöglinge, die vor jedem Arzt auspuken, über die Bartscherer in Doktorhüten,
über die **schöne Rarität**, **schöne Spielebät** seiner anatomischen Präparaten, über
die galonirten Bäuche unteoretischen Lehrer, über seine Autorschaft, über seine
Latinität ohne Latein, über seine medizinische Pfuscherei, . . . über seinen Haß
gegen alle Aerzte, und endlich über das ganze medizinisch-chirurgische Treibhaus,
durch daß er alle Aerzte aus der Welt hinaus zu **treiben** hoffet'. Richter, *Affenland*,
pp. 64–8 (boldface in the original).

38 For the late eighteenth-century debate about luxury, see e.g. Christopher J.
Berry, *The idea of luxury: a conceptual and historical investigation* (Cambridge:
Cambridge University Press, 1994).

39 For an overview of entertainment genres see Gerhard Tanzer, *Spectacle müssen
sein: Die Freizeit der Wiener im 18. Jahrhundert* (Vienna: Böhlau, 1992). In contemporary Austrian, 'Hetz' is still synonymous with 'fun'.

40 '[M]agische Experimente', 'mit lebenden Meerschweinchen gefüllt', 'eine
Taschenuhr in ein 16jähriges Mädchen verwandeln'. Bibliothek der Stadt
Wien (BSW), Konvolut D64522: 'Programme und Ankündigungen von
Sehenswürdigkeiten und Schaustellungen'.

41 'Da stehn eine Menge Leut um den Thurm herum, und die treiben ihrn Spaß mit
den Narrn, die zum Fenster heraus sehn'. Joseph Richter, *Die Eipeldauer Briefe*,
ed. Eugen von Pannel (Munich: Georg Müller 1917 [1785–1813]), vol. 1, p. 212.

42 Richter's Eipeldauer (see below) calls them 'Foltär', 'Robatsbär', Rossau'/'Russo'.

43 'Auch ist in diesem Kabinett eine weibliche lebensgroße Figur, anatomisch bear-
beitet, befindlich, welche eine schwangere Frau vorstellt, und die gegen doppel-
tes Legegeld zerlegter gezeiget wird'. BSW, Konvolut D64522: 'Programme und
Ankündigungen von Sehenswürdigkeiten und Schaustellungen'. For the tension
between education and entertainment in eighteenth-century experimental natural
history shows see e.g. Oliver Hochadel, *Öffentliche Wissenschaft. Elektrizität in
der deutschen Aufklärung* (Göttingen: Wallstein, 2003); Simon Schaffer, 'Natural
philosophy and public spectacle in the eighteenth century', *History of science*
21:1 (1983), pp. 1–43; Barbara Maria Stafford, *Artful science: enlightenment,
entertainment, and the eclipse of visual education* (Cambridge, Mass.: MIT Press,
1994).

44 'Geister Erscheinungen zeigen, in der Hoffnung, daß Kenner und Liebhaber . . .
sich dadurch gänzlich überzeigen, wie manche Menschen vor einiger Zeit auf die
betrüglichste Art getäuscht worden sind'; BSW, Konvolut D64522: 'Programme
und Ankündigungen von Sehenswürdigkeiten und Schaustellungen'.

45 'Gut gewählte Stellungen', 'Liebhaber', BSW, Konvolut D64522: 'Programme und
Ankündigungen von Sehenswürdigkeiten und Schaustellungen'.

46 '[S]o manche Attitüden, deren Anblick bei den meisten Christen unserer Zeit die
guten Lehren ihrer respektive Fastenprediger über den Haufen geworfen hätte';

'daß es wider alle Sittlichkeit sei, irgendeinen Menschen so etwas sehen zu lassen'. Richter, *Eipeldauer*, vol. 1, pp. 373–4.

47 See e.g. a broadsheet of the 'Große Kunst-Gallerie' in the Prater gardens: 'Man wird bey den Gestalten dieser Gallerie weder in Hinsicht des Colorits, der Augen, der Haare, ihrer Stellungen und Bekleidung, noch etwas zu wünschen finden, und . . . wir [werden] unwillkürlich bey diesen zu der Stimmung gebracht, die der lebendige Charakter-Ausdruck ihrer originell contrastirenden Physiognomien in der wirklichen Welt hervorbringen würde, wir werden mit dem Lacher lachen, wir werden mit dem Gähner einen kleinen Hang zum Gähnen nicht unterdrücken können'. BSW, Konvolut D64522: 'Programme und Ankündigungen von Sehenswürdigkeiten und Schaustellungen'. For a contemporary study of expressions of emotions in late-eighteenth-century Vienna see also the 'character heads' by sculptor Franz Xaver Messerschmidt (1736–83). Michael Krapf (ed.), *Franz Xaver Messerschmidt, 1736–1783* (Ostfildern-Ruit: Hatje Cantz, 2003).

48 '[W]ilde Thier', 'Riesen und Zwergl', 'Mißgeburten'; 'damit sich d'neugierigen Weiber dran habn ersehn können'; Richter, *Eipeldauer*, vol. 1, p. 191.

49 '[D]'Frau vom Haus'; Richter, *Eipeldauer*, vol. 1, p. 191. For the 'waxwork moment', the moment of uncertainty before a spectator decides that a wax model is not real, see Uta Kornmeier, 'Almost alive. The spectacle of verisimilitude in Madame Tussaud's waxworks', in Roberta Panzanelli (ed.), *Ephemeral bodies: wax sculpture and the human figure* (Los Angeles: Getty Research Institute, 2008), pp. 67–82.

50 'Die Tag hat mich mein Frau Gemahlinn in d'Wahringergassn mitgnommen, wo d'Josephinische Akidemi ist, und da warn ein Menge schöne Sachen z'sehn, und da warn so viel tausend Menschen da, daß s'so gar d'Wacht übern Haufen gworfn haben. Da sind ein Menge gläserne Flaschen da gstanden, und die sind mit Brandwein angfüllt gwesen, und da sind wunderbare Sachen drin ghenkt, und da sind d'Fraunzimmer vor einigen Flaschen gar nicht weg z'bringen gwesen. Ein Sechswochenkind ist auch in so einer Flaschen ghenkt; das war aber nicht so groß, als's Sechswochenkind von meiner Frau Gemahlinn'; 'Das wird wohl was anders gwesen seyn, und kein Sechswochenkind; aber ein dummen Eipeldauer ists ja z'verzeihn, wenn er schwarz für weiß nimmt'. Richter, *Eipeldauer*, vol. 1, pp. 247–8.

51 Horn, 'eine Akademie in Absicht der Erweiterung', pp. 216–17.

52 Erna Lesky, 'Das Bild des vollkommenen Chirurgen bei Brambilla', in *Giovanni Alessandro Brambilla nella cultura medica del Settecento Europeo*, ed. Centro per la storia dell'Università di Pavia (Milan: La Goliardica, 1980), pp. 23–7, on p. 24.

53 Thomas Broman, *The transformation of German academic medicine 1750–1820* (Cambridge: Cambridge University Press, 1996), p. 67.

54 'Der wahre Verstand ist ohngefähr dieser: 'Wenn wir Aerzte mit uns selbst ehrlich sein wollen, so könne wir nicht läugnen, daß wir der Chirurgie in jedem Betracht ein Bisschen zu nahe getreten sind. Die Medizin hat gewiß keinen Vorrang vor der Chirurgie, das erkennen wir wohl, aber unser Interesse erfoderte [sic] es,

dies den Leuten nicht merken zu lassen. Es hat uns Mühe genug gekostet, bis man ihnen beigebracht hat, die Chirurgie sei nur eine unterthänigste Dienstmagd von der Madame Medizin. Würden sich unsere jährliche Einnahmen so hoch beloffen haben, wenn wir den Narrenstreich begangen hätten, die Chirurgen von ihren Sklavenketten loszumachen . . .? . . . Nein, nein! Die Chirurgen . . . bleiben Barbierer, und wir, wir Aerzte bleiben in unserm Flor und Ansehen, welches wir auf Kosten der Chirurgie erworben haben.' Anon., *Drey interessante Fragen als ein Aufschluß zu den neuern Anstalten in den österreichischen Staaten. Die Medizin und Chirurgie betreffend* (s.l. 1788), pp. 38-9.

55 For these tropes, see also e.g. the ten-page praise of the virtues of the physician in Johann Christoph Hackel, *Anleitung zum zweckmäßigen Gebrauche der zur Erhaltung der Gesundheit, des Lebens, und Wachsthumes der menschlichen Körpers nothwendigen Dinge, mit Beyfügung der wesentlichen Grundregeln, nach welchen der Mensch bevorstehenden, oder schon wirklich vorhandenen Krankheitsgefahren vorbauen, und den Tod von hohem Alter so weit, als möglich, hinaus fristen kann. . .* (Vienna: Johann Carl Schuender, 1797-98), pp. 353-63.

56 Johann Peter Franz Xaver Fauken, *Entwurf zu einer Einrichtung der Heilkunde* (Göttingen: Johann Christian Dieterich, 1794), and Philiatros [Johann Peter Franz Xaver Fauken], *Tableau des études de medecine de Vienne comme elles etoient, comme elles sont, comme elles devroient etre. Avec une memoire sur l'Academie Militaire de Vienne, et sur la Faculté de Medecine* (s.l. 1794). Philiatros ('friend of science') was the pseudonym chosen by Rabelais in his French translation of Galen, and a character in physician Fernel's dialogue 'De abdictis rerum causis'. Fauken repeatedly highlighted his erudition, in contrast presumably to Brambilla's lack of Greek and weak Latin.

57 'Staatsbürger'; 'die Wirthschaft und den Vortheil des Staates befördern'; Fauken, *Entwurf*, p. 3.

58 '[E]ine kindische, und für gelehrte männlich denkende Männer unanständige Zänkerey; ein wahrhaft Gelehrter und Weiser betrachtet dergleichen Luftstreiche, wie die erwachsene Person die Seifenblasen der Kinder'; Fauken, *Entwurf*, p. 34.

59 'Halbgott', Fauken, *Entwurf*, pp. 12, 26.

60 'Les gens eclairés savent qu'il est tres difficile d'acquerir des connoissances necessaires pour exercer dignement la Medecine'. Philiatros [Fauken], *Tableau*, p. 19.

61 'Les anciens Medecins, qui etoient tout ensemble grands Philosophes, ont reconnu combien il est difficile qu'un seul homme suffise a l'etude de toute la Medecine, et c'est pourquoi ils en ont separé la partie qui guerit par l'operation de la main, et qu'on appelle Chirurgie; jugeant que le Medecin et le Chirurgien auroient toujours assés [*sic*] de peine a acquerir la capacite que l'un et l'autre doit avoir'. Philiatros [Fauken], *Tableau*, p. 21.

62 '[N]ur ein *Spielwerk* für Kinder und für Leute [. . .], welche von der Wissenschaft gar keine Begriffe haben, und dergleichen Sachen betrachten, wie das Kind die Puppe'. Fauken, *Entwurf*, p. 24 (italics A.M.).

63 See e.g. anonymous contributions in the journal *Medicinisch-chirurgische Zeitung* (1794), vol. 2, pp. 325ff; vol. 3, pp. 49ff.

64 The Josephinum teachers on the commission were Böcking, Gabriely, Hunczovsky, Plenk and J.A. Schmidt.

65 'Die Medizin und Chirurgie . . . beruhen auf einerlei Grundsätzen; sie sind nicht nur verwandt, sondern machen vielmehr ein unzertrennliches Ganzes aus'; 'Es gab von Anbeginn bis jetzt nur eine Heiekunst, gleichwie es von Anbeginn bis jetzt nur eine nach immer gleichen Gesetzen organisirte und wirkende Natur gab'. 'Protokoll der unterthänigsten Militär-Sanitäts-Kommission, die Verbesserung der k.k. Josephs-Akademie und des gesamten k.k. Militär-Sanitätswesens betreffend', Vienna, 2 May 1795, quoted from J. Habart, *Unser Militär-Sanitätswesen vor hundert Jahren* (Vienna, 1896), p. 58.

66 'Die beständigen anatomischen und chirurgischen Übungen an Leichen sind zur Bildung der Feldärzte eine so unentbehrliche Sache, dass der Mangel an solchen Übungen bisher eine Mitursache war, dass sich keine geschickten und beherzten Ärzte bilden konnten', 'Protokoll', quoted from Habart, *Militär-Sanitätswesen*, p. 73.

67 '[Z]um Abscheu und Ärgernis des Publikums, ein Arm oder Fuß einer Leiche unterwegs verlohren gegangen sayn', HHS, Studienrevisionshofkommission (1795–1803), box 26, 'Gutachten des Hofraths und Professors Johann Peter Frank, in Rücksicht auf das medicinische und chirurgische Studium', p. 121. I would like to thank Sonia Horn for alerting me to the Studienrevisionshofkommission's existence. For the rise of clinical medicine in late eighteenth-century Vienna see Othmar Keel, *L'avènement de la médecine clinique moderne en Europe, 1750–1815: Politiques, institutions et savoirs* (Montréal: PUM, 2001).

68 See e.g. Anon., 'Nachricht von der neuen Kayserlich-Königlich Josephinischen medicinisch chirurgischen Academie zu Wien', *Medicinisches Journal* 9 (1786), pp. 3–21, especially p. 9.

69 'Unglückseliger Weise setzte der Kaiser sein Vertrauen in einen Mann, der unstreitig unter die verworrensten, und verwirrendsten Köpfe des achtzehnten Jahrhunderts gehört', *Medicinisch-Chirurgische Zeitung* 2 (1794), p. 325. 'Diese prächtige Akademie hat keine anatomische Uebungs-Anstalt, weder eine chirurgische, noch medicinische Klinik', ibid., pp. 61–2. 'Theils hat er [Brambilla] geradezu bey seinen Einrichtungen das Unentbehrliche dem voluptuösen Luxus aufgeopfert', ibid., vol. 3 (1794), p. 61. 'Aber zeigt diese Einrichtung denn nicht sonnenklar, daß er in der That von dem Satze ausgegangen, um Chirurgie zu studieren, und auszuüben, bedürfe der Studierende keine andere Vorkenntnisse, als Anatomie', ibid., vol. 2 (1794), p. 325.

70 'Freilich ist bei einer so theuren Sammlung blos anatomischer Präparaten mehr Luxus, als wahrer Reichthum; aber bei alledem kann das Vorräthige zur nützlichen Übersicht dienen'. Haus- Hof- und Staatsarchiv Vienna (HHS), Studienrevisionshofkommission (1795–1803), Karton 26, 'Gutachten des Hofraths und Professors Johann Peter Frank, in Rücksicht auf das medicinische und chirurgische Studium', 31 October 1798, pp. 134–5.

71 'L'utilità di questi Preparati è grande, perchè i Chirurghi della Scuola hanno un continuo esercizio anche nell'Anatomia più fina, e siccome nell'estate non si permette la Notomia fresca, il Professore d'Anatomia deve spiegarla in questa stagione sulle figure di Cera, che si pongono sul tavolo nell'Anfiteatro'. G.A. Brambilla, *Appendice alla storia della chirurgia austriaca militare* (Pavia: Pietro Galeazzi, 1800), p. 74.

72 '[D]urch ihr rohes Betragen in [den angehenden Chirurgen] jeden wissenschaftlichen Keim auf immer [unterdrückt]', Hunczovsky, *Rede*, p. 15.

73 'Bey der Aufnahme dieser Zöglinge wird sowohl auf die Eigenschaften des Körpers als jene der Seele Rücksicht genommen, und man ist ebenso aufmerksam auf ihr sittliches Betragen, als man es in der Folge auf die Fortschritte wird, die sie in den Wissenschaften machen'. Hunczovsky, *Rede*, p. 21.

74 For the use of phantoms in eighteenth-century obstetrical training see Gerhard Ritter, 'Das geburtshilfliche Phantom im 18. Jahrhundert', *Medizinhistorisches Journal* 1 (1966), pp. 127–43; Urs Boschung, 'Geburtshilfliche Lehrmodelle. Notizen zur Geschichte des Phantoms und der Hysteroplasmata', *Gesnerus* 38 (1981), pp. 59–68. Phantoms continued to have a customer base in Vienna despite the criticism: see e.g. Johann Bauer, *Verzeichniß der neuesten und brauchbaresten chirurgischen Verbandstücke und Maschinen, die verfertigt werden bey Johann Bauer, chirurgischen Maschinist und Bandagist . . .* (Vienna, 1803), entry no. 261, 'Das künstliche Phantome oder die Geburtsmaschine zum Unterrricht in der Geburtshülfe, fl. 70'. For 'new surgeons' attempts at demarcation in England see Christopher Lawrence, 'Democratic, divine and heroic: the history and historiography of surgery', in Christopher Lawrence (ed.), *Medical theory, surgical practice. Studies in the history of surgery* (London and New York: Routledge, 1992), pp. 1–47, esp. p. 4.

75 Sonia Horn, 'Wiener Hebammen 1643–1753', *Studien zur Wiener Geschichte* (= Jahrbuch des Vereins für Geschichte der Stadt Wien), 59 (2003), pp. 35–102.

76 Jürgen Schlumbohm, '"The pregnant women are here for the sake of the teaching Institution": The Lying-in Hospital of Göttingen University, 1751 to *c.*1830', *Social history of medicine* 14:1 (2001), pp. 59–78; Hans-Ch. Seidel, *Eine neue Kultur des Gebärens: Die Medikalisierung von Geburt im 18. und 19. Jahrhundert in Deutschland* (Stuttgart: Franz Steiner, 1998).

77 'Die Hebammen wollten das Kind nach ihrer Art holen; die Akkuschörs behaupteten, diese Art wäre nicht methodisch; die Hebammen hießen die Akkuschörs methodische Narren; die Akkuschörs bewiesen es ihnen sehr gelehrt, daß sie keine wären; die Hebammen fielen ihnen endlich in die Haare; die Akkuschörs warfen diese an Boden; die Handlangerinnen halfen den Hebammen. [. . .] Die Hebammen hatten den Akkuschörs die Perrücken und ihre Haare ausgerupfet; diese hatten der Hebammen Hauben und einige Stücke von ihren Kleidern in Händen; die Handlangerinnen blaue Augen und gebäulte Köpfe [. . .]. Alle schnoben, um sich zu erholen, und Fräulein Eselin indessen – starb sehr methodisch'. Huber, *Esel*, vol. 1, pp. 44–5.

78 'Durch ihr gütiges Betragen, weise Anordnungen und Geschicklichkeit retteten sie manche theure Gemahlinn, sie erhielten den Kindern ihre Mütter, sie gaben der Mutter den Lohn ihrer beschwerlichen Arbeit. Sie erhielten Thronfolger zum Wohl des Staates.' Raphael Steidele, *Abhandlung von der Geburtshülfe* (Vienna: von Trattner, 1803), vol. 4 ('Vom Gebrauch der Instrumente'), 'Vorbericht' (no pagination).

79 For critical views in late eighteenth-century Austria on the training with dummies see Erna Lesky, 'Theorie und Praxis, aufgezeigt an den Wiener geburtshilflichen Lehrkanzeln 1752–1859', *Gesnerus* 1:2 (1983), pp. 99–107.

80 'Doch muß der Lehrer besorgt seyn, mehrere Leiche von Weibern, und ungebohrenen Kindern zu solchem Endzwecke zu verwenden, und zu verhüten, daß die Schüler sich in der künstlichen Puppe Handgriffe angewohnen, welche sie sich in einer lebenden Gebährenden nur mit Gefahr für diese, oder für ihr Kind, erlauben würden'. HHS, Studienrevisionshofkommission (1795–1803), Karton 26, 'Gutachten des Hofraths und Professors Johann Peter Frank, in Rücksicht auf das medicinische und chirurgische Studium', 31 October 1798, p. 276.

81 'Alle Maschinen heissen nichts; ja sie sind vielen Lehrlingen mehr schädlich als nützlich, weil sie sich die gröbste Behandlungsart unwillkürlich angewöhnen'. Steidele, *Geburtshülfe*, vol. 4 ('Vom Gebrauch der Instrumente'), 'Vorbericht' (no pagination).

82 Present-day medical modelling for training purposes still grapples with this problem. For a responsive 'dummy patient' developed to familiarise students with the distressful situation of emergencies see Jerome Groopman, 'A model patient; How simulators are changing the way doctors are trained', *New Yorker*, 2 May 2005. For the continuing close relationship between surgeons' tools and their bodily practice see Rachel Prentice, 'The anatomy of a surgical simulation: the mutual articulation of bodies in and through the machine', *Social studies of science* 35 (2005), pp. 837–66.

83 See e.g. Karl Asmund Rudolphi, *Bemerkungen aus dem Gebiet der Naturgeschichte, Medicin und Thierarzneykunde, auf einer Reise durch einen Theil von Deutschland, Holland und Frankreich gesammelt...* (Berlin: Realschulbuchhandlung, 1804); Johann Friedrich Osiander, *Nachricht von Wien über Gegenstände der Medicin, Chirurgie und Geburtshilfe* (Tübingen: Christian Friedrich Osiander, 1817).

84 Joseph Scherer, *Tabulae anatomicae, quae exhibent musaei anatomici Academiae Caes. Josephinae praeparata cerea* (Vienna 1817–21); Anton Römer, *Handbuch der Anatomie des menschlichen Körpers* (Vienna: Heubner, 1831).

85 For a similar rejection of Specola-style wax models at the Muséum d'histoire naturelle in the 1790s for being too close to popular entertainment, see Emma C. Spary, 'Forging nature at the republican Muséum', in Lorraine Daston and Gianna Pomata (eds), *The faces of nature in enlightenment Europe* (Berlin: Berliner Wissenschafts-Verlag, 2003), pp. 163–80.

86 Despite this rapprochement between physicians and surgeons the Josephinum continued to exist as an autonomous institution until 1874, accepting students until 1859. Jantsch, *Gründung des Josephinums*, pp. 57–8.

6

Regime changes in Tuscany and at La Specola, 1790–1814

In 1790, Grand Duke Pietro Leopoldo departed for Vienna to succeed his brother Joseph as Austrian emperor Leopold II, leaving Tuscany in the care of his second son Ferdinando. Over the course of the next 25 years, and especially in the aftermath of the French Revolution, Tuscany went through numerous regime changes. Throughout these changes, the museum managed to ensure its costly existence in a state with massive financial and political problems. The models' rejection in Vienna indicates the fragility of the artificial anatomies' status as useful representations of the body – how, then, can their survival in Florence be accounted for? Analysing how the museum's naturalists and administrators continued to justify the utility of the artificial anatomies in different political contexts, and how changing governments envisioned the function of the public museum and its collections, this last chapter argues that the interpretive flexibility of the models proved beneficial for their survival.

Naturalists tried to instrumentalise regime changes to push their own agenda for the museum as a place for public education. However, regime changes could be both an opportunity and a threat for the museum and its model workshop. While museum naturalists' competency to evaluate and authorise the models was not challenged, they could not always maintain the authority to determine the artificial anatomies' purpose. The changing success of the museum's administration in aligning itself with governments gives evidence for the continuities between enlightened absolutism and the French Revolution, with regard to the function and treatment of natural knowledge. The events between 1799 and 1814 show that the ideological similarities between enlightened absolutism and the French Revolution helped to sustain the museum as an institution where natural expertise was created, exercised, and displayed. In these negotiations, models could serve as a point of reference for the museum's direction to articulate its alignment with the new regime.

Tuscany under Ferdinando III, 1790–99

In response to the French Revolution, Pietro Leopoldo and his advisers tried to push their reforms further, convinced that these measures would increase public happiness and thus forestall public unrest. This strategy backfired, however, since the accelerated pace of change heightened the population's sense of insecurity – just as Joseph II had frequently overestimated the public acceptance of rationalising measures like the introduction of reusable coffins in Austria. In 1790, after Joseph's death, the Tuscan Grand Duke succeeded his brother as Holy Roman Emperor Leopold II. In Vienna, the zealous enlightener's quest for public happiness had to give way to attempts to control the volatile international situation.[1] Shortly after Pietro Leopoldo's departure, the rift in public opinion with regard to his far-reaching reforms became openly visible.[2] Popular outcry arose against the reforms, which were held responsible for food shortages: 'Bread, flour, and all as before!'[3] On 7 March 1791 Leopold's second son officially succeeded his father as Grand Duke Ferdinando III of Tuscany. With Leopold II's early death in 1792, Ferdinando was free of his father's strong influence.

The new Grand Duke's politics in the 1790s responded to the increasingly vocal popular unrest and to the complicated European politics of the revolutionary wars. Tuscany's military was weak; the Grand Duchy initially retained its neutrality, as its Mediterranean port of Livorno was used by both the French and the British navies. The occasional occupation of the important harbour by the French army, and its defence, posed a heavy financial burden on Tuscany, especially since trade was strongly diminished. Against the recommendations of the Accademia dei Georgofili and the Consiglio di Stato, Ferdinando retreated from his father's politics of nature. Where Pietro Leopoldo had introduced free trade, his son returned to imposing restrictions on trade in grains and basic foods, since some members of government, and the general public, had considered free trade in grain to be the cause of rising grain prices.

In this period of economic and political insecurity, a number of 'miracles', such as the sudden brightening of a darkened image of the Madonna in a chapel in Arezzo, fuelled popular religion. Already in 1780, Uffizi director Pelli had criticised Pietro Leopoldo's radical anti-spectacular legislation and predicted that 'the people want spectacles and celebrations to pacify the senses and uplift them from their misery'.[4] Popular enlightenment had not extinguished such needs, and the Church used these events to foster religious devotion.[5] Under these circumstances, the new Grand Duke's politics were increasingly pro-nobility and pro-clergy. Public debt was on the rise, both because of the financial strains imposed by the wars, and because Ferdinando was less frugal than his father and predecessor.

Pro-Leopoldian intellectuals in Tuscany considered Ferdinando's politics to be a step backwards; many proclaimed sympathies for the aims of the French Revolution, for instance at the salon of Giovanni Fabbroni's wife Teresa Pelli Fabbroni. At the same time, they adopted a moderate stance with regard to political change, and argued that, unlike France, a total democratisation of Tuscany was unnecessary because Pietro Leopoldo's reforms had progressive aims that were similar to those of the revolutionaries, and because a strong enlightened monarch would be more successful in carrying out reforms that would benefit all parts of society equally.[6] At the museum, Fontana continued his work on the detachable wood anatomy to realise the artificial anatomies' civilising mission, but he did not succeed in gaining additional financial support from the grand-ducal court for this project. The production of new waxes slowed down considerably since artisans were occupied by the wood project.[7] At La Specola, as elsewhere in Tuscany, preservation of the status quo was the order of the day. This would change with the French invasion of Tuscany in 1799.

The French occupation, 1799–1801

On 12 March 1799, the French Directorate declared war on Austria, now ruled by Pietro Leopoldo's eldest son Francis II, and on his brother Ferdinando's Grand Duchy of Tuscany. Less than two weeks later, France occupied Tuscany with an army of 7000. Ferdinando was exiled to Vienna, and a French provisional government was installed, headed by military commander General Gaultier with the former French ambassador to Tuscany, the moderate Charles de Reinhard, as political and civil authority. During the occupation, French revolutionary ideals had to take a back seat behind political considerations over the balance of power in Europe. Tuscany was not republicanised, but kept in limbo under a military occupation as potential trading material for the French Directorate's negotiations with other European powers. Therefore, the local administration was kept largely intact.

Since the occupation did not result in reforms after the model of the new French Republic, Reinhard's moderate, church- and nobility-friendly politics managed to alienate both the anti-French general population and pro-revolutionary Tuscans, who had hoped that the new regime would reanimate Pietro Leopoldo's reforms, which had largely been dormant under Ferdinando. The French did not endear themselves either when they emptied the state's coffers and extracted repeated contributions from the population. By the end of May, the occupation had already cost Tuscany a staggering 8 million

Lire, equivalent to almost all of the state's total annual revenue of 9 million.[8] The French military government and its detractors alike tried to win public support. Despite Pietro Leopoldo's campaign for education, illiteracy was still widespread, and the Church proved most successful at popular enrolment. Religious authorities recognised the importance of tradition and customs that were dismissed by the old Grand Duke and the new revolutionaries.[9] Church leaders thus presented food shortages as divine punishment for the impiety of the republicans and the passivity of Tuscans against them.[10] Subsequently, popular uprisings throughout Tuscany rallied around the pro-Catholic outcry of 'Viva Maria!'[11]

The French invasion started a pattern of interaction between the museum's administration and the government which would characterise La Specola throughout the various regime changes that followed, until the restoration of 1814. Every new regime requested an inventory of all state institutions. Museum directors and affiliates such as anatomist Mascagni used this interest to try to enrol new governments in their own vision of La Specola's future as a place for public education. Such visions, both imagined and realised, con-stituted different relationships between state, experts, and the public at the museum. Within these constellations, the function of the anatomical models changed. As in Vienna, the models' accuracy was not challenged through-out these institutional changes; however, the artificial anatomies were not necessarily integrated into systems of knowledge production.

The day after the invasion, eighteen French soldiers set up camp at La Specola in the porters' rooms, and received lamps, firewood and cooking utensils paid from the museum's budget. After the entrances had been sealed and the museum's current monetary assets determined, the museum's keys were officially handed over to the French commissary Abrâm, and passed on to Fontana, who openly professed pro-revolutionary sympathies. The museum could, of course, no longer be subordinate to the (abandoned) grand-ducal court; instead, it was submitted under the authority of the municipality of Florence, which declared that the museum should continue its work as far as possible with its remaining assets.[12] During the absence of Fabbroni, who was attending a congress on the metric system in Paris as a member of the Tuscan delegation, Fontana used his alliance with the French to take charge of the entire museum again, and to reiterate his disciplinary rules, backed by the new military government's muscle.[13] In accordance with his earlier attempts to discipline the modellers, he once more posted a set of rules which reconfirmed artisans' duty to be punctual, and to refrain from gossiping and wandering around, reiterating his conviction that 'the perfection of the works does not permit distractions'.[14]

Without Fabbroni's supervision, Fontana, once more, set upon his devil-may-care course of financial management. Less than a month after the introduction of the new administration, the museum's accountant Parlini had to remind the director that they would run out of money within a few days.[15] Fontana countered that the museum should continue its model and instrument production of pieces already started, since otherwise the employees would receive their wages to no advantage of the museum.[16] However, political events prevented any further development: counter-revolutionary troops seized Florence, and arrested the pro-French Fontana on 8 July 1799. He was officially suspended by the Florentine senate, and all work at the museum came to a halt.[17] During this period, all expenses that went beyond mere conservation were prohibited.[18] When requested by the senate to evaluate the wood project, anatomist Bonicoli once more affirmed his earlier judgement that the wood anatomy could never be carried to the same degree of 'subtlety' as the waxes, and therefore should not be continued.[19]

Shortly afterwards the French army once more prevailed and repossessed the city, but the provisional government was keen not to alienate the locals further. The French asserted their high regard for Tuscany's artistic and scientific heritage and declared that 'all public institutions of the state which keep precious monuments of the arts and sciences will be respected, and preserved for the benefit of the nation'.[20] Fontana was reinstated as director, but this time once more under the economic supervision of Fabbroni, who had returned from Paris.[21] During the first invasion, the soldiers billeted at the museum had caused some damage with open fires and petty theft, but this time, in accordance with the government's proclamation of protection, La Specola no longer had to serve as soldiers' quarters.[22] French officials such as the commander-in-chief Murat visited the museum, thus demonstrating the new administration's interest, and the provisional government repeatedly stressed its support of scientific institutions of public education.[23] Significantly, the new administration put its money where its mouth was, and provided financial support, albeit under the warning to 'adopt the strictest economy'.[24] To augment state contributions, the military administration instructed local religious orders such as the Vallombrosani and Benedictines to 'donate' to the museum.[25]

Despite the otherwise fairly desolate financial situation of Tuscany, and of the museum's budget, Fontana used the French occupation to further his own goals for the wood anatomy. In many respects, the interests of the French revolutionary regime in natural history and natural philosophy for the new republic were identical to those which Pietro Leopoldo has pursued. Revolutionary politicians, such as the members of the Committee on Public Education, regarded the revolution as the realisation of the Enlightenment, and maintained that public education in natural laws would transform subjects into citizens of the republic. At the same time, knowledge of natural laws was considered to further material improvement through technological progress. Finally, public displays of nature should convey the function of nature as the source for political authority, and serve to give an image of the new nation.[26]

La Specola, under Pietro Leopoldo, had thus anticipated the goals of the revolutionaries. Already in the early 1790s, the French government, informed about the Florentine models by 'ideal visitor' Desgenettes, had professed an interest in Fontana's model production, and had ordered copies of the anatomical waxes, which the director produced in a private initiative at his own home. In 1801, model production was taken up again because Napoleon, then First Consul, had once more expressed interest in the waxes and the wood anatomy project.[27] He ordered the Tuscan provisional government to pay an additional 12,000 Lire to Fontana for materials and workers' wages, and to provide him with a building near the museum for his workshop.[28] Fontana took up production in a house not far from the museum in via Maggio,[29] and received permission to use museum models and tools for the models intended for France.[30] Napoleon's backing thus allowed the director to pursue the wood anatomy project further.[31] Fontana's powerful ally, the First Consul, publicly demonstrated his interest and support during a visit to the museum on 29 December 1801, at which Fontana guided him through the exhibition accompanied by all the employees.[32] The director's alliance with the new regime had paid off. Siena anatomist Mascagni, who had supported Fontana earlier in the production of models representing the lymphatic system, pursued a similar strategy. He openly professed sympathies for the new regime, and used his alliance with the French to push his own agenda at the museum. He requested, and received, permission to reorganise (or, as the disgruntled Fabbroni remarked, 'disorganise') the collection of preparations of lymphatic and blood vessels to which he had contributed.[33] The new regime thus enabled Fontana and Mascagni, the two expert naturalists who had publicly proclaimed sympathies for the French occupation, to realise their own visions for the model collection.

The Kingdom of Etruria, 1801–8

However, the museum's status was soon endangered by the accession of a new regime, which was far less concerned with public enlightenment than either Pietro Leopoldo or the French had been. Following the stipulations of the Peace of Lunéville, in 1801 Tuscany was turned into a new political entity, the Regno d'Etruria. To further the alliance between Spain and the French Republic, the satellite kingdom went to the Spanish Bourbon Ferdinando, Duke of Parma, who passed it on to his son Lodovico. The large public debt was the most urgent of Tuscany's problems in these years, occupying the government and independent commentators alike.[34] At that time, Tuscany had accumulated a debt of over 142 million Lire, and the new kingdom's government was forced to demand further extraordinary payments from the population, and to sell crown property. The king called in an economic consulting deputation, appointing mostly local advisers. Fabbroni was among the members of the deputation, and became director of the mint in 1802.[35]

Recent wars notwithstanding, European travellers and locals continued to flock to the museum on their visits to Florence.[36] Echoing Pietro Leopoldo's strategy forty years earlier, the new Bourbon sovereigns used Tuscany's scientific and artistic heritage, and the museum's international fame, to place themselves in line with previous dynasties. On his ascent to the Etrurian throne, Lodovico aligned himself with previous regimes by stressing his protection of intellectual and cultural life:

> Yours is the country of the arts and sciences. The new sovereign who is coming to govern here has drawn the attention of Europe with his taste for the sciences, and the arts ... His ascent to the Throne foretells you all the glorious successes which rendered Tuscany famous under the Reign of the Medici, and of Leopoldo.[37]

However, it is not clear whether he intended to carry out any measures regarding the sciences which went beyond these legitimatory pronouncements. Lodovico did not take action immediately, and his early death prevented any further development.

King Lodovico's demise in 1803, so soon after his ascent to the throne, prompted a more conservative turn in Tuscan politics as his widow Maria Luisa became regent for her three-year-old son. This development affected many areas of Tuscan political and cultural life. It posed a new challenge for the museum, its model collection and its naturalists, but also an opportunity for some, especially Fabbroni, to pursue their plans for the role of experts at the museum. The Spanish Bourbons had already revoked most of Pietro Leopoldo's secularising ecclesiastical legislation soon after their accession – a move unopposed by the French since the First Consul at that time tried to reconcile with the Pope. After her husband's death, the Queen, who was prone to public demonstrations of her faith, donned a nun's habit. Political action in Etruria was increasingly influenced by the Queen's conservative clerical advisers, and Maria Luisa's course diverged from the reformist suggestions of the pro-Leopoldian local advisers whom her late husband had hired.

Fabbroni and his colleagues in the economic deputation put forward ideas for improvement which were based on their liberal creed, supporting the right of property, the position of landowners, and free trade, and Fabbroni was considered a likely candidate for the position of minister of finance by his peers.[38] However, the Queen, who increasingly relied on her conservative Spanish advisers, was suspicious of the deputation's activities, and the influence of its members on public opinion. Her reaction to this development was similar to Pietro Leopoldo's response to the increasing demands for agency of the Chamber of Commerce: she dissolved the deputation in 1805. Administration continued to be chaotic during Maria Luisa's reign. The Queen's actions were observed closely by Napoleon's sister Elisa Baciocchi, who reigned over Lucca and Piombino, territories to the North and South of Tuscany, and the French hold on Etruria tightened.

During the early years of the nineteenth century, La Specola was in disarray like the general administration. Fontana was now in his 70s, his health was declining, and he was occupied exclusively with the production of the models for Paris at his private workshop. According to Fabbroni, he did not set foot in the museum between 1801 and 1803.[39] The vice-director himself was occupied in various ways, especially as a member of the economic commission, and as the new director of the mint. In addition, he battled against the museum's physical decline, combating an insect infestation, which had set in during his sojourn in Paris and which had done serious damage to the museum's books and furniture.[40]

Giuseppe Pelli, Fabbroni's father-in-law, lamented the museum's descent into chaos: 'Everything goes in a desultory manner, and casually, without order.'[41] In his view this disarray was due to the current regime's neglect; after all, the French invasions had left the museum intact. The new dynasty's stance as protector of the sciences was no more than lip-service. Lodovico had not united the museum's collection with his own, as promised, and his successor queen Maria Luisa did not provide the funding that would be necessary to develop it further. Thus, at this point, 'all the expenses made by Leopoldo were wasted, and did not serve for anything but a sterile show'. The anatomical waxes still constituted a 'beautiful series', but they did not serve for the teaching of anatomy. The museum's deterioration was exacerbated further, in Pelli's view, by the 'spirit of charlatanish disorganization' of director Fontana (which Pelli had complained about throughout the previous decades), 'our current poverty', and his son-in-law Fabbroni's 'excess of occupations'.[42]

Instead of furthering the museum's development as a public institution, the new dynasty blurred the demarcation between private and public collections, which Pietro Leopoldo had attempted to strengthen. Rather than donating their private collection, the Bourbons used the museum employees' experience with the preservation of *naturalia* for their own cabinet of curiosities. In 1805, La Specola's administrators were charged with overseeing the maintenance of the Bourbons' precious natural historical objects, while stressing that this collection would nevertheless remain at the palace, rather than contribute to public education.[43]

Despite the Etrurian regime's retreat from public science, Fabbroni did not give up on his plan to create a new forum for the performance of expertise by introducing teaching at the museum (see Chapter 4). In the regime's early years, after the king had hired advisers from the ranks of the local administration, Fabbroni still had hopes that the middle-class civil servants whom Pietro Leopoldo had installed would retain their agency at court. The vice-director used his initial influence with the new regime, and probably Fontana's lack of allies within it, to realise his earlier idea to introduce teachers to render the anatomical models instructive and useful through active mediation.[44] Fontana had thrown in his lot with the French and the wood anatomy project, and abandoned the supervision of wax modelling. The anatomist Filippo Uccelli, a nephew of Fabbroni who had worked as a dissector for the model workshop and the hospital Santa Maria Nuova, was made anatomy teacher at the Royal Museum in 1804.[45] He was instructed to continue the supervision of model production, and to use the collection of waxes to teach a course on anatomy, primarily for medical students during the summer months, when the work with real cadavers was suspended.[46] Apparently, in practice, Uccelli also performed daily anatomical demonstrations using the models.[47] He immediately set about shaping the museum's zoological collection according to his teaching activities, adding new wet specimens, wax models, and skeletons.[48]

The museum experienced its very own regime change when Fontana passed away on 10 March 1805. Like Antonio Cocchi, Fontana was dissected, and his status as a celebrated scholar was confirmed when he was buried in the chapel of Santa Croce with Galileo and Michelangelo.[49] Immediately after Fontana's death (and before Fabbroni's official election as interim director on 19 March 1805), custodian Raddi used Fontana's demise to suggest to Fabbroni a purging of the museum according to their own priorities. He advocated getting rid of the pathology models (which Fabbroni as well had considered inappropriate for an anatomical collection), to discard some of the lymphatic vessel preparations by Mascagni, which he deemed neither 'instructive' nor 'useful', and to purge the collection of duplicate waxes. Furthermore, Raddi advocated closing off some walls between the rooms of the anatomical model collection to streamline visitors' passage through the exhibition.[50] Fabbroni's response is not recorded, and later documents indicate that this purge was not carried out, at least not completely. Earlier statements show that Fabbroni agreed, in principle, with Raddi's assessment; it is, therefore, likely that these measures were not realised owing to his 'excess of occupations' rather than a lack of approval.

After a short interim period with Fabbroni as acting director, in 1806 the position went to the nobleman Count Girolamo de' Bardi (1777–1829), who would retain it through the following governments of the French Empire and the restoration period.[51] As the heir of one of Florence's pre-eminent noble families, Bardi was elected court chamberlain in line with Maria Luisa's policy of installing noblemen and clergy into offices. Bardi agreed with Fabbroni on the importance of public education, and of the mediating presence of expert naturalists, and used his influence at court to advance the museum's transformation into a teaching institution. In early 1807, Bardi submitted a proposal for turning the museum into a lyceum (*liceo*), a teaching institution endowed with six teaching chairs. With this transformation, the new director hoped to use the collections for public education after the model of the Collège de France, a teaching institution open to everybody free of charge, which offered lectures in a variety of branches of natural science without conferring degrees.[52]

In addition to following the model of the French institution, Bardi also promoted a change to the content of the subjects represented at La Specola, which would align it with current trends of scientific research in France. His argument for the continuation of anatomical model production, despite the high costs, rested to a large degree on the rise of comparative anatomy, which was fostered by the current tsar of French natural history Georges Cuvier. Cuvier promoted comparative anatomy, for instance with his *Leçons d'anatomie comparée* (1800–5), as a means to reconstruct the laws that regulated the animal economy through explanations of the functions of its constituent parts.[53] In accordance with Cuvier's claims for the uses of comparative anatomy to provide functional accounts of (human and animal) bodies, Bardi argued that it was 'necessary' to supplement Uccelli's course on human anatomy with comparative demonstrations of the anatomy of animals 'for the greatest advantage of physiology'.[54] Bardi's plan was 'approved in all its parts' by Queen Maria Luisa, probably at least in part because she wanted to ingratiate herself with the French, at whose grace she reigned over 'Etruria'.[55] In addition, like other sovereigns before her, the Queen exploited the museum as a showpiece of her magnificence.

The opening ceremony of the new *liceo* was staged in detail, down to the sequence and number of genuflections. In the presence of foreign ambassadors and high court officials, the Queen signed a special edition, in leather, of the museum's books, and subsequently an account of the ceremony was published.[56] A great hall was adorned with the portraits of famous Florentines, most prominently Galileo and explorer Amerigo Vespucci, drawing attention once more to Tuscany's long scientific tradition.[57] This choreography rearticulated the museum's representational function. Already, under Pietro Leopoldo, the museum had constituted a representation of the sovereign. However, where the Grand Duke had considered the very existence of the museum as a place for public enlightenment a sufficient display of his magnanimity, the Bourbon regime turned the museum into a stage for courtly spectacle, thus using the collection as a display of legitimacy in a different way.

Bardi's initiative won him the title of 'Director and general superintendent of public education for the Kingdom of Etruria' ('Direttore e Soprintendente Generale della Pubblica Istruzione nel Regno di Etruria').[58] However, this title seems to have been largely decorative, since despite Bardi's repeated suggestions for educational reforms, with the exception of the foundation of the *liceo* the Bourbons did not introduce any further changes.[59]

But at the museum, at least, Bardi's plans came to fruition. Six professors took up their new teaching post, lecturing on physics (Giovanni Babbini), astronomy (Domenico de' Vecchi), chemistry (Giuseppe Gazzeri), zoology and mineralogy (Filippo Nesti), botany (Ottaviano Targioni Tozzetti), and anatomy (Filippo Uccelli).[60] Fulfilling his uncle Fabbroni's vision of the mediating expert, Uccelli gave daily lectures for his new course on comparative anatomy, using the corpses of humans and animals, skeletons, and anatomical waxes of humans and animals.[61] Under his guidance, the modellers now increasingly turned to animal models as required for Cuvierian comparative anatomy; for the years 1807 until 1811, Uccelli reported the completion, or current production, of wax models of animals such as the silkworm, snail, turkey, chicken, whiting, goat, cat, and cuttlefish – many of them selected in accordance with Cuvier's works.[62] However, the anatomist lamented a shortage of means which, he claimed, caused 'serious inconveniences' for the progress of instruction.[63]

While documentation for this period is patchy, there is no evidence that the collaboration between Uccelli and the modellers was as fraught with tension as it had been during Fontana's time. The new anatomist may have shared his uncle Fabbroni's tendency to put more trust in the modellers' abilities than the old director – and he did not demand the same degree of autonomy as Fontana had done. The increasing recognition of their contribution to the production of artificial anatomies, and Fontana's absence, encouraged the modellers to be more vocal in their own claims for model authorship. Early descriptions of the models, such as those by Fontana's ideal visitors Desgenettes and Wichelhausen, did not mention the modellers by name, but this changed around 1800. Marco Lastri's account of Florence's cultural riches *Osservatore fiorentino sugli edifizi della sua patria* explicitly mentioned Susini as the artist responsible for the anatomical models.[64] In his first report, Uccelli praised the 'truth' and 'elegance' of the waxes produced by 'our peerless artists Signor Clemente Susini and Signor Francesco Calenzoli' – praise echoed by Giovanni Prezziner in his 1810 *Storia del pubblico studio e delle società scientifiche e letterarie di Firenze*.[65] Susini used his reputation to claim the waxes, the most admired part of the museum, as his work. In a request for a raise, for instance, he contended that '*his* works . . . are the most peculiar object of the establishment, and are admired by connoisseurs'.[66]

His assistant Calenzuoli, who had been Susini's apprentice, claimed similar authorship; he too cited visitors' recognition of the models as the works of Susini and himself when requesting a raise in salary, or other favours.[67] The modellers' increased status as artists rather than artisans was evident not only in these claims to authorship. In addition, Susini's increasing status was furthered by, or expressed through, a part-time position as instructor at the Accademia delle Belle Arti, which he held at least since 1799; he was also one of the judges for the Academy's prize competitions for art students.[68] By the time of his death in 1814, Susini was publicly acknowledged as an artist. An obituary in the *Gazzetta di Firenze* praised him as a 'celebrated modeller' and a 'worthy artist'. The anonymous author referred to the anatomical waxes as Susini's work, and considered the models' accuracy to be his achievement:

> his works leave nothing more to be desired, be it in the beauty which he gave to the most revolting things, be it for the truth and accuracy, and for the insight of these works.[69]

Under the French Empire, 1808–14

Another regime change posed a potential danger to director Bardi's recent achievement of turning the museum into a teaching institution, and prompted him once more to rearticulate the museum's function for the state. Maria Luisa was relieved of her artificial new kingdom by the French when she disobeyed their orders to uphold the blockade against Britain and its allies.[70] In 1808, Tuscany was formally divided into three *départements*, which were incorporated into the French Empire. The new regent was Napoleon's sister Elisa, Grand Duchess of Tuscany from 1809, who promised to her brother 'to second Your Majesty's grand and liberal visions for the arts and sciences'.[71]

Tuscan law and administration were amalgamated with, and subordinated to, the French system under Consigliere di Stato Dauchy. These measures were carried out zealously, but they were often subject to bad organisation and ambiguous distributions of responsibilities.[72] The new government's pressure for change threatened the Royal Museum, especially since education was monopolised by the state under the French imperial university system. The eminent naturalist Georges Cuvier, whose studies in comparative anatomy had inspired La Specola's recent zoological waxes, was put in charge of the reorganisation of the former university at Pisa as an Imperial Academy, and of uniting Tuscan educational institutions with the imperial system of *Écoles supérieures*.[73] This reform of the education system not only brought about institutional, but also curricular changes, in favour of the natural sciences and mathematics: The new *université* system created for the first time a separate faculty of sciences at Pisa to provide a technical education for engineers.[74] Once more, as during the French invasions of 1799–1800, the new government emphasised its protection of cultural institutions; and the destruction or damage of 'public monuments of the sciences and the arts' was now punishable with two years of prison.[75]

As with previous regime changes, the new administration requested reports from all public institutions. Already, on 25 January 1808, the Consigliere di Stato demanded that the museum's administration address the following points:

> What is the precept of this establishment, both in relationship to the scope of its foundation, and also with respect to public education, to which it has lately been directed. What is its budget, and what allowances does this consists of. Who are the persons destined to teach there.[76]

This time, however, Bardi was not as keen to contribute information and suggestions as the new government was to receive it: only a week later, he was admonished by the court administration to deliver the requested report, which was still outstanding.[77] This delay may be due to the fact that he had achieved the institutional changes he had advocated for the museum. Submission under the centralised French system of public education and administration would have limited the recent institutional achievement. And indeed, already two months after the initial enquiry, the museum's financial administration and accountability were subordinated to the office for the general conservation of public buildings, which, as Bardi told professor of chemistry Giuseppe Gazzeri, gave him 'no little displeasure'.[78] This subordination under civil administration occasionally caused friction. When the museum managed to stay under budget in 1812, for instance, Bardi wanted to use the surplus for the publication of a volume of annals containing scientific papers by museum professors. However, his superiors in the civil administration would not allow it, preferring to divert the money elsewhere.[79]

While this submission curtailed the museum's autonomy to some degree, Bardi managed to avoid its integration into the centralised *université* system by drawing on a French precedent, the Muséum d'histoire naturelle in Paris. In 1812, the resident inspector of Florence reminded the director of the imperial decree of 1808 which had given the *université* the monopoly on public educa- tion, and which had therefore put all institutions of public education under its central administration. The inspector argued that owing to this decree, 'the teachers of the Museum are necessarily subjected under the Imperial University', and that they were under the jurisdiction of the director of the University of Pisa.[80] Bardi therefore had to comply with the Pisa director's request for information concerning the professors employed at the museum.[81]

At this point, La Specola's good contacts with Paris scientific institutions helped Bardi convince the inspector that the Florentine museum's profes- sors should be treated differently from university lecturers. Since Tuscany's incorporation into the French Empire, museum naturalists had repeatedly communicated their activities to the Institut de France, both in person and by mail, and they knew the empire's scientific landscape well.[82] Once more, the continuities of Pietro Leopoldo's enlightened absolutist ideology of natural law with that of the French Revolution proved beneficial for the museum's contin- ued existence, enabling Bardi to highlight La Specola's similarities to another great institution. The museum's director could convince the inspector that his institution and its experts should be treated as a special case. Following Bardi's reasoning, the inspector accepted that the Florence museum was 'established after the same principles as the Muséum of the Jardin des Plantes in Paris', that is, the Muséum d'histoire naturelle, which had been founded by the French revolutionaries in 1793. The Paris Muséum was not part of the *université*, and therefore 'the university [had] no right whatsoever' to the direction of La Specola, which belonged immediately to the Crown.[83]

The Restoration after 1814

Under the French Empire, the museum's immediate link to the Crown pro- tected La Specola's naturalists from submission to the French *université*. After yet another regime change, however – the restoration of the Habsburg-Lorraine dynasty – the same perspective on the museum as a royal possession led to the demise of the museum as a space for experts in state service. After Napoleon's defeat in 1814, Ferdinando III was reinstated to the Tuscan throne. The years in exile at the Viennese court of his brother, the increasingly conservative Francis II, had extinguished whatever motivations for reform he had once pos- sessed. His course of action on reinstatement was to announce the 'return to the old order' of 1799 in all aspects of Tuscan legislation and culture. In the cul- tural sector this meant a return to the old collegial system of higher education, which was 'to be based on the Catholic religion and the purity of its morals, obedience to the Sovereign, and respect for public authorities'.[84]

The museum received a particularly hard blow: On 22 June 1814, even before the Grand Duke's actual return to Florence, his plenipotentiary Rospigliosi ordered the museum to return to 'the order, and system, which was in effect at the time of Our Most Beloved Sovereign's departure, who has always considered this establishment an annex to his own residence, and for his private pleasure'. Where Pietro Leopoldo had reinforced the public character of the museum, Ferdinando insisted on La Specola as his personal possession. The place where he had received instruction from Fontana and other tutors as a child was no longer to be a place of learning for everybody. Within a week, La Specola's teaching chairs were abolished and all courses terminated; employees whose living quarters were in the museum had to leave; and the museum's budget was once more fixed at 32,000 Lire.[85] On 4 July 1814, these orders were put into effect.[86]

Faced with this backlash, Bardi appealed to the Grand Duke to reopen the museum as a teaching institution by describing its successes over the past years. His arguments rested on three main points: an appeal to Ferdinando's esteem of science, invocation of public opinion, and the museum's utility for the state as a teaching institution. In all three cases, however, his appeal fell on deaf ears.

Upon the Grand Duke's actual return to the capital, the director sent a report of the museum's changes since Ferdinando's exile, together with suggestions for further improvement. Once more he tried to align the museum's interest with those of the sovereign and his subjects. Bardi claimed that his initiative to move Queen Maria Luisa to found a *liceo* at La Specola had been inspired by Ferdinando's own attempts to improve public education, as well as by 'the shared wish of civilised and patriotic persons'.[87] This argument was supported by contemporary testimonies such as history professor Giovanni Prezziner's recent account of public education in Florence, which stressed that, as a teaching institution, the museum was 'far more useful to the public'.[88] The additional expenses of the new institute, the museum director argued, had also contributed to the improvement of the collection. Bardi submitted a 'prospect of the improvements made at the Royal Museum from 1807 to 1814', a list which contained new inventions such as Volta's electrometer and a galvanic pile to demonstrate that the museum had kept abreast of scientific development while carrying out its teaching mission with success.[89] Developing his claim to scientific relevance further, Bardi singled out the museum's celebrated model collection and highlighted that the museum had conducted lectures in human anatomy using the 'rich collection of waxes'. He stressed that the institution of a chair of comparative anatomy was in response to the fact that this discipline had recently become 'indispensable for natural history'.[90]

To support his plea to resume instruction at La Specola further, Bardi cited the 'enthusiasm' of the Tuscan people for the new teaching institution, which, he claimed, was of dual use. It completed the scientific studies of young men returning from university, just as medical students completed their studies by the practical courses held at the hospital Santa Maria Nuova. It also provided an opportunity for scientific education for those whose circumstances did not allow them to attend a university in the first place. The director particularly stressed that the local nobility had benefited much from the courses, which had enticed them to take to academic studies. While Bardi did not expand on this point, he may have wished to imply that the improvement of noblemen's education could help Ferdinando to reinstate the nobility to administrative positions while maintaining the advantages of Pietro Leopoldo's previous policy to create a class of well-trained civil servants from the ranks of commoners.

Thus, the nobility in Bardi's accounts could be made useful for the state by making them more like the middle class; and the museum could once more serve to eradicate the differences between different groups of society, thus integrating the nobility as a productive part of the state. Good attendance at the lectures was proof, Bardi argued, of the very positive public reception of the museum as a teaching institution. Surely, the director continued, the discontinuation of classes had only been due to the circumstances (which he did not specify). The public, he assured his sovereign, continued to hope that this measure was only temporary.[91]

However, Bardi's appeal to the sovereign's wish to patronise the sciences, to public opinion, and to considerations of social utility was in vain. For Ferdinando, the museum's representative function could be maintained without any changes from the system which had been in place in the late 1790s. Even less: La Specola no longer needed to be a place for the active production of scientific knowledge in order to fulfil its representational function. To be sure, Ferdinando did not revoke all changes that had been made since his departure, especially in the field of economic legislation. However, he did not take into account public opinion to the same degree as previous governments.

Unlike Pietro Leopoldo and the French, the reinstated Grand Duke had no interest in the levelling of social rank and the creation of an enlightened public through science education. Courses in comparative anatomy were restricted to medical students and transferred to the hospital Santa Maria Nuova, which received the materials previously used by Uccelli in his lectures at the museum. The separation of the museum's representational function from the collection's contribution to education thus mirrored the spatial separation of parts of the model collection. The production and maintenance of waxes continued under Susini's former assistant Calenzuoli, but it was no longer integrated into a concerted plan for public education. The museum and its famous model collection became an arrested showpiece of Tuscan scientific and artistic achievements for noble and well-to-do visitors, a display of princely splendour, much like the Medici *Wunderkammer*, which the Habsburg dynasty had inherited 80 years previously.[92]

Conclusion

During the repeated regime changes between 1799 and 1814, museum naturalists attempted to increase, or at least maintain, their agency, either by professing to act on behalf of the state or by assuming the voice of the public. Their successes and failures made it clear, however, that the state, in the shape of sovereigns or government officials, dictated the museum's fate. Ferdinando's refusal to use the Royal Museum as a place for public education, in particular, illustrates the limits of museum naturalists' ability to instrumentalise political change by articulating the museum in line with the new regime's political goals. The returning Grand Duke's response shows that this instrumentalisation required a willingness on the part of the sovereign or his/her administrators to go along with experts' aims – either his willingness to let the museum's director determine the institution's purpose, or at least a shared vision for the purpose of the museum and its model collection. To a lesser degree, this was a problem during the reign of Etruria under Maria Luisa as well, where Bardi's suggestions for educational reforms had frequently fallen on deaf ears. The crucial difference between Bardi's partial success with Maria Luisa in the establishment of the *liceo* and his complete failure with Ferdinando in its maintenance was the background presence, in Maria Luisa's case, of France.

The efforts of Fontana, Mascagni, and Bardi show that local power structures and alliances played an important role for naturalists' ability to instrumentalise new regimes. At the same time, however, until the restoration in 1814, actors at the museum could also appeal to France directly or indirectly. Where the local government was headed by the French (as in the case of the French occupation and Tuscany's inclusion into the Empire), or dependent on their support (as in the case of Etruria), it was possible for museum employees to align themselves with Paris in two ways. The naturalists could make use of their personal contacts with savants in Paris. In addition, on the conceptual level, La Specola had from its inception incorporated many enlightenment goals shared by the French regimes during and after the revolution. Museum experts and French government representatives found common ground in their views on the importance of natural knowledge in state service, as central to public education, to political legitimation, and to material improvement through innovation. The museum's naturalists drew especially on the anatomical models as the most celebrated elements at La Specola to illustrate these shared assumptions and aims of enlightened absolutism and the French Revolution. The artificial anatomies also permitted greater alignment with French post-revolutionary science through the introduction of comparative anatomy as a new field of expertise.

The appeal to France ceased to be efficient on the resumption of the old regime under Grand Duke Ferdinando III. While normal human anatomy remained with the museum as representative showpieces of Tuscan artisanal and scientific tradition, the pathological and comparative models were transferred to institutions for professional training, such as the hospital Santa Maria Nuova. This separation indicates the changing relationship of the naturalist to the state and to the public. Model production had already brought to the fore a tension between expert naturalists and general audiences when it came to authorising the models: claims that natural knowledge was accessible to everybody were contradicted by naturalists' claims to special abilities. Fabbroni, in particular, highlighted this distinction in his aims for changing exhibition practice at the museum. In his plans for a new way of employing the anatomical models for public education, Fabbroni implied that an enlightened public could not be created solely on the basis of visual perception of the artificial anatomies: rather, this vision had to be guided by expert naturalists.

Through Fabbroni's and successor Bardi's efforts, for a brief period, model use at the museum became a process mediated by knowledgeable teachers rather than a presumably unmediated encounter between object and audience. Museum's naturalists' agency, such as it was, derived in part from this tension between generally accessible and exclusive knowledge. This ambivalence made it possible for the experts to claim to speak for public opinion – to represent, in effect, the opinion the public ought to have if it was fully enlightened. When Ferdinando did away with reference to public opinion as a basis for political legitimacy and political action, the naturalists' agency diminished accordingly.

Notes

1 For Leopoldo's Austrian reign, see e.g. Lettner, Gerda. *Das Rückzugsgefecht der Aufklärung in Wien, 1790–1792* (Frankfurt am Main: Campus, 1988).
2 Gabriele Turi, *'Viva Maria'. Riforme, rivoluzione e insorgenze in Toscana (1790–1799)* (2nd edn, with postscript, Bologna: Il Mulino, 1999), postscript, pp. 325–53.

3 'Pane, farina e tutto come prima'. Luigi Mascilli Migliorini, 'L'età delle riforme', in *Storia d'Italia*, vol. 13/2 (Il Granducato di Toscana. I Lorena dalla Reggenza agli anni rivoluzionari), ed. Giuseppe Galasso (Torino: UTET, 1997), pp. 249–421, on p. 401.

4 '[I]l popolo . . . vuole gli spettacoli, e le feste per pascere i sensi, e per sollevarsi de' suoi mali'. BNCF, Pelli 'Efemeridi', Serie II, vol. VIII (1780), p. 1364.

5 Carlo Mangio, 'Tra conservazione e rivoluzione', ibid., pp. 425–509, on p. 456.

6 See e.g. Fabbroni's *Epicrisi della 'Vita pubblica e privata di Pietro Leopoldo'* (1787), and his *De la Toscane* (1799). Renato Pasta, *Scienza politica e rivoluzione. L'opera di Giovanni Fabbroni (1752–1822) intellettuale e funzionario al servizio dei Lorena* (Florence: Olschki, 1989), pp. 420ff.

7 La Specola, '1793. Giornale dei Modellatori', '1796. Giornale dei Modellatori', '1797. Giornale dei Modellatori', '1798. Giornale dei Modellatori'.

8 Mangio, 'Conservazione', p. 477.

9 Turi, *'Viva Maria'*, postscript, pp. 325–53.

10 Mangio, 'Conservazione', p. 485.

11 Turi, *'Viva Maria'*.

12 IMSS–ARMU, Filza di negozi dell'anno 1799, fol. 98, fol. 110, fol. 120.

13 IMSS–ARMU, Filza di negozi dell'anno 1799, fol. 17; IMSS–ARMU, Filza di negozi dell'anno 1799, fol. 116 (doc. 87). For Fontana's calling on the French authorities see IMSS–ARMU, Filza di negozi dell'anno 1799, fol. 145, 7 June 1799.

14 'Che restano vietate le ciarle, e le conversazioni tra i Lavoranti in Cera, e quelli in Legno etc, come pure di andare gli uni nelle Stanze degli altri, perche la perfezione dei Lavori non ammette distrazioni'. IMSS–ARMU, Filza di negozi dell'anno 1799, fol. 120 (doc. 87).

15 IMSS–ARMU, Filza di negozi dell'anno 1799, fols 124–125 (10 May 1799).

16 IMSS–ARMU, Filza di negozi dell'anno 1799, fol. 148.

17 IMSS–ARMU, Filza di negozi dell'anno 1799, fol. 56, fol. 48, fol. 44.

18 IMSS–ARMU, Filza di negozi dell'anno 1800, fol. 17.

19 '[S]ottigliezza'; IMSS–ARMU, Filza di negozi dell'anno 1800, fol. 16.

20 '[T]utti gli Stabilimenti Pubblici dello Stato di Toscana, nei quali si conservano Monumenti preziosi delle Belle Arti [added: e Scienze] saranno rispettati, e conservati a favore della Nazione', IMSS–ARMU, Filza di negozi dell'anno 1800, fol. 18 (doc. 15).

21 IMSS–ARMU, Filza di negozi dell'anno 1801, fol. 71.

22 IMSS–ARMU, Filza di negozi dell'anno 1799, fol. 24, fol. 30.

23 IMSS–ARMU, Filza di negozi dell'anno 1801, fol. 116 (24 January 1801); e.g. IMSS–ARMU, Filza di negozi dell'anno 1801, fol. 7, fol. 71.

24 '[A]dottare la più stretta economia'; IMSS–ARMU, Filza di negozi dell'anno 1801, fol. 7.

25 IMSS–ARMU, Filza di negozi dell'anno 1801, fol. 12.

26 For education's role for the formation of the republican citizen see e.g. Charles

C. Gillispie, *Science and polity in France: the revolutionary and Napoleonic years* (Princeton: Princeton University Press, 2004), p. 153; Emma C. Spary, *Utopia's garden. French natural history from old regime to revolution* (Chicago and London: University of Chicago Press, 2000), pp. 10–14; for material innovation, see e.g. Gillispie, *Revolutionary and Napoleonic years*, pp. 195–209; for displays of nature as source of authority and image of the nation, see e.g. Spary, *Utopia's garden*, ch. 5, 'The spectacle of nature: the Muséum d'Histoire Naturelle and the Jacobins'. For a selection of Italian texts from the late 1790s which aimed to educate the populace in the new revolutionary tenets, see Luciano Guerci, *'Mente, cuore, coraggio, virtù repubblicane': educare il popolo nell'Italia in rivoluzione (1796–1799)* (Torino: Tirrenia Stampatori, 1992).

27 Jacqueline Sonolet, 'À propos d'un mannequin anatomique en bois: Napoléon Bonaparte et Felice Fontana', in Congresso internazionale sulla ceroplastica nella scienza e nell'arte, *La ceroplastica nella scienza e nell'arte: atti del I congresso internazionale Firenze, 3–7 giugno 1975* (Florence: Olschki, 1977), pp. 443–58.

28 IMSS–ARMU, Filza di negozi dell'anno 1801, fol. 16ff (20 March 1801).

29 Ibid., fol. 60.

30 Ibid., fol. 58.

31 Ibid., fol. 41.

32 Ibid, fol. 73, report by custodian Raddi.

33 IMSS–ARMU, Filza di negozi dell'anno 1801, fol. 2 (doc. 2), 26 January 1801, for the government's permission to Mascagni. Ibid., fols 3–6, for a copy of Mascagni's plan, and Fabbroni's remark in the margins. See also Patrizia Ruffo, 'Paolo Mascagni e il Reale Museo di Fisica e Storia Naturale di Firenze', in *La scienza illuminata: Paolo Mascagni nel suo tempo (1755–1815)*, ed. Francesca Vannozzi (Siena: Nuova imagine, 1996), pp. 241–51.

34 See e.g. a publication by the (exiled) former grand-ducal adviser Gianni, *Discorso sul Debito Publico* (1801); and the anonymous *De la Toscane* (1799), which Renato Pasta has attributed to Fabbroni: Pasta, *Scienza politica rivoluzione*, pp. 420ff.

35 The new dynasty initially appointed mostly Tuscans into government offices; Fabbroni was elected Director of the Mint on 2 August 1802.

36 See e.g. IMSS–ARMU, Filza di negozi dell'anno 1801, fols 113–38; Filza di negozi dell'anno 1802, fol. 54, fol. 55; Filza di negozi dell'anno 1803, fol. 2. fol. 47.

37 'La vostra Patria è quella delle Arti, e delle Scienze. Il nuovo Monarca che viene a governarvi ha attirato gli sguardi d'Europa col suo gusto per le Scienze, e per le Arti . . . Il suo avvenimento al Trono vi presagisco tutti i successi gloriosi, che illustrarono la Toscana sotto il Regno dei Medici, e di Leopoldo'; *Gazzetta Toscana*, no. 31, 1801.

38 See e.g. Fabbroni's *Provvedimenti annonari* of June 1804. Romano Paolo Coppini, *Il Granducato di Toscana. Dagli 'anni francesi' all'Unità. Storia d'Italia*, vol. 13/3, ed. Giuseppe Galasso (Torino: UTET, 1993), p. 63.

39 Pasta, *Scienza politica rivoluzione,* p. 468.

40 Giovanni Fabbroni, *Nuovo Giornale dei Letterati di Pisa* 12 (1806), pp. 418ff.

41 ('[Tut]to va a salti, e senza ordine p[er] casualità'); BNCF, manuscript collection NA 1050, Pelli, 'Efemeridi', II serie, vol. 32/1 (1804), 17 January 1804, fol. 26v.

42 BNCF, manuscript collection NA 1050, Pelli, 'Efemeridi', Serie II, vol. 32/1 (1804), 79v–80r, 26 February 1804: 'Fra gli stabilimenti, che non soffersero nelle nostre Invasioni Francesi vi fù certo il R. Gabinetto di Fisica. Egli dunq[ue] si mostra intatto, ma non vi si è voluta riunire la raccolta scelta, e pregievole, che portò seco Lodovico. . . . quindi è che la tanta spesa fatta da Leopoldo con un locale poco felice t[ut]ta è gettata, e non serve che ad una sterile comparsa. Le Preparazioni anatomiche in cera formano una bella serie ma q[ue]ste pure non servono ad insegnare l'Anatomia. . . . Lo *spirito di ciarlatanesca disorganizazione* d[e]l famoso Fontana, ora la Povertà nostra e la *soprabondanza di occupazioni* d[e]l Sig.r Fabbroni' (Italics A.M.).

43 '[P]revio l'esatto Inventario estima di tutti gli oggetti che compongono il Gabinetto di Storia naturale annesso al Quartiere che abita S.M.tà il Re in tempo d'inverno, onde costì sempre della proprietà privata del med.o presso la M.tà S., ne sia riunita l'amministrazione al'Pubblico Gabinetto Fisico, avendo in conseguenza appartenere a quel Soprintendente Economico l'invigilare alla sua conservazione'; IMSS–ARMU, Filza di negozi dell'anno 1804/05, fol. 27 (doc. 17).

44 Pasta, *Scienza politica rivoluzione,* p. 494.

45 IMSS–ARMU, Filza di negozi dell'anno 1804/05, fol. 19 (doc. 12).

46 Ibid., fol. 15–16 (doc. 11), 'Istruzioni pel Dissettore, ed Istruttore di Anatomìa del R. Museo di Fisica'.

47 IMSS–ARMU, Filza di negozi dell'anno 1810, fol. 121–22 (doc. 64), 22 June 1810. The sources do not indicate who the audience for these daily demonstrations was; it may have been both regular museum visitors and medical students who participated in the lecture courses.

48 Giovanni Prezziner, *Storia del pubblico studio e delle società scientifiche e letterarie di Firenze* (Florence: Carli 1810), vol. II, pp. 264–5.

49 Anon., 'Anecdotes of the celebrated Felix Fontana', *Weekly entertainer, or agreeable and instructive repository* 45 (1805), pp. 594–5.

50 IMSS–ARMU, Filza di negozi dell'anno 1804/05, fol. 30–1 (doc. 20), suggestions by custodian Raddi to Fabbroni, 16 March 1805.

51 Simone Bonechi, 'Un proprietario toscano tra scienza, rivoluzione e filantropismo: Girolamo de'Bardi (1777–1829)', *Nuncius* 10:1 (1995), pp. 51–97.

52 ASF, Acquisti e Doni, 232. For the Collège see Gillispie, *Revolutionary and Napoleonic years,* pp. 306–11.

53 For the life and works of Cuvier and his notion of comparative anatomy, see e.g. William Coleman, *Georges Cuvier, zoologist. A study in the history of evolution theory* (Cambridge, Mass.: Harvard University Press, 1964); Toby A. Appel, *The Cuvier-Geoffroy debate. French biology in the decades before Darwin* (New York and Oxford: Oxford University Press, 1987); Martin Rudwick, *Georges Cuvier, fossil bones, and geological catastrophes: new translations and interpretations of the primary texts* (Chicago: University of Chicago Press, 1997).

54 IMSS–ARMU, Filza di negozi dell'anno 1807, fol. 63–8 (doc. 19/20), 26 February
    1807: 'per sommo vantaggio della Fisiologia'.
55 IMSS–ARMU, Filza di negozi dell'anno 1807, fol. 41–56 (doc. 16).
56 IMSS–ARMU, Filza di negozi dell'anno 1807, fol. 191 (doc. 86), 'Formulario p La
    Funzione della Solenne Apertura del Liceo'. The published account is in *Omaggi
    alle Maestà . . . per l'apertura del R. Liceo eretto nel Museo Reale di Fisica e Storia
    Naturale . . .*(Florence: Piatti, 1807), cited from Luigi Zangheri, *Feste e apparati
    nella Toscana dei Lorena, 1737–1859* (Florence: Olschki, 1996), p. 193.
57 Giovanni Prezziner, *Storia del pubblico studio e delle società scientifiche e letterarie
    di Firenze* (Florence: Carli 1810), vol. II, p. 260.
58 IMSS–ARMU, Filza di negozi dell'anno 1807, fol. 77 (doc. 26).
59 A recent account summarises the period as 'stagnant' in the field of education:
    Gianfranco Bandini, 'Gli anni francesi e l'educazione in Toscana', in *La Toscana
    e l'educazione. Dal Settecento a oggi: tra identità regionale e laboratorio nazionale*,
    ed. Franco Cambi (Florence: Le Lettere, 1998), pp. 131–47, on p. 132.
60 N.N. *Annali del Museo Imperiale di Fisica e Storia Naturale di Firenze per il
    MDCCCVIII.* vol. 1 (Florence: Giuseppe Tofani, 1808).
61 IMSS–ARMU, Filza di negozi dell'anno 1810, fol. 121–2 (doc. 64), 22 June 1810,
    'Spese per le lezioni e altre preparazioni di Anatomia Comparata'. Many of the
    animals chosen for wax models were examples used by Cuvier in his *Anatomie
    comparée*.
62 IMSS–ARMU, Filza di negozi dell'anno 1811, fol. 163–4 (doc. 82), 'Nota degli
    Oggetti di cui è stato l'Imp.e, e R.e Museo arrichito per la parte d'Anatomia
    Comparata dall'Anno 1807 fino al presente'.
63 '[G]ravi inconvenienti'; IMSS–ARMU, Filza di negozi dell'anno 1811, fol. 162
    (doc. 81), 5 September 1811.
64 [Lastri, Marco]. *L'osservatore fiorentino sugli edifizi della sua patria.* Third
    edition, based on second edition of 1797. (Florence: Gaspero Ricci).
65 '[V]erità', 'eleganza', 'nostri incomparabili Artisti Signor Clemente Susini e Signor
    Francesco Calenzoli'; Uccelli, Filippo. 'Rapporto del Professore di Anatomia com-
    parata Filippo Uccelli', in *Annali del Museo imperiale di fisica e storia naturale di
    Firenze per il MDCCCVIII*, vol. 1 (Florence: G. Tofani, 1808), p. 2; also Giovanni
    Prezziner, *Storia del pubblico studio e delle società scientifiche e letterarie di Firenze*
    (Florence: Carli 1810), vol. II, p. 264.
66 IMSS–ARMU, Filza di negozi dell'anno 1807, fol. 289–90 (doc. 114): '*le sue
    Opere* qualunque elle siano, son l'oggetto il più particolare di tale stabilimento, e
    l'ammirazione degli Intendenti' (Italics A.M.).
67 IMSS–ARMU, Filza di negozi dell'anno 1810, fol. 226 (doc. 108), n.d., but end of
    1810: 'I Lavori che sono nel I. Museo di Cera fatti da Susini, e Calenzoli'; IMSS–
    ARMU, Filza di negozi dell'anno 1814, fol. 143 (doc. 216), n.d. (but probably
    December 1814): 'il Sig.re Ferrini, il Sig.re Susini, ed Io medesimo che siamo i
    primi in quest'Arte'.
68 ABA, pezzo G, no. 65, 1, 'Individui componenti l'Accademia delle Belle Arti'(7

April 1799); Pezzo H, doc. 12, 'Concorso Semestrale del Settembre 1802 e Programmi per il Concorso Triennale del 1803'.

69 '[I]l celebre modellatore'; 'valente artista'; 'nei suoi lavori nulla più resta a desiderare si per il bell'aspetto che dava anche alle cose più ributtanti, si per la verità, e esattezza, come per l'intelligenza dei detti lavori'. *Gazzetta di Firenze,* no. 124, 15 October 1814, supplement.

70 Romano Paolo Coppini, *Il Granducato di Toscana. Dagli 'anni francesi' all'Unità. Storia d'Italia,* vol. 13/3, ed. Giuseppe Galasso (Torino: UTET, 1993) (abbreviated as Coppini, *Anni francesi*), p. 81.

71 '[À] seconder les vues grandes et liberales de Votre Majesté pour les arts et les sciences'; Archives Nationales Paris, AF IV, 1716, Dossier 1, Ins. 144, 17 September 1808; quoted from Coppini, *Anni francesi,* p. 81.

72 Edgardo Donati, *La Toscana nell'Impero napoleonico* (2 vols, Florence: Polistampa, 2008), vol. 2, p. 913.

73 For Cuvier's activities during the educational reform of Tuscany under the Empire see Dorinda Outram, *Georges Cuvier. Vocation, science, and authority in postrevolutionary France* (Manchester: Manchester University Press, 1984). A more general account of the French reforms on all levels of education is Bandini, 'Anni francesi'.

74 Gianfranco Bandini, 'Gli anni francesi e l'educazione in Toscana', in Franco Cambi (ed.), *La Toscana e l'educazione. Dal Settecento a oggi: tra identità regionale e laboratorio nazionale* (Florence: Le Lettere, 1998), pp. 131–47 (abbreviated as Bandini, *Anni francesi*), p. 160.

75 '[M]onumens publiques des sciences et arts', Bandini, 'Anni francesi', p. 138.

76 'Qual è l'Istituto di codesto stabilimento, tanto in rapporto allo scopo della Fondazione, quanto in riguardo all'altro dell'Istruzione Pubblica, al quale è stato modernamente diretto. Quale la sua Dote, ed in quali assegnamenti consista. Quali siano le persone destinatevi ad insegnare'. IMSS–ARMU, Filza di negozi dell'anno 1808, fol. 15 (doc. 7).

77 IMSS–ARMU, Filza di negozi dell'anno 1808, fol. 24 (doc. 14), 1 February 1808.

78 IMSS–ARMU, Filza di negozi dell'anno 1808, fol. 74 (doc. 38), 'Copia d'Articolo Contenuto nel Decreto emanato, nel di 8. Marzo 1808, da S.Ecc.a il Sig.re Consigliere di Stato Dauchy Amministrator Generale della Toscana'. IMSS–ARMU, Filza di negozi dell'anno 1809, fol. 110 (doc. 58), letter by Bardi from Paris, 31 July 1809: 'Questa cosa mi ha dato non poco dispiacere'.

79 IMSS–ARMU, Filza di negozi dell'anno 1812, fol. 87/88 (doc. 47), 'Stato degli Acquisti fatti nell'Imperial Museo di Fisica e Storia Naturale di Firenze dall'Anno 1807 fino al 1812'.

80 'Ai tessuti del decreto i professori del Museo sono necessariamente sottoposti all'università Imperiale'; 'si son Compresi nel Corcondario dell'Accademia di Pisa, e sotto la immediata giurisdizione del Sig. Rettore della medesima'; IMSS–ARMU, Filza di negozi dell'anno 1812, fol. 2 (doc. 2).

81 Ibid., fol. 10 (doc. 5).

82 See e.g. IMSS–ARMU, Filza di negozi dell'anno 1809, fol. 90 (doc. 44), letter by Bardi from Paris, 19 June 1809, mentioning a favourable report on the museum by a commission 'p[er] ordine d[e]ll'Istituto sopra il Volume degli Annali da me presentati'. Also IMSS–ARMU, Filza di negozi dell'anno 1811, fol. 118 (doc. 64), for the Institut de France receiving the museum's annals (1 July 1811).

83 IMSS–ARMU, Filza di negozi dell'anno 1812, fol. 33 (doc. 18), 12 June 1812: 'S.E. [l'Intendant General de la Couronne] a pensé que le Musée Imperial de Florence etant établi d'après les mêmes principes que le Musée du Jardin de Plantes de Paris l'université n'avait aucun droit à la direction de cet Etablissement qui d'allieurs appartient à la Couronne'.

84 Decree of 9 November 1814: 'ritorno all'antico'; the first article of the decree stipulates: 'L'insegnamento che dovrà darsi nell'università di Pisa avrà per base la religione cattolica e la purezza della sua morale, l'obbedienza al Sovrano e il rispetto alle pubbliche autorità'. Quoted from Coppini, *Anni francesi*, p. 194. For education in the early years of the restoration see Franco Cambi, 'L'Ottocento. Introduzione', in *La Toscana e l'educazione. Dal Settecento a oggi: tra identità regionale e laboratorio nazionale*, ed. Franco Cambi (Florence: Le Lettere, 1998), pp. 151–60.

85 '[R]icondurre il Museo a quell'ordine, ed a quel sistema, che era in vigore all'epoca della partenza da Firenze del Nostro Amatissimo Sovrano, il quale ha sempre considerato questo stabilimento, come un Annesso alla propria residenza, e di suo privato piacere'. IMSS–ARMU, Filza di negozi dell'anno 1814, fol. 72 (old pagination fol. 92–93).

86 IMSS–ARMU, Filza di negozi dell'anno 1814, fol. 79 (old pagination fol. 109).

87 IMSS–ARMU, Filza di negozi dell'anno 1814, fol. 117–21 (old pagination fol. 171–7), on fol. 117: 'Furono queste stesse disposizioni di VAI e R, ed il comune desiderio delle persone colte, ed amanti della gloria del nostro Paese che io feci presente a Sua Maestà La Regina Reggente per invitarla ad estendere i vantaggi della pubblica istruzione.'

88 '[D]i gran lunga più vantaggioso al Pubblico', Giovanni Prezziner, *Storia del pubblico studio e delle società scientifiche e letterarie di Firenze* (1810), p. 259.

89 'Prospetto degli Aumenti fatti nel R. Museo dal 1807 fino al 1814', IMSS–ARMU, Filza di negozi dell'anno 1814, fol. 120–1. Other names mentioned are Chladni, Gay-Lussac, Wallaston, Morichini, and Rumford. IMSS–ARMU, Filza di negozi dell'anno 1814, fol. 120–1.

90 IMSS–ARMU, Filza di negozi dell'anno 1814, fol. 117–21 (old pagination fol. 171–7), on fol. 117v: 'Anatomia comparata, Scienza divenuta oramai indispensabile per la Storia Naturale'.

91 'Essendo stata, in forza delle circostanze, sospesa quest'istruzione, il pubblico si è lusingato sempre che la misura non fosse che momentanea'. IMSS–ARMU, Filza di negozi dell'anno 1814, fol. 117–21 (old pagination fol. 171–7), on fol. 118.

92 See e.g. the visit of the Duchess of Parma in IMSS–ARMU, Filza di negozi dell'anno 1816, fol. 70 (no doc. no), 31 August 1816.

Conclusion

La Specola's modelling enterprise entailed more than the production of artificial bodies. It was the central element in an attempt to create a new kind of
institution – a space for expertise in state service devoted to the production
of natural knowledge, its communication to the public and, ultimately, the
shaping of the citizen. Like some contemporaneous art collections, the Royal
Museum was organised in a way that contributed to the articulation of national
identity.[1] The exhibition of models, specimens and instruments provided a
link between Tuscan nature and the new ruling dynasty by displaying national
ingenuity, national resources, and the sovereign as the force to make them
productive in the service of the public. It also attempted to direct visitor behaviour and understanding in such a way as to turn audiences into model citizens.
Initially, the museum's ambitious mission was thus to advance public enlightenment and public happiness. However, this mission and the role of model
experts changed, responding to institutional pressures and to the conceptual
contradictions of expertise in state service.

Chapter 1 argued that Pietro Leopoldo's politics of nature, tested in his
Tuscan 'laboratory', assumed that legitimate political action had to be based on
natural laws. If the government followed these laws, the result would be social
harmony and prosperity: an increase in public happiness. These assumptions
were shared by many eighteenth-century contemporaries such as director of
the Uffizi art gallery Giuseppe Pelli, who emulated the Grand Duke's mission of
public enlightenment at his own home, or the Florentine obstetrician Giuseppe
Galletti, investigated in Chapter 2, who provided an important early impulse
to establish a collection of wax models in Tuscany to improve the training of
medical professionals.

Anatomy, in particular, was considered a model science by many Tuscans
following the arguments of local physician Antonio Cocchi, which were discussed in Chapter 2. Asked to develop proposals for medical reforms by the
Regency government which preceded Pietro Leopoldo's reign, Cocchi claimed

that anatomy could be useful to the state in a number of ways. Founded equally on theoretical knowledge and practical experience, anatomy could provide facts that were useful for the improvement of public health and arts and manufacture. At the same time, the analytical-deductive method used by anatomists was the most reliable method of knowledge production and should therefore be adopted to improve other areas of expertise in state service. According to Cocchi, anatomists were as useful to the state for *how* they acquired knowledge as for *what* they knew: they were indeed 'model experts'.

Medical reforms during the Regency and under Pietro Leopoldo changed medical training accordingly to integrate practical and theoretical elements, aiming to improve the practice of physicians, surgeons, obstetricians and midwives. But Pietro Leopoldo was also intent on exploiting the improving potential of the anatomical method in fields beyond medicine and public health. In new and reformed institutions such as the agricultural academy the Georgofili, the Chamber of Commerce and the Museum of Physics and Natural History 'La Specola', the Grand Duke attempted to institutionalise expertise based on a reliable analytical-deductive method that would deliver true and useful knowledge in state service. The sovereign's measures shaped concepts of the state, the public, the expert, and their relationship. This was the case especially where the realisation of political ideas posed practical problems. The Grand Duke frequently faced two core problems: the control of experts and their claims to authority, and the constitution of the public. In order to support public enlightenment his responses included the introduction of anti-spectacular legislation to direct the public's attention towards educational alternatives such as the Royal Museum. With regard to the institutionalisation of scientific expertise in state service, analysed in Chapter 1, Pietro Leopoldo soon found that those who possessed authoritative natural knowledge could use it to claim more political agency for themselves. His experience with these new cadres of experts brought the problem of expert control to the fore, especially at the new Chamber of Commerce, where this struggle eventually led to its dissolution. It is not surprising, then, that the sovereign's measures for public health tightly intermeshed the support of medical expertise with administrative surveillance.

Similar administrative surveillance was introduced at La Specola to control modelling practice, investigated in Chapter 3. This surveillance caused clashes of different images of the scientist in state service, and it prompted naturalists to articulate their role vis-à-vis the court and the museum's artisans. Initially, museum director Fontana presented himself as an autonomous natural philosopher whose honour was tied to his truth claims. However, his status as employee at a state institution made this stance impossible. Under pressure to adhere to the court's administrative procedures Fontana resorted to a self-presentation akin to the new image of the genius in an attempt to justify his continuing resistance to surveillance. His vice-director Fabbroni responded very differently, attempting instead to meet the court's expectations. He took great pains to present himself as an employee in state service whose honour depended on a history of reliable service to the state and adherence to its administrative conventions. His interactions with the court show how his articulations of expertise were simultaneously attempts to define state interest. Fabbroni argued that a proper expert had to prioritise the state's interests over personal ones such as Fontana's honour. The naturalist had to conform to standardised procedures to produce knowledge that was intelligible and accessible to the administration on its own terms. His knowledge and skills had to be matched by appropriate comportment in order to be useful to the state. Thus, personal features of the naturalist remained central to all these changing articulations of the expert's role.

Chapter 4 argued that the naturalist's position as an expert in state service was defined not only in model production, but also in model use, especially in naturalists' responses to the problems of controlling model reception by visitors in order to create public enlightenment. Fontana maintained that the presence of a knowledgeable naturalist was indispensable for creating accurate representations, but not necessary for the visitor's front-stage encounter with the artificial anatomies. In his view, the exhibition of accurate and suitable models would, by itself, enable visitors to see the underlying laws of nature for themselves. However, practical experience showed that, left to their own devices, visitors interpreted the models in a variety of ways, not all of them in accordance with the museum's enlightenment mission. The director maintained this position even when faced with discrepancies between his own expectations and visitors' comportment. Fontana's response was to change the models' features. He attempted the development of wooden models which would allow hands-on use. While the new material would thus alter practices of model use, it left the naturalist's role apparently unchanged. With the wooden anatomies, as with the waxen ones, Fontana maintained that the naturalist's job was to guarantee the representations' accuracy, submitted only to the judgement of his peers. In response to the museum's lack of success with its educational mission, Fontana's second-in-command Fabbroni created a different image of the relationship between expert and public. He claimed that the naturalist's presence was necessary not only back-stage, in model production to ensure the validity and efficacy of the objects, but also front-stage, mediating visitors' encounters with the artificial anatomies. This mediating presence, Fabbroni insisted, was indispensable in turning the encounter to pedagogical account. Thus, the audience for natural laws would become an audience for expertise.

Articulations of experts' utility for the state were inseparable from articulations of the utility of the models themselves, in model production, in model display, and in their transfer to the medico-surgical academy in Vienna. In all cases, the models' interpretive flexibility could be used to support or to undermine experts' claims to authority and public utility. Fontana maintained that models could only be useful as tools of public enlightenment if they were perfectly accurate. The model expert's main function, then, was to ascertain the accuracy of the models – and he required a high degree of autonomy to do this. Fabbroni, on the other hand, argued that the models could only be useful if they were accompanied by explanations from a model expert who mediated the artificial anatomies to the public.

In comparison, Chapter 5 shows how, in Vienna, discussions of the models' utility contributed to articulations of professional authority and expertise in state service in a very different way, which ultimately led to their rejection, or at least lack of public endorsement. Physicians and educated middle-class commentators criticised the models to highlight the impossibility of general public enlightenment, and thus to underline the necessity of experts for the polity. Medical practitioners' discussions of artificial anatomies also helped articulate their claims to expertise and authority by explaining why they, in particular, were well suited to be the caretakers of public health. Labelling the models as toys branded them as uneducational, artificial luxuries created by an over-zealous and erratic sovereign. These toys, critics argued, could appeal only to an ignorant public in thrall to the artificial, more interested in entertainment than in education, and to the equally ignorant and uncivilised barber-surgeons. As such, the waxes were not acceptable to enlightened physicians, or to the new generation of surgeons who aligned themselves with physicians by stressing their civilisation, their compassion, and their utility for the state.

The models' interpretive flexibility became especially salient during regime changes following the French Revolution, analysed in Chapter 6. No matter whether Tuscany was occupied by the French republican army, a satellite state under Spanish rule, or part of the French Empire, fundamental problems such as the tension between expert knowledge as exclusive and accessible, the control of experts in state service, and the tension between models as education and entertainment remained salient at the public museum. During numerous regime changes between 1799 and 1814, museum naturalists attempted to increase or at least maintain their agency by rearticulating the utility of the models. The model experts supported these articulations by either professing to act on behalf of the state or by assuming the voice of the public. Museum naturalists' agency, such as it was, derived in part from the tension between generally accessible and exclusive knowledge. This ambivalence made it possible for the experts to claim to speak for public opinion – to represent, in effect, the opinion the public ought to have if it were fully enlightened. Similarly, Viennese intellectuals and medical professionals implied that their rejection of the Florentine models was the appropriate response, rather than the artificial anatomies' popular success with the ignorant general public. However, their successes and failures made it clear that, ultimately, the state, in the shape of sovereigns or government officials, dictated the museum's fate. When Ferdinando of Habsburg-Lorraine was restored to the Tuscan throne, he did away with references to nature and the public as a basis for political legitimacy and political action, and the naturalists' agency diminished accordingly.

There remains for consideration the subsequent fate of La Specola's wax anatomies, and those aspects of model production and display which have continued to be significant to the present day. Exquisitely crafted wax anatomies have been joined by mass-produced models together with new techniques of specimen preservation since the end of the eighteenth century, while debates continued over the need to provide audiences for models with expert guidance. Performers and audiences also continued in their attempts to balance education and entertainment, science and spectacle, the mundane and the morbid. Model makers and model users concerned themselves with the materiality of displays, knowing that the choice between different substances, such as wax, wood, papier-mâché or plastic, affects the reception and meaning of displays.

Returning to Florence after fifteen years in Austrian exile, Grand Duke Ferdinando of Tuscany no longer shared his father Pietro Leopoldo's belief in the improving powers of nature and public enlightenment. For a quarter of a century, he had witnessed how the French Revolution and its aftermath had thrown Europe into chaos, from the execution of his aunt Marie Antoinette in Paris to Napoleon's imperial ambitions. A cultish reverence of nature was no guarantee of social harmony and political stability; and public enlightenment was a slippery slope into mob rule. Displays of princely authority, the restored sovereign reasoned, were more important than general public education. However, the anatomical waxes of La Specola and their producers had left an impression on many who saw them, heard or read about them, and they continued to shape a variety of enterprises in the following centuries.

Take for instance the case of the artist Antonio Serantoni, who had worked as an illustrator for anatomist Paolo Mascagni.[2] In searching for a new source of income after Mascagni's death he retrained as a wax sculptor and began producing imitations of the Specola waxes. Fellow Italian Antonio Sarti took Serantoni's works on tour.[3] Throughout the nineteenth century, Serantoni's wax models drew crowds around Europe; the show's centrepiece was the

'Florentine' or 'Medicean' Venus. Like Fontana, the advertisers of the travelling Venus claimed that accurate models would convey anatomical knowledge more rapidly than textbooks: 'executed after the best Models of the Gallery of *Florence*', 'the unlearned as well as the learned' would 'in less than a quarter of an hour' learn *'more . . . than at a Course of Lectures on Anatomy'*.[4]

The travelling showmen were ultimately swayed by Fabbroni's argument for mediation, however, and included explanations delivered by an expert. In 1855, for instance, the models were used to educate visitors about 'the evil effects of Tight Lacing, Excessive use of Tobacco, and Immoderate Drinking', with demonstrations by a member of the Royal College of Surgeons.[5] Other successors followed Fontana's line of reasoning, assuming that models could by themselves be educational if they were suitable representations of the human body. Consider the case of the French doctor Louis Auzoux. As a medical student in Paris in the early 1820s, he encountered a copy of Fontana's detachable wooden model at the medical faculty of the French capital, and he decided to improve on Fontana's idea. To create models for anatomical auto-didacticism, Auzoux developed a robust paper paste which allowed for the serial production of detachable models. Brightly coloured and extensively labelled, the Auzoux papier-mâché models were soon distributed globally, and were the forerunners of today's plastic anatomical models for the classroom.[6]

Whether instructed by experts or left to their own devices, audiences continue to receive models in different ways. The artificial anatomies' interpretive flexibility frequently enabled models to travel between different contexts and audiences. In the nineteenth century, for instance, models of pathological anatomy which showcased the effects of diseases such as syphilis in drastic detail often migrated from medical schools to fairground shows, on display to medical students and healthcare professionals, to curious lay audiences and to soldiers, the primary targets of many late nineteenth-century public health campaigns highlighting the dangers of venereal diseases.[7] The tension between education and entertainment thus never left displays of anatomy.

More recently, Gunther von Hagens's 'Body Worlds' exhibition of anatomical preparations provides a prime example of this ambivalence, as pensive visitors contemplate the modern *memento mori* of a smoker's lung while excited teenagers enjoy the thrill of touching real corpses. Audiences still discover the body through viewing and contemplation, a mix of learned observation and macabre spectacle. 'Body Worlds' also demonstrates the persistence of fundamental problems concerning the creation and display of anatomical representations.[8] Just as claims to accuracy of the anatomical waxes at La Specola had to be supported through a combination of tools, techniques and networks, so analysts have investigated similar constructions of authority in von Hagens' rhetoric of authenticity.[9] Where locals in late eighteenth-century Florence and Vienna complained about the open traffic of body parts in the service of anatomical learning, today's audiences and regulatory bodies question the ethics of using bodies as the raw materials for anatomical displays. Furthermore, scholars have highlighted how the plastinated specimens of von Hagens, like Fontana's waxes, are indebted to the conventions of anatomical representations established over centuries, despite their rhetoric of innovation.[10]

Throughout the development of artificial anatomies, the models' materiality presented both opportunities and obstacles. Wax was durable and malleable, and enabled the creation of a permanent overview of every possible aspect of human anatomy, presented as a living body rather than a corpse. But wax models also posed a challenge to anatomists and administrators when it came to controlling the skills and resources necessary for their production. Furthermore, modellers were repeatedly faced with a fundamental feature of modelling: no model ever fully replicates the original it is supposed to replace. In some respects, the difference between model and original was desirable – wax bodies, for instance, offered convincing visual sensations, but, as many museum visitors reported with relief, they lacked the stench of a real body. Divorced from the odour of the dissecting room, the Florentine models were palatable to a wide range of users, in line with the museum's mission of public enlightenment.

Where model makers and model users perceived the discrepancy between model and original to be problematic, they resorted to a number of different strategies: a change of materials, the development of new forms of intermediality, or attempts to police model use and reception through disciplinary measures. Already in the eighteenth century, obstetricians from du Coudray to Galli had experimented with a wide range of materials, from glass to leather, in their attempts to create obstetric phantoms which answered their requirements for practical training. At La Specola, Fontana attempted to solve the apparent shortcomings of his anatomical waxes by turning to the more durable wood, which would enable the manual 're-membering' of the body. Two decades later, Auzoux pursued a similar strategy replacing wood with the more pliable papier-mâché. At the end of the nineteenth century, the embryologist Wilhelm His returned to the use of wax, combining the traditional material with new techniques to achieve very different goals for his series of enlarged models of embryo development.[11]

Another strategy employed to overcome the potential defects of a particular material, and to bridge the gap between model and original in suitable ways, was the resort to intermediality. At La Specola, Fontana addressed the problem that visitors could not 'dissect' the fragile waxes by developing a mode of presentation which would enable a synoptic overview through the calculated combination of multiple models, images, and texts. The Royal Museum's method of combining different media and spatial arrangements to provide synoptic views of the body remains salient in anatomical teaching until today. As Elizabeth Hallam has highlighted, anatomy teachers continue to explore new juxtapositions of different media and materials, borrowing techniques from artisanal and domestic traditions, from writing to knitting, to pursue their aim of achieving representations of the body which suit their specific purposes and contexts.[12] Twenty-first century projects similarly exploit the possibilities of new media. A recent project of the University of Florence, for instance, uses the wax models of La Specola as the basis for an interactive CD-ROM aimed at helping medical students to learn basic anatomy – a virtual dissection, or a museum in cyberspace.[13]

Materials and presentation strategies shaped how model users understood and interacted with the body itself. Nineteenth-century anatomists could perceive of the body as a 'book', and the process of dissection as similar to the act of reading, turning pages as in a textbook, or in the layered anatomical prints then used by medical students to grasp the respective situation of organs in the body.[14] Similarly, some eighteenth-century obstetricians had greeted the use of phantoms with scepticism, arguing that the training with these inanimate simulations of female bodies would encourage students to coarse and unfeeling practice on living patients.

Finally, strategies to close the gap between model and original, at times, included not only the addition of other materials and media, but also disciplinary measures intended to police model use and reception. At the Florentine museum, this began with the introduction of guards and locks, and culminated in the introduction of teachers to mediate encounters with the artificial anatomies. Other institutions such as Guy's Hospital in London, which housed Joseph Towne's nineteenth-century anatomical waxes, purposefully restricted the audience for its model collections to avoid the taint of the fairground, which had undermined the Florentine models' reception in Vienna.[15]

The changing fate of La Specola's models highlights the fragility of expert authority, and the mutual constitution of notions of expertise, the public, and the state. In Florence and Vienna, the authority of experts depended on how relations between expertise, the public and the state were articulated in particular institutional, political, and cultural contexts. Influential works in science and techology studies and museum studies have proposed a rupture between absolutism and liberal democracies with respect to the articulation of scientific expertise in state service.[16] In contrast, the case of the anatomical models indicates the existence of important continuities between enlightened absolutism and later regimes. Fundamental problems of expertise, such as the tension between generally accessible and exclusive knowledge, and the limitation of experts' authority, traversed different polities and periods.

Articulations of expertise were thus shaped by political theories and institutional requirements, by conceptual contradictions and practical demands in model production, display and use. Such performances were a delicate balancing act between different perspectives: individuals professed, alternately, to represent the interest of the state, the voice of the public, or their own opinion. These changing images of the scientist in state service shared one central aspect: the continuing importance of personal features. Fontana's anatomical genius was innovative and independent; Fabbroni's naturalist-administrator was unselfish and reliable; the Viennese doctors were empathetic and civilised. While modern concepts of scientific authority claim that it should be accorded on the basis of impersonal considerations, historical analyses such as the present case study of La Specola's anatomical models show how authority continues to be based in individual moral features. Only the conventions of its performance change.[17]

Notes

1 For the contribution of art museums, as spaces to enact citizenship, to the emergence of national identities see Carol Duncan, *Civilizing rituals: inside public art museums* (London and New York: Routledge, 1995), especially Chapter 2, 'From the princely gallery to the public art museum. The Louvre Museum and the National Gallery, London'.

2 P[ietro] Vannoni, *Biografia di Antonio Serantoni* (Florence: V. Batelli, 1838); [Paolo Mascagni], *Anatomia universale ... rappresentata con tavole ... ridotte a minori forme di quelle della grande edizione pisana per Antonio Serantoni* (Florence: V. Batelli, 1833).

3 John Johnson Collection of Printed Ephemera, Bodleian Library, Oxford (hereafter JJC), Waxworks 3 (21), handbill 'Anatomical Representation of a female figure, Modelled from the Venus De Medicis, by Antonio Scrantoni, of Florence, private inspection for ladies ...' (The Cosmorama [London], 209, Regent Street, [1834]); JJC, Waxworks 3 (53), handbill 'The Florentine Anatomical Museum...' (Florentine anatomical museum [London], 27, Margaret Street, Regent Street [1839]); and numerous similar entries. For Sarti's anatomical show and others in nineteenth-century England, see Alberti, 'Wax bodies. Art and anatomy in Victorian medical museums', *Museum history journal* 2:1 (2009), pp. 7–35; A.W. Bates, '"Indecent and demoralising representations": public anatomy museums in mid-Victorian England', *Medical history*, 52:1 (2008), pp. 1–22.

4 JJC, Waxworks 3 (62), handbill 'Superb anatomical Venus dite Medicis' ([s.n.], [London], [No. 89 Strand opposite Southampton Street], January 1828).

5 JJC, Waxworks 3 (22), handbill 'If individuals only know how much misery might be avoided by the possession of such information about themselves, as that taught by the lecturer, by the aid of the Florentine Venus' ([1855]).

6 Aubrey B. Davis, 'Louis Thomas Jerôme Auzoux and the papier maché anatomical model', in Congresso internazionale sulla ceroplastica nella scienza e nell'arte, *La ceroplastica nella scienza e nell'arte: atti del I congresso internazionale Firenze, 3–7 giugno 1975* (Florence: Olschki, 1977), pp. 257–79; Bart Grob, *The world of Auzoux: models of man and beast in papier-mâché* (Leiden: Museum Boerhaave, 2000).

7 For pathological models and public anatomy displays in the nineteenth century, see e.g. Thomas Schnalke, *Diseases in wax: the history of the medical moulages*, trans. K. Spatschek (Chicago: Quintessence, 1995); Bates, '"Indecent and demoralising representations"', pp. 1–22; Maritha Rene Burmeister, *Popular anatomical museums in nineteenth-century England* (PhD dissertation, Rutgers University, 2000).

8 For multidisciplinary perspectives on 'Body Worlds', see most recently the contributions in T. Christine Jespersen, Alicita Rodríguez and Joseph Starr (eds), *The anatomy of body worlds: critical essays on the plastinated cadavers of Gunther von Hagens* (Jefferson, NC: McFarland & Co., 2009).

9 See e.g. José van Dijck, 'Bodyworlds: the art of plastinated cadavers', *Configurations* 9:1 (2001), pp. 99–126.

10 E.g. Stephen Johnson, 'The persistence of tradition in anatomical museums', in Jespersen et al. (eds), *Body worlds*, pp. 68–85. For von Hagens' eighteenth-century precursor in theatrical anatomical preparations Honoré Fragonard see especially Jonathan Simon, 'Honoré Fragonard, anatomical virtuoso', in Bernadette Bensaude-Vincent and Christine Blondel (eds), *Science and spectacle in the European Enlightenment* (Aldershot: Ashgate, 2008), pp. 141–58.

11 Nick Hopwood, 'Giving body to embryos: modeling, mechanism, and the microtome in late-nineteenth-century anatomy', *Isis* 90 (1999), pp. 462–96; Hopwood, *Embryos in wax: models from the Ziegler studio* (Cambridge: Whipple Museum of the History of Science, University of Cambridge, 2002).

12 Elizabeth Hallam, 'Anatomy display: contemporary debates and collections in Scotland', in Andrew Patrizio and Dawn Kemp (eds), *Anatomy acts: how we come to know ourselves* (Edinburgh: Birlinn, 2006), pp. 119–38; Hallam, *Anatomy museum. Death and the body displayed* (London: Reaktion, forthcoming 2011), especially Chapter 7, 'Paper, wax and plastic'. I am grateful to Elizabeth Hallam for making her work available to me before publication.

13 Enzo Brizzi, Marta Poggesi and Eleonora Sgambati, 'Museo di Storia Naturale Sezione zoologica "La Specola". Studio dell'anatomia umana attraverso le cere del Museo "La Specola"' (CD-ROM, Università degli Studi di Firenze, Centro Servizi Informatici dell'Ateneo Fiorentino, 2005).

14 Hallam, *Anatomy museum*, Chapter 7, 'Paper, wax and plastic'.

15 Alberti, 'Wax bodies', especially p. 33.

16 See e.g. Ezrahi, *Descent of Icarus*; 'Introduction', in Tony Bennett (ed.), *The birth of the museum: history, theory, politics* (London and New York: Routledge, 1995).

17 Similarly, Steven Shapin refers to changing 'modes of authority' in his recent investigation of scientific authority in late modernity. Shapin, *Scientific life* (2008), p. 4.

Bibliography

Primary sources

Abhandlungen der Kais. Königl. Medicinisch-Chirurgischen Josephs-Academie zu Wien, vol. 1 (Vienna: Albert Camesina, 1787).

Abhandlungen der Kais. Königl. Medicinisch-Chirurgischen Josephs-Academie zu Wien, vol. 2 (Vienna: Albert Camesina, 1801).

Aglietti, Francesco (ed.). *Memorie per servire alla storia letteraria e civile* (Venice, 1796).

Albrecht, Johann Friedrich Ernst. *Die Affenkönige oder die Reformation des Affenlandes* (Vienna: Wucherer, 1788).

'Anecdotes of the celebrated Felix Fontana', *Weekly Entertainer, or Agreeable and Instructive Repository* 45 (1805), pp. 594–5.

Annali del Museo Imperiale di Fisica e Storia Naturale di Firenze per il MDCCCVIII (v. 1, Florence: Giuseppe Tofani, 1808).

Annali del Museo Imperiale di Fisica e Storia Naturale di Firenze per l'anno MDCCCIX (v. 2, Florence: Guglielmo Piatti, 1810).

Bandi, e ordini da osservarsi del Granducato di Toscana pubblicati in Firenze dal dì primo Gennaio MDCCLXXX. a tutto Dicembre MDCCLXXXI (Florence: Gaetano Cambiagi, 1782).

Baretti, Joseph [Giuseppe]. *A Dictionary of the English and Italian Languages*, v. 1 (London, 1760).

Bauer, Johann. *Verzeichniß der neuesten und brauchbaresten chirurgischen Verbandstücke und Maschinen, die verfertiget werden bey Johann Bauer, chirurgischen Maschinist und Bandagist* (Vienna, 1803).

Beckford, Peter. *Familiar letters from Italy, to a friend in England* (London: J. Easton, 1805).

Bellini, Lorenzo. *Discorsi di anatomia ora per la prima volta stampati dall'originale esistente nella libreria Pandolfini . . . colla prefazione di Antonio Cocchi . . .* (Florence: Francesco Moücke, 1741–44).

Bienvenu, François. *Prospetto di un corso familiare di fisica sperimentale da dimostrarsi in 21. Lezione. Adattato all'intendimento di qualunque persona.* (Florence: Gaetano Cambiagi, 1792).

Brambilla, Giovanni Alessandro. *Rede, die er bey der Eröfnung der neuen k.k. medizi-nisch-chirurgischen Akademie 1785 gehalten hat* (Vienna: Gräffer, 1785).

Brambilla, G[iovanni] A[lessandro]. *Appendice alla storia della chirurgia austriaca militare* (Pavia: Pietro Galeazzi, 1800).

Brooke, N. *Observations on the Manners and Customs of Italy, with Remarks on the Vast Importance of British Commerce on that Continent* (London: T. Cadell and W. Davies, 1798).

Canovai, Stanislao and Gaetano del Ricco. *Elementi di fisica matematica dedi-cati all'Altezze Reali di Ferdinando-Giuseppe, Carlo-Luigi, Alessandro-Leopoldo Arciduchi d'Austria, Principi di Toscana ec.ec.ec.* (Florence: Pietro Allegrini, 1788).

Cariche occupate in Firenze dal Prof. Lorenzo Nannoni ed opere del medesimo pubblicate (Florence: Borgognissanti, 1809).

Cocchi, Antonio. *Dell'anatomia discorso* (Florence: Zannoni, 1745).

Cocchi, Antonio. 'Lettera intorno all'educazione e al genere di vita degl'Inglesi.' *Biblioteca Italiana*, vol. I (1816[1724]), pp. 188–98.

Cocchi, Antonio. *Antonio Cocchi: scritti scelti*, ed. Simone Contardi (Florence: Giunti, 1998).

Cocchi, Antonio. *Relazione dello Spedale di Santa Maria Nuova di Firenze*, ed. Maria Mannelli Goggiolo (Florence, Casa Editrice Le Lettere, 2000).

Cocchi, Raimondo. *Lezioni fisico-anatomiche recitate pubblicamente in Firenze nel teatro del Regio Spedale di Santa Maria Nuova dal Dottore Raimondo Cocchi già professore di Anatomìa in detto Spedale* (Livorno: Tommaso Masi, 1775).

Condillac, Étienne Bonnot de. *Traité des sensations* (London [Paris?], 1754).

Coudray, A.M. le Boursier du. *Abrégé de l'art des accouchemens* (Paris, 1759).

Desgenettes, Nicolas-René. *Analyse du système absorbant ou lymphatique* (Montpellier: Martel, 1791).

Desgenettes, Nicolas René. 'Observations sur l'enseignement de la medicine dans les hôpiteaux de la Toscane', *Journal de Médecine, Chirurgie et Pharmacie* 91 (1792), pp. 233–56.

Desgenettes, Nicolas René. 'Réflexions générales sur l'utilité de l'anatomie artificielle; et en particulier sur la collection de Florence, et la necessité d'en former de sem-blables en France', *Observations sur la physique, sur l'histoire naturelle et sur les arts* 43 (1793), pp. 81–94.

Desgenettes, Nicolas-René. 'Remarques sur le passage suivant, inséré dans le journal de médecine, chirurgie et pharmacie, cahier de mars 1806, tome XI, page 459: 'La réputation de l'illustre Cocchi n'a pas encore franchi les Alpes'. Par R. Desgenettes, docteur et professeur en médecine, etc', *Journal de Médecine, Chirurgie et Pharmacie* 11 (1806), insert.

Drey interessante Fragen als ein Aufschluß zu den neuern Anstalten in den österreichi-schen Staaten. Die Medizin und Chirurgie betreffend (s.l., 1788).

Dupaty, Charles. *Sentimental Letters on Italy, written in French by President Dupaty, in 1785. Published in Rome in 1788, and translated the same year by J. Povoleri* (London: Crowder & Bew, 1789).

Duverney, M. and Jacques Fabien Gautier D'Agoty (ills*), Myologie complette en couleur et grandeur naturelle: composée de l'Essai et de la Suite de l'Essai d'anatomie, en tableaux imprimés; ouvrage unique, utile et necessaire aux etudians & amateurs de cette science* (Paris: L Gautier, 1746).

'Ein Wort zu seiner Zeit, die k.k. medic. chirurg. Josephinische Akademie zu Wien betreffend', *Medicinisch-chirurgische Zeitung* 2 (1794), pp. 325ff; 3 (1794), pp. 49ff.

Eustace, John C. *A Classical Tour Through Italy An. MDCCCII* (Leghorn, 4th edn, 1817).

Fauken, Johann Peter Franz Xavier. *Entwurf zu einer Einrichtung der Heilkunde* (Göttingen: Johann Christian Dieterich, 1794).

Follini, Vincenzo and Modesto Rastrelli. *Firenze antica e moderna illustrata* (Florence: Iacopo Grazioli, 1798–1802).

Fontana, Felice. *Richerche fisiche sopra il veleno della vipera* (Lucca: Jacopo Giusti, 1767).

Fontana, Felice. *Richerche filosofiche sopra la fisica animale* (Florence: Gaetano Cambiagi, 1775).

Galvani, Luigi. *Aloysii Galvani De Manzoliniana supellectili oratio: habita in Scientiarum et Artium Instituto cum ad anatomen in tabulis ab Anna Manzolina perfectis publice tradendam aggrederetur anno MDCCLXXVII* (Bologna [1777]).

Gori, Antonio Francesco. *Museum Florentinum exhibens insignora vetustatis monumenta quae Florentiae sunt* (Florence: M. Nestenus and F. Moucke, 1731–62).

Gruner, Christian Gottfried. 'Vorzüge und Alterthum der Chirurgie. Ein Problem', *Almanach für Aerzte und Nichtaerzte für das Jahr 1788* (Jena: Cuno, 1788), pp. 203–16.

Gruner, Christian Gottfried. 'Kann die Fakultät Doctoren der Wundarznei machen?', *Almanach für Aerzte und Nichtaerzte für das Jahr 1788* (Jena, 1789), pp. 248–69.

Hackel, Johann Christoph. *Anleitung zum zweckmäßigen Gebrauche der zur Erhaltung der Gesundheit, des Lebens, und Wachsthumes der menschlichen Körpers nothwendigen Dinge, mit Beyfügung der wesentlichen Grundregeln, nach welchen der Mensch bevorstehenden, oder schon wirklich vorhandenen Krankheitsgefahren vorbauen, und den Tod von hohem Alter so weit, als möglich, hinaus fristen kann* (Vienna: Johann Carl Schuender, 1797–98).

Herder, Johann G. *Plastik* (Riga: Hartknoch, 1778).

Herder, Johann G. *Italienische Reise. Briefe und Tagebuchaufzeichnungen 1788–1789* (Munich: Deutscher Taschenbuch Verlag, 1988).

Huber, Franz Xaver. *Der blaue Esel* (Berlin and Leipzig, 1786).

Hunczovsky, Johann. *Anweisung zu chirurgischen Operationen. Für seine Vorlesungen bestimmt* (Vienna: Rudolph Graeffer, 1785).

Hunczovsky, Johann. *Ueber die neuere Geschichte der Chirurgie in den k.k. Staaten. Eine Rede, gehalten am 8ten November 1787, als die k.k. Josephinische medicinisch-chirurgische Akademie zu Wien den Gedächtnistag ihrer Stiftung und Uebersetzung zum zweytenmale feyerte* (Vienna: Rudolph Graeffer, 1787).

[Lastri, Marco]. *L'osservatore fiorentino sugli edifizi della sua patria.* (3rd edn, based on 2nd edn of 1797. Florence: Gaspero Ricci, 1821).

Malaspina, Carlo Maurizio di. 'Descrizione del viaggio di Giovan Battista Malaspina nell'anno 1785 ed 86', *Miscellanea Fiorentina di Erudizione e Storia. Pubblicata da Iodoco Del Badia* 1:6 (June 1886).

Mascagni, Paolo. *Vasorum lymphaticorum corporis humani historia et iconographia* (Siena: Carli, 1787).

[Mascagni, Paolo]. *Anatomia universale . . . rappresentata con tavole . . . ridotte a minori forme di quelle della grande edizione pisana per Antonio Serantoni* (Florence: V. Batelli, 1833).

Meisel [Josef Valentin Sebastian Eybel]. *Herr und Frau von Wachs oder ein lustiges Gespräch zwischen zwey wächsernen Opfermännln* (Vienna: Joseph Edlen von Kurzbeck, 1782).

Moore, John. *View of Society and Manners in Italy: with Anecdotes Relating to Some Eminent Characters* (2 vols, London, 1781).

'Nachricht von der neuen Kayserlich-Königlich Josephinischen medicinisch chirurgischen Academie zu Wien, in einem Schreiben an den Hofr. Baldinger, in Marburg, vom 18 März, 1786', *Medicinisches Journal* 9 (1786).

Nannoni, Angelo. *Dissertazioni chirurgiche* (Paris, 1748).

Nannoni, Lorenzo. *Trattato d'anatomia, fisiologia e zootomia* (Siena: Bindi, 1788–91).

Osiander, Johann Friedrich. *Nachricht von Wien über Gegenstände der Medicin, Chirurgie und Geburtshilfe* (Tübingen: Christian Friedrich Osiander, 1817).

Philiatros [Johann Peter Franz Xaver Fauken]. *Tableau des études de medecine de Vienne comme elles etoient, comme elles sont, comme elles devroient etre. Avec une memoire sur l'Academie Militaire de Vienne, et sur la Faculté de Medecine* (s.l., 1794)

[Pignotti, Dr Lorenzo]. *Istruzioni Mediche per le genti di campagna* (Florence: Giuseppe Tofani, 1784).

Prezziner, Giovanni. *Storia del pubblico studio e delle società scientifiche e letterarie di Firenze* (v. 2, Florence: Carli, 1810).

'Protokoll der unterthänigsten Militär-Sanitäts-Kommission, die Verbesserung der k.k. Josephs-Akademie und des gesamten k.k. Militär-Sanitätswesens betreffend [1795]'. Reprinted in J. Habart, *Unser Militär-Sanitätswesen vor hundert Jahren* (Vienna 1896), n.p.

Regolamento del Regio Arcispedale di Santa Maria Nuova di Firenze (Florence: Gaetano Cambiagi, 1783).

Regolamento dei Regi Spedali di Santa Maria Nuova e di Bonifazio (Florence: Gaetano Cambiagi, 1789).

[Richter, Joseph]. *Das Affenland oder der Doktor Fanfarone* (s.l., 1787).

Richter, Joseph. *Die Eipeldauer Briefe*, ed. Eugen von Pannel (Munich: Georg Müller, 1917 [1785–1813]).

Römer, Anton. *Handbuch der Anatomie des menschlichen Körpers* (Vienna: Heubner, 1831).

Rudolphi, Karl Asmund. *Bemerkungen aus dem Gebiet der Naturgeschichte, Medicin und Thierarzneykunde, auf einer Reise durch einen Theil von Deutschland, Holland und Frankreich gesammelt* (Berlin: Realschulbuchhandlung, 1804).

Saggio del Real Gabinetto di Fisica, e di Storia Naturale di Firenze (Rome: Giovanni Zempel, 1775).

Scherer, Joseph. *Tabulae anatomicae, quae exhibent musaei anatomici Academiae Caes. Josephinae praeparata cerea* (Vienna: Wappler and Beck, 1817–21).

Shaw, George. *General Zoology; or Systematic Natural History* (London: G. Kearsley, 1800).

Sismondi, Jean-Charles-Léonard Simonde de. *Tableau de l'agriculture toscane* (Geneva: J.J. Pasehoud, 1801).

Smith, James Edward. *A Sketch of a Tour on the Continent* (2nd edn, 2 vols, London 1807).

Steidele, Raphael. *Lehrbuch von der Hebammenkunst* (3rd edn, Vienna: Trattner, 1784).

Stendhal, *Rome, Naples et Florence* (vol. 1, 3rd edn, Paris: Delaunay, 1826).

Uccelli, Filippo. 'Rapporto del Professore di Anatomia comparata Filippo Uccelli', in *Annali del Museo imperiale di fisica e storia naturale di Firenze per il MDCCCVIII* (vol. 1, Florence: G. Tofani, 1808).

Vannoni, P[ietro]. *Biografia di Antonio Serantoni* (Florence: V. Batelli, 1838).

Vigée-Lebrun, Elisabeth. *The Memoirs of Elisabeth Vigée-Lebrun*, trans. Siân Evans (Bloomington: Indiana University Press, 1989).

Walker, Adam. *Ideas Suggested on the Spot, in a Late Excursion Through Flanders, Germany, France, and Italy* (London, 1790).

Walpole, Horace. *Horace Walpole's correspondence with Sir Horace Mann*, ed. W. S. Lewis, Warren Hunting Smith and George L. Lam (London: Oxford University Press; New Haven: Yale University Press, 1954–71).

Weiskopf, Hieronimus. *Kritische Bemerkung über den bei den Jakoberinnen zu Wien öffentlich zur Schaugestellten unverwesten Körper der Nonne Magdalena, Baronin von Walterskirchen* (Augsburg, 1786).

Wichelhausen, Engelbert. *Ideen über die beste Anwendung der Wachsbildnerei, nebst Nachrichten von den anatomischen Wachspräparaten in Florenz und deren Verfertigung, für Künstler, Kunstliebhaber und Anthropologen* (Frankfurt am Main: J.L.E. Zessler, 1798).

Winckelmann, J.J. *Reflections on the Painting and Sculpture of the Greeks: with Instructions for the Connoisseur, and an Essay on Grace in Works of Art* (London: Millar, 1765 [1755]).

Yvon, Claude. 'Attention', in Denis Diderot and Jean le Rond d'Alembert (eds), *L'Encyclopédie de Diderot et d'Alembert: ou Dictionnaire raisonné des sciences, des arts et des métiers* (Paris: Briasson, David, Le Breton and Durand, 1751–72), vol. 1, pp. 840–3.

Zedler, Johann Heinrich (ed.). *Grosses vollständiges Universal-Lexicon aller Wissenschafften und Künste* (Halle and Leipzig: Zedler, 1732–54).

Secondary sources

Abbri, Ferdinando. *Science de l'air: Studi su Felice Fontana* (Cosenza: Brenner, 1991).

Accademia delle scienze. *I materiali dell'Istituto delle Scienze* (Bologna: CLUEB, 1979).

Alberti, Samuel J.M.M. 'The museum affect: visiting collections of anatomy and natural history in Victorian Britain', in Bernard Lightman and Aileen Fyfe (eds), *Popular science: Nineteenth-century sites and experiences* (Chicago: Chicago University Press, 2007), pp. 371–403.

Alberti, Samuel J.M.M. 'Wax bodies. Art and anatomy in Victorian medical museums', *Museum history journal* 2:1 (2009), pp. 7–35.

Albertone, Manuela. 'Introduzione', *Studi settecenteschi* 24 (2004), 'Fisiocrazia e proprietà terriera', ed. Manuela Albertone, pp. 11–22.

Albertone, Manuela (ed.). *Studi settecenteschi* 24 (2004), 'Fisiocrazia e proprietà terriera'.

Alder, Ken. *Engineering the revolution: Arms, Enlightenment, and the making of modern France, 1763–1815* (Princeton: Princeton University Press, 1997).

Aleardi, A., G. Germano, C. Marcetti, and N. Solimano (eds). *L'Ospedale e la città. Dalla fondazione di S. Maria Nuova al sistema ospedaliero del 2000* (Florence: Polistampa, 2000).

Ammerer, Gerhard and Hanns Haas (eds), *Ambivalenz der Aufklärung. Festschrift für Ernst Wangermann* (Munich: Oldenbourg, 1997).

Anderson, Benedict. *Imagined communities* (London and New York: Verso, 1991 [1983]).

Anderson. M.S. 'The Italian Reformers', in H.M. Scott (ed.), *Enlightened absolutism. Reform and reformers in later eighteenth-century Europe* (Ann Arbor: University of Michigan Press, 1990), pp. 55–74.

Appel, Toby A. *The Cuvier-Geoffroy debate. French biology in the decades before Darwin* (New York and Oxford: Oxford University Press, 1987).

Armaroli, Maurizio (ed.). *Le cere anatomiche bolognesi del Settecento* (Bologna: CLUEB, 1981).

Arneth, Alfred von. *Joseph II. und Leopold von Toscana. Ihr Briefwechsel von 1781 bis 1790* (Vienna: Wilhelm Braumüller, 1872).

Ars ostetricia bononiensis. *Catalogo e inventario del museo ostetrico Giovan Antonio Galli* (Bologna: CLUEB, 1988).

Artusi, Luciano and Silvano Gabbrielli. *Feste e giochi a Firenze* (Florence: Becocci, 1976).

Ash, Eric H. 'Introduction: expertise and the early modern state', *Osiris* 25 (2010).

Ash, Eric H. *Power, authority, and expertise in Elizabethan England* (Baltimore: Johns Hopkins University Press, 2004).

Ashworth, William J. *Customs and excise: trade, production, and consumption in England, 1640–1845* (Oxford: Oxford University Press, 2003).

Azzaroli Puccetti, Maria Luisa, Benedetto Lanza, and Ludmilla Bontempelli. 'La Venere scomponibile', *Kos* 1 (1984), pp. 65–94.

Baggiani, Daniele. 'Progresso tecnico e azione politica nella Toscana leopoldina: La Camera di Commercio di Firenze (1768–1782)', in Giulio Barsanti, Vieri Becagli and Renato Pasta (eds), *La politica della scienza. Toscana e stati italiani nel tardo settecento* (Florence: Olschki, 1996), pp. 67–99.

Bandini, Gianfranco and Alessandro Mariani. 'Accademie, eruditi, biblioteche e ceto intellettuale', in Franco Cambi (ed.), *La Toscana e l'educazione. Dal Settecento a oggi: tra identità regionale e laboratorio nazionale* (Florence: Le Lettere, 1998), pp. 55–73.

Bandini, Gianfranco. 'Gli anni francesi e l'educazione in Toscana', in Franco Cambi (ed.), *La Toscana e l'educazione. Dal Settecento a oggi: tra identità regionale e laboratorio nazionale* (Florence: Le Lettere, 1998), pp. 131–47.

Barnes, Barry. 'The conventional component in knowledge and cognition', in Nico Stehr and Volker Meja (eds), *Society and knowledge: Contemporary perspectives in the sociology of knowledge* (New Brunswick: Transaction Books, 1984), pp. 185–208.

Barnes, Barry, David Bloor, and John Henry. *Scientific knowledge. A sociological analysis* (Chicago: University of Chicago Press, 1996).

Barsanti, Giulio, Vieri Becagli, and Renato Pasta (eds). *La politica della scienza. Toscana e stati italiani nel tardo settecento* (Florence: Olschki, 1996).

Bates, A.W. '"Indecent and demoralising representations": public anatomy museums in mid-Victorian England', *Medical history*, 52:1 (2008), pp. 1–22.

Batten, Charles. *Pleasurable instruction: Form and convention in eighteenth-century travel literature* (Berkeley: University of California Press, 1978).

Beales, Derek. *Joseph II*. (Cambridge: Cambridge University Press, 1987).

Becagli, Vieri. 'Economia e politica del sapere nelle riforme leopoldine. Le Accademie', in Giulio Barsanti, Vieri Becagli, and Renato Pasta (eds), *La politica della scienza. Toscana e stati italiani nel tardo settecento* (Florence: Olschki, 1996), pp. 35–66.

Becagli, Vieri. 'Georg-Ludwig Schmid d'Auenstein e i suoi *Principes de la législation universelle*: oltre la fisiocrazia?', *Studi settecenteschi* 24 (2004), 'Fisiocrazia e proprietà terriera', ed. Manuela Albertone. pp. 215–52.

Becker, Peter and William Clark (eds). *Little tools of knowledge: Historical essays on academic and bureaucratic practices* (Ann Arbor: University of Michigan Press, 2001).

Bedini, Silvio. 'The fate of the Medici-Lorraine scientific instruments', in Silvio Bedini, *Patrons, artisans and instruments of science, 1600–1750* (Aldershot and Brookfield: Ashgate/Variorum, 1999).

Bellatalla, Luciana. *Pietro Leopoldo di Toscana granduca-educatore. Teoria e pratica di un despota illuminato* (Lucca: Maria Pacini Fazzi, 1984).

Bennett, Tony (ed.). *The birth of the museum: History, theory, politics* (London and New York: Routledge, 1995).

Bensaude-Vincent, Bernadette and Christine Blondel (eds), *Science and spectacle in the European Enlightenment* (Aldershot: Ashgate, 2008).

Beretta, Marco (ed.). *From private to public: Natural collections and museums* (Canton, Mass.: Science History Publications, 2005).

Berg, Maxine. *The machinery question and the making of political economy, 1815–1848* (Cambridge: Cambridge University Press, 1980).

Berry, Christopher J. *The idea of luxury: A conceptual and historical investigation* (Cambridge: Cambridge University Press, 1994).

Berti Logan, Gabriella. 'Women and the practice and teaching of medicine in Bologna in the eighteenth and early nineteenth centuries', *Bulletin of the history of medicine* 77:3 (2003), pp. 506–35.

Biagioli, Mario. *Galileo, courtier. The practice of science in the culture of absolutism* (Chicago: The University of Chicago Press, 1993).

Blankertz, Herwig. *Die Geschichte der Pädagogik. Von der Aufklärung bis zur Gegenwart* (Wetzlar: Büchse der Pandora, 1982).

Bloor, David. *Wittgenstein: A social theory of knowledge* (New York: Columbia University Press, 1983).

Bodi, Leslie. *Tauwetter in Wien: zur Prosa der österreichischen Aufklärung 1781–1795* (Frankfurt am Main: S.Fischer, 1977).

Bohr, Michael. *Die Entwicklung der Kabinettschränke in Florenz* (Frankfurt am Main: Peter Lang, 1993).

Bonechi, Simone. 'Un proprietario toscano tra scienza, rivoluzione e filantropismo: Girolamo de' Bardi (1777–1829)', *Nuncius* 10:1 (1995), pp. 51–97.

Borroni Salvadori, Fabia. 'Memorialisti e diaristi a Firenze nel periodo leopoldino (1765–1790)', *Annali della Scuola Normale Superiore di Pisa*, Classe di Lettere e Filosofia, 3rd series, 9:3 (1979), pp. 1189–291.

Borroni Salvadori, Fabia. 'Committenti scontenti, artisti litigiosi nella Firenze del Settecento', in *Mitteilungen des Kunsthistorischen Institutes in Florenz*, 39:1 (1985), pp. 129–58.

Boschung, Urs. 'Geburtshilfliche Lehrmodelle. Notizen zur Geschichte des Phantoms und der Hysteroplasmata', *Gesnerus* 38 (1981), pp. 59–68.

Boutier, Jean, Brigitte Marin and Antonella Romano (eds). *Naples, Rome, Florence: Une histoire compare des milieux intellectuels italiens (XVIIe–XVIIIe siècles)* (Rome: École française de Rome, 2005).

Brambilla, Elena. 'La medicina del Settecento: dal monopolio dogmatico alla professione scientifica', in Franco Della Peruta (ed.), *Storia d'Italia*, vol. 7 (Malattia e medicina) (Turin: Einaudi, 1894), pp. 5–147.

Brau, Jacqueline. 'La professionalization de la santé dans la Toscane des Lumières, 1765–1815', *Revue d'histoire moderne et contemporaine* 41:3 (1994), pp. 418–39.

Broman, Thomas H. 'Rethinking professionalization: Theory, practice, and professional ideology in eighteenth-century German medicine', *The journal of modern history* 67 (1995), pp. 835–72.

Broman, Thomas H. *The transformation of German academic medicine 1750–1820* (Cambridge: Cambridge University Press, 1996).

Broman, Thomas H. 'The Habermasian public sphere and "science in the Enlightenment"', *History of Science* 26 (1998), pp. 123–49.

Broman, Thomas H. 'Medical science', in *The Cambridge history of science*, vol. 4, 'Eighteenth-century science', ed. Roy Porter (Cambridge University Press, 2003), pp. 463–84.

Bruni, Luigino and Pier Luigi Porta. '*Economia civile* and *pubblica felicita* in the Italian Enlightenment', *History of political economy* 35, annual supplement (2003), pp. 361–85.

Brunner, Otto, Werner Conze and Reinhart Koselleck (eds). *Geschichtliche Grundbegriffe. Historisches Lexikon zur politisch-sozialen Sprache in Deutschland* (Stuttgart: Klett-Cotta, 1978).

Bucci, Mario. *Anatomia come arte* (Florence: Edizioni d'Arte Il Fiorino, 1969).

Büll, Reinhard. *Das große Buch vom Wachs. Geschichte, Kultur, Technik* (Munich: Georg D. W. Callwey, 1977).

Burmeister, Maritha Rene. *Popular anatomical museums in nineteenth-century England* (PhD thesis, Rutgers University, 2000).

Cambi, Franco. 'La pedagogia illuministica in Toscana: tra politica, economia, religione', in Franco Cambi (ed.), *La Toscana e l'educazione. Dal Settecento a oggi: tra identità regionale e laboratorio nazionale* (Florence: Le Lettere, 1998), pp. 39–53.

Cambi, Franco. 'L'Ottocento. Introduzione', in Franco Cambi (ed.), *La Toscana e l'educazione. Dal Settecento a oggi: tra identità regionale e laboratorio nazionale* (Florence: Le Lettere, 1998), pp. 151–60.

Cambrosio, Alberto, D. Jacobi, and P. Keating. 'Ehrlich's "beautiful pictures" and the controversial beginnings of immunological imagery', *Isis* 84 (1993), pp. 662–99.

Casalini, Eugenio. *La SS. Annunziata di Firenze. Studi e documenti sulla chiesa e il convento* (Florence: Convento della SS. Annunziata, 1971).

Centro per la storia dell'Università di Pavia. *Giovanni Alessandro Brambilla nella cultura medica del Settecento Europeo* (Milan: La Goliardica, 1980).

Chaplin, Simon. 'Nature dissected, or dissection naturalized? The case of John Hunter's museum', *Museum and society* 6:2 (2008), pp. 135–51.

Chiswick, Harvey. *The limits of reform in the Enlightenment: Attitudes toward the education of the lower classes in eighteenth-century France* (Princeton: Princeton University Press, 1981).

Ciuffoletti, Zeffiro. 'I moderati toscani e la tradizione leopoldina', in Clementina Rotondi (ed.), *I Lorena in Toscana* (Florence: Olschki, 1989), pp. 121–38.

Clark, William, Jan Golinski and Simon Schaffer (eds), *The Sciences in Enlightened Europe* (Chicago and London: University of Chicago Press, 1999).

Clark, William. 'On the ministerial registers of academic visitations', in Peter Becker and William Clark (eds), *Little tools of knowledge: Historical essays on academic and bureaucratic practices* (Ann Arbor: University of Michigan Press, 2001), pp. 95–140.

Clarke, Adele and Joan Fujimura. 'What tools? Which jobs? Why right?', in Adele Clarke and Joan Fujimura (eds), *The right tools for the job: At work in twentieth-century life sciences* (Princeton: Princeton University Press, 1992), pp. 3–44.

Cochrane, Eric. *Tradition and Enlightenment in the Tuscan academies, 1691–1800* (Chicago: University of Chicago Press, 1961).

Cochrane, Eric. *Florence in the forgotten centuries 1527–1800. A history of Florence and the Florentines in the age of the Grand Dukes* (Chicago and London: University of Chicago Press, 1973).

Coleman, William. *Georges Cuvier, zoologist. A study in the history of evolution theory* (Cambridge, Mass.: Harvard University Press, 1964).

Collins, Harry. *Changing order. Replication and induction in scientific practice* (London: Sage, 1985).

Collins, Harry and Robert Evans. *Rethinking expertise* (Chicago: University of Chicago Press, 2007).

Congresso internazionale sulla ceroplastica nella scienza e nell'arte. *La ceroplastica nella scienza e nell'arte: atti del I congresso internazionale, Firenze, 3–7 giugno 1975* (Florence: Olschki, 1977).

Contardi, Simone. 'Unità del sapere e pubblica utilità: Felice Fontana e le collezioni di fisica dell'Imperiale e Regio Museo', in Giulio Barsanti, Vieri Becagli, and Renato Pasta (eds), *La politica della scienza. Toscana e stati italiani nel tardo settecento* (Florence: Olschki, 1996), pp. 279–94.

Contardi, Simone. 'Felice Fontana e l'Imperiale e Regio Museo di Firenze. Strategie museali e accademismo scientifico nella Firenze di Pietro Leopoldo', in Ferdinando Abbri and Marco Segala (eds), *Il ruolo sociale della scienza (1789–1830)* (Florence: Olschki, 2000), pp. 37–56.

Contardi, Simone. *La Casa di Salomone a Firenze. L'Imperiale e Reale Museo di Fisica e Storia Naturale (1775–1801)* (Florence: Olschki, 2002).

Contardi, Simone. 'L'artigianato fiorentino al servizio della scienza', in Riccardo Spinelli (ed.), *La grande storia dell'Artigianato*, vol. 5 (Il Seicento e il Settecento), (Florence: Giunti, 2002), pp. 85–99.

Contardi, Simone. 'Linnaeus institutionalized: Felice Fontana, Giovanni Fabbroni, and the natural history collections of the Royal Museum of Physics and Natural History of Florence', in Marco Beretta and Alessandro Tosi (eds), *Linnaeus in Italy: The spread of a revolution in science* (Uppsala studies in history of science, 34), (Sagamore Beach, MA: Watson Pub. International LLC, 2007), pp. 113–28.

Contini, Alessandra: '"La naissance n'est qu'effet du hazard". L'educazione delle principesse e dei pricipi alla corte leopoldina', in Sergio Bertelli and Renato Pasta (eds), *Vivere a Pitti. Una reggia dai Medici ai Savoia* (Florence: Olschki 2003), pp. 389–438.

Coppini, Romano Paolo. *Il Granducato di Toscana. Dagli 'anni francesi' all'Unità. Storia d'Italia*, ed. Giuseppe Galasso, vol. 13:3 (Torino: UTET, 1993).

Dacome, Lucia. '"Un certo e quasi incredibile piacere": cera e anatomia nel Settecento', *Intersezioni*, 25:3 (2005), pp. 415–36.

Dacome. Lucia. 'Women, wax and anatomy in the "century of things"', *Renaissance studies* 21:4 (2007), pp. 522–50.

Daston, Lorraine. *Eine kurze Geschichte der wissenschaftlichen Aufmerksamkeit* (Munich: Carl-Friedrich-von-Siemens-Stiftung, 2001).

Daston, Lorraine and Peter Galison. 'The image of objectivity', *Representations* 40 (1992), pp. 81–128.

Daston, Lorraine and Katherine Park. *Wonders and the order of nature, 1150–1750* (New York: Zone Books, 1998).

Daston, Lorraine and Gianna Pomata (eds). *The faces of nature in Enlightenment Europe* (Berlin: BWV-Berliner Wissenschafts-Verlag, 2003).

Davis, Audrey B. 'Louis Thomas Jerôme Auzoux and the papier maché anatomical model', in *La ceroplastica nella scienza e nell'arte: atti del I congresso internazionale Firenze, 3–7 giugno 1975* (Florence: Olschki, 1977), pp. 257–79.

De Benedictis, Cristina. *Per la storia del collezionismo italiano. Fonti e documenti* (Florence: Ponte alle Grazie, 1995).

De Ceglia, Francesco. 'Rotten corpses, a disembowelled woman, a flayed man. Images of the body from the end of the 17th to the beginning of the 19th century. Florentine wax models in the first-hand accounts of visitors', *Perspectives on science* 14:4 (2006), pp. 417–56.

De Chadarevian, Soraya. 'Models and the making of molecular biology', in Soraya de Chadarevian and Nick Hopwood (eds), *Models: The third dimension of science* (Stanford: Stanford University Press, 2004), pp. 339–68.

De Chadarevian, Soraya and Nick Hopwood (eds). *Models: The third dimension of science* (Stanford: Stanford University Press, 2004).

De Renzi, Silvia. 'Medical expertise, bodies and the law in early modern courts', *Isis* 98 (2007), pp. 315–22.

Dear, Peter. 'Mysteries of state, mysteries of nature: authority, knowledge and expertise in the 17th century', in Sheila Jasanoff (ed.), *States of knowledge. The co-production of science and social order* (London and New York: Routledge, 2004), pp. 206–24.

Dear, Peter. *The intelligibility of nature: How science makes sense of the world* (Chicago: University of Chicago Press, 2006).

Dennis, Michael A. 'Graphic understanding: instruments and interpretation in Robert Hooke's "Micrographia"', *Science in context 3* (1989), pp. 309–64.

Didi-Huberman, Georges (1999a). 'Wax flesh, vicious circles', in Museo zoologico La Specola. *Encyclopaedia Anatomica. Vollständige Sammlung anatomischer Wachse. Museo di Storia Naturale dell' Universita di Firenze, sezione di zoologia La Specola* (Cologne: Taschen, 1999), pp. 64–74.

Didi-Huberman, Georges (1999b). *Ouvrir Vénus – nudité, rêve, cruauté* (Paris: Gallimard, 1999).

Dieckmann, Herbert. 'Diderot's conception of genius', *Journal of the history of ideas* 2:2 (1941), pp. 151–82.

Donati, Edgardo. *La Toscana nell'Impero napoleonico* (2 vols, Florence: Polistampa, 2008).

Donnison, Jean. *Midwives and medical men: A history of the struggle for the control of childbirth* (2nd edn, New Barnet: Historical Publications, 1988).

Dooley, Brendan. *Science and the marketplace in early modern Italy* (Lanham: Lexington, 2001).

Duchhardt, Heinz. 'Die Absolutismusdebatte – eine Antipolemik', *Historische Zeitschrift* 275 (2002), pp. 323–31.

Dürbeck, Gabriele. 'Empirischer und ästhetischer Sinn: Strategien der Vermittlung von Wissen in der anatomischen Wachsplastik um 1800', in Gabriele Dürbeck, Bettina Gockel, Susanne B. Keller, Monika Renneberg, Jutta Schickore, Gerhard Wiesenfeldt, and Anja Wolkenhauer (eds), *Wahrnehmung der Natur, Natur der Wahrnehmung. Studien zur Geschichte visueller Kultur um 1800* (Dresden: Verlag der Kunst, 2001), pp. 35–54.

Duncan, Carol. *Civilizing rituals: inside public art museums* (London and New York: Routledge, 1995).

Ezrahi, Yaron. *The descent of Icarus. Science and the transformation of contemporary society* (Cambridge, Mass.: Harvard University Press, 1990).

Ferrone, Vincenzo. *The intellectual roots of the Italian Enlightenment: Newtonian science, religion, and politics in the early eighteenth century* (Atlantic Highlands: Humanities Press, 1995).

Fileti Mazza, Miriam and Bruna Tomasello, *Antonio Cocchi: primo antiquario della Galleria fiorentina, 1738–1758* (Modena: F.C. Panini, 1996).

Fileti Mazza, Miriam and Bruna Tomasello. *Galleria degli Uffizi 1758–1775: la politica museale di Raimondo Cocchi* (Modena: Panini, 1999).

Fileti Mazza, Miriam and Bruna Tomasello. *Galleria degli Uffizi 1775–1792: un laboratorio culturale per Giuseppe Pelli Bencivenni* (Modena: Panini, 2003).

Filippini, Nadia Maria. 'Eine neue Vorstellung vom Fötus und vom Mutterleib (Italien, 18. Jahrhundert)', in Barbara Duden, Jürgen Schlumbohm, Patrice Veit (eds), *Geschichte des Ungeborenen. Zur Erfahrungs- und Wissenschaftsgeschichte der Schwangerschaft, 17.–20. Jahrhundert* (Göttingen: Vandenhoeck & Ruprecht, 2002), pp. 99–128.

Findlen, Paula. *Possessing nature: Museums, collecting, and scientific culture in early modern Italy* (Berkeley: University of California Press, 1994).

Focaccia, Miriam. *Anna Morandi Manzolini: Una donna fra arte e scienza. Immagini, documenti, repertorio anatomico* (Biblioteca di Nuncius n. 65) (Florence: Olschki, 2008).

Forti, Alberto (ed.). *L'Imperiale e Regio Museo di Fisica e Storia Naturale di Firenze: indicazioni per un metodo di lettura e per una soluzione museografica* (Florence: Angelo Pontecorboli, 1995).

Foucault, Michel. *Discipline and punish* (New York: Vintage Books, 1995 [1975]).

Fox-Genovese, Elizabeth. *The origins of physiocracy. Economic revolution and social order in eighteenth-century France* (Ithaca and London: Cornell University Press, 1976).

Francoeur, Eric. 'The forgotten tool: the design and use of molecular models', *Social studies of science* 27 (1997), pp. 7–40.

Furrer, Rita. 'Die Restaurierung anatomischer und geburtshilflicher Wachsmodelle im Wiener Josephinum', *Restauratorenblätter* 2:1 ('Mirabilia und Curiosa') (2000), pp. 105–16.

Geach, P.T. *Reference and generality. An examination of some medieval and modern theories* (3rd edn, Ithaca and London: Cornell University Press, 1980 [1962]).

Gelbart, Nina Rattner. *The king's midwife. A history and mystery of Madame du Coudray* (Berkeley, Los Angeles, London: University of California Press 1998).

Gentilcore, David. *Medical charlatanism in early modern Italy* (Oxford: Oxford University Press, 2006).

Gilbert, Ruth. *Early modern hermaphrodites. Sex and other stories* (Basingstoke and New York: Palgrave, 2002).

Gillispie, Charles C. *Science and polity in France at the end of the Old Regime* (Princeton: Princeton University Press, 1980).

Gillispie, Charles C. *Science and polity in France: The Revolutionary and Napoleonic years* (Princeton: Princeton University Press, 2004).

Goffman, Erving. *The presentation of self in everyday life* (New York: Anchor Books Doubleday, 1959).

Golan, Tal. *Laws of men and laws of nature: The history of scientific expert testimony in England and America* (Cambridge, Mass.: Harvard University Press, 2004).

Golinski, Jan. *Making natural knowledge: Constructivism and the history of science* (Cambridge: Cambridge University Press, 1998).

Gori, Pietro. *Le feste fiorentine attraverso i secoli* (Florence: Bemporad, 1926).

Graber, Frédéric. 'Inventing needs: expertise and water supply in late eighteenth- and early nineteenth-century Paris', *British journal for the history of science* 40 (2007), pp. 315–32.

Griesemer, James R. 'The role of instruments in the generative analysis of science', in Adele Clarke and Joan Fujimura (eds), *The right tools for the job: At work in twentieth-century life sciences* (Princeton: Princeton University Press, 1992), pp. 47–75.

Griesemer, James R. 'Three-dimensional models in philosophical perspective', in Soraya de Chadarevian and Nick Hopwood (eds), *Models: The third dimension of science* (Stanford: Stanford University Press, 2004), pp. 433–42.

Grob, Bart. *The world of Auzoux: Models of man and beast in papier-mâché* (Leiden: Museum Boerhaave, 2000).

Gröger, Helmut. 'Die Sammlung anatomischer und geburtshilflicher Wachsmodelle als Lehrmittel', in Manfred Skopec and Helmut Gröger (eds), *Anatomie als Kunst. Anatomische Wachsmodelle des 18. Jahrhunderts im Josephinum in Wien*, (Vienna: Christian Brandstätter, 2002), pp. 125–49.

Groopman, Jerome. 'A model patient: How simulators are changing the way doctors are trained', *New Yorker* (2 May 2005).

Guerci, Luciano. *La discussione sulla donna nell'Italia del Settecento. Aspetti e problemi* (Torino: Tirrenia Stampatori, 1988).

Guerci, Luciano. *La sposa obbediente. Donna e matrimonio nella discussione dell'Italia del Settecento* (Torino: Tirrenia Stampatori, 1988).

Guerci, Luciano. *'Mente, cuore, coraggio, virtù repubblicane': educare il popolo nell'Italia in rivoluzione (1796–1799)* (Torino: Tirrenia Stampatori, 1992).

Haas, Norbert, Rainer Nägele, and Hans-Jörg Rheinberger (eds). *Aufmerksamkeit* (Eggingen: Klaus Isele, 1998).

Habermas, Jürgen. *Strukturwandel der Öffentlichkeit* (Frankfurt am Main: Suhrkamp, 1990 [1962]).

Hagner, Michael. 'Aufmerksamkeit als Ausnahmezustand', in Norbert Haas, Rainer Nägele and Hans-Jörg Rheinberger (eds), *Aufmerksamkeit* (Eggingen: Klaus Isele, 1998), pp. 273–94.

Hagner, Michael. 'Enlightened monsters', in William Clark, Jan Golinski, and Simon Schaffer (eds), *The sciences in enlightened Europe* (Chicago and London: University of Chicago Press, 1999), pp. 175–217.

Hahn, Roger. *The anatomy of a scientific institution: The Paris Academy of Sciences, 1666–1803* (Berkeley: University of California Press, 1971).

Hallam, Elizabeth. 'Anatomy display: contemporary debates and collections in Scotland', in Andrew Patrizio and Dawn Kemp (eds), *Anatomy acts: How we come to know ourselves* (Edinburgh: Birlinn, 2006), pp. 119–38.

Hallam, Elizabeth. *Anatomy museum. Death and the body displayed* (London: Reaktion, forthcoming 2011).

Harig, Georg (ed.). *Chirurgische Ausbildung im 18. Jahrhundert* (Abhandlungen zur Geschichte der Medizin und der Naturwissenschaften, Heft 57) (Husum: Matthiesen Verlag, 1990).

Haynes, Clare. 'A 'natural' exhibitioner: Sir Ashton Lever and his holophusikon', *British journal for eighteenth-century studies* 24 (2001), pp. 1–14.

Henderson, John. *The Renaissance hospital. Healing the body and healing the soul* (New Haven and London: Yale University Press, 2006).

Hess, Volker, Eric Engstrom and Ulrike Thoms (eds). *Figurationen des Experten: Ambivalenzen der wissenschaftlichen Expertise im ausgehenden 18. und frühen 19. Jahrhundert* (Frankfurt: Peter Lang, 2005).

Hildebrand, Reinhard. 'Der menschliche Körper als stilisiertes Objekt. Anatomische Präparate, Modelle und Abbildungen im 18. Jahrhundert', in Rüdiger Schultka and Josef N. Neumann (eds), *Anatomie und anatomische Sammlungen im 18. Jahrhundert* (2007), pp. 197–222.

Hilgartner, Stephen. *Science on stage: expert advice as public drama* (Stanford: Stanford University Press, 2000).

Hill, Kate. '"Roughs of both sexes": the working class in Victorian museums and art galleries', in Simon Gunn and Robert J. Morris (eds), *Identities in space: contested terrains in the Western city since 1850* (Aldershot: Ashgate, 2001), pp. 190–203.

Hill, Kate. *Culture and class in English public museums, 1850–1914* (Aldershot: Ashgate, 2005).

Hochadel, Oliver. *Öffentliche Wissenschaft. Elektrizität in der deutschen Aufklärung* (Göttingen: Wallstein, 2003).

Hooper-Greenhill, Eilean. *Museums and the shaping of knowledge* (London: Routledge, 1992).

Hopwood, Nick. 'Giving body to embryos: modeling, mechanism, and the microtome in late-nineteenth-century anatomy', *Isis* 90 (1999), pp. 462–96.

Hopwood, Nick. *Embryos in wax: models from the Ziegler studio* (Cambridge: Whipple Museum of the History of Science, University of Cambridge, 2002).

Hopwood, Nick. 'Artist versus anatomist, models against dissection: Paul Zeiller of Munich and the revolution of 1848', *Medical history* 51 (2007), pp. 279–308.

Horn, Sonia. 'Wiener Hebammen 1643–1753', *Studien zur Wiener Geschichte* (= Jahrbuch des Vereins für Geschichte der Stadt Wien), 59 (2003), pp. 35–102.

Horn, Sonia. '"eine Akademie in Absicht der Erweiterung der medizinisch-chirurgischen Wissenschaft . . .": Hintergründe für die Entstehung der medizinisch-chirurgischen Akademie "Josephinum"', in Wolfgang Schmale, Renate Zedinger, and Jean Mondot (eds), *Josephinismus – eine Bilanz/Échecs et réussites du Joséphisme* (= Das Achtzehnte Jahrhundert und Österreich, vol. 22) (Bochum: Winkler, 2008), pp. 215–44.

Ilting, Karl-Heinz. 'Naturrecht', in Otto Brunner, Werner Conze, and Reinhart Koselleck (eds), *Geschichtliche Grundbegriffe. Historisches Lexikon zur politisch-sozialen Sprache in Deutschland* (Stuttgart: Klett-Cotta, 1978).

Impey, Oliver and Arthur MacGregor (eds). *The origins of museums: The cabinet of curiosities in sixteenth and seventeenth-century Europe* (Oxford: Clarendon Press, 1985).

Jackson, Myles. *Spectrum of belief: Joseph von Fraunhofer and the craft of precision optics* (Cambridge, Mass.: MIT Press, 2000).

Jantsch, Marlene. *Die Gründung des Josephinums. Seine Bedeutung für die Entwicklung der Chirurgie und des Militärswesens in Österreich* (Vienna: Hollinek, 1956).

Jasanoff, Sheila. 'Science, politics, and the renegotiation of expertise at EPA', *Osiris* 7 (1992), pp. 195–217.

Jasanoff, Sheila. *The fifth branch. Science advisers as policymakers* (Cambridge, Mass.: Harvard University Press, 1990).

Jasanoff, Sheila. 'The idiom of co-production', in Sheila Jasanoff (ed.), *States of knowledge. The co-production of science and social order* (London and New York: Routledge, 2004), pp. 1–12.

Jespersen, T. Christine, Alicita Rodríguez, and Joseph Starr (eds), *The anatomy of body worlds: critical essays on the plastinated cadavers of Gunther von Hagen* (Jefferson, NC: McFarland & Co., 2009).

Johns, Adrian. *The nature of the book: Print and knowledge in the making* (Chicago: University of Chicago Press, 1998).

Johnson, Stephen. 'The persistence of tradition in anatomical museums', in T. Christine Jespersen, Alicita Rodriguez, and Joseph Starr (eds), *The anatomy of body worlds: critical essays on the plastinated cadavers of Gunther Von Hagen* (Jefferson, NC: McFarland, 2009), pp. 68–85.

Johnson, Virginia W. *The lily of the Arno: Or Florence, past and present* (Boston: Estes and Lauriat, 1891).

Jordanova, Ludmilla. 'Museums: representing the real?', in George Levine (ed.), *Realism and representation. Essays on the problem of realism in relation to science, literature, and culture* (Madison: University of Wisconsin Press, 1993), pp. 255–78.

Jordanova, Ludmilla. *Sexual visions: Images of gender in science and medicine between the eighteenth and twentieth centuries* (Madison: University of Wisconsin Press, 1989).

Kaplan, Steven. 'Physiocracy, the state, and society: the limits of disengagement', in Peter Katzenstein, Theodore Lowi, and Sidney Tarrow (eds), *Comparative theory and political experience* (Ithaca and London: Cornell University Press, 1990), pp. 23–62.

Keel, Othmar. 'La scuola di Santa Maria Nuova modello per l'Europa e nella Francia della Rivoluzione', in Enrico Ghidetti and Esther Diana (eds), *La bellezza come terapia: arte e assistenza nell'ospedale di Santa Maria Nuova a Firenze: atti del Convegno internazionale, Firenze, 20–22 maggio 2004* (Florence: Polistampa, 2005), pp. 313–75.

Keel, Othmar. *L'avènement de la médecine clinique moderne en Europe, 1750–1815: Politiques, institutions et savoirs* (Montréal: PUM, 2001).

Kirchenberger. 'Chronologie der Josefs-Akademie', *Dr. Wittelshöfer's Der Militärarzt* (Separatabdruck), 4 (1885) and following.

Kleindienst, Heike. *Ästhetisierte Anatomie aus Wachs. Ursprung – Genese – Integration* (PhD dissertation, University of Marburg, 1989).

Kleindienst, Heike. '"Pester Venus"' – Expedition einer anatomischen Schönheit', *Anatomischer Anzeiger, Jena* 171 (1990), pp. 147–52.

Knoefel, Peter K. 'Antonio Scarpa, Felice Fontana, and the wax models for Pavia', *Medicina nei secoli* 16 (1979), pp. 219–34.

Knoefel, Peter K. *Felice Fontana, 1730–1805: An annotated bibliography* (Trento: Società di Studi Trentini di Scienze Storiche, 1980).

Knoefel, Peter K. *Felice Fontana. Life and works* (Trento: Società di Studi Trentini di Scienze Storiche, 1984).

Koerner, Lisbet. *Linnaeus: Nature and nation* (Cambridge, Mass.: Harvard University Press, 1999).

Kornmeier, Uta. 'Almost alive. The spectacle of verisimilitude in Madame Tussaud's waxworks', in Roberta Panzanelli (ed.), *Ephemeral bodies: wax sculpture and the human figure* (Los Angeles: Getty Research Institute, 2008), pp. 67–82.

Krapf, Michael (ed.). *Franz Xaver Messerschmidt, 1736–1783* (Ostfildern-Ruit: Hatje Cantz, 2003).

Krüger-Fürhoff, Irmela Marei. *Der versehrte Körper. Revisionen des klassizistischen Schönheitsideals* (Göttingen: Wallstein, 2001).

Landes, Joan B. 'Wax fibres, wax bodies, and moving figures: artifice and nature in eighteenth-century anatomy', in Roberta Panzanelli (ed.), *Ephemeral bodies: wax sculpture and the human figure* (Los Angeles: Getty Research Institute, 2008), pp. 41–66.

Lankheit, Klaus. *Die Modellsammlung der Porzellanmanufaktur Doccia. Ein Dokument italienischer Barockplastik* (Munich: Bruckmann, 1982).

Lanza, Benedetto, Azzaroli Puccetti, Maria Luisa, Poggesi, Marta, and Martelli, Antonio. *Le cere anatomiche della Specola* (Florence: Arnaud, 1997).

Latour, Bruno. 'Drawing things together', in Michael Lynch and Steve Woolgar (eds), *Representation in scientific practice* (Cambridge, Mass.: MIT Press, 1990), pp. 19–68.

Law, John. 'On the methods of long-distance control: vessels, navigation, and the Portuguese route to India', in John Law (ed.), *Power, action and belief. A new sociology of knowledge?* (London: Routledge, 1986), pp. 234–63.

Lawrence, Christopher. 'Democratic, divine and heroic: the history and historiography of surgery', in Christopher Lawrence (ed.), *Medical theory, surgical practice. Studies in the history of surgery* (The Wellcome Institute Series in the History of Medicine) (London and New York: Routledge, 1992), pp. 1–47.

Lawrence, Ghislaine. 'An obstetric phantom', *Lancet* 358:9296 (2001), p. 1916.

Lemire, Michel. *Artistes et mortels* (Paris: Chabaud, 1990).

Lesky, Erna. 'Wiener Lehrsammlungen von Wachspräparaten', *Gesnerus* 33 (1976), pp. 8–20.

Lesky, Erna. 'Das Bild des vollkommenen Chirurgen bei Brambilla', in Centro per la storia dell'Università di Pavia (ed.), *Giovanni Alessandro Brambilla nella cultura medica del Settecento Europeo* (Milan: La Goliardica, 1980), pp. 23–7.

Lesky, Erna. 'Theorie und Praxis, aufgezeigt an den Wiener geburtshilflichen Lehrkanzeln 1752–1859', *Gesnerus* 1:2 (1983), pp. 99–107.

Lettner, Gerda. *Das Rückzugsgefecht der Aufklärung in Wien, 1790–1792* (Frankfurt am Main: Campus, 1988).

Licoppe, Christian. *La formation de la pratique scientifique: le discours de l'expérience en France et en Angleterre, 1630–1820* (Paris: La Découverte, 1996).

Litchfield, R. Burr. *The emergence of a bureaucracy: The Florentine patricians 1530–1790* (Princeton: Princeton University Press, 1986).

Lynch, Michael. *Scientific practice and ordinary action: Ethnomethodology and social studies of science* (New York: Cambridge University Press, 1993).

Macdonald, Sharon. *Behind the scenes at the Science Museum* (Oxford: Berg, 2002).

Macdonald, Sharon. 'Accessing audiences: visiting visitor books', *Museum and Society* 3 (2006), pp. 119–36.

Maerker, Anna. 'The tale of the hermaphrodite monkey: classification, state interests and natural historical expertise between museum and court, 1791–4', *British journal for the history of science* 39:1 (2006), pp. 29–47.

Magherini, Graziella. *La sindrome di Stendhal* ([Florence]: Ponte alle Grazie, 1989).

Mah, Harold. 'Phantasies of the public sphere: rethinking the Habermas of historians', *Journal of modern history* 72 (2000), pp. 153–82.

Mangio, Carlo. 'Tra conservazione e rivoluzione', in Giuseppe Galasso (ed.), *Storia d'Italia*, vol. 13:2 (Il Granducato di Toscana. I Lorena dalla Reggenza agli anni rivoluzionari) (Torino: UTET, 1997), pp. 425–509.

Marland, Hilary (ed.), *The art of midwifery: Early modern midwives in Europe* (The Wellcome Institute series in the history of medicine) (London: New York: Routledge, 1993).

Mascilli Migliorini, Luigi. 'L'età delle riforme', in Giuseppe Galasso (ed.), *Storia d'Italia*, vol. 13:2 (Il Granducato di Toscana. I Lorena dalla Reggenza agli anni rivoluzionari) (Torino: UTET, 1997), pp. 249–421.

Massey, Lyle. 'On waxes and wombs. Eighteenth-century representations of the gravid uterus', in Roberta Panzanelli (ed.), *Ephemeral bodies: wax sculpture and the human figure* (Los Angeles: Getty Research Institute, 2008), pp. 83–106.

Mazzolini, Renato G. and Giuseppe Ongaro (eds). *Epistolario di Felice Fontana*, vol. 1. Carteggio con Leopoldo Marc'Antonio Caldani (Trento: Società di Studi Trentini di Scienze Storiche, 1980).

Mazzolini, Renato G. 'Fontana, Gasparo Ferdinando Felice', in *Dizionario biografico degli italiani*, vol. 42 (Rome: Istituto della Enciclopedia Italiana, 1997), pp. 663–9.

Mazzolini, Renato G. 'Plastic anatomies and artificial dissections', in Soraya de Chadarevian and Nick Hopwood (eds), *Models: The third dimension of science* (Stanford: Stanford University Press, 2004), pp. 43–70.

Mazzolini, Renato G. 'Visitors to Florence's R. Museum of Physics and Natural History from September 1784 to October 1785', *Nuncius* 21:2 (2006), pp. 337–48.

McTavish, Lianne. *Childbirth and the display of authority in early modern France* (Aldershot: Ashgate, 2005).

Meinel, Christoph. 'Molecules and croquet balls', in Soraya de Chadarevian and Nick Hopwood (eds), *Models: The third dimension of science* (Stanford: Stanford University Press, 2004), pp. 242–75.

Messbarger, Rebecca. 'Waxing poetic: Anna Morandi Manzolini's anatomical sculptures', *Configurations* 9 (2001), pp. 65–97.

Messbarger, Rebecca. *The century of women: Representations of women in eighteenth-century Italian public discourse* (Toronto: University of Toronto Press, 2002).

Messbarger, Rebecca. 'Re-membering a body of work: anatomist and anatomical designer Anna Morandi Manzolini', *Studies in eighteenth-century culture* 32 (2003), pp. 123–54.

Messbarger, Rebecca. 'As who dare gaze the Sun: Anna Morandi Manzolini's wax anatomies of the male reproductive system', in Paula Findlen, Wendy Wassyng Roworth, and Catherina M. Sama (eds), *Italy's eighteenth century: Gender and culture in the age of the Grand Tour* (Stanford: Stanford University Press, 2009), 251–74.

Miller, Edward. *That noble cabinet. A history of the British Museum* (London: André Deutsch, 1973).

Möller, Horst. *Vernunft und Kritik. Deutsche Aufklärung im 17. und 18. Jahrhundert* (Frankfurt am Main: Suhrkamp, 1986).

Monza, Francesca. 'Le arti al servizio delle scienze: la ceroplastica', in Angelo Stella and Gianfranco Lavezzi (eds), *Esortazioni alle storie* (Milan: Cisalpino, 2001), pp. 629–42.

Morelli Timpanaro, Maria Augusta. *Autori, stampatori, librai. Per una storia dell'editoria in Firenze nel secolo XVIII* (Florence: Olschki, 1999), p. 204.

Mukerji, Chandra. 'Cartography, entrepreneurialism, and power in the reign of Louis XIV: the case of the Canal du Midi', in Pamela H. Smith and Paula Findlen (eds), *Merchants and marvels: Commerce, science, and art in early modern Europe* (New York and London: Routledge, 2002), pp. 248–76.

Mülder-Bach, Inka. *Im Zeichen Pygmalions. Das Modell der Statue und die Entdeckung der 'Darstellung' im achtzehnten Jahrhundert* (Munich: W. Fink, 1998).

Museo zoologico La Specola. *Encyclopaedia Anatomica. Vollständige Sammlung anatomischer Wachse. Museo di Storia Naturale dell' Universita di Firenze, sezione di zoologia La Specola* (Cologne: Taschen, 1999).

Newman, Karen. *Fetal positions: Individualism, science, visuality* (Stanford: Stanford University Press, 1996).

Nicoletti, G. (ed.), 'Periodici toscani del Settecento', *Studi italiani* 14 (2002), pp. 363–411.

Nyhart, Lynn K. 'Science, art, and authenticity in natural history displays', in Soraya de Chadarevian and Nick Hopwood (eds), *Models: The third dimension of science* (Stanford: Stanford University Press, 2004), pp. 307–35.

Nys, Liesbet. 'The public's signatures: Visitors' books in nineteenth–century museums', *Museum History Journal* 2:2 (2009), pp. 143–61.

Olmi, Giuseppe. '"A wonderful collection indeed!" The Royal Museum of Florence in the testimony of two travelers', *Nuncius* 21:2 (2006), pp. 349–68.

Outram, Dorinda. *Georges Cuvier. Vocation, science, and authority in post-revolutionary France* (Manchester: Manchester University Press, 1984).

Outram, Dorinda. *The body and the French Revolution: Sex, class and political culture* (New Haven, London: Yale University Press, 1989).

Palmer, Robert R. *The improvement of humanity. Education and the French Revolution* (Princeton: Princeton University Press, 1985).

Pancino, Claudia. *Il bambino e l'acqua sporca; La 'machine' de Coudray ou l'Art des accouchements au XVIIIe siècle* (Rouen: Point de vues, 2005).

Pancino, Claudia and Jean d'Yvoire. *Formato nel segreto. Nascituri e feti fra immagini e immaginario dal XVI al XXI secolo* (Rome: Carocci, 2006).

Panzanelli, Roberta. 'Compelling presence. Wax effigies in Renaissance Florence', in Roberta Panzanelli (ed.), *Ephemeral bodies: wax sculpture and the human figure* (Los Angeles: Getty Research Institute, 2008), pp. 13–40.

Panzanelli, Roberta (ed.). *Ephemeral bodies: Wax sculpture and the human figure* (Los Angeles: Getty Research Institute, 2008).

Pasta, Renato. *Scienza politica e rivoluzione. L'opera di Giovanni Fabbroni (1752–1822) intellettuale e funzionario al servizio dei Lorena* (Florence: Olschki, 1989).

Pasta, Renato. 'L'Accademia dei Georgofili e la riforma dell'agricoltura', *Rivista storica Italiana* 105 (1993), pp. 484–501.

Pasta, Renato. 'Scienza e istituzioni nell'età leopoldina. Riflessioni e comparazioni', in Giulio Barsanti, Vieri Becagli, and Renato Pasta (eds), *La politica della scienza. Toscana e stati italiani nel tardo Settecento* (Florence: Olschki, 1996), pp. 1–34.

Pasta, Renato. '"L'Ospedale e la città": Riforme settecentesche a Santa Maria Nuova', *Annali di storia di Firenze* 1 (2006), pp. 83–98.

Pearce, Susan M. (ed.). *Museums, objects and collections: A cultural study* (Washington, DC, Smithsonian Institution Press, 1993).

Pellegrini Boni, Luisa. 'Strutture e regolamenti della Galleria nel periodo di Pietro Leopoldo', in *Gli Uffizi: quattro secoli di una galleria. Convegno internazionale di studi. Fonti e documenti*, Florence: Olschki 1982), pp. 267–311.

Poggi, Stefano and Maurizio Bossi (eds). *Romanticism in science. Science in Europe, 1790–1840* (Dordrecht, Boston, London: Kluwer, 1994).

Prentice, Rachel. 'The anatomy of a surgical simulation: the mutual articulation of bodies in and through the machine', *Social studies of science* 35:6 (2005), pp. 837–66.

Price, Don K. *The scientific estate* (Cambridge, Mass.: Harvard University Press, 1965).

Rabier, Christelle (ed.). *Fields of expertise: A comparative history of expert procedures in Paris and London, 1600 to present* (Newcastle: Cambridge Scholars Publishing, 2007).

Ravenni, Gian Bruno. 'Il Settecento tra lumi e rivoluzione. L'educazione del popolo, dalle feste agli opuscoli, al teatro', in Franco Cambi (ed.), *La Toscana e l'educazione. Dal Settecento a oggi: tra identità regionale e laboratorio nazionale* (Florence: Le Lettere, 1998), pp. 91–102.

Righini, Benvenuto. *I periodici fiorentini (1597–1950). Catalogo ragionato* (Florence: Sansoni antiquariato, 1955).

Riskin, Jessica. 'Eighteenth-century wetware', *Representations* 83 (2003), pp. 9–125.

Ritter, Gerhard. 'Das geburtshilfliche Phantom im 18. Jahrhundert', *Medizinhistorisches Journal* 1 (1966), pp. 127–43.

Ritvo, Harriet. *The platypus and the mermaid, and other figments of the classifying imagination* (Cambridge, Mass.: Harvard University Press, 1997).

Riva, Alessandro. *Flesh & wax: The Clemente Susini's anatomical models in the University of Cagliari* (Nuoro: Ilisso, 2007).

Rowland, Ingrid. *The scarith of Scornello: A tale of Renaissance forgery* (Chicago: University of Chicago Press, 2004).

Rudwick, Martin. *Georges Cuvier, fossil bones, and geological catastrophes: New translations and interpretations of the primary texts* (Chicago: University of Chicago Press, 1997).

Ruffo, Patrizia. 'Paolo Mascagni e il Reale Museo di Fisica e Storia Naturale di Firenze', in Francesca Vannozzi (ed.), *La scienza illuminata: Paolo Mascagni nel suo tempo (1755–1815)* (Siena: Nuova imagine, 1996), pp. 241–51.

Schaffer, Simon. 'Natural philosophy and public spectacle in the eighteenth century', *History of science* 21 (1983), pp. 1–43.

Schaffer, Simon. 'Scientific discovery and the end of natural philosophy', *Social studies of science* 16 (1986), pp. 387–420.

Schaffer, Simon. 'Measuring virtue: eudiometry, enlightenment and pneumatic medicine', in Andrew Cunningham and Roger French (eds), *The medical Enlightenment of the eighteenth century* (Cambridge: Cambridge University Press, 1990), pp. 281–318.

Schaffer, Simon. 'Self evidence', *Critical inquiry* 18 (1992), pp. 327–62.

Schaffer, Simon. 'Experimenters' techniques, dyers' hands, and the electric planetarium', *Isis* 88 (1997), pp. 456–83.

Schaffer, Simon. 'Enlightened automata', in William Clark, Jan Golinski, and Simon Schaffer (eds), *The sciences in enlightened Europe* (Chicago and London: University of Chicago Press, 1999), pp. 126–65.

Schaffer, Simon. 'Fish and ships: models in the age of reason', in Soraya de Chadarevian and Nick Hopwood (eds), *Models: The third dimension of science* (Stanford: Stanford University Press, 2004), pp. 71–105.

Schiebinger, Londa and Claudia Swann (eds). *Colonial botany: Science, commerce, and politics in the early modern world* (Philadelphia: University of Pennsylvania Press, 2005).

Schiebinger, Londa. *Nature's body. Gender in the making of modern science* (Boston: Beacon Press, 1993).

Schiff, Ugo. 'Il museo di storia naturale e la facolta di scienze fisiche e naturale di Firenze', *Archeion* 9 (1928), pp. 3–36, 81–95, 290–324, 483–496.

Schlumbohm, Jürgen. '"The pregnant women are here for the sake of the teaching institution": The lying-in hospital of Göttingen University, 1751 to *c.*1830', *Social history of medicine* 14:1 (2001), pp. 59–78.

Schmidt, Gabriela. *Geburtshilfliche Wachpräparate des Josephinums* (Vienna, Munich, Bern: Wilhelm Maudrich, 1997).

Schmidt, Gabriela. 'Sul contributo di Paolo Mascagni alla collezione viennese delle cere anatomiche nel Josephinum', in Francesca Vannozzi (ed.), *La scienza illuminata: Paolo Mascagni nel suo tempo (1755–1815)* (Siena: Nuova immagine, 1996), pp. 101–9.

Schnalke, Thomas. *Diseases in wax: the history of the medical moulages*, trans. K. Spatschek (Chicago: Quintessence, 1995).

Schnalke, Thomas. 'Vom Modell zur Moulage. Der neue Blick auf den menschlichen Körper am Beispiel des medizinischen Wachsbildes', in Gabriele Dürbeck, Bettina Gockel, Susanne B. Keller, Monika Renneberg, Jutta Schickore, Gerhard Wiesenfeldt, and Anja Wolkenhauer (eds), *Wahrnehmung der Natur, Natur der Wahrnehmung. Studien zur Geschichte visueller Kultur um 1800* (Dresden: Verlag der Kunst, 2001), pp. 55–69.

Schnalke, Thomas. 'Der expandierende Mensch – Zur Konstitution von Körperbildern in anatomischen Sammlungen des 18. Jahrhunderts', in Frank Stahnisch and

Florian Steger (eds), *Medizin, Geschichte und Geschlecht. Körperhistorische Rekonstruktionen von Identitäten und Differenzen* (Stuttgart: Franz Steiner, 2005), pp. 63–82.

Scott, H.M. 'Reform in the Habsburg monarchy, 1740–90', in H.M. Scott (ed.), *Enlightened absolutism. Reform and reformers in later eighteenth-century Europe* (Ann Arbor: University of Michigan Press, 1990), pp. 145–87.

Scott, James C. *Seeing like a state: How certain schemes to improve the human condition have failed* (New Haven: Yale University Press, 1998).

Scotti, Aurora. 'Malati e strutture ospedaliere dall'età dei Lumi all'Unità', in Franco Della Peruta (ed.), *Storia d'Italia*, vol. 7 (Malattia e medicina), (Turin: Einaudi, 1988) pp. 237–96.

Secord, James A. 'Monsters at the Crystal Palace', in Soraya de Chadarevian and Nick Hopwood (eds), *Models: The third dimension of science* (Stanford: Stanford University Press, 2004), pp. 138–69.

Seidel, Hans-Ch. *Eine neue Kultur des Gebärens: Die Medikalisierung von Geburt im 18. und 19. Jahrhundert in Deutschland* (Stuttgart: Franz Steiner, 1998).

Shapin, Steven. *A social history of truth* (Chicago and London: University of Chicago Press, 1994).

Shapin, Steven. 'Pump and circumstance: Robert Boyle's literary technology', *Social studies of science* 14 (1984), pp. 481–520.

Shapin, Steven. *The scientific life. A moral history of a late modern vocation* (Chicago and London: University of Chicago Press, 2008).

Shapin, Steven and Christopher Lawrence (eds). *Science incarnate*. Chicago: University of Chicago Press, 1998).

Shapin, Steven and Simon Schaffer. *Leviathan and the air-pump: Hobbes, Boyle and the experimental life* (Princeton: Princeton University Press, 1985).

Shea, William (ed.). *Science and the visual image in the Enlightenment* (Canton, Mass.: Science History Publications, 2000).

Sheriff, Mary. *The exceptional woman. Elisabeth Vigée-Lebrun and the cultural politics of art* (Chicago: University of Chicago Press, 1996).

Simon, Jonathan. 'Honoré Fragonard, anatomical virtuoso', in Bernadette Bensaude-Vincent and Christine Blondel (eds), *Science and spectacle in the European Enlightenment* (Aldershot: Ashgate, 2008), pp. 141–58.

Siraisi, Nancy. 'Vesalius and human diversity in De Humani Corporis Fabrica', *Journal of the Warburg and Courtauld Institute*, 57 (1994), pp. 60–88.

Skopec, Manfred. 'Anatomie in Wachs', in Manfred Skopec and Helmut Gröger (eds), *Anatomie als Kunst. Anatomische Wachsmodelle des 18. Jahrhunderts im Josephinum in Wien* (Vienna: Christian Brandstätter Verlag, 2002), pp. 31–73.

Sloan, Philip. 'John Locke, John Ray, and the problem of the natural system', *Journal of the history of biology* 5 (1972), pp. 1–53.

Smith, Pamela. *The business of alchemy. Science and culture in the Holy Roman Empire* (Princeton: Princeton University Press, 1994).

Smith, Pamela. *The body of the artisan. Art and experience in the Scientific Revolution* (Chicago and London: University of Chicago Press, 2004).

Sommer, Hubert. *Génie. Zur Bedeutungsgeschichte des Wortes von der Renaissance zur Aufklärung* (Frankfurt: Peter Lang, 1998).

Sonnenfels, Joseph von. *Grundsätze der Polizey, Handlung und Finanz* (3 vols, Vienna 1769–76).

Sonolet, Jacqueline. 'À propos d'un mannequin anatomique en bois: Napoléon Bonaparte et Felice Fontana', in Congresso internazionale sulla ceroplastica nella scienza e nell'arte, *La ceroplastica nella scienza e nell'arte: atti del I congresso internazionale Firenze, 3–7 giugno 1975* (Florence: Olschki, 1977), pp. 443–58.

Spary, Emma C. *Utopia's garden. French natural history from Old Regime to Revolution* (Chicago and London: University of Chicago Press, 2000).

Spary, Emma C. 'Forging nature at the republican Muséum', in Lorraine Daston and Gianna Pomata (eds), *The faces of nature in enlightenment Europe* (Berlin: Berliner Wissenschafts-Verlag, 2003), pp. 163–80.

Spary, Emma C. 'Of nutmegs and botanists: the colonial cultivation of botanical identity', in Londa Schiebinger and Claudia Swan (eds), *Colonial botany: Science, commerce, and politics in the early modern world* (Philadelphia: University of Pennsylvania Press, 2005), pp. 187–203.

Stafford, Barbara Maria. *Artful science: Enlightenment, entertainment, and the eclipse of visual education* (Cambridge, Mass.: MIT Press, 1994).

Starn, Randolph. 'A historian's brief guide to new museum studies', *The American historical review* 110:1 (2005), pp. 68–98.

Stehr, Nico and Volker Meja (eds). *Society and knowledge. Contemporary perspectives in the sociology of knowledge* (New Brunswick: Transaction Books, 1984).

Stekl, Hannes. 'Ambivalenzen von Bürgerlichkeit', in Gerhard Ammerer and Hanns Haas (eds), *Ambivalenz der Aufklärung. Festschrift für Ernst Wangermann* (Munich: Oldenbourg, 1997), pp. 33–48.

Stendhal, *Rome, Naples et Florence* (3rd edn, vol. 1, Paris: Delaunay, 1826).

Strickland, Stuart Walker. 'Reopening the texts of romantic science: the language of experience in J.W. Ritter's *Beweis*', in Kostas Gavroglu, Jean Christianidis, and Efthymios Nicolaidis. *Trends in the historiography of science* (Dordrecht: Kluwer, 1994), pp. 385–96.

Strickland, Stuart Walker. 'The ideology of self-knowledge and the practice of self-experimentation', *Eighteenth-century studies*, 31:4 (1998), pp. 453–71.

Tanzer, Gerhard. *Spectacle müssen sein: Die Freizeit der Wiener im 18. Jahrhundert* (Vienna: Böhlau, 1992).

Thomas, Keith. *Man and the natural world: Changing attitudes in England 1500–1800* (Oxford: Oxford University Press, 1983).

Thorpe, Charles. 'Disciplining experts: scientific authority and liberal democracy in the Oppenheimer case', *Social studies of science* 32 (2002), pp. 525–62.

Timpanaro, Maria Augusta Morelli, *Autori, stampatori, librai. Per una storia dell'editoria in Firenze nel secolo XVIII* (Florence: Olschki, 1999), p. 204.

Tribby, Jay, 'Body/building: living the museum life in early modern Europe', *Rhetorica* 10:2 (1992), pp. 139–63.

Tuck, Richard. *Natural rights theories. Their origin and development* (Cambridge: Cambridge University Press, 1979).

Turi, Gabriele. *'Viva Maria'. La reazione alle riforme leopoldine* (1790–1799) (Florence: Olschki, 1969).

Turi, Gabriele. *'Viva Maria'. Riforme, rivoluzione e insorgenze in Toscana (1790–1799)* (2nd edn, with postscript, Bologna: Il Mulino, 1999).

Vagnarelli, Rita. 'Evoluzione e modifiche della fabbrica della Specola attraverso le piante storiche', in Angelo Forti (ed.), *L'Imperiale e Regio Museo di Fisica e Storia Naturale di Firenze: indicazioni per un metodo di lettura e per una soluzione museografica* (Florence: Angelo Pontecorboli, 1995), pp. 29–42.

Van Dijck, José. 'Bodyworlds: the art of plastinated cadavers', *Configurations* 9:1 (2001), pp. 99–126.

Vannozzi, Francesca. 'Dall'arte empirica alla sperimentazione sistematica. Il 'nuovo' medico del settecento riformatore', in Enrico Ghidetti and Esther Diana (eds), *La bellezza come terapia: arte e assistenza nell'ospedale di Santa Maria Nuova a Firenze: atti del Convegno internazionale, Firenze, 20–22 maggio 2004* (Florence: Polistampa, 2005), pp. 295–311.

Venturi, Franco. *Italy and the Enlightenment* (New York: New York University Press, 1972).

Venturi, Franco. *Settecento riformatore* (Turin: Einaudi, 1969–84).

Walker, Margot. *Sir James Edward Smith, 1759–1828* (London: Linnean Society of London, 1988).

Wandruszka, Adam. *Leopold II.* (2 vols, Vienna and Munich: Herold, 1963).

Weber, Giorgio. *Aspetti poco noti della storia dell'anatomia patologica tra '600 e '700: William Harvey, Marcello Malpighi, Antonino Cocchi, Giovanni Maria Lancisi: verso Morgagni* (Florence: Olschki, 1997).

Werrett, Simon. 'Wonders never cease: Descartes's Météores and the rainbow fountain', *British journal for the history of science*, 34 (2001), pp. 129–47.

Wilson, Adrian. *The making of man-midwifery: childbirth in England, 1660–1770* (Cambridge, Mass.: Harvard University Press, 1995).

Wittgenstein, Ludwig. *Philosophische Untersuchungen/Philosophical Investigations*, (Oxford: Blackwell, 1997 [1936]).

Wokler, Robert. 'The nexus of animal and rational: socio-biology, language, and the Enlightenment study of apes', in Sabine Maasen, Everett Mendelsohn, and Peter Weingart (eds), *Biology as society, society as biology: Metaphors* (Dordrecht: Kluwer, 1995), pp. 81–103.

Wolkenhauer, Anja. '"Grausenhaft wahr ist diese wächserne Geschichte": Die Wachsfiguren von Don Gaetano Zumbo zwischen Kunst und medizinischer Anatomie', in Gabriele Dürbeck, Bettina Gockel, Susanne B. Keller, Monika Renneberg, Jutta Schickore, Gerhard Wiesenfeldt, and Anja Wolkenhauer (eds), *Wahrnehmung der Natur, Natur der Wahrnehmung. Studien zur*

Geschichte visueller Kultur um 1800 (Dresden: Verlag der Kunst, 2001), pp. 71–85.

Woodmansee, Martha. *The author, art, and the market: Rereading the history of aesthetics* (New York: Columbia University Press, 1994).

Wyklicky, Helmut. *Das Josephinum: Biographie eines Hauses. Die medicinisch-chirurgische Josephs-Akademie seit 1785 das Institut für Geschichte der Medizin seit 1920* (Vienna: Brandstätter, 1985).

Zanca, A. *Le cere e le terrecotte del Museo di storia della scienza di Firenze* (Florence: Arnaud, 1981).

Zangheri, Luigi. *Feste e apparati nella Toscana dei Lorena, 1737–1859* (Florence: Olschki, 1996).

Zullino, M. Luciana. 'L'organizzazione museologica della Specola nelle varie epoche', in Alfredo Forti (ed.), *L'Imperiale e Regio Museo di Fisica e Storia Naturale di Firenze: indicazioni per un metodo di lettura e per una soluzione museografica* (Florence: Angelo Pontecorboli, 1995), pp. 43–5.

Index

academies 8, 19, 24–6, 33, 37, 40–1, 104, 196
academy of science, Tuscany 25, 29, 37
Academy of Sciences, Paris 104
accountability 96, 100, 106, 197
accuracy 10–11, 30, 66, 83–107 *passim*, 120, 123, 128, 130, 132, 135, 138, 151–2, 158, 172, 188, 196, 211–13
administration
    government 21, 23–4, 27, 30, 32, 56, 92–103 *passim*, 106–7, 118, 155, 157, 187, 189, 192, 196–8, 200–2, 210–11
    public health 62–3, 70
    Royal Museum 8, 12, 30–1, 35, 37, 83, 92–103 *passim*, 106–7, 122–3, 125, 136, 185, 188–202 *passim*, 210–11, 215
agency
    of civil servants 193
    of institutions 25–7, 37, 70, 192, 210
    of modellers 103
    of naturalists 119, 137, 201–2, 212–13
Agricultural Academy *see* Georgofili
anatomy
    comparative 124, 165, 194–5, 197, 200, 202
    displays since 1800 213–16
    illustrations 61, 85–9, 99, 213
    method 56–8, 70

textbooks 85, 124, 135, 152, 171, 173, 214, 216
theatre 61, 64
training 53, 55, 61–67 *passim*, 70, 89, 172, 202, 209–10, 215–16
utility 55, 57–9, 85–7
animal models 124, 194–5
animals 1, 20, 31, 36–9, 57, 84, 124–6, 158, 162, 194–5
art 30–1, 34, 50, 119, 127, 132–3, 137, 168, 196, 209
artisans 93
    see also artists; Calenzuoli; Carmine; guilds; modellers; sculpture; Susini
artists 1, 3–4, 50, 66, 68, 88, 91, 129
    see also artisans; Ferrini; Gautier d'Agoty; Michelangelo; modellers; Vigée-Lebrun
attention 10, 97–100, 105, 113n.61
audience
    discipline 10, 133–7
    emotions 163
    frameworks 118, 125–7, 162–3
    gender 163
    responses to models 127–33, 138, 163–5, 214–15
    see also public; visitors
authority
    of experts 6, 8–10, 12, 24–7, 59, 70, 118, 137, 153–74 *passim*, 188, 210, 212, 216–17

authority (*cont.*)
 limits of 7, 9, 22
 in model production 10, 71, 83–107
   passim, 118, 129, 137, 185, 215
 political 7, 19, 21–7, 40, 70, 190, 199,
   213
 and status in early modern natural
   philosophy 89–92
 see also legitimacy
autonomy 24, 29, 37, 52, 93, 95, 102, 105,
   107, 195, 197, 210, 212

Baciocchi, Elisa 192, 196
Bartolini, Luigi 101
Becchini, Giuseppe 101
Benedict XIV 65–6, 68
Biagioli, Mario 90
Bienvenu, François 126–7, 136
bladders used for phantoms 66
Bonicoli, Tommaso 35, 104–5, 112n.51,
   135, 189
Botanical Garden
 at the Royal Museum 35, 124
 at Santa Maria Nuova 64–5
Brambilla, Giovanni 151–2, 156–69
   passim, 173, 174n.1
 view on surgery 157–59
British Museum 30, 121, 136
Broman, Thomas 166
Buchan, William, *Domestic Medicine* 59
budget 11, 50, 92, 101–2, 105, 188–9,
   197, 199
 see also expenses

cabinets 30–1, 38, 68, 124–6, 162,
   193
 see also Wunderkammer
Calenzuoli, Francesco 86, 91, 196, 201
Camera di Commercio *see* Chamber of
   Commerce
Cappelletti, Niccolò 93–4
Carmine, Felice 93
carnival 38–9, 125
celebrations, courtly 38, 125–6

Chamber of Commerce (Camera di
   Commercio) 9, 20, 24, 26–7, 29,
   37, 40, 70, 101, 192, 210
charlatans and mountebanks 19, 39, 59
chemistry 20, 29–31, 33, 64, 123, 165,
   195, 197
 see also experiments; laboratory;
   Lavoisier
classification 35, 124
clay 66, 69
Cocchi, Antonio 10, 51–70 *passim*, 193,
   209–10
Cocchi, Raimondo 62, 69
collections, systematised 34, 64, 123–4
Collegio Medico, Florence 55, 64
Committee on Public Education, France
   189–90
Condillac 27
control
 of artisans 29, 83–107 *passim*, 210, 215
 of experts 8–9, 24–7, 39, 70, 83–107
   passim, 210, 212
 of naturalists 29–30, 83–107 *passim*
 of public 20, 38–9, 137, 211
 of sovereign 22
corpses
 comparison with models 128, 172, 215
 competition for 65, 89
 in obstetric training 172
 public responses 88, 168, 214
 public viewing 63, 126
 supply 65, 89, 92, 104, 168
 as teaching material 61–2, 64, 168, 193,
   195
 used in modelling 87–9, 92
Cuvier, Georges 194–5, 197

De'Bardi, Count Girolamo 137, 194–201
deception *see* illusion
delays 92, 95, 101, 105–6
demonstrations 123–4, 134, 193, 214
Desgenettes, René 64, 87, 89, 95, 128–29,
   132, 190, 195
Diderot, Denis 99

directors of the Royal Museum *see* Fontana, Fabbroni, De'Bardi
discipline 35, 83, 88, 93, 95–8, 100, 105–6, 120, 123, 126–7, 130, 188, 215–16
see also control
display
of authority 39–40, 118, 190, 195, 201, 209
of expertise 10, 118–38 *passim*, 185
improvement 133–137
of models 1, 50, 66–7, 84–6, 92, 95, 100, 118–38 *passim*, 151–2, 212–17
of nature 19–20, 30, 37, 162–3, 190, 209
obscene 154, 163
synoptic approach 137
systematisation at Uffizi 34, 141n.28
see also audience; entertainment; exhibition; public; spectacle
dissection 1, 53, 61–5, 124, 169, 216
of Cocchi 62
of Fontana 193
see also corpses
drawings 29, 124
in education 29
of models 1, 84, 88, 91, 120, 124, 127, 129
Du Coudray, A.M. Le Boursier 53, 66, 215
Dupaty, Charles 29, 131

education
medical 53, 55, 61–5, 67–70, 89, 128, 156, 168–9, 202, 209–10
obstetrics 53, 61, 65–6, 70, 170–2, 215–6
of princes and nobility 23, 28–9, 119, 200
public *see* public education
role of mediation 36, 120, 123
surgery 11, 53, 61–5, 70, 151, 153–7, 168–9, 172
see also entertainment; public
empathy 161, 170

entertainment 38–9, 50, 122, 125–7, 137–8, 151, 153, 161–5, 172–3, 212–14
see also cabinets; carnival; celebrations; display; education; shows; theatre
erudition 36, 55–6, 58–9, 68, 125, 152, 167
evaluation 6, 8, 35, 56, 91–8 *passim*, 104–6, 118, 135, 137, 153, 185, 189
see also judgment
expenses 86, 100–2, 122, 168, 189, 192, 194, 199
see also budget
experiments
political 7, 9, 21, 28
scientific 21, 28–31, 33, 39, 58–9, 91, 126–7, 162
expert, category 8

Fabbroni, Giovanni *passim*
background 33
Fauken, Johann Peter 166–8
Ferdinando III, Grand Duke 28–9, 103–4, 126, 185–7, 198–202, 213
Ferrini, Giuseppe 67–8, 86, 94, 96, 100
Fontana, Felice *passim*
background 31
Francis II (arch-duke Francesco) 29, 167–8, 187, 198
Francis Stephen, emperor 19, 21, 30, 56
Frank, Johann Peter 52
French Revolution 3, 11–12, 30, 64, 103, 162, 185–9 *passim*, 198, 202, 212–13

Gagli, Luigi 34, 93, 97–8, 122–3, 136
Galileo 37, 56, 90f, 193–4
Galletti, Giuseppe 65–7
Gautier d'Agoty, Jacques Fabien 61
gender 161, 163, 167, 171
General Hospital, Florence *see* Santa Maria Nuova
genius 83, 98–100, 102, 106–7, 128, 211, 217

Georgofili (agricultural academy in
        Florence) 9, 20, 24–6, 29, 33, 37,
        40, 70, 101, 186, 210
Gianni, Francesco Maria 21, 23, 28, 37,
        100
Giorgi, Ferdinando 31, 91
Giusti, Giuseppe 31
glass 1, 66, 125, 158, 164, 215
Grand Tour 50, 53, 129–33 *passim*
guided tours 87, 89, 120–4, 127–8
Guidetti, Giacinto 4, 88–9
guilds 21, 26, 38, 53, 93, 156–7, 165

Hallam, Elizabeth 216
honour 90–1, 104, 106f, 123, 127, 159
    Fabbroni 33, 102, 107, 211
    Fontana 90f, 95, 104, 106–7, 210–11
    sovereign's 51, 90–1, 104
    see also reputation; self-image
Hunczovsky, Johann 152, 157, 169–70

illusion 163–4
Innocenti (Florentine orphanage) 88, 127
instruments 20, 29–32, 35–7, 57–8, 62, 68,
        86, 119, 123, 152, 156–8, 171–2
    see also tools
intelligibility 6, 68, 85, 99, 107, 119, 123,
        128, 157, 211
interpretive flexibility 10–12, 71, 119, 130,
        174, 185, 212, 214
ivory 66

Joseph II, emperor 11, 27, 29, 95, 103,
        151–74 *passim*, 185–6
Josephinum (medico-surgical academy in
        Vienna)
    collections 157
    foundation 154–7
    investigation into 168
    new direction 169
    see also Brambilla
judgment 8, 36, 85, 87, 89–90, 100, 103–5,
        132, 135, 138, 162, 171, 189, 211
    see also evaluation

labels 124
laboratory 53, 64, 123, 131
    Tuscany as 21–3, 127, 209
labour 83, 88, 92, 96
Lavoisier, Antoine 31, 91
layout of exhibition 123
leather 53–4, 66, 194, 215
lectures
    anatomy 55, 61, 126, 136, 195,
        199–200, 214
        see also Cocchi; Uccelli
    at Josephinum 152
    public 55, 58, 126–7, 136, 194
    at Santa Maria Nuova 55, 61, 64–5
lecturers
    itinerant 19, 126–7
    at Royal Museum 195
legitimacy 5–9 *passim*, 19–29 *passim*, 52,
        57, 68, 71, 83, 91, 105, 118, 191,
        195, 202, 209, 213
Lelli, Ercole 66
liceo, Royal Museum as 194–5, 199, 201
Locke, John 27–8
Lodovico I, king 191–2
London 26, 30, 31, 32, 37, 55, 121, 132,
        216
Louis XV, king 53
luxury 151, 153, 162, 169, 173, 212

Magistrato di Sanità, Florence 64
Malpighi, Marcello 56–7
Manetti, Saverio 62
Manzolini, Giovanni 66
Maria Luisa, queen 191–201 *passim*
Maria Teresa, empress 21
Mascagni, Paolo 31, 35, 86, 89–90, 103–5,
        129, 188, 190, 193, 201, 213
materials 50, 53, 69, 86, 92–4, 96, 100,
        102, 105, 133–5, 190, 211–16
        passim
    accounting for 96, 100, 102, 121
    for medical instruction 65, 152, 200,
        215
    of obstetric models 53, 66

see also clay; glass; ivory; leather; papier-
mâché; pigments; silk; silver;
sponges; turpentine; wax; wood
Matteucci, Antonio 96, 99, 106, 118
maturity 160-2, 167
mediation 29, 36, 85, 118-19, 131, 136,
138, 162, 172, 193-5, 202,
211-12, 214, 216
Medici 19-21, 29, 34, 55, 60, 68, 90-1,
125-6, 129, 191, 201
memento mori 34, 66-7, 214
Michelangelo 50, 56, 193
microcosm, museum as 20, 36, 84, 157
midwives 52-3, 60, 63, 65-6, 69-70, 153,
156, 170-2, 210
see also Galletti; obstetrics; phantoms
modellers 91-2
recognition 195-6
see also artisans; Calenzuoli; Cappelletti;
Ferrini; Lelli; Morandi Manzolini;
Susini; Zumbo
modelling 86-90
based on illustrations 86, 124, 129
conceptual and practical problems 5
contributors 91-2
delays 92, 95, 101, 105-6
different perspectives on 92-3
idealised account 87-8
as purposive activity 6
skills 10, 34, 94-5, 97, 105
models
ambivalence 6
detachable 11, 162, 187
see also dissection
gestures 3, 50, 86
interpretive flexibility 10-12, 71, 119,
130, 174, 185, 212, 214
obstetrics (phantoms) 53-4, 66, 171-2,
215-16
pathological 157
travelling shows 213-14
see also corpses; display; evaluation;
judgment; utility
Morandi Manzolini, Anna 66

Muséum d'histoire naturelle, Paris 30, 136,
198
museum studies 7, 119, 130, 216

Nannoni, Angelo 61-2
Nannoni, Lorenzo 89, 112n.51
Napoleon 147n.108, 190, 192, 196, 198,
213
national identity 37, 40, 209
natural history 21, 24, 29, 36, 38, 56-7, 59,
120, 123-4, 126, 130, 132, 137,
162, 189, 193-4, 200
natural law
intelligibility of 5, 11, 27, 36, 39-40, 68,
85, 137-8, 157, 190, 211
role for the polity 5-7, 9, 21-3, 37,
39-40, 68, 190, 198, 209
universality 37, 84-5
nobility 28, 30, 33, 56, 83, 90, 122, 125-7,
129, 153, 186-7, 194, 200-1

objects 30, 34, 51, 88, 97, 122, 163-5, 193,
211
acquisition 32, 119
display 1, 10, 36, 84, 118-20, 123, 125,
132, 136-8
role in education 29, 34, 170, 202
security 123
see also porters
see also instruments; models; specimens
observation 6-7, 9, 20, 56, 58, 62-4, 96-7,
125, 127, 131-2, 136, 158, 165,
214
obstetrics 10, 52-4, 60-70, 89, 129, 152-3,
157, 169-72, 209-10, 215-16
see also Galletti; midwives; phantoms
orphanage (Istituto degl'Innocenti) 88, 127

papier-mâché 214
Paris 32, 37, 104, 136, 156, 188-9, 192,
198, 201, 213-14
Parlini, Giovanni 189
Pasta, Renato 33, 40
patronage 32, 68, 83, 90-1, 103, 166, 200

pedestals 1, 50, 120, 123, 129
Pelli, Giuseppe 28, 31, 33f, 39, 58, 69, 93,
    99, 126–7, 186, 192, 209
Pelli Fabbroni, Teresa 28, 33, 187
perfection of models 84, 89, 95, 98, 102,
    104, 118, 120, 128, 133, 135, 188,
    212
    see also accuracy
periodicals 27–8, 57–9, 68–9, 120, 154,
    166
    medical 57–59
phantoms (obstetric models) 53–4, 66,
    171–2, 215–16
    materials 53, 66, 215
    resistance to 171–2, 216
physicians 10, 11, 34–5, 52–3, 56, 59, 89,
    121–2
    in Vienna 11, 151–74 *passim*, 212
    see also education, medical
physics 29, 31, 36, 57, 59, 67–8, 85, 195
physiocracy 6, 9, 21, 23–4, 37
Pietro Leopoldo, Grand Duke *passim*
    on education 28–9
    on reforms as experiments *see*
        experiments, political
pigments 50, 86
Pisa, university 31, 55, 67, 197–8
plants 20, 29, 33, 53, 124
population growth 52–3, 57–9, 63, 66,
    155–6, 171–2
pornography 163
porters 35, 101, 106, 121–2, 188
pregnancy and fetal development 10, 50,
    52–3, 66, 89, 123, 132, 162, 164,
    215
Priestley, Joseph 32, 63
public
    'attestive' 6–7
    see also audience; visitors
public education
    and French Revolution 189–90
    in health and medicine 59, 68
    role of expert 11, 119, 136–7, 194, 202
    scepticism 153–4, 160, 164–5, 173

    in Tuscan press 27–8
    utility 28, 36, 39–40, 194, 199, 213
public happiness 4–5, 7, 9, 20, 23, 25, 52,
    57, 58, 62, 83, 131, 152, 160, 186,
    209
public health
    administration 63, 70
    in Austria 152, 154–9 *passim*, 173
    in Tuscany 53, 55–9 *passim*, 62–3,
        69–70, 210
public opinion 40–1, 154, 186, 192,
    199–200, 202, 213

Raddi, Giuseppe 193
reforms 23–7, 60–5
    in Austria 152–7
    see also Chamber of Commerce;
        experiments; public health
relics 37, 119, 126, 132, 154
religion
    and education 198–9
    popular 186, 188
representation 5–7, 9
    and authority 95–9, 102, 106, 118, 214
    conventions 129, 215
    in education 84–5, 119, 133, 214
    and intertextuality 215–16
    see also accuracy; drawings; models
reputation 31, 56, 69, 84, 99, 102–3, 128,
    130, 132, 161, 166, 169
    see also honour; self-image
Richter, Joseph 159–67 *passim*
Rosenberg, Franz Xaver 19, 21
Royal Museum of Physics and Natural
        History, Florence
    employees 34–5, 86, 91–2, 95, 101–6
        passim, 189–90, 192–3, 199, 201
    see also artisans; directors; modellers;
        porters

Santa Maria Nuova (general hospital,
        Florence) 33, 53–65 *passim*, 69,
        88–9, 96, 126–7, 193, 200, 202
    see also Cocchi; medical education

Santissima Annunziata (Florentine church) 67, 126

satire 11, 151–4 *passim*, 159–67 *passim*, 171

Scarpa, Antonio 31, 89–90

Schmidt, J.A. 152

Schnalke, Thomas 124

science and the state 6–8

science and technology studies 7, 40–1, 216

sculpture 1, 34, 66–7, 86, 90, 94, 105, 126, 128, 132–3, 213–14

self-image
  experts' 32, 85
    see also honour; reputation
  middle class 154, 165

sensationalism 27–9, 84, 120, 137

Shapin, Steven 8

Sheriff, Mary 131

showcases 1, 50, 88, 92, 125, 137, 151, 192

Siena 21, 26, 28, 55, 103, 190

silk 92, 151

silver 94

Smith, James Edward 132

Sömmering, Samuel Thomas 86, 157

Sonnenfels, Joseph von 155

sovereignty 22, 40–1

specimens 5, 30, 32, 35, 37–8, 85, 88–9, 96, 99, 119, 123–6, 132–3, 137, 163, 193, 209, 213, 215

'Specola' as name for Royal Museum 12n.3, 20

spectacle 20
  in Florence 38–9, 125
  policing of 38–9
  travelling shows 38, 126, 162–3, 213–14
  in Vienna 161–5
  see also entertainment; theatre

sponges 66

standardisation
  of administrative practice 95, 102
  of display 125
    see also showcases

state interests 37, 58, 107, 189, 211, 217

Steidele, Raphael 171–2

Störck, Anton von 155

superstition 154

surgery
  conflicts with medicine 151–74 *passim*
  legal status in Austria 156–7
  training 53, 55, 61–2, 64–6, 70, 129, 151–74 *passim*, 210
  utility 60, 65, 151–2, 157–9, 212

surveillance 70, 93, 96, 128, 152, 155, 210–1

Susini, Clemente 86, 89, 91, 93–5, 100, 104–5, 195–6, 201

Swieten, Gerard van 156

Targioni Tozzetti, Giovanni 36

technology 7, 26, 36–7, 39–40, 190

theatre 33, 38–9, 162

tickets 121, 123

tools 84, 86
  modellers as 88, 95, 98, 105
  for modelling 11, 86–7, 92, 190, 214
  see also instruments

touch 10, 66, 69, 94, 96–8, 119, 123, 126, 132–4, 158, 167, 172, 211, 214

Towne, Joseph 216

toys 34, 93–4
  models as 11, 151–74 *passim*, 212

traditions
  artistic and artisanal 34, 37, 66–7, 69, 202, 215–16
  medical 70, 99, 165, 170
  religious 126, 188
  scholarly and scientific 19, 36–7, 56, 67–8, 69, 121, 195, 202

transparency 96, 106
  see also accountability

trust 8, 59, 94, 102–3, 106, 130, 195

turpentine 86, 93–4

Uccelli, Filippo 193–6, 200

Uffizi (Florentine art museum) 31, 33–4, 56
  see also Pelli, Giuseppe

utility
  of models 7, 9, 11, 51–2, 67–9, 84, 105,
      120, 129, 133, 135, 153, 161, 169,
      173, 185, 212
  of natural knowledge 7, 11, 36, 51,
      199–200, 212
  see also anatomy; surgery

Venus 1, 34, 50, 123, 214
Vienna 7, 11, 19, 30, 103, 126, 138,
      151–74 *passim*, 185–8, 212,
      215–16
Vigée-Lebrun, Elisabeth 131
visibility 68, 84–5, 120, 125
visitors 5, 20, 122, 130–2
  admission 121–2
  'ideal visitors' 128–9
      see also audience; flexibility
      interpretive; public

wax 67
  connotations 50, 126, 162–4
  in model production 50, 86, 88, 93–4,
      103, 124, 133–5, 189, 211,
      215–16
wax busts 34, 93, 126
Wichelhausen, Engelbert 87, 89, 95,
      128–9, 132, 195
Winckelmann, Johann Joachim 34
wood 1, 53–4, 66, 69, 86, 92, 124–5,
      128, 188, 213
wood model 11, 69, 103–5, 133–8,
      187, 189–90, 193, 211,
      214–15
Wunderkammer 20, 30, 201

Zuccagni, Attilio 35
Zumbo, Gaetano 34–5, 37, 67